TURBULENCE, EMPOWERMENT AND MARGINALISATION IN INTERNATIONAL EDUCATION GOVERNANCE SYSTEMS

STUDIES IN EDUCATIONAL ADMINISTRATION

Series Editors: Gaëtane Jean-Marie and Ann E. Lopez

Studies in Educational Administration presents monographs and edited collections along the broad themes of educational leadership, management and administration.

The series presents research conducted across a diverse range of contexts and locations. Proposals are invited for authored or edited books from scholars in all stages of their careers for work that will help us to advance the educational administration field, and will be of use to both researchers and school administrators and teachers.

Forthcoming Publications

Orly Shapira-Lishchinsky, *International Aspects of Organizational Ethics in Educational Systems*

Izhar Oplatka and Khalid Arar (eds), *Emotion Management in Teaching and Educational Leadership: A Cultural Perspective*

Interested in publishing in this series? Please contact Gaëtane Jean-Marie and Ann E. Lopez at sea@uni.edu

TURBULENCE, EMPOWERMENT AND MARGINALISATION IN INTERNATIONAL EDUCATION GOVERNANCE SYSTEMS

EDITED BY

ALISON TAYSUM
University of Leicester, UK

KHALID ARAR
Al-Qasemi Academic College of Education, Israel

United Kingdom – North America – Japan – India – Malaysia – China

Emerald Publishing Limited
Howard House, Wagon Lane, Bingley BD16 1WA, UK

First edition 2019

Copyright © 2019 Emerald Publishing Limited

Reprints and permissions service
Contact: permissions@emeraldinsight.com

British Library Cataloguing in Publication Data
A catalogue record for this book is available from the British Library

ISBN: 978-1-78754-676-9 (Print)
ISBN: 978-1-78754-675-2 (Online)
ISBN: 978-1-78754-677-6 (Epub)

Printed and bound by CPI Group (UK) Ltd, Croydon, CR0 4YY

ISOQAR certified
Management System,
awarded to Emerald
for adherence to
Environmental
standard
ISO 14001:2004.

Certificate Number 1985
ISO 14001

INVESTOR IN PEOPLE

Contents

We would like to dedicate this book to God, to all the senior-level leaders who participated in this research and who work in our noble profession and to all people who work for social justice with courage and prudence for peace in our time.

Preface and Acknowledgements

A community of scholars is needed in order to further such a significant and complex project such as this; many highly valued colleagues contributed directly or indirectly to the construction, design and refinement of this book. The discussion on how governance at different levels can improve access to education for excluded communities has gradually developed between the editors of the book and many other participants over the last decade; the hope is that this book will contribute to the discourse on fairness for these excluded communities in education. Our voyage of discovery began with cyclic research, which deepened through internal school discourse concerning the complexity of this issue and its communal, socio-cultural and national aspects. Our many partners in this quest included Professor Daniel Muijs representing Belgium, Professor Rui Yang from China; Dr Emir Mahmoud from Egypt; Professor Mika Risku from Finland; Professor Danielle Zay from France; Professor Marc Beutner and Mr Rasmus Pecheul from Germany; Dr Michalis Kakos, Dr Despina Karakatsani, Professor Nektaria Palaiologou and Dr Dora Katsamori from Greece; Professor Anikó Fehérvári from Hungary; Professor Ewelina K. Goździk from Poland; Dr Dorina Goceami from Romania; Professor Anna Nedyalkova from Bulgaria; Dr Geraldine Vadna Murrel-Abery from Guyana; Professor Stephan Huber and Professor Guri Skedsmo from Switzerland; Dr Priti Chopra and Mr Rajesh Patek from India; Dr Khalid Arar presenting an Arab perspective of Israel, Dr Zvei Berger presenting a Jewish perspective of Israel, Professor Roberto Serpieri, Dr Emiliano Grimaldi and Dr Barbara Segatto from Italy; Professor Kenji Maehara from Japan; Professor Aigerim Mynbyeva, Professor Yenar Onalbekov and Dr Zarina Yelbayeva from Kazakhstan; Dr Kaeunghun Yoon from South Korea Professor Hauwa Imam from Nigeria, Dr Samuel McGuinness, Dr Jessica Bates, Dr Stephen Roulston, Dr Una O'Connor, Dr Catherine Quinn and Mr Brian Waring from Northern Ireland; Dr Mohammed Ilyas Khan, Dr Muhammad Iqbal Majoka and Dr Asima Iqbal from Pakistan; Dr Kathy Harrison, Professor Gerry McNamara, Professor Joe O'Hara and Dr Barney O'Reilly from the Republic of Ireland; Professor Segei Trapitsin, Professor Victoria Pogosian, Professor Elena Pushkinova, Dr Elena Tropinova and Professor Victor Timchenko from Russia; Professor Freddy James and Dr June George from Trinidad and Tobago; Dr Ana Patrícia Almeida from Portugal; Dr Sarah Sands-Meyer from Strasbourg; Mr Shailen Popat, Dr Tania Hart, Mr Ian Potter, Mr Kenny Dunkwu and Dr Alison Taysum from England; The Feast including Founder and Chair of Trustees Dr Andrew Smith from England; Mr Tim Fawssett from Australia; Ms Mayssa Haidar leader of Model United Nations from Lebanon; and Dr Carole Collins Ayanlaja, Dr Warletta Brookins and Dr Pam Angelle from the United States (Taysum, 2012, 2014; Taysum et al., 2017). The project owes its success to these colleagues demonstrated by the generation of new knowledge in our publications and grant applications. The in-depth socio-historiographical analysis of the 30 nation states that have contributed to the education project has afforded the depth of comparative analysis that connects with Paulston (2000). These analyses have enabled us to have a deeper understanding of the five case studies presented in this book that have underpinned our impact strategy meetings with senior-level leaders, for example in Southside Chicago, that puts knowledge generated in this book to action.

International, independent and critical friends to whom we owe our gratitude, each from their own viewpoint and world view, have peer-reviewed the chapters. All authors have responded to the feedback which has enriched and sharpened our observations on education systems as dynamic systems influenced by many different stakeholders and representing 'momentary' consensus between them. The external international peer-review process was conducted along with our team's internal peer-review process, which has enhanced the trustworthiness of the research and the quality dimensions (Bridges, 2016; Levin, 2004; Oancea & Furlong, 2007; Pollard, 2008).

Our viewpoint on the role of governance stemmed from examination of the school and its activity on the micro-level and the work of policy-makers at the political macro-level and developed through discussion circles and workshops in conferences at the European Education Research Association Annual Conferences (Taysum, 2012, 2013, 2014; Taysum et al., 2015, 2016, 2017), The British Educational Research Association Annual Conferences, the American Educational Research Association Annual Conferences and the British Educational Leadership, Management and Administration Society Doctoral Interest Group (2018). During these workshops, we tried to develop through an international research community, representing different societies, cultures and worldviews on education governance systems. We examined education governance systems in contexts where contested projects compete in the education field: projects that aim to maintain social stratification, to serve a particular national scheme and to strengthen partition between religions and cultures in contrast to projects that aim to challenge this discourse with the development of social cohesion and multicultural discourse, strengthening democratic processes including social justice and fairness through recognition, participation and equal distribution of human wealth and seeing diversity as socio-culture enrichment.

The strong commitment of the authors of the different chapters permitted deep observation of the complexity involved at the level of the individual classroom and school and also at the level of the state. The work of these various authors allowed us to develop our research approaches and methodologies and to attribute meaning to the current reality to develop tools to improve participation in school decision-making and the implementation of processes in praxis and to develop our theoretical conceptualisation including the development of a model that would provide a space for containment and constructive critical discussion. We found that we were able to understand this complex reality by applying the lens of 'Turbulence Theory' (Gross, 2014). This wide-branching project allowed us as a research community to become more aware of the role of governance in different states and cultures and to develop different approaches concerning its role in school work.

We would like to sincerely thank the authors of the calls for the Horizon 2020 education projects. We highly recommend the rich reading of the Horizon 2020 calls and the associated documentation whether the reader wishes to apply for Horizon 2020 funding or not. Our reason is because, in our view, they have been written by some of the most enlightened minds of our time and offer valuable insights for any individual interested in the relationship between knowledge of our evolving world, and the practice of our evolving world and putting knowledge to action for the betterment of our world's economic, cultural, political and ecological good sustainability.

Finally, Alison Taysum would particularly like to thank Dr Dieter Krohn and Dr Kirsten Malmquist for being patient teachers during the socratic facilitator's training, and her fellow socratics on the course who explored virtue and character through our Socratic Dialogues. She would also like to thank Professor Yusef Waghid Professor Ron Glass, Professor Charles Slater, Professor James Conroy, Professor Michael Apple, Professor Ikuo Komatsu Professor Masaaki Katsuno, Dr Ueda Midori, Dr Hiroko Hirose, Professor Dr Kathy Harrison, Professor Chie Nakajimar, Professor Gerry McNamara and Professor Jo O'Hara, for their wisdom and support of the development of the ideas in this book.

British Educational Leadership, Management and Administration Society Doctoral Research Interest Group (BELMAS DRIG) (2018) Empowering Young Societal Innovators for Equity and Renewal; Reviewing Strategies to improve education in diverse communities. Global Kitchens: South Side Chicago, US, in April.

References

Bridges, D. (2016). *Philosophy in educational research: Epistemology, ethics, politics and quality*. E-book: Springer.

Taysum, A. (2012). *Convener of a large symposium in two parts: 'Globalization, Policy and Agency: Eight Nation states working together to Further Understand their Political Sociologies of Education'*. European Conference for Educational Research, Cadiz, September.

Levin, B. (2004). Marking research matter more. *Education Policy Analysis Archives*, *12*(56). Retrieved from https://scholarcommons.usf.edu/cgi/viewcontent.cgi?referer=https://www.google.com/&httpsredir=1&article=1517&context=coedu_pub. Accessed on 17 October 2018.

Oancea, A., & Furlong, J. (2007). Expressions of excellence and the assessment of applied and practice-based research. *Research Papers in Education*, *22*(2), 119–137.

Paulston, R. (2000). Imagining comparative education: Past, present and future. *Compare: A Journal of Comparative and International Education*, *30*(3), 353–367.

Pollard, A. (2008). *Quality and capacity in UK education research.* Report of the first meeting of the UK's Strategic Forum for Research in education, 16 and 17 October, Harrogate.

Taysum, A. (2013). *Convener of a large symposium in two parts; 'International Boundary Crossing Study of Teachers' and Students' Participation in Institutional Processes and Practices".* European Conference for Educational Research. Istanbul, September.

Taysum, A. (2014). *Convener of a large symposium in two parts: 'International Boundary Crossing Study Of Higher Education Institutions working in Partnership with Schools To Improve Participation In Processes And Practices Chair: Jan Heystek (Stellenbosch University) Discussant: Carole Collins Ayanlaja (Chicago, Superintendent).* European Conference for Educational Research, Porto.

Taysum, A. (2015). *Convener of a large symposium in two parts with Arar, K., Collins-Ayanlaja, C., Harrison, K., Imam, H., Murrel-Abery, V., Mynbayeva, A., Yelbayeva, Z. 'A Theory of Young People's Participation in Systems and Learning from International Boundary Crossing Action-Resarch Project.* European Conference for Educational Research. Budapest, Hungary. September.

Taysum, A. (2016). *Convener of a large symposium in two parts with McNamara (Chair), Risku, M., Collins Ayanlaja, C., Iddrisu, M.T., Murrel-Abery, J.V., Arar, K., Masry-Herzallah, A., Imam, H., Chopra, P., McGuinness, S. Theoretical underpinnings of an education and skills model for participation and cooperation in the Youth Field; empowering Europe's young innovators.* European Conference for Educational Research, Dublin, Ireland, August.

Taysum, A. (2017). *Convener of a large symposium in two parts with Arar, K., Masry-Herzallah, A., Collins Ayanlaja, C., Brookins, W., McGuinness, S., Bates, J., Roulsten, S., O'Connor, U., James, F., and George, J., Taysum, A. Turbulence in Six International Education Governance-Systems: Comparing Knowledge to Action for Equity, Peace and Renewal.* European Conference for Educational Research, Copenhagen, Denmark, August.

Foreword

When I served as chief of curriculum and instruction for the Vermont Department of Education, I was asked to lead that state's curriculum reform program, with the goal of setting a broad learning agenda for all of our schools. The central question we posed to 5,000 people in over 50 forums around our small state boiled down to this: *What do we need to know and be able to do in order to be successful?* But what is meant by the word *we*? Is it a singularity, *we* meaning each one of us considering our separate well-being and the preparations the lone individual needs or is it a group *we*? If so what are the boundaries of that *we*? Or most broadly, is it a universal *we* connecting the well-being and preparation of our human family so that we define the knowledge and abilities that are our common responsibilities?

At that time, my colleagues and I argued that the top priority of our school systems was to provide the next generation of citizens with the knowledge and abilities they needed to sustain and improve democratic societies locally, nationally and around the world. Therefore, it is the third use of the word *we* that mattered most. We were hardly alone in this conclusion. Consider the aspirational vision outlined in such documents as the United Nations' Universal Declaration of Human Rights (United Nations, 1948) or the spirit of the heroic civil rights leader Fannie Lou Hamer when she taught us that 'Nobody's free until everybody's free' (1971).

It is clear to me that the authors of this book are aiming at the third definition as well, namely the needs that *we* writ large, have to be successful. If this is the case, *we* again meaning all of us, need to consider the needs and aspirations of those whose hands are not within grasping distance of the levers of power. Just as importantly, we need to examine the historic circumstances that have led to current inequities for marginalised communities. For the authors, this means considering the pattern of events in the specific international cases in their research as well as connecting these findings to theoretical work that seeks to establish clear patterns of power shifting first from one group to another, all the while sustaining or even elevating inequities.

Into this caldron of political and social turbulence come the educators, specifically those senior leaders and supervisors charged with harmonising elements of school system bureaucracies with publics who may have very different agendas. All of this often comes amidst inequalities of resources. It is, therefore, no mystery why conditions of heightened turbulence exist (Gross, 2014).

The authors have used Turbulence Theory and specifically the four levels of turbulence it depicts as a consistent theoretical lens with which to describe the dramatic struggles of their protagonists. They have also considered the three drivers of turbulence: positionality, cascading and stability in their thoughtful analysis. By so doing, they make it clear that every event does not lead to an extreme level of turbulence and therefore help us to understand the times that modest adjustments are called for as distinguished from stronger measures in the case of more challenging situations. This analysis leads to specific suggestions for innovations such as robust, equity-oriented mentoring networks and the empowerment of a new generation of social renewal activists. Helping educators around the world learn to work with the inevitable turbulence of their profession in ways such as these is why I developed Turbulence Theory in the first place and why I continue to explore ways it can be employed.

But the authors do more than reflect on turbulence in isolation. Their carefully selected international cases, taken individually and as a whole, provide a multi-dimensional lens with which we can better understand and respond to inequities in our school systems. Whether they are examining the challenges facing African American women superintendents in the United States, depicting the pressures confronting Arab educational supervisors in Israel, or considering the conditions meeting curriculum reform leaders in Trinidad and Tobago, the authors faithfully connect the three concepts found in the title of this book: Turbulence, Empowerment and Marginalisation. This dedication to the book's theme is clearly found as well in the English case of Black Asian Minority Ethnicity (BAME) chief executive officers' (CEO) determination to support their communities and in the examination of educational leaders helping to guide communities in Northern Ireland towards peaceful coexistence. In this way, authors do the world's educational community and the wider public a true service.

Returning to the question of what do we mean by *we*? I would say that that acquiring the knowledge and skills to respond, adapt and even thrive amidst the heightened turbulence of our era is something that *we* all need. This seems even more the case for educators seeking to promote equity in their work with marginalised populations. This book is a rich resource for just such a study. I commend it to you.

Steven Jay Gross
Professor Emeritus
Temple University

References

Gross, S. J. (2014). Using turbulence theory to guide actions. In C. M. Branson & S. J. Gross (Eds.), *Handbook on ethical educational leadership* (pp. 246–262). New York, NY: Routledge.

Hamer, F. L. (1971, July 10). "Nobody's Free Until Everybody's Free." Speech Delivered at the Founding of the National Women's Political Caucus, Washington, DC.

United Nations. (1948). *Universal declaration of human rights* (General Assembly Resolution 217 A). Retrieved from http://www.un.org/en/universal-declaration-human-rights/. Accessed on 29 April 2018.

PART I
CONCEPTUALISING TURBULENCE, EMPOWERMENT AND MARGINALISATION

Chapter 1

Turbulence, Empowerment and Marginalised Groups

Alison Taysum and Khalid Arar

Abstract

This introduction sets the scene for the study by explaining the rationale for presenting a comparative analysis of five nation states' governance systems; England, Northern Ireland, Arabs in Israel, Trinidad and Tobago and the United States, with Nigerian interests represented in the research design. The context is that of a global phenomenon of a Black–White achievement gap (Wagner, 2010). The quality is world leading in terms of originality, significance and rigour. We present a theory of colonisation between groups with different interests, which includes nation states colonising other nation states, and dominant groups within nation states colonising marginalised groups. We also explored how dominant groups within educational governance systems may colonise marginalised groups within education governance systems. We theorised colonisation using Karpman's Triangle (1968) identifying that different groups can be oppressor, and/or victim, and/or rescuer, and these roles may shift as changes occur in power and economic influence. We present the Empowering Young Societal Innovators for Equity and Renewal Model (Taysum et al., 2012, 2013, 2014, 2015, 2016, 2017) with five principals for equity and renewal. We explain the turbulence that senior-level leaders experience and how education governance systems need to empower their autonomy as credentialed educational professionals' with track records of school improvement. Impact strategies to optimise students' learning and students' outcomes, and build the community's values of social justice, courage and prudence need to underpin social mobility. These innovations are only possible if they are informed by grass roots participatory philosophical inquiry, that is informed by and informs

Turbulence, Empowerment and Marginalisation in International
Education Governance Systems, 3–28
doi:10.1108/978-1-78754-675-220181002

policy, and is carefully monitored for quality assurance against the highest of educational professional standards.

Keywords: Democracy; equity; peace; achievement gap; reparation

The aim of this book is to present a comparative analysis of five nation states' governance systems to understand how governance systems empower key agents of change in school communities, from marginalised groups, to Empower Young Societal Innovators for Equity, and Renewal (EYSIER), for peace. The nation states in alphabetical order are England, Arabs in Israel, Northern Ireland, Trinidad and Tobago, and the United States (US). The context is that of a global phenomenon of a Black-White achievement gap (Wagner, 2010). The research quality is world leading in terms of originality, significance and rigour in the way we address an identified gap in the knowledge regarding issues of race, gender, religion, language and culture, socio-economic status, citizenship, migrant and refugee status. We agree with Bridges (2016) that our research is international and does not assume knowledge of the author's national educational system. Therefore, we provide a full education historiographical policy history in three editions of *IJSE* (2012a, 2014, and 2017), which underpins the education project, and we reference these historiographical policy histories in this book. We also agree with Bridges (2016) that the local and particular case is absolutely necessary so that research makes sense to researchers in their own contexts at the state level, district level, school level and classroom level. We present local and particular cases in full, invite the reader to connect with the issues and then present an international comparative analysis. We also want to address what Bridges (2016, p. 431) calls: 'the unequal power across the global community when it comes to the production of research (including educational research) and in the very definition of what will count as research'. Our research team has chosen to partner with each other to try to see beyond the unequal distribution of cash-rich nation states' power, and to work together to transcend the rhetoric and practices of Western epistemologies, to co-create communities of research that do not require adherence to existing norms (Bridges, 2016; Rizvi, 2009; Taysum & Iqbal, 2012). As a research team of 17 international researchers working in six nation states, we have always strived to work collaboratively with open minds in our engagement with the literature. Professor Hauwa Imam from Nigeria contributed to the research design of our education project and wanted to contribute a chapter to the book. Most senior public officers she approached were reluctant to participate with the research on educational governance systems that prevented a full Nigerian case from being presented. Professor Imam was able to conduct an interview with two senior public officers, which revealed that intersectionalities of discrimination exist in curriculum implementation practices in the schools. Professor Imam is included in this book as a key member of the research team and contributor to the design of the research.

We continue to be committed to our research project steered by a moral compass that assures an ethical framework revealed throughout the book. We are very grateful to all colleagues who participated in this research in a collaborative endeavour to understand how we can EYSIER.

The book has three parts. The first part titled 'Introductory Chapter: Turbulence, Empowerment and Marginalised Groups' focuses on the introduction to turbulence in governance systems, a review of the literature and the research methodology. The second part titled 'Five International Cases of Turbulence, Empowerment and Marginalisation' presents each case of compulsory education systems K-12 in alphabetical order: an English Case, a Northern Irish Case, an Arabs in Israel Case, a Trinidad and Tobago Case and a US Case. The third part titled 'Turbulence, Empowerment and Marginalisation: Knowledge to Action' presents a comparative analysis and a theory of empowerment through governance systems, conclusions and recommendations.

The objectives of the book are to present five international cases of how governance systems empower key agents of change in school communities to EYSIER for peace. Each of the five international cases takes a humanist approach and collect narrative biographies of over 50 senior-level leaders who represent marginalised communities with intersectionalities of discrimination based on race, gender, religion, culture, language, socio-economic status and legal documented status regarding citizen or refugee within five different international education governance systems. We take a culturally sensitive approach to the phenomenological study (Bridges, 2016). The data analysis was informed by Collins Ayanlaja's approach to and engagement with data analysis and this section draws from the data analysis section written up by Collins Ayanlaja in the US case study chapter. For the purposes of this research between six and fifteen respondents were identified in each case. In ethnography, the recommended sample size is approximately 30–50 interviews, whereas, in phenomenology, the recommended sample size is 'six interviews' (Mertens, 1998, p. 271).

According to Kilbourn (2006), the phenomena that we aim to understand are filtered through a point of view in a qualitative study. Thus, the theoretical frameworks aforementioned are important as guideposts for the analysis. Interpretations are always filtered through one or more lenses or theoretical perspectives that we use for 'seeing'; reality is not something that we find under a rock (p. 545). As researchers, we acknowledge that we all have positions in the research and we have worked hard to ensure we do not curb our open-mindedness through the internal and external review process. We are mindful that Lie (2011) cautions that Western-educated intellectuals in struggles to counter racism may perpetuate marginalisation. Lie (2011, p. 251) suggests 'Majority and minority groups often share the same language, religion, and culture. The potentially contradictory claims of belonging and exclusion generate the particularities and paradoxes of minority identity'. We have always worked closely to develop a collaborative diverse research team, and we have always critically reflected on our research design, findings and impact strategies to ensure we are not perpetuating a discourse of marginalisation in our efforts to work for equity, renewal and a participatory post-racial society (Dewey, 2016;

Rich, 2013). Taysum and Collins Ayanlaja led a British Educational Leadership Management and Administration Society Doctoral Research Interest Group on 11 April 2018 in Chicago with senior Chicago public school leaders. The feedback from these senior leaders was that our impact strategies offered in this book are specific, measurable, achievable and realistic, and the senior leaders are interested in working with us to implement them. The voices of those from public schools are vital to this book. Therefore, we represent the voices of senior leaders in the generation of new knowledge, and we represent the voices of senior leaders who believe the impact strategies we propose can work.

All five cases were shared by the team at The European Conference for Educational Research (ECER), 2017, held in Denmark (Taysum et al., 2017). During that time, we were able to explore the macro-level of categorisation and theme identification. Taysum had developed a research design and interview schedule to ask how policy and governance systems supported the work of senior-level leaders, how the senior-level leaders perceived networks of support from experts and mentors and what culture change was required for school improvement for equity, renewal and social mobility. Thus, we had data from five international cases that addressed these questions and we were able to talk through the similarities and differences within cases and between cases. Our comparative analysis revealed a common thread that ran through each of the cases, and across the cases which enabled us to begin to pull together the international cross-cultural comparison of the findings in Chapter 10.

Conclusions arose through reflection whereby the researchers were aware of the need to construct and revisit categories, look for similarities, uncover negative evidence and notice patterns (Stainback & Stainback, 1988 in Mertens, 1998). Each team then sent their cases to Taysum who distributed them for internal and external review following a timetable she had created and agreed with all reviewers. Taysum then engaged with a meta-analysis of the five cases using a constant comparative method (Mertens, 1998). Whilst the authors of the five cases responded to the reviews to improve their chapters, Taysum followed Huberman's (1994) approach to qualitative analysis to create a descriptive picture of the comparative analyses. Understandings grew out of a creative process whereby Taysum identified what was significant and insignificant and how the ideas could be succinctly represented for the reader (Patton, 2015). Working with a diverse research team was vital for representing different world views in the research, along with participants, and external reviewers from different faiths and none: Islam, Judaism, Sikhism, Hinduism, Christianity and from different nation states to diminish the possibility of bias that would impact an accurate analysis. Taysum sent the analysis she had completed to Arar which underpinned a dialogue through a Skype meeting. Taysum then wrote the comparative analysis chapter and sent it to Arar, and we then developed it collaboratively.

The five cases in Chapters 4 through 9 identify the roles and categorise the kinds of 'turbulence' (Gross, 2014) the senior-level leaders experience. Each case analyses how these senior-level leaders navigate the turbulence. Finally, each case reveals how the governance systems empower or disempower senior-level leaders in school communities to EYSIER for peace (Horizon, 2020). A new impact strategy of empowerment through knowledge to action to EYSIER for Peace is presented.

The five nation states were chosen because they are connected by histories of colonialism as identified by Taysum (2017) that has marginalised groups based on different groups' race, ethnicity, culture, religion, economic resources, owner- ship of land and inheritance with the drawing of geographical boundaries. Strategies of colonisation include an oppressor creating victims, who require rescuers (Karpman, 1968). However, Karpman suggests that such roles are switched and the victim, perhaps of colonisation, can become the oppressor by colonising. The victims created by colonisation may seek a rescuer, but when that rescuer does not deliver, they are quickly perceived as an oppressor by the victim. At the same time, the rescuer needs victims to rescue and may sabotage the emancipation of the victim because they need victims to fulfil their need to be a rescuer. Oppressors can blame their victims and can be very controlling, angry and unpleasant. These bullies do not solve any problems. Karpman calls this a triangle of drama. Those in this triangle need to recognise the role they are playing in the triangle. Just one person becoming enlightened with the think- ing tools they need to recognise their role, and through becoming more mature, shift out of their role(s), can empower themselves to gain the resources they need to step out of the shadows and meet their own needs. From this position of strength, they can empower others to recognise their role in the triangle and emancipate themselves from it by working collaboratively.

Colonialism in Trinidad and Tobago is summed up by Besson (2011, p. 1) in 'The Caribbean History Archives' who states:

> African slavery and European colonisation in the Caribbean are in separable. Africans and Spanish-born blacks arrived in the islands along with Columbus and the earliest Spanish settlers and enslaved Africans soon became the major work force for the mines, plantations and ranches established in the Hispanic Caribbean in the 16th century.

Besson and Brereton (2010) identify Trinidad's African-born population came from Western Africa, Angola and Central Congo, and Muslims came from sub-Saharan Africa. England's role in this slave trade and in colonisation could also be seen in Ireland and was instrumental in causing the flight of the Earls in Ulster (Hull, 2012), underpinned by the Statutes of Kilkenny 1367 AD which Figgis (1918, p. 1) identifies:

> made it punishable by death to: speak the Irish language, to wear the Irish fashion of dress, to wear beards as did the Irish, to ride a horse barebacked, to have an Irish name, to take judgment by Irish law, to marry an Irish man or woman, to interchange chil- dren in fosterage as did the Irish, to entertain any Irish poet or minstrel, or to hear Irish history, to admit an Irishman to

> sanctuary, to permit an Irishman to graze cattle, or to graze cattle
> on an Irish man's land, to cease at any time to war upon the
> Irish, or to hold any manner of commerce with an irishman.

An apartheid was created in Ireland and the attempted annihilation of the Irish identity. The sectarian conflict in Ireland between Irish Catholics and English Protestants was carried out on a wider scale with the defeat of the Spanish Armada by the English, in the English Channel. Douglas and Barrett (2009) argue that the hurricane force winds off the Coast of Ireland on 21 September 1588, and the challenges of navigating the Irish coast caused in total the loss of 24 ships and 5,000 men, which was a far greater loss than the Spanish losses in the English Chanel. The defeat of the Catholic Spanish challenged the rule of the Spanish Inquisition that had the power to trial and kill people guilty of heresy who had not converted to Catholicism (Karman, 2014; Pym, 2012). Karman identifies that there was a problem in defining heresy and there were no clear laws to this regard. Individuals in communities could be informers for the inquisition making community life one of potential fear that a neighbour might accuse a neighbour of heresy. Indeed, Edwards (2012, p. 47) identifies that 'interior prayer and intense devotion indicating a personal relationship with God could be seen as 'wrong'. There is no space to discuss the extent to which this murder of human beings for heresy is connected with the murder of human beings who are deemed as heretics by Islamic Violent Fundamentalism feeding terrorism such as the 11 September 2001 attacks on New York and Washington (Osman, 2016). Osman (2016) also identifies The Islamic State of Iraq and Syria (ISIS) are 'cyber jihadists' (p. 71) who have hacked US Military Command and therefore have the potential to cause further cyber-attacks and other kinds of attacks which may be blamed on other nation states causing international conflict as an impact strategy to divide and conquer and undermine peace in our time (Taysum & Murrel-Abery, 2017). Neither is there space to discuss how Catholics elect their spiritual leader the Pope, and The British monarch as the defender of the faith for the Church of England is a hereditary role, and how in Islam some consider a new leader should be elected (Sunni), whilst others (Shia) consider the caliph must be the Holy Prophet's (Peace Be Upon Him) descendants (Rogerson, 2010). Rather, the aim of this chapter is to provide an explanation for the choice of these nation states for this project and for this book.

The flight of the Earls of Ulster in 1603 at the end of a 9-year war was the last ditch attempt for independence in Ireland from English domination and marks the end of the old Gaelic governance systems in Ireland and the end of an Irish epoch (Gaston, 2014). In 1609, Protestant English and Presbyterian Scots settlers were imported to Ireland by the orders of King James VI (Scotland) who is one and the same with King James I (England and Ireland). The settlers who dispossessed all rebel leaders of their lands changed the way the land was managed, which arguably predicated the famine in Ireland along with the external influence of the British Government with the Corn Laws (Harley, 2008). Harley identifies that The Corn Laws imposed tariffs on imported food and grain to

England to gain economic and political influence and power. Two principles underpinned these regulations: first to protect domestic interests and second to generate revenue for the state. However, these steep import duties made it too expensive to import food and grain, even when food supplies were short. The impact of these import duties was to raise the cost of living for the British people, which, in turn, depressed economic growth in other domestic sectors. The experience of damaging high import duties resulted in what Floud and Johnson call distress (2004; pp. 189–190):

> Political and economic events brought the tariff to the forefront of parliamentary concern in the early 1840s. Severe economic recession created distress in manufacturing districts and, by curtailing revenue from customs and excises, brought a crisis in government finance. Distress strengthened the already powerful political challenge, mainly outside of parliament, to the corn laws – a particularly iniquitous tax on the poor's food for the benefit of the rich. In 1842 Prime Minister Peel acted decisively to strengthen government finance and unexpectedly reintroduced the income tax, which provided revenue that permitted tariff reform; the corn laws and the timber duties were modified. Return of prosperity allowed Peel to undertake further tariff reform in 1845 – including the removal of the import tax on raw cotton and lowering of the sugar duties [...] Almost immediately Benjamin Disraeli, who emerged as the leader of the protectionist majority of the Tory party that split from Peel, recognised that the reimposition of protection would subject the established order – the Tory's overwhelming concern – to savage and perhaps fatal popular attack (Blake, 1966: 278–84). On the other side of the House, Whigs, Radicals and Peelites, despite their many differences, all opposed protectionism [...] Britain's unwavering free trade supported expansion of world trade for more than half a century.

Identifying that the tariffs on imports to protect national interests logically appeared sound, however, history reveals import tariffs ultimately stood as a barrier to liberalism, contributed to causing famines and led to economic stagnation, and migration. In the case of the Irish Famine, the high imposed import duties now stand as a symbol of oppression for Irish Nationalist Groups. To escape the famine, large numbers of starving and sick Irish people migrated to the United States, many via Canada because this was a cheaper passage. The horrific conditions on the ships gave them the name of 'coffin ships' (Irish Genealogy Tool Kit, 2018). The conflict in Northern Ireland between Catholic groups and Protestant groups arguably grows out of protectionism from annihilation, has its roots in this Irish-English socio-political and economic history and connects Ireland with the United States through migration.

English colonialism was predicated by the conflict between the nations of the UK, prior to that England was colonised by the Norse men, or Vikings, prior to that England was colonised by the Barbarians (Scotts and Pitts) and prior to that England was colonised by the Romans (Halsall, 2007). Thus, the desire for England to colonise the rest of the world may have originated from a fear of annihilation experienced during the first five centuries from the Romans, Barbarians, Vikings and neighbouring countries. Indeed, the fear of annihilation from the Barbarians was so great that the English wrote to Rome saying they had the choice to jump from the cliffs, drown in the sea or have their throats cut by the Barbarians (Halsall, 2007). Interestingly, the Romans may have colonised England in response to protecting themselves by gaining economic and political influence and power from the colonialism of the Greeks of the fifth-century BC (Halsall, 2007). Halsall (2007) suggests the Greeks colonisation was driven by a desire for economic and political influence and power.

This introduction is not an apology for colonialism and how it appears to seek economic and political influence and power. Rather, the introduction invites the reader to consider how groups of people seek power in an impact strategy of colonialism as a possible response to previous experiences of colonisation by the other. Thus, Karpman's Triangle (1968) helps us understand the socio-historiographical relationships between different partners of this educational project that shapes the reality of marginalisation nowadays.

Arabs in Israel has been chosen as a case because of the similar religious segregation experienced nowadays that Northern Ireland experiences and is seeking to overcome. Comparing and contrasting cases where different segregation occurs, and looking at socio-cultural and economic histories helps reveal how oppressors may be seeking to protect themselves from previous oppression and marginalisation. Prior to the Balfour agreement (1917) and the religious segregation of Arabs and Jews in Israel, the Jewish people had been oppressed. The Jewish Virtual Library (2018, p. 1) states:

> Jews were mentioned in documents in 945 and 992 forbidding Venetian captains from accepting Jews onboard their ships. In 1252, Jews were not allowed to settle in the main part of the city […], The Senate decided to expel the Jews from the city in 1394 due to fears of Jewish encroachment in certain economic spheres. They were allowed to work in the city for limited two-week intervals. Those who were not moneylenders were allowed to remain in the city, albeit with certain restrictions. Jews were forced to wear various markings on their clothing to identify themselves as Jews. In 1394 they had to wear a yellow badge, it was changed to a yellow hat in 1496 and to a red hat in 1500. Other anti-Jewish laws including the prohibition against owning land (enacted in 1423) and from building a synagogue […] In 1516, the doges, Venice's ruling council, debated whether Jews should be allowed to remain in the city. They decided to let the Jews remain, but

their residence would be confined to Ghetto Nuova, a small, dirty island; it became the world's first ghetto. The word 'ghetto' is from the Italian getto meaning 'casting' or Venetian geto meaning 'foundry'. Jews of Italian and German origin moved into this ghetto. The latter came to Venice because of persecution in their communities, while the former came from Rome and from the South, where they faced anti-Semitism.

At these times, Venice had become an apartheid state, and the Jews were segregated from other communities and were not allowed to own land. Oppression of Jews continued and Cesarani (2011, p. 1) states: In April 1933, Hitler permitted an organised boycott of Jewish businesses and his government enacted a string of laws that gradually excluded the Jews from government employment and public life.

Under the Nuremberg Laws of 1935 German Jews were reduced to subject status and lost the rights of citizens. Germany became, in effect, an apartheid state.

Aly and Heim (2008) suggest German economists argued overpopulation in Poland due to an influx of refugees, and 'people disabled by the state'[1] who were labelled as 'useless eaters' contributed to economic inefficiencies. A strategy to address this was to exploit labour, and when that failed, to kill labour and replace the Polish population with ratios of one Polish person to two German people and as much as one Polish person to 10 German people (Aly & Heim, 2008). Using this analysis, Aly and Heim (2008) argues Helmut Meinhold, The Reich's economic advisor, argued for widespread German population starvation at the end of World War II. The intellectual logic of his proposition was to address the overpopulation in Germany in the same way it had been addressed in Poland. Aly and Heim (2008, p. 183) state:

Meinhold now saw in Germany the economic chaos he had previously seen in Poland: severe overpopulation due to the influx of refugees, destruction of production facilities and lack of capital. In his terms, the erosion of manpower due to the war had not kept pace with the erosion of capital, at least not as far as the Germans were concerned. Consequently there were too many people living in Germany in 1945 for their combined labour resources to be exploited to the full with the capital that remained.

---

[1]There is no space to critique: (1) the social model where people are disabled by the state, and (2) the medical model where people are located in a deficit model where disabled people are seen to be 'in deficit, or 'deficient' (Crutchley, 2018). Our position is to take the social model adopting the UK Government (2010) Equality Act.

The number of Jewish women, men and children murdered in the Holocaust in Germany, Poland, Lithuania and elsewhere is difficult to state exactly, but the consensus appears to be around 6 million, though this is still probably a conservative estimate (Aly & Heim, 2008). The state of Israel was created in 1948 and Berger (2014) identifies mass immigration to Israel saw a clash of different cultures between Socialist and Capitalist groups, Jews from Europe and Jews from the Middle East. Berger (2014, p. 90) describes 'serious ideological gulfs between socialist and capitalist factions, as well as between the predominantly secular majority and the various religiously observant communities'. In addition, the Palestinian Arabs became refugees with the creation of the Israeli state in 1948 (Cohen, 2000). The ensuing apartheid has left Arabs in Israel needing to protect their human rights, including protecting their rights to own land and protecting their identities from annihilation. Emira who contributed to this education project (2014, p. 20) identifies Egypt got involved to try to protect Arabs in Israel:

> The continuing 'Arab-Israeli confrontation forced Egypt to spend approximately forty percent of its 1975 budget on arms' (McLaughlin, 1978, p. 886). (at the same time of) external debts (Fan, Al-Riffai, El-Said, Yu, & Kamaly, 2007). Unlike the Socialist programme of Nasser's regime in the previous policy era, the foundations of liberalisation of the economy were laid in 1974 'to open up the economy to foreign investment and protect investments against nationalisation and confiscation' (Licari, 1997, p. 13). To assist the economic crisis Egypt had to ask in January 1977 the International Monetary Fund (IMF) for financial support, which was agreed on a condition that Egypt would raise taxes and reduce subsidies, which led to riots in the same month by 'the unhappy working masses and the students' (Feiler, 2003, p. 193). Although these planned reforms were cancelled, the government had to resort to a bigger budget deficit to avoid political instability Feiler (2003).[2]

Nation states have been involved with the segregation of Palestinians from Jewish people since the creation of Israel in 1948, including the occupation of the West Bank and Gazza Strip, which has continued to marginalise the Palestinian people in Israel in different life spheres including segregation between Jewish and Arab education (Arar, 2012).

This brief historical analysis, which is explored in great depth in 26 international peer-reviewed articles commissioned and edited by Taysum in the *Italian Journal of Sociology of Education* (2012a, 2014, 2017), identifies the reasons why

---

[2]There is no space to discuss the impact of the Arabs in Israel's segregation from Jews in Israel on other nation states in the Middle East and beyond. An Egyptian perspective has been given here because Emira collaborated in the education project.

these nation states where chosen based on their inter-relationships with each other. England has been a victim of colonisation experiencing apartheid and marginalisation and has moved from a position of being colonised to one of colonisation and oppressor. The shift in the role was perhaps made possible by learning from the colonisers how to colonise and how to protect the interests of an identity from annihilation and gain economic, and political power and influence. England played a significant part in the slave trade of human beings from Africa to the West Indies and the US, which has been documented by Taysum and Murrel-Abery (2017). England also played a significant part in the abolition of slavery, which may place England as a rescuer on Karpman's Triangle (1968). The working people in the thriving cotton mills in Manchester refused to touch cotton picked by slaves in a union initiative leading to a cotton famine. The huge sacrifice by the working people of Manchester, who could not feed their families without the work, was recognised in President Abraham Lincoln's (1863) letter to 'the working people of Manchester', which states:

> I cannot but regard your decisive/utterances upon the question as an instance of sublime Christian heroism which has/not been surpassed in any age or in any country. It is indeed an energetic/and re-inspiring assurance of the inherent truth and of the ultimate and universal/triumph of justice, humanity and freedom (...) I hail this interchange of sentiments/therefore, as an augury that whatever else may happen, whatever misfortune/may befall your country or my own, the peace and friendship which now exists/ between the two nations will be as it shall be my desire to make them, perpetual.

In summary England has been the victim of an apartheid state, and the persecutors of an apartheid state, and rescuers of people from an apartheid state. England was the victim of an apartheid state with the Romans and the Vikings etc. Trinidad and Tobago has been colonised by the Spanish, the French, the Dutch and the English, used to traffic slaves and experienced an apartheid. Jewish people have been colonised and experienced apartheid in Europe including Italy, Germany, Poland and Lithuania and been victims of massive war crimes and annihilation of six million Jewish people during the Holocaust. Jewish Israeli people have been colonisers, and Arabs in Israel have become refugees, thus creating an apartheid state. The Island of Ireland has been colonised by the English with Ulster being the focus of the Flight of the Earls, creating an apartheid state that was also sectarian, based on Catholics and Protestants. Marginalisation in Northern Ireland continues today with what might be called an apartheid state.

The US has played a significant part in slave trafficking and segregation of Black human beings from White human beings, and an effective apartheid existed under US law. The *Red Scott* v. *Sanford* (1857) (United States Supreme Court, 1857) decision stated Americans descended from African slaves could not be citizens of the US. The 'one drop of blood rule', called an hypodescendent rule, meant if a White male slave owner had a child with a Black female slave, their child would be categorised as Black. Their Black child had no rights to property or wealth of her or his White father (Lee and Bean, 2010). The US abolished slavery with the 13th Amendment to the US Constitution in 1865, Public Law US Code 38–11, Stat. 567; Public Law 38–52 13, Stat. 774–775 (Historical Archives, United States House of Representatives, 1865, p. 1), and the 14th Amendment to the Constitution, Public Law US Code 14, Stat. 358–359, which further declared:

> all persons born or naturalized in the U.S. were citizens and that any state that denied or abridged the voting rights of males over the age of 21 would be subject to proportional reductions in its representation in the U.S. House of Representatives. Approved by the 39th Congress (1865–1867) as H.J. Res. 127; ratified by the states on July 9, 1868. (Historical Archives, United States House of Representatives, 1868, p. 1).[3]

Whilst the 14th Amendment was contested, particularly by the states of the defeated Confederacy, the threat of not being represented at the US House of Representatives forced the former Confederate states to ratify the 14th Amendment. However, Louisiana and Tennessee legalised the 'one drop of blood rule' again in 1910 that ensured any person classified as 'mixed race' would be classified as Black (Lee & Bean, 2012). The implication of this for families during segregation was that a White father would be segregated from his child in society if the mother of the child was categorised as Black. Lee and Bean (2012) affirm that by 1925 most states in the US had institutionalised this race law into practice. In 1930, the US Census classified all mixed-race 'Black' people as 'Negro'. Schools in the US have operated under a desegregation policy since 1967 although desegregation in schools legally ended in 1954 with the *Brown* v. *Board of Education* (United States Supreme Court, 1954).

De Gruy (2005) identifies that human beings who are dominated through slavery, colonisation, segregation and marginalisation are not able to protect their families from harm and possible annihilation because they are dominated by others who do not recognise them (Payne, 2008). Taysum in the English case of this book argues dominant cultures may maintain a status quo unnaturally privileging themselves through institutional customs located in historical epochs regulated by geographical borders and statistics. These structures are so entrenched the unnatural and socially constructed privilege affording extra entitlement, may appear natural (Bourdieu, 2000; Dewey, 2016; De Gruy, 2005).

---

[3]There is no space here to talk about the other colonisations that have existed throughout the epochs of time and Taysum is currently exploring this.

An example of evidence of privilege in society today is that eight men have the same wealth as 50% of the world's poorest people (Oxfam, 2017).

The reason for choosing the five nation states as the focus of this book and the other 25 who have engaged in the education project is because these nation states, with institutional customs located in historical epochs and regulated by geographical borders and statistics, are linked with each other in Karpman's Triangle (1968). The roles they take as oppressors, and/or victims and/or rescuers have located different groups as dominant and/or marginalised particularly if they have switched roles within Karpman's Triangle. Looking back, sociopolitical and economic Governance impact strategies have lacked a moral compass that assures an ethical framework: when human beings have been colonised to increase the power and economic wealth of the coloniser; when human beings have been starved, or left to die to address over-population; when mercantile law with import taxes has stagnated economic growth and led to starvation of populations; when migrants and refugees are marginalised within societies that may already have marginalised groups based on race, ethnicity, culture, language, religion, gender, those disabled by society, gay lesbian, bisexual or transgender (GLBT), and/or any of the protected characteristics of the UK Equality Act (UK Government, 2010).

At a time of mass migration nowadays with 244 million global migrants in 2015 (International Organisation for Migration, 2018), and 65.6 million forcibly displaced people world wide, and 22 million refugees (The United Nations Refugee Agency, 2018) a challenge emerges which this book begins to address: How can educational governance systems organise the education of marginalised groups together with dominant groups in times of turbulence to EYSIER at a local level, state level and global level for peace in our time?

This book presents new descriptions and understandings of the ways in which senior leaders of education governance systems EYSIER in the five nation states. The states are connected by a web of colonisation and colonising that may be understood using Karpman's (1968) Triangle of oppressor, victim and rescuer. We recognise that the construct of peace in such a world is complex and that the current Governance Systems of nation states are perhaps seeking to position themselves as number one in the world league tables of wealth and power amongst nations, and to protect themselves from a threat of economic, political and cultural colonisation from the other. Such an ideology within governance systems that does not trust in cooperation between nation states for the common good and peace is likely to be replicated in education policy and regulated through International Education Assessors (2017) where groups compete for the highest ranks in the educational league tables that may, unintentionally, provoke an outcome of divide and conquer (Taysum & Murrel-Abery, 2017). This book is interested in developing young people to be the hope of the future and to challenge the structures and the agents that are perpetuating the roles of Karpman's Triangle that may be causing mistrust, conflict and war. We seek to understand the extent to which equity and renewal in constructive and sustainable ways for peace in our time might be explored in a curriculum that prepares young people, within inter-generational contexts, to understand the codes of human behaviour and make informed choices to change attitudes and behaviours for equity and renewal, and peace in our time.

We seek to describe and understand, in a step by step way first, what thinking tools senior-level leaders say they need, and second, what support they say they require from infrastructure, policy, budgets and networks of autonomous professional experts and experts in becoming. We then seek to describe and understand what impact strategies they say they need for culture change and how to implement these change strategies and build capacity in education governance systems to EYSIER within such an education project.

The education model EYSIER was developed with international partners representing 30 nation states, including Australia, Belgium, Bulgaria, China, Egypt, England, Finland, France, Germany, Greece, Guyana, Hungary, India, the Arab perspective of Israel, the Jewish perspective of Israel, Italy, Japan, Kazakhstan, Lebanon, Nigeria, Northern Ireland, Pakistan, Poland, Portugal, Republic of Ireland, Romania, Russia, South Korea, Trinidad and Tobago and the United States (Taysum, 2012a; Taysum, 2014a, b, 2017). Analyses conducted with these nation states from five continents from the end of World War II to the present day in the three issues of the *Italian Journal of Sociology of Education* reveal a pattern (2012a, 2014, 2017). First, new performance management systems often create education governance systems where 'doing things right' using what Adler (1941) calls intellectual virtues is prioritised over 'doing the right thing' which Adler (1941)[4] calls primary virtues of fortitude, or courage, prudence and social justice. Evidence from the historical international comparative analyses in the three issues of the *Italian Journal of Sociology of Education* (2012a, 2014, 2017) reveals that there is a lack of alignment between the values of school leaders working for social justice with courage and prudence using moral and intellectual virtues, on the one hand, and performance systems driven by quantitative data and education governance systems that require the implementation of performance systems (Ball, 2004), on the other. A pragmatic consequence for pupils is that they are also trained to play the system using intellectual virtues, rather than solving societal problems using both moral and intellectual virtues together for a sustainable and stable cultural, economic, political and ecological model (Taysum, 2012c; Taysum, 2013, 2014; Taysum et al., 2015, 2016, 2017).

Students playing the game know the key performance indicators they need to meet in a narrow range of subjects to be first. Their scores during their academic career may be correlated, even predicted by their socio-economic status related to their post-codes. Those with high socio-economic status are high achievers, and those with low socio-economic status do not know how to play the game and are marginalised with few real chances for social mobility (Arnova, Torres, & Franz, 2013; Taysum, 2012b; Taysum & Gunter, 2008; Waite, Rodríguez, & Wadende, 2015).

---

[4]Adler's (1941) primary virtues and secondary intellectual virtues helped theorise emergent themes from the comparative analysis of the five cases and are further explored in the Comparative Analysis Chapter of the book.

The global distribution of knowledge concerning education from cash-rich countries has had a tremendous impact on what is taught and tested in schools, and how they are organised in all countries and, in particular, nation states that are marginalised in the global politics because they are not cash rich (Moloi, Gravett, & Petersen, 2009). Comparative studies focusing on statistics, for example, the Programme of International Students Assessment (Organisation for Economic and Cooperation and Development, 2017) and Trends in International Mathematical and Science Study (TIMSS) (International Education Assessors, 2017) and Progress in International Reading Literacy Study (PIRLS) (IEA, 2017) examine the output of national education systems through a global lens. However, these studies do not shed light on the socio-economic or political context that shapes the values and acts of particular legislation; the fair funding formulas that underpin the allocation of funds to the construction of infrastructure, the education governance systems and the organisation of processes and practices of the education system within nation states and between nation states in the international community (Taysum & Iqbal, 2012). Intellectual and cultural colonisation that may lack moral and ethical frameworks (Adler, 1941) may be driven through education policy and into the curriculum and classroom metaphorically like a post person delivers mail. The danger is the deliverology (Barber, 2015) leapfrogs the role of an autonomous professional teacher as a researcher in the classroom focusing on the inquiry into students' progress in their learning. At the same time, deliverology potentially prevents the opportunity to talk back in the co-construction of meaning within participatory assessment for learning processes and practices (Bridges, 2016; Stenhouse, 1975). Such an approach commodifies education (Darling-Hammond & Lieberman, 2012; Waite et al., 2015) where people with cash-rich post-codes can afford the commodity 'education' to sustain their extra entitlement in the socio-economic system. Perhaps consideration could be given to the kinds of quantitative data that could usefully help benchmark progress of strategies for equity and renewal. In the US by the fourth quartile of 2015, national statistics revealed 72.2% of White folk were homeowners and 41.9% of Black folk were homeowners (United States Census Bureau, 2016). Setting targets for improved homeownership or a reduction in prison populations might be useful.

The innovative EYSIER offers a Charter Mark that benchmarks progress towards achieving five principles of the model (Taysum, 2012c; Taysum, 2014a, b; Taysum et al., 2015, 2016, 2017). The EYSIER model was built on Taysum's research projects since 2001 and has been developed and refined over five years with an international research team of 30 nation states. The EYSIER model represents many different cultural heritages of people moving to Europe and throughout the world with histories of being colonised and colonising over the past 5,000−10,000 years.

The five first principles of the EYSIER Model are as follows:

(1) inclusion to realise social justice and recognition for all (Adler, 1941; Fraser, 2000; Marshall & Gerstl-Pepin, 2005; Morgan, 2017);
(2) respect to realise social justice (Barnett, 2000; Taysum & Gunter, 2008);

(3) trust in the search for truth (Barnett, 2000; Carter, 2005; Möllering, 2001; Pring, 2000; Wagner, 2010);

(4) courage to engage in prudent dialogue to co-create constructive cross-cultural critique of alternative world views to arrive at a shared multicultural world view of how to live together for peace in our time (Adler, 1941; Darling-Hammond & Rothman, 2011; Gerstl-Pepin & Aiken, 2012; Ishii, Klopf, & Cooke, 2007); and

(5) the generation of new knowledge that prudently synthesises traditional and new knowledge to enable the re-imagining of new futures where young people are mobilisers of stable and sustainable socio-economic change for equity and renewal (Harrison, Taysum, McNamara, & O'Hara, 2016; Taysum, 2012b).

The schemes of work that meet each of the principles mentioned above through our developed action research approach (Bridges, 2016; Taysum, 2012c; Taysum, 2014a, b; Taysum et al., 2015, 2016, 2017) are being developed by Taysum (2018), along with a rationale for the EYSIER. The rationale focuses on how the education project empowers senior educational leaders, school and college staff, families, students and community partnerships (Epstein et al., 2002). The aims of this book are to understand if EYSIER was further tested for proof of concept and found successful, would the senior-level leaders in education governance systems be empowered to implement the model, which has been the focus of weekly discussions between Taysum and Collins Ayanlaja over the past five years and from which the focus of this book emerged.

Taysum was struck by the relevance of Gross (2014) Turbulence Theory at Professor Steven Gross' presentation at a BELMAS Annual Conference meeting in 2016. Taysum and Gross talked about Turbulence Theory, and Taysum presented the ideas of reading the enablers and challenges of the senior-level leaders' articulated experiences through Gross (2014) Turbulence Theory to the research team. After discussing this with all research partners in this book, we concurred Turbulence Theory provided a typology that allowed us to categorise the level and the impact of the challenges these senior-level leaders and key agents of change need to navigate as they mediate between the levels of the education governance systems. Gross (2014, p. 248) theory of turbulence states that 'turbulence can be described as "light" with little or no movement of the craft. "Moderate" with very noticeable waves. "Severe" with strong gusts that threaten control of the aircraft. "Extreme" with forces so great that control is lost and structure damage to the craft occurs'. The findings from all cases were read through the theory of turbulence. The findings reveal the state of the education governance systems and their impact on empowering cosmopolitan citizens (Waghid & Smeyers, 2014) to participate fully and freely in societal interactions and cooperations between diverse groups (Dewey, 2016). This book was imperative because we cannot move forward with the education model EYSIER until:

• We have described and understood the turbulence in education governance systems in different nation states as experienced by senior-level leaders seeking to empower marginalised groups for equity and renewal.

- We have described and understood how the turbulence empowers or disempowers senior-level educational leaders to work for equity and renewal.
- We have considered what support these senior-level leaders need to implement educational leadership, learning and change to EYSIER.
- We have considered how people have come to be marginalised through a process of colonisation with oppressors, and/or victims, and/or rescuers so we can offer those engaging with EYSIER a context and a brief overview of the codes of human behaviour that reveals two sides: first, driven by fear humans may seek to protect the self/group from annihilation from the other and second, humans, who trust in the divine if they have faith, and/or trust in humanism if they have no faith, may seek to co-create liberal infrastructures and liberal agents where hard work of all kinds is rewarded, and the vulnerable are lifted up through education and renewed with socially just opportunities to work for a good life.
- We have considered how the principals of EYSIER seek to replace the fear within societal systems for social justice, inclusion, respect, trust and courage to engage in dialogue with the other within a global cultural heritage of conflict, to re-imagine a shared world view with an overarching shared moral compass that assures an ethical framework for equity and renewal.

We now turn to how the aims of the book meet the professional challenge by asking four research questions: first, how do senior leaders of educational governance systems who are from and represent marginalised groups in society describe and understand how School Governance Systems empower or disempower them to develop school communities as societal innovators for equity and renewal? Second, how do these senior-level leaders of education governance systems describe and understand the role mentors and/or advocates play to support their navigation through the turbulence? Third, to what extent, do these senior-level leaders of education governance systems believe a cultural change is required to empower them in school and college communities including staff, families, students and community partnerships to EYSIER? Finally, what theories of knowledge to action emerge regarding how these senior-level leaders might successfully navigate turbulence to empower marginalised groups for equity and renewal for all in public corporate education governance systems?

Each research team presenting a case study in this book from England, Northern Ireland, Arab Israel, Trinidad and Tobago and the United States adopted the same methodologies so that the same data collection tools were administered in each context. At each stage of the development of the research, the research team engaged with dialogue via email, telephone calls or face-to-face meetings at conferences to discuss and develop the research design and the data collection tools until a consensus was reached. The consensus on the research design enabled us to assure cultural relevancy for each context in our research design, which assured we conducted empirical research that was trustworthy and provides the reader with the warrants for the claims we make (Gunter, 2005; Levin, 2004; Oancea & Furlong, 2007; Pollard, 2008). Thus, replicating the same research design in each case optimised the quality dimensions of a comparative analysis within each case and between the five cases.[5] Each case was conducted in accordance with the British Educational Research Association (BERA) (2011) Guidelines for Ethical Framework, the American Educational Research Association ethical framework (2010), the ethical codes of each researcher's University and nation state. The quality dimensions, therefore, focus on the trustworthiness of the logical, empirical, ethical and moral research, and each case study presented in this book was peer-reviewed internally by the researchers and externally by a network of experts.

Education is a cultural project that consists of histories, narratives and all faiths and none. All senior leaders from marginalised groups that we talked to in this research stated their faith, and religion was central to their service as an educational leader. The faiths represented by our researchers and within the research include Islam, Judaism, Sikhism, Hinduism, Christianity and no faith where a humanitarian approach is taken. Our questions help us generate new understandings about what values underpin these leaders' behaviours and to understand how their values align with legislation, education policy and the values found in education governance systems.

A central part of sustaining work in school and system improvement is developing the capacity of schools and colleges, and system leaders to recognise, foster and implement innovative educational leadership, learning and change to optimise learning within the learning communities. Education governance systems can empower and develop leaders and thereby contribute to the implementation of innovation in research and practice. By creating and empowering collaborative networked learning communities that support the ongoing professional learning and professional development of individual practitioners, and professional associations, it is possible to deepen existing and emergent pathways for bridging any knowledge–practice gaps in instructional leadership practice. Thus, each case study examines a local and particular senior level of educational leaders.

The English case researched and written by Alison Taysum examines how Black, Asian Minority Ethnic (BAME) chief executive officers (CEOs) of multi-academy trusts (MATs) navigate the turbulence when leading MATs to optimise students' learning and mobilise and empower communities for democracy in education (Dewey, 2016). The BAME people in England are categorised as belonging to marginalised groups. Marginalised groups include children living in poverty in England who are more likely to be in poor health, overweight, obese, suffer from asthma, have poorly managed diabetes, experience mental health problems and die early (Boseley, 2017). About 3.7 million children in the UK are below the poverty line, that is over 25% of children, and 1.7 million of these are in severe poverty (Barnardos, 2017).

---

[5]The BERA Ethical Guidelines were revised and the fourth edition published in June 2018 after the research was complete for this book.

The Northern Ireland case study, researched and written by Samuel McGuinness, Jessica Bates, Una O'Connor Stephen Roulston, Catherine Quinn and Brian Waring, is located in a society, emerging from recent conflict, which continues to display considerable division. The case study, which forms this chapter, was undertaken within the context of school partnerships and shared campuses forged through the shared education programme in Northern Ireland. Eight school principals were interviewed to explore the manner in which they undertook their roles and to categorise the kinds of 'turbulence' they experience – for example, in terms of strength and whether turbulence is light, moderate, severe or extreme (Gross, 2014). The team examined how the governance systems sanction them to empower school communities to become societal innovators for equity peace and renewal.

The Arab in Israel case was researched and written by Khalid Arar and Asmahan Masry. The authors identify that the Arab education system and Jewish education system are not only segregated but also unequal in both means and outputs. The difference between the Jewish and Arab systems, and the volatile apartheid environment in which the Arab education system is situated affirmed the need to read the data through Gross (2014) Turbulence Theory. Gross Turbulence Theory helped to better understand how those attempting to lead Arab education can overcome the constrictive reality and sustain deep democratic reform in such a turbulent era. The findings reveal that these senior-level leaders were able to steer a course through the turbulence with a moral compass that assured an ethical framework for the Arab education system underpinning greater success. Turbulence necessitates the leadership's intervention to influence the organisation's daily life, functioning and outputs (Gross, 2014; Harvey, Cambron-McCabe, Cunningham, & Koff, 2013). The study examines the perceptions of superintendents as administrative officers with professional educational credentials and proven track records as outstanding teachers and organisers of school improvement. The case focuses on how these senior-level leaders have, in many cases, succeeded in reducing the existing Arab–Jewish achievement gap. These officers have lead curriculum reform to enhance Arab students' achievements while finding solutions to cope with the competing interests within the education system.

The Trinidad and Tobago case was researched and written by Freddy James and June Gordon and is based on a component of a larger research project that was an independent review of the primary school curriculum renewal exercise that was carried out in Trinidad and Tobago (T&T) under the seamless education system (SES). The SES is a programme sponsored by the Inter-American Development Bank (IDB). The actual curriculum renewal exercise occurred during the period December 2012 to July 2013, and the review was commissioned two years later. This component of the review examines the relationships between policy-makers in education governance systems and the agencies charged with the responsibility to revise the curriculum. It further examines the interactions among these various agencies and uses this platform to explore how these agencies functioned to engender educational change through education governance systems in the process of revising the primary school curriculum.

Agencies refer to sections/units/divisions and personnel within the national education governing body, the Ministry of Education (MoE), that were involved in the revision process.

The US Case was researched and written by Carole Collins Ayanlaja, Warletta Brookins and Alison Taysum. The review of the literature identifies that there is a dearth of qualitative research on Women of Colour in decision-making positions in education systems and particularly on their role as top Chief Executives of education system leadership. To address this gap and to make a new contribution to knowledge, this chapter focuses on 14 African American superintendents currently seated or retired within the last academic year prior to the commencement of the study. The chapter generates new understandings into how these Black women navigate intersectionalities of discrimination. Horsford (2012) draws on Crenshaw (1989) to make the case that socially constructed identities include race, gender, cultural heritage, class, language, faiths and none, GLBT and those recognised as disabled by society and all those with protected characteristics in the UK Equality Act (UK Government, 2010), in a context of a Black–White achievement gap. Superintendents are empowered, or otherwise, to lead curriculum transformation to support the educational success of Black young people, young people of Colour, religiously divided young people and all young people with protected characteristics (UK Government, 2010). Turbulence Theory allows the authors to categorise the impact of the interplay between the superintendent, policy and the school board as light, moderate, severe or extreme in empowering the Superintendents to EYSIER.

Our position in the research presented in this book is that we are inspired by Bridges (2016) who suggests research should empower and mobilise individual professionals in their local and particular contexts. Thus, practitioners at different levels of the education system need to have the thinking tools to apply research in their own contexts on a rainy afternoon in November, only if it helps them connect with their own research in situ to inform school improvement. We are also inspired by Berger (2014, p. 110) who suggests:

> While educational policy is determined on the national level, it is often influenced by developments on the ground, e.g. community initiatives or efforts of groups committed to a particular educational, social or cultural agenda. In Israel, teachers, academics, social activists, parents and pupils themselves have all engaged in such initiatives at various periods in Zionist and Israeli history. I have argued here that 'grass-roots' initiatives have significant potential for meaningful educational reform. The commitment and creative thinking exhibited by these educational activists creates new alternatives for educational practice. Rather than creating bureaucratic obstacles to innovation, governmental bodies should encourage choice initiatives, while carefully guarding their regulatory role to ensure that fundamental societal values (such as equality of educational opportunity) are consistently upheld.

Thus, the following chapters of Part I conceptualise turbulence, empowerment and marginalisation in international educational governance systems and provide the research design for the project. The Part II consists of six chapters that reveal: first, how senior-level leaders in five different nation states describe turbulence in their education governance systems; second, how these senior-level leaders articulate the kinds of support they ideally want, and the support they actually get at the infrastructural level, the resources level and the agency level to navigate the turbulence of the different education governance systems; third, how these senior-level leaders wish to put their professional credentials, professional expertise and proven track records in school improvement to action and mobilise school communities for EYSIER. The Part III presents an international comparative analysis chapter presenting knowledge to action with impact strategies and a final conclusion chapter.

References

Adler, M. (1941). *A dialectic of morals: Towards the foundations of political philosophy.* Notre Dame, IN: University of Notre Dame.

Aly, G., &Heim, S. (2008). *Architects of annihiliation: Auschwitz, and the logic of destruction.* Kindle Version.

American Educational Research Association. (2010). Code of ethics. *Educational Researcher, 40*(3), 145–156.

Arar, K. (2012). Israeli education policy since 1948 and the State of Arab Education in Israel. *Italian Journal of Sociology of Education, 4*(1), 113–145.

Arnova, R. F., Torres, C. A., & Franz, S. (2013). *Comparative education: The dialectic of global and local.* Lanham, MD: Rowan & Littlefield.

Ball, S. (2004). *The Routledge Falmer reader in sociology of education.* London: Routledge.

Barber, M. (2015). *Deliverology in practice: How education leaders are improving student outcomes.* London: Corwin.

Barnardos. (2017). Child poverty. Retrieved from https://www.barnardos.org.uk/what_we_do/our_work/child_poverty/child_poverty_what_is_poverty/child_poverty_statistics_facts.htm. Accessed on 23 April 2017.

Barnett, R. (2000). *Higher education: A critical business.* Buckingham: The Society for Research into Higher Education & Open University Press.

Berger, Z. (2014). Negotiating between equality and choice – A dilemma of Israeli educational policy in historical context. *Italian Journal of Sociology of Education, 6*(2), 88–114.

Besson, G. (2011). *The Caribbean history archives.* Retrieved from http://caribbeanhistoryarchives.blogspot.co.uk/2011/08/african-slavery.html. Accessed on 14 April 2018.

Besson, G., & Brereton, B. (2010). *The Trinidad Book.* Trinidad and Tobago: Paria Publishing Company Ltd.

Blake, R. (1966). *Disraeli.* London: Eyre and Spottiswood, London.

Boseley, S. (2017). *Poverty in the UK jeopardising children's health, warns landmark report. The Guardian.* Retrieved from https://www.theguardian.com/society/2017/jan/25/poverty-in-the-uk-jeopardising-childrens-health-warns-landmark-report. Accessed on 23 April 2017.

Bourdieu, P. (2000). *Pascalian meditations.* Cambridge: Polity Press.

Bridges, D. (2016). *Philosophy in educational research: Epistemology, ethics, politics and quality.* E-book: Springer.

British Educational Research Association. (2011). *Ethical guidelines for educational research.* London: BERA.

Carter, P. L. (2005). *Keepin' it real: School success beyond Black and White.* New York, NY: Oxford University Press.

Cesarani, D. (2011). *From persecution to genocide.* The BBC. Retrieved from http://www.bbc.co.uk/history/worldwars/genocide/radicalisation_01.shtml. Accessed on 14 March 2018.

Cohen, H. (2000). *The present absent: The Palestinian refugees in Israel since 1948.* Jerusalem: Van Leer Institute [Hebrew].

Crenshaw, K. (1989). Demarginalizing the intersection of race and sex: A Black feminist critique of antidiscrimination doctrine, feminist theory, and antiracist politics. *University of Chicago Legal Forum, 140,* 139–167.

Crutchley, R. (2018). *Special needs in the early years partnership and participation.* London: Sage.

Darling-Hammond, L., & Lieberman, A. (Eds.) (2012). *Teacher education around the world: Changing policies and practices (teacher quality and school development).* London: Routledge.

DeGruy, J. (2005). *Post traumatic slave syndrome: America's legacy of enduring injury and healing.* Portland: Joy DeGruy.

Dewey, J. (2016). *Democracy and education.* New York, NY: Macmillan.

Douglas, K., & Barrett, K. (2009). *The downfall of the Spanish Armada in Ireland.* Dublin: Gill & Macmillan.

Dred Scott v. Sandord 60 U.S. (19 How.)393 (1857).

Fraser, N. (2000). *Justice interruptus: Rethinking key concepts of a post-socialist age.* London: Routledge.

Edwards, J. (2012). The Spanish inquisition refashioned: The experience of Mary I's England and the Valladolid tribunal, 1559. *Hispanic Research Journal, 13*(1), 41–54.

Emira, M. (2014). Higher education in Egypt since World War II: Development and challenges. *Italian Journal of Sociology of Education, 6*(2) 8–35.

Epstein, J. L., Sanders, M. G., Simon, B. S., Salinas, K. C., Jansorn, N. R., & Van Voorhis, F. L. (2002). *School, Family, and Community Partnerships: Your Handbook for Action* (2nd ed.). Thousand Oaks, CA: Corwin Press.

Fan, S., Al-Riffai, P., El-Said, M., Yu, B., & Kamaly, A. (2007). Public spending, growth, and poverty reduction in Egypt: A multi-level analysis. In A. Ali & S. Fan (Eds.), *Public Policy and Poverty Reduction in the Arab Region* (pp. 117–168). Safat: The Arab Planning Institute. Retrieved from http://www.ifpri.org/sites/default/files/publications/arabregion.pdf

Feiler, G. (2003). *Economic relations between Egypt and the gulf oil states, 1967–2000: Petro wealth and patterns of influence.* Brighton: Sussex Academic Press.

Figgis, D. (1918). *The historic case for Irish independence.* The Library of Ireland. Retrieved from http://www.libraryireland.com/IrishIndependence/10.php. Accessed on 14 March 2018.

Floud, R., & Johnson, P. (2004). *The Cambridge economic history of modern Britain volume I industrialisation, 1700–1860.* Cambridge: Cambridge University Press.

Fraser, N. (2000). *Justice interruptus: Rethinking key concepts of a post-socialist age.* London: Routledge.

Gaston, B. (2014). *The flight of the earls.* E-book: Kindle Edition.

Gerstl-Pepin, C., & Aiken, J. (2012). *Social justice leadership for a global world.* Charlotte, NC: Information Age Publishing.

Gross, S. J. (2014). Using turbulence theory to guide actions. In C. M. Branson & S. J. Gross (Eds.), *Handbook on ethical educational leadership* (pp. 246–262). New York, NY: Routledge.

Gunter, H. (2005). Conceptualising research in educational leadership. *Educational Management Administration and Leadership, 33*(2), 165–180.

Halsall, G. (2007). *Barbarian migrations and the Roman West 376–568.* Cambridge: Cambridge University Press.

Harley, K. (2008). Trade: Discovery, mercantilism and technology. In R. Floud & P. Johnson (Eds.), *The Cambridge Economic History of Great Britain* (Vol. 1). Cambridge: Cambridge University Press.

Harrison, K., Taysum, A., McNamara, G., & O'Hara, J. (2016). The degree to which students and teachers are involved in second-level school processes and participation in decision making: An Irish case study in Irish studies in education. *Irish Educational Studies, 35*(2), 155–173.

Harvey, J., Cambron-McCabe, N., Cunningham, L. L., & Koff, R. H. (2013). *The superintendent's fieldbook* (2nd ed.). Thousand Oaks, CA: Corwin.

Historical Art and Archives. (1968). The fourteenth amendment to the US Constitution. Retrieved from http://history.house.gov/Exhibitions-and-Publications/BAIC/Historical-Data/Constitutional-Amendments-and-Legislation/. Accessed on 15 March 2018.

Horizon. (2020). 2015. CO-CREATION-01-2017: Education and skills: Empowering Europe's young innovators. Retrieved from https://ec.europa.eu/research/participants/portal/desktop/en/opportunities/h2020/topics/co-creation-01-2017.html. Accessed on 30 May 2017.

Horsford, S. D. (2014). This bridge called my leadership: An essay on Black women as bridge leaders in education. In S. D. Horsford & L. C. Tillman (Eds.), *Intersectional identities and educational leadership of Black women in the USA* (pp. 11–22). Abingdon: Routledge. [Reprint of article in *International Journal of Qualitative Studies in Education*].

Huberman, B. (1994). *Qualitative Data Analysis: An Expanded Sourcebook.* London: Sage.

Hull, E. (2012). *Early Christian Ireland (Epochs of Irish History book2).* Kindle Edition: AlbaCraft Publishing.

Institute of Educational Assessors. (2017). *Progress in international reading literacy study.* Retrieved from http://www.iea.nl/pirls. Accessed on 18 March 2018.

Institute of Education Assessors. (2017). Trends in international mathematics and science study. Retrieved from http://www.iea.nl/timss. Accessed on 18 March 2018.

International Organisation for Migration. (2018). World migration report (2018) Switzerland: Migration agency. Retrieved from https://publications.iom.int/system/files/pdf/wmr_2018_en.pdf. Accessed on 18 March 2018.

Irish Genealogy Tool Kit. (2018). Irish Immigration to America 1846 to the early 20th century. Retrieved from https://www.irish-genealogy-toolkit.com/Irish-immigration-to-America.html. Accessed on 18 March 2018.

Ishii, S., Klopf, D., &Cooke, P. (2007). Worldview in intercultural communication: A religio-cosmological approach. In L.Samovar, R. Porter, & E. McDaniel

(Eds.), *Intercultural Communication a Reader*. Boston, MA: Wadsworth Cengage Learning.

Jewish Virtual Library. (2018). *Venice early history and the Ghetto*. Retrieved from http://www.jewishvirtuallibrary.org/venice-italy-jewish-history-tour.

Karman, H. (2014). *The Spanish inquisition: A historical revision*. London: Yale University Press.

Karpman, S. (1968). Fairy tales and script drama analysis. *Transactional Analysis Bulletin, 7*(26), 39–43.

Kilbourn, B. (2006). The qualitative doctoral dissertation proposal. *Teachers College Record*. Retrieved from https://www.tcrecord.org/AuthorDisplay.asp?aid=16939. Accessed on 05 January 2018.

Lee, J., & Bean, F. (2010). *The diversity paradox. Immigration and the colour line in twenty-first century America*. New York, NY: Russell Sage Foundation.

Lee, J., & Bean, F. (2012). A postracial society or a diversity paradox. *Du Bois Review: Social Science Research on Race, 9*(2), 419–437.

Levin, B. (2004). Making research matter more. *Education Policy Analysis Archives, 12*(56), 1–20.

Licari, J. (1997). *Economic reform in Egypt in a changing global economy*. OECD Development Centre. Retrieved from http://www.oecd.org/countries/egypt/1922293.pdf. Accessed on August 7, 2018.

Lie, J. (2011). Modern peoplehood: On race, racism, nationalism, ethnicity, and identity. UC Berkeley. Retrieved from https://escholarship.org/content/qt73c5c0cg/qt73c5c0cg.pdf. Accessed on 30 March 2018.

Lincoln, A. (1863). Revealing histories, remembering slavery. Retrieved from http://revealinghistories.org.uk/the-american-civil-war-and-the-lancashire-cotton-famine/places/statue-of-abraham-lincoln-lincoln-square-manchester.html. Accessed on 18 March 2018.

Marshall, C., & Gerstl-Pepin, C. I. (2005). *Re-framing educational politics for social justice*. Boston, MA: Pearson/Allyn and Bacon.

Mertens, D. (1998). *Research methods in education and psychology*. London: Sage.

Möllering, G. (2001). The nature of trust. From Georg Simmel to a theory of expectations, interpretation, and suspence. *Sociology, 35*(2), 403–420.

Moloi, K., Gravett, S., & Petersen, N. (2009). Globalization and its impact on education with specific reference to education in South Africa. *Educational Management Administration and Leadership, 37*(2), 278–297.

Morgan, D. (2017). *An unbroken educational apartheid legacy; Chicago's South Suburban predominantly black communities of color*. Kindle Edition.

Oancea, A., & Furlong, J. (2007). Expressions of excellence and the assessment of applied research. *Research Papers in Education, 22*(2), 119–137.

Organisation for Economic and Cooperation and Development. (2017). *Programme of International Students Assessment*. Retrieved from http://www.oecd.org/pisa/. Accessed on 18 March 2018.

Osman, T. (2016). *Islamism what it means for the middle east and the world*. Cornwall: Yale University Press.

Oxfam. (2017). *Just eight men own the same wealth as half the world*. January 16, 2017. Retrieved from https://www.oxfam.org/en/pressroom/pressreleases/2017-01-16/just-8-men-own-same-wealth-half-world. Accessed on December 23, 2017.

Patton, M. (2015). *Qualitative research and evaluation methods integrating theory and practice*. London: Sage.

Payne, C. (2008). *So much reform, so little change: The persistence of failure in urban schools*. Harvard: Harvard Education Press.

Pollard, A. (2008). Quality and capacity in UK education research. Report of the first meeting of the UK's Strategic Forum for Research in education, 16th and 17th October, Harrogate.

Pring, R. (2000). *Philosophy of Educational Research*. London: Continuum.

Pym, R. (2012). The Irishman, the Gypsy, and 'the Olivares Girl'. *Hispanic Research Journal*, *13*(1), 71–82,

Rich, W. (2013). The post-racial society is here. *Recognition, Critics and the Nation State*. London: Routledge.

Rizvi, F. (2009). Internationalisation and the assessment of research quality in education. In A. C. Besley (Ed.), *Assessing the Quality Of Educational Research In Higher Education: International Perspectives*. Rotterdam: Sense.

Rogerson, B. (2010). *The Heirs of the Prophet Muhammad, and the roots of the Sunni-Shia Schism*. Abacus; Digital original edition: Kindle edition.

Stainback, S., & Stainback, W. (1988). *Understanding and conducting qualitative research*. Dubuque, IA: Kendall/ Hunt Pub. Co.

Stenhouse, L. (1975). *An introduction to curriculum research and development*. London: Heinemann.

Taysum, A. (2012a). 'Editorial and editor' 'Learning from international educational policies to move towards sustainable living for all' in China, England, France, Israel, Italy, Nigeria, Northern Ireland, Republic of Ireland, Russia, United States. *Italian Journal of Sociology of Education 4*(1), 1–10. Retrieved from http://ijse.padovauniversitypress.it/issue/4/1

Taysum, A. (2012b). *Evidence informed leadership in education*. London: Continuum.

Taysum, A. (2012c). *Convener of a large symposium in two parts: 'Globalization, policy and agency: Eight Nation states working together to further understand their political sociologies of education'*. European Conference for Educational Research, Cadiz, September.

Taysum, A. (2013). *Convener of a large symposium in two parts; 'International boundary crossing study of teachers' and Students' participation in institutional processes and practices'*. European Conference for Educational Research. Istanbul, September.

Taysum, A. (2014a). *Convener of a large symposium in two parts: 'International boundary crossing study of higher education institutions working in partnership with schools to improve participation in processes and practices chair: Jan Heystek (Stellenbosch University) Discussant: Carole Collins Ayanlaja (Chicago, Superintendent)*. European Conference for Educational Research, Porto.

Taysum, A. (2014b). 'Editorial and editor 'Learning from international education policies to move towards education systems that facilitate sustainable full economic, cultural and political participation in Egypt, Finland, Greece, Israel (Jewish perspective), Japan, Kazakhstan, and South Korea. *Italian Journal of Sociology of Education*, *6*(2), 1–7. Retrieved from http://ijse.padovauniversitypress.it/issue/6/2.

Taysum, A. Convener of a large symposium in two parts with Arar, K., Collins-Ayanlaja, C., Harrison, K., Imam, H., Murrel-Abery, V., Mynbayeva, A., Yelbayeva, Z (2015). *A theory of young people's participation in systems and learning from international boundary crossing action-resarch project.* European Conference for Educational Research. Budapest, Hungary. September.

Taysum, A. Convener of a large symposium in two parts with McNamara (Chair), Risku, M., Collins Ayanlaja, C., Iddrisu, M.T., Murrel-Abery, J.V., Arar, K., Masry-Herzallah, A., Imam, H., Chopra, P., McGuinness, S. (2016). *Theoretical underpinnings of an education and skills model for participation and cooperation in the Youth Field; empowering Europe's young innovators.* European Conference for Educational Research, Dublin, Ireland, August.

Taysum, A. Convener of a large symposium in two parts with Arar, K., Masry-Herzallah, A., Collins Ayanlaja, C., Brookins, W., McGuinness, S., Bates, J., Roulsten, S., O'Connor, U., James, F., and George, J., Taysum, A. (2017). *Turbulence in six international education governance-systems: Comparing knowledge to action for equity, peace and renewal.* European Conference for Educational Research, Copenhagen, Denmark, August.

Taysum, A. (2017). Introduction to the special section. External influences on education systems and education system leadership. *Italian Journal of Sociology of Education, 9*(2), 1–8.

Taysum, A., & Gunter, H. (2008). A critical approach to researching social justice and school leadership in England. *Education, Citizenship and Social Justice, 3*(2), 183–199.

Taysum, A., & Iqbal, M. (2012). What counts as meaningful and worthwhile policy analysis. *Italian Journal of Sociology of Education, 4*(1), 11–28.

Taysum, A., & Murrel-Abery, G. V. (2017). Shifts in education policy, administration and governance in Guyana 1831–2017. Seeking 'A-political' agenda for equity and renewal. In A. Taysum (Ed.), *Italian Journal of Sociology of Education, 9*(2), 55–87.

Taysum, A. (2018). A Deweyen framework moral training for democracy in education. In C. Lowery & P. Jenkin (Eds.), A Dewey Handbook Of Dewey's Education Theory and Practice. Rotterdam: Sense Publishing.

The United Nations Refugee Agency. (2018). Figures at a glance. Retrieved from http://www.unhcr.org/uk/figures-at-a-glance.html. Accessed on 17 March 2018.

UK Government. (2010). *Equality act.* London: HMSO.

United States Supreme Court. (1857). The Red Scott V Sanford.

United States Supreme Court. (1954). Brown v. board of education, 347 U.S. 483 (1954). Retrieved from http://caselaw.lp.findlaw.com/scripts/getcase.pl?court=US&vol=347&invol=483. Accessed on May 2010.

US Census Bureau. (2016). *Residential vacancies and homeownership in the fourth quarter 2015.* Retrieved from http://www.census.gov/housing/hvs/files/currenthvspress.pdf. Accessed on 26 April 2016.

Waghid, Y., & Smeyers, P. (2014). Re-envisioning the future: Democratic citizenship education and Islamic education. *Journal of Philosophy of Education, 48*(4), 539–558.

Wagner, T. (2010). *The Global Achievement Gap.* New York, NY: Basic Books.

Waite, D., Rodríguez, G., & Wadende, A. (2015). Globalization and the business of educational reform. In J. Zajda (Ed.), *Second International Handbook In Globalization, Education and Policy Research* (pp. 353–374). Dordrecht: Springer.

Chapter 2

Literature Review – Turbulence in Education Governance Systems

Khalid Arar and Alison Taysum

Abstract

This chapter identifies that distributed leadership is about sharing power for political pluralism. Distributed leadership has a comprehensive commitment to bringing different groups with different interests, different languages and dialects, different knowledge bases, different metaphysical knowledge and different religions, or no religion, together through provisional agreement on key principals of political pluralism. Marginalised groups may not feel like they belong and may be vulnerable to ideologies that give them a sense of being disconnected from community. Such a position stands as a barrier to political pluralism and shared world views. The situation might be ignored in schools because developing political liberalism through participatory, evidence-informed leadership that is logical, moral and ethical requires time, and agents need to be prepared for such identity work. However, the problem cannot be ignored if community members seek to belong with risky gangs, and are vulnerable to radicalisation, which is very dangerous for them and for their communities. Empowering others may be achieved by developing their capability to ask good questions, and apply collaborative critical thinking for solving social and personal problems. Such empowerment requires shifts from hierarchical teaching of standardised knowledge that is right or wrong to doing the right thing as mature citizens in becoming. The chapter also identifies that it cannot be assumed that leaders are willing or able to distribute leadership, or that doing so would be a panacea for navigating the turbulence faced by their schools to empower societal innovators for equity and renewal. Rather, we concur with Leithwood et al. (2008) who advocate for a thoughtful and purposeful approach to developing leadership for school improvement.

Keywords: Democracy; equity; political pluralism; empowerment; peace

Turbulence, Empowerment and Marginalisation in International
Education Governance Systems, 29–48
Copyright © 2019 by Emerald Publishing Limited
doi:10.1108/978-1-78754-675-220181003

In the first chapter, we explained how the research quality in this book is world leading in terms of originality, significance and rigour in the way we address an identified gap in the knowledge regarding issues of race, gender, religion, language and culture, Socio-Economic Status (SES), citizenship, migrant and refugee status. We presented a theory of colonisation between groups with different interests which included nation states colonising other nation states, and dominant groups within nation states colonising marginalised groups. We also explored how dominant groups in national education governance systems may colonise marginalised national education governance systems and how dominant groups within educational governance systems may colonise marginalised groups within education governance systems. We theorised colonisation using Karpman's Triangle (1968) identifying that different groups can be oppressor, and/or victim, and/or rescuer, and these roles may shift as changes occur in power and economic influence. We presented the Empowering Young Societal Innovators for Equity and Renewal (EYSIER) Model (Taysum 2012a, Taysum 2013, 2014a, 2015, 2016, 2017a) with five principals for equity and renewal. We identified that it would be futile to seek proof of concept for this model if senior-level leaders in educational governance systems did not have the professional autonomy to implement the model that may disrupt inequitable power relationships. Therefore, this book seeks to gain insights into the extent to which senior-level leaders are able to replace any fears within societal systems with impact strategies for social justice, inclusion, respect, trust and courage to re-imagine a shared world view with an overarching shared moral compass that assures an ethical framework for equity and renewal. We presented our position in the research which is education governance systems need to promote the autonomy of educational professionals' with track records of school improvement and whose praxis is informed by grass roots inquiry that is informed by and informs policy. These innovations need to be carefully regulated to uphold societal values and optimise learning for all for equity, renewal and peace in our time.

In this second chapter, we examine Gross' (2014) Theory of Turbulence and provide an explanation regarding why we chose to read our findings through this theory in the light of a critical review of the literature of the kinds of turbulence found in governance systems. The aim of this chapter is to generate new understandings of turbulence and the kinds of turbulence the literature reveals exists currently in education governance systems and the possible causes of this turbulence. To deliver on the aims first, we consider how the Turbulence Theory identifies different levels of turbulence to help shed new light on how senior educational leaders of marginalised groups are empowered in education governance systems. Second, we consider the role advocates and mentors play in supporting senior educational leaders through this turbulence. Third, we consider what kinds of cultures exist in education governance systems, and their origins.

In the preparation of this research, we commissioned 21 international researchers, many of which are part of our international research team, to research the educational policy histories of their respective nation states, and their findings were published in three special editions of the *International Journal of the Sociology of Education*. Their international peer reviewed articles focused on understanding the shifts in education policy, the rationale for these shifts and the pragmatic consequences, or impact of these shifts in each of the nation states (Taysum, 2012a, 2014a, 2017a,b). Our findings revealed that the senior leaders interfacing between education policy, education governance systems and schools' and colleges' staff, parents and students were doing the work during periods of government reforms. These changes occurred against a backdrop of changing cultures from welfarist approaches to neoliberalism, competition, and the impact of market forces and trends of deregulation.

Rapid socio-economic and political changes in the modern world have necessitated continual re-evaluation of the role and strategies of nation states' educational systems in preparing students to become mature citizens (Taysum 2012b, 2014b; 2017b; Waghid & Smeyers, 2014). Mature citizens have the critical and reflective thinking tools required to ask good questions, problem solve, and make evidence informed, logical, moral and ethical decisions (Taysum, 2016). Such dispositions for decision making are necessary for citizens' full and free interactions, and cooperation with society's sustainable economic, cultural and political institutions (Dewey, 2016). The perpetual change in education systems and consequential turbulence felt throughout the systems in and of itself may be destabilising. However, the impetus for change is arguably being amplified by global transmission of knowledge, mobilised through the mass media that emphasise the gaps between education systems in different countries and name and shame those education systems with children with poor educational performance. Gaps are revealed between different education systems within nation states related to key performance indicators. These key performance indicators are mapped to students' education outcomes in a narrow range of subjects focusing on home language, and maths. These scores may be correlated, even predicted by SES related to post codes (Arnova, Torres, & Franz, 2013; Waite, Rodríguez, & Wadende, 2015).

The global distribution of knowledge concerning education from cash-rich countries has had a tremendous impact on what is taught and tested in schools and how they are organised in all countries and in particular nation states that are marginalised in the global politics because they are not cash rich (Moloi, Gravett, & Petersen, 2009). Comparative studies focusing on statistics, for example, the Programme of International Students Assessment (OECD, 2017) and Trends in International Mathematical and Science Study (TIMSS) (Institute of Educational Assessors, 2017) and Progress in International Reading Literacy Study (PIRLS) (IEA, 2017) examine the output of national education systems through a global lens. However these studies do not shed light on the socioeconomic, or political context that shape the values and acts of particular legislation, the fair funding formulas that underpin the allocation of funds to the construction of infrastructure, the education governance systems and the organisation of processes and practices of the education system within the international community (Taysum & Iqbal, 2012). Intellectual and cultural colonisation that may lack moral and ethical frameworks (Adler, 1941) may lead to the commodification of education (Darling-Hammond & Lieberman, 2012; Waite et al., 2015).

The busyness of a school or college to optimise learning becomes eclipsed by those who see schools and colleges as a business opportunity to make profits and pay dividends to nameless shareholders (Diamond, 2012). These shareholders are disconnected from their financial investment in the local and particular school communities, and can only measure success by the size of their dividends. The shareholders are therefore deprived of having a personal commitment to these schools and colleges and their communities, and deprived of the opportunity to personally care about the schools' and colleges' students' achievements, or failures in the education of all our future generations (Diamond, 2012). These kinds of disconnects disturb the balance between schools and colleges, on the one hand, providing funders' shareholders with a return on their investments, and on the other hand, the noble purpose of professional educators' answering a public service vocational call to work for democracy in education systems (Dewey, 2016). Such systems that seek democracy do so through inclusionary processes and practices (Harrisson, Taysum, McNamara, & O'Hara, 2016) that respect all citizens and trust in the good order of funding, the priorities of organising education, how these are regulated and students' educational outcomes (Brooks & Normore, 2010).

The global community has undergone rapid socio-economic and technological change in the last half century. Senior leaders who interface between policymakers, leaders of education governance systems, school staff, parents, children, tax paying community stakeholders and funders' nameless shareholders operate in constantly changing and challenging environments (Arar, Turan, Barakat, & Oplatka, 2017; Waite et al., 2015). In this context, the senior leaders from marginalised groups, the focus of this book, play a key role in navigating turbulence and developing staff and students' dispositions so that they care about the self, the other, feel stable in their own identity to navigate turbulence and feel connected to their communities (Taysum, 2017c; Arar & Massry-Herzallah, 2017; Collins Ayanlaja, Brookins, & Taysum, 2017; McGuinness et al., 2017; James & Gordon, 2017). Providing opportunities to help staff and students also become stable means that senior leaders need to develop cultures within which opportunities for growth can be realised and young people can become mature moral citizens (Adler, 1941). Such opportunities transcend opportunities to develop intellectual capacity to pass high stake tests.

Glazer (2005) identifies that minoritised groups experience inequalities and that questions need to be asked to first, describe the experiences of minoritised groups, and second to steer philosophical inquiry into problem solving for equity and renewal. Wagner (2010) identifies that Black children are not achieving their full potential and accessing pathways within the education system to prosperity. Wagner argues that a Black-White achievement gap is a global phenomenon. Dewey (1916) identifies there are groups within society who do not aim to redress inequalities, perhaps because they might lose their greater entitlement. These groups may wish to be Masters of others and their strategies to achieve this may be almost invisible, but prevent people from enjoying their human rights. Duty may be transformed into obedience achieved through hierarchical processes and practices that the Masters may dominate remotely (Rousseau, 1762).

We seek to describe and understand the experiences of senior educational leaders who are from marginalised groups. We wish to describe and understand the extent to which these senior leaders believe they are empowered by education governance systems to do the right thing for democracy in education, or they are disempowered to obediently do what they are told to do within systems with a logic that may be difficult to challenge. Our research therefore seeks to establish if generating and mobilising knowledge to action is possible within de-centralised control of school systems that are effectively centralised. The centralisation process comes through what Early, Bubb, Eddy-Spicer, Crawford, and James (2017) call accountability regimes, and centrally controlled school systems, which may have become the remote Masters of education governance systems.

We want to explore the literature regarding the best that has been thought and said about the lived experiences of educational senior leaders developing long term strategies for school improvement when they are relentlessly required to adapt to, lead, and navigate the implementation of government attempts to reform the schools in light of the socio-economic-technological dynamics identified previously. We also want to interrogate the literature to understand how education governance systems support their senior leaders in the navigation of the turbulence. We are particularly interested in how senior leaders from marginalised groups are empowered to build bridges to co-create cultures of democracy in education (Dewey, 2016) between: nameless funders and shareholders seeking financial returns on investment from public education; the government accountable to the tax payer regarding how they spend the tax payers money on education; education policy; education governance systems; school and college professional leaders of professional educators; the professional educators themselves; school and college parents; students and the local communities.

To understand the challenge senior leaders of marginalised groups face in supporting school principals and advocating for them at local and state level in these education systems in a state of flux we have chosen to read the data from the case studies through Steven Gross' (2014) Turbulence Theory.

Turbulence Theory

Turbulence Theory proposed by Gross (2014) provides different levels of challenges and opportunities superintendents and chief executive officers face in education systems. In his attempt to understand educational innovation and change, Gross posed four key questions: '(1) How might the levels of disturbance facing innovating schools be described so that different degrees of challenge could be compared? (2) How might the emotional strength of that disturbance be more thoroughly understood? (3) How might the school look at its own disturbance in a measured way so that reasoned action could be more likely? (4) Might there be a positive aspect to the disturbances facing schools that decide to innovate, or was turbulence always a detrimental force to be avoided or at least diminished?' (Gross, 2014, p. 248).

These four questions have helped guide the case studies' investigations which are understood using Gross' metaphor of four different levels of aircraft flight turbulence: *Light*: little or no movement of the craft, translated into the atmosphere or culture at school: little or no interruption to regular work, and minor signs of stress. *Moderate*: noticeable waves, translated into widespread awareness of the issue and specific sources of turbulence. *Severe*: strong gusts that threaten control of the craft, translated into fear for, and of the organisation, widespread community protests and a sense of crisis. *Extreme*: forces so great that control is lost and structural damage to the craft occurs, which can be translated into structural damage to the very functioning of the organisation.

Light or moderate levels of turbulence in education governance systems arguably allow for logical, evidence informed, moral and ethical data gathering, and analysis, as a means of working through the problems, whereas in a state of severe or extreme turbulence no such opportunity is available, since the need for a speedy, well considered response is crucial.

Senior Leaders' Navigating Turbulence

The superintendent or CEO is expected to manage the school system effectively and also to act as a strong pedagogic/instructional leader. Superintendents or CEOs are expected to have broad knowledge of optimising learning, to be able to lead change (Maxfield et al., 2008) and empower school principals to empower staff to EYSIER (Taysum et al., 2016).

These expectations from superintendents and CEOs grow in parallel to their own desire to react and function excellently in complex environments (Lewis, Rice, & Rice, 2011) with different levels of turbulence. As part of the superintendents' and CEOs' duties, they need to understand and react appropriately to the sometimes conflicting demands of different stakeholders in the field to do 'more' and 'better' (Maxfield et al., 2008).

The role of the superintendent or CEO is considered one of the most demanding and essential roles in the education system (Grissom & Anderson, 2012). They are responsible for the identification and understanding of the challenges and future opportunities that stem from the different government-imposed reforms and they are also the leaders responsible for constant development of high quality learning streams that foster learning and leadership in others (Arar, 2015; Grogan & Shakeshaft, 2011).

Thus, the superintendent and CEO simultaneously fulfil two roles as a pedagogic leader focusing on improvement of the learning-teaching processes, and as a systemic leader, who sees the schools' leaders and staff under their area of jurisdiction as a productive professional network organised to work with full and free interactions and cooperation within their institutions (Dewey, 2016). In other words, the superintendent or CEO acts as an inspector, facilitator, counsellor, pedagogue, expert, advocate and diplomatic interface between local governance systems that may include school boards, and the school leadership, staff, parents and students. The superintendent and CEO ensures schools' compliance with government regulations and supervises principal–teacher relations, but also acts as a professional mentor, guiding, instructing and counselling the principal and staff on their day to day professional processes and practices. The aim of this work is to optimise students' learning whilst assisting principals and staff with their professional learning and development, and keeping an eye on succession planning, which is a role that necessitates trust relations (Fergusson, 1998).

As part of the supervisory role, the superintendent or CEO acts to co-create work and learning environments and cultures with principals to develop the school according to defined standards, pooling the resources of the schools in their area of jurisdiction and analysing the application of resources to develop essential learning opportunities in the schools to empower all students to optimise their learning and outcomes. Their roles include the following:

(1) supervisory and follow-up visits to check the schools' compliance with regulations;
(2) guide schools to ensure the quality of students' achievements;
(3) collect data concerning the implementation of standardised work in schools and report to their superiors/governance systems/school board;
(4) put in place and operate shared work processes between the schools, and local governments and ensure that all students have opportunities to optimise learning and achievements (Avidov-Ungar, 2016).

The regional superintendent or CEO translates general policies usually from the Ministry of Education for the particular needs of the different schools, and this is especially important because of the diversity and range of cultures in different societies. To do this, the superintendent may decode and analyse unique local cultures and trends and use this information to create a comprehensive picture of the situation for their superiors that can help them to understand the genuine status of the field in order to improve/sustain its policies and modify them as necessary. A state of structured tension exists between the superintendents' supervisory and mentoring roles. As a result of the onerous burden imposed on the superintendents by their many functions, they naturally tend towards their regulatory role that involves supervision and control over the school, serving as a channel to pass down instructions from 'above' to the schools, and delivering reports to their superiors on the extent of compliance with the stipulated goals. In parallel, the superintendents' ability to serve as a mentor and partner for the school principals is weakened. They may be seen more and more as an external, threatening figure, which focuses on demands for outputs and results and obedience to government directives but is apathetic to the daily difficulties with which the schools have to cope.

The role of the superintendent is arguably a role that embodies ambivalence and the need to cope with contradictory expectations with observational education, a concept derived from the field of philosophy. Observational education connects with Plato in the 'Allegory of the Cave'. One of the main ideas expressed in the allegory is that the philosopher or the person who undertakes the responsibility of teaching others must be able to observe and see any things that seem to contradict what is seen as real and accepted in the socio-cultural context in which he/she acts. The superintendent forms the overall evaluation of the situation through observation and collection of data in different ways and through fruitful dialogue with the principal and the school staff. All this helps the superintendent to shape and consolidate policies in a down-up direction, to identify and expose conflicts and obstacles delaying change,and pushing it forward under the shared leadership of the principal, and the superintendent towards the achievement of new goals, or the appropriate implementation of government reforms.

Empowering Through Distributive Leadership

Distributed leadership was conceived in the early twenty-first century as a theoretical and analytical framework for studying school leadership, one that would explicitly focus attention on how leadership was enacted in schools, as an activity spread across the entire social and spatial context (Spillane, Halverson, & Diamond, 2001) and the way in which these procedures are distributed between different persons including teacher leadership, democratic leadership, shared leadership or collaborative leadership (Harris, 2013).

Distributed leadership in schools and education systems has the potential to empower community members to co-construct pedagogical relationships and partnerships that provide opportunities to share their identity schemas hallmarked by political pluralism and liberalism (Ball, 1994; Rawls, 2005). Rawls (ibid.) argues political liberalism is a distributed power share for all free and equal citizens where no culture or religion is favoured for, of, or by people of a free state. Rawls argues that to achieve a working definition of political liberalism all citizens will need to have a comprehensive conception of a society characterised by sustainable justice and fairness over generations and for generations. The justice is realised by community members developing innovative strategies for equity and renewal that identify and address intersectionalities of discrimination (Arar, 2015; Taysum, 2012c). The premise is that they will be inserted into the world without prior knowledge of their role, which aims to ensure citizens co-construct an equitable world that they will then inhabit (Rawls, 2005).

Top-down hierarchical leadership that ignores community members' voices prevents young people being able to understand and practice political liberalism in the school education system (Bolden, 2011). Hierarchical structures will not prepare young people to be mature societal innovators for equity, and renewal as adults, with the principals of political liberalism (Gronn, 2009). Top-down hierarchical processes and practices do not induct young people into critical thinking and educated debate. Being told what to do does not empower young people to develop cultures that empower young people to problem solve as independent autonomous young people (Wagner, 2010). For example the young people will not have experienced the impact of engaging in dialogue with diverse and/or marginalised groups with different languages or dialects, or with conflicting conceptualisations of world views, and what is good (Lewin, 1946). For example, the Arabic language has many dialects and these dialects can present barriers to giving and receiving clear understanding between different groups. Under these conditions, of paramount import is finding ways and means to engage in deep dialogue so that different groups can represent their different interests to reach a provisional consensus on key principles together. The key principles include tolerating each other without fear, and tolerating differences by agreeing to disagree, whilst not harming anyone (Darling-Hammond & Rothman, 2011; Gerstl-Pepin & Aiken, 2012; Ishii, Klopf, & Cooke, 2007). Moving from hierarchical relationships to flatter pedagogical relationships and partnerships characterised by deep dialogue (Saran & Niesser, 2004) may create the conditions to sustain individuals' open mindedness to optimise their learning and learning outcomes (Crawford, 2012). Indeed, if this learning is accompanied by a deep understanding of market economies, the young people have the potential to renew their local economies, cultures and politics and are truly empowered as young societal innovators for equity and renewal. Flatter pedagogical relationships have the potential to release staff, parents, and students' talents that principals can trust and depend upon, underpinning a shared ability to organise and effectively run public schools (Donaldson, Marnik, Mackenzie, & Ackerman, 2009). Devos, Tuytens, and Hulpia (2014) show that secondary principals in particular depend on all stakeholders including junior administrators, department coordinators and informal teacher leaders to contribute to leading schools. Moreover, Timperley (2005) argues an heroic leadership model of one is limited in effectiveness, and not sustainable.

Distributed leadership is challenging because it requires pedagogical relationships and partnerships between leaders, teachers, students, parents and stakeholders that underpin the navigation of the intersectionalities of race, ethnicity, culture, gender, class and religion through educated debate that critiques multifarious world views (Harrison et al., 2016; Williams, 2016). Delivering standardised curriculums in a top-down hierarchical way does not require the navigation of these place-based intersectionalities and therefore does not provide opportunities for young people to connect their knowledge with the curriculum. A consequence is students and teachers are prevented from co-creating authentic cultural alignment (Harrison et al., 2016). Learning how to co-create authentic cultural alignment is important to achieve peaceful disagreement in diverse communities that is psychologically, emotionally, physically and spiritually healthy and positively reaffirming (UNICEF, 1948).

A recent cooperative investigation between an Arab researcher from Israel and an English researcher documented and compared two principals' experiences during a culture change from hierarchical system leadership to distributed system leadership in an Arab high school in Israel and an English high school

(*International Journal of Leadership in Education*, under review). Evidence reveals that both the Arab education hierarchical system in Israel and the English hierarchical education system are experiencing conflict in what *The Economist* (2016) calls the 'Post-Truth World'. Essentially these education systems are in a state of turbulence due to the need to change and adapt to the reality of this world. The findings revealed the senior leaders were not supported by national policy or by accountability regimes, but were supported by the academy through postgraduate research and participatory action research. The evidence-informed intervention strategies that emerged from the action research were developed in partnership between the academy, senior leaders and their staff. These intervention strategies empowered the teachers and students to integrate a standardised curriculum with participatory pedagogical partnerships between teachers and students that included students' social contexts (Dewey, 1897). The increased empowerment correlated with significantly increased student achievement and examination results for all students involved. The research attempted to understand how principals can navigate their schools through such a cultural shift and indicated that distributed leadership helped to empower young people as societal innovators for equity and renewal (Horizon 2020, 2015). These leaders took a risk in implementing the action research project because it was not supported by the education governance systems. The English principal identified they alleviated fear of the education system by having back up strategies for their future, in case they were sacked for poor student performance.

The literature reveals that developing partnerships to conduct philosophical inquiries empowers and motivates school communities to build capacity for the language of community cohesion within a political pluralism (Rawls, 1999). Empowerment focuses on developing independent, critical and resilient problem-solvers who can co-create societal equity and renewal (Taysum, 2012a, 2013, 2014c, 2015, 2016, 2017a). Where leaders, professional researchers, teachers and students are empowered and have trust in an education system (Hallinger & Heck, 2010a, 2010b; Klar, Huggins, Hammonds, & Buskey, 2016; Mifsud, 2017; Woods, Bennett, & Harvey, 2004; Möllering, 2001; Barnett, 2000; Wagner, 2010) that respects their respective and diverse world views (Barnett, 2000; Darling-Hammond & Rothman, 2011; Gerstl-Pepin & Aiken, 2012; Ishii et al., 2007), they are likely to build good pedagogical relationships and partnerships based on respect and inclusion in an iterative way that builds more good relationships in virtuous upward-moving circles (Marshall & Gerstl-Pepin, 2005). The generation of new knowledge requires courage in a system that punishes failure, and the new knowledge needs to be synthesised prudently with the traditional knowledge, to enable the re-imagining of new futures where young people are mobilisers of stable and sustainable social change for equity and renewal and peace in the real world (Adler, 1941; Bhaskar, 2013; Taysum, 2012b, 2018).

The Impact of Distributed Leadership as a Process of Empowerment

Distributed leadership realised through participatory processes and practices requires people to know themselves, as Socrates argued (Brown, 2009). Knowing the self can lead to a sense of security in the self-hood, or identity, to enable the self to deeply listen to the narratives of others. Being self-aware and having self-control and being able to regulate the self, based on self evaluation, are important characteristics for a quiet ego for establishing and attaining realistic goals (Kesebir, 2014). Kesebir continues those who were not self-focused and had realistic expectations understood the self on a deep level in relation to the other, and were more likely to share control and distribute leadership. Those keen to distribute leadership and empower others sought to reach a mutual understanding with others, which Harris' (2012) research indicates can lead to cultural alignment. Angelle (2010) suggested that relationships are not only important to the practice of distributed leadership, but can also influence organisational culture, including efficacy, increased trust, job satisfaction, and teacher intent to stay. She added that organisational culture could be improved if relationships were respected within the practice of distributed leadership. Mascall, Leithwood, Straus, and Sacks (2008) said for distributed leadership to be effective, there must be relational trust.

Nappi (2014) stated that the overall culture of a school campus, including aspects of principal, teacher and student success, is more likely to improve with the dedicated practice of distributed leadership. Distributed leadership variables such as leadership of formal leaders, teacher leaders, the cooperation of leadership teams and participative decision-making help improve the relational climate within a school culture as well as the principal's and teachers' commitment to the school (Devos et al., 2014).

Nevertheless, the notion of distributed leadership might just be used as a mask by policy producers and government officials to ease in their agenda as a normalising discourse in schools. Despite the fact that Gunter and Forrester (2008) recognise distributed leadership as the 'officially sanctioned model of good practice' (p. 32) advocated by English government departments, they suggest that it reflects normative narratives. These narratives are part of the English government's rhetoric that power and autonomy are being shared with schools, whereas in reality accountability regimes centralise power through what Ball (2004) calls New Public Management. Hartley (2007) regarded distributed leadership as 'yet another sign of an institutional isomorphism' (p. 211) where isomorphism is borrowed from mathematics and means to form equity. Gunter and Forrester (2008) detected a control imperative in the professional practice of 'policy entrepreneurs', concluding that the primacy of the single person remains, with distribution enacted as a form of delegation taking on a hierarchical guise. Some critics of distributed leadership inquire whether it offers a genuine alternative to other forms of leadership or whether it serves as 'the emperor's new clothes' (Bolden, 2011, p. 254) or a stratagem to society's demand for equity and purpose. Gronn (2009) noted how the term 'distributed can inadvertently mislabel a situation in which the influence of a number of individuals continues to be significant' (p. 285).

Distributed leadership can affect more than just relationships and school culture; it can affect social justice issues facing students in minority-majority high schools, particularly when adopting Rawls' (2005) political liberalism. Distributed leadership that recognises all groups, including minoritised groups can benefit aspiring and practicing school leaders because it connects the social mission of most schools to realise democracy in education (Dewey, 2016) to the practice of everyday leadership activity (Brooks, Jean-Marie, Normore, & Hodgins, 2007). Jackson and Marriott (2012) indicated that urban schools, which practice leadership in a less distributed way, could end up with disturbing educational outcomes from an equity perspective. For them, poorly performing urban schools and struggling free school-lunch-eligible students, are often associated with leadership that fails to either understand or implement distributed leadership from an organisational perspective. Brooks et al. (2007) found that the practice of distributed leadership by formal and informal leaders, especially as it pertains to context-specific and situationally bound issues, has the potential to improve some aspects of social justice within minority–majority schools.

People who perpetuate hierarchical systems do not distribute leadership and thus prevent Rawls' notion of political liberalism from being realised. To sustain the hierarchical structures, self-focused leaders may control their environment and control knowledge sharing of the environment and of different worldviews (Stenhouse, 1975). Hierarchical leaders may perpetuate what Pring (2007) calls evaluative cultures. Evaluative cultures find alternative cultures and their prime principles inadequate, and exclude them. Excluding others underpins protectionist dispositions, racism and xenophobia, which may influence how citizens view political pluralism. Hierarchical leaders are positioned to sustain hierarchies because they are not inculcated into dispositions of distributed leaders by the very nature of the structures that structure their agency. Hierarchical leaders may find empowering themselves to get to know themselves, and empowering others to get to know themselves, very challenging. Hierarchical leaders arguably need support in navigating evaluative cultures in their schools and locales and in transforming their own dispositions to be evaluative, develop multicultural dispositions and bridge different cultures for democracy in education (Dewey, 2016; Taysum & Slater, 2014).

Principals are being encouraged to distribute leadership to increase schools' organisational capacities, and enhance student growth and learning, and extend this to including parents in decision making (Epstein, et al., 2002). Extant research on distributed leadership practices provides an emerging basis for adopting such approaches (Klar et al., 2016). Yet, relatively less attention has been paid to examining the principal's role in fostering the leadership capacities of others to create the aptitude for distributed leadership. Thus, distributed leadership is about sharing power for political pluralism, and Taysum & Slater, 2014has a comprehensive commitment to bringing different groups with different interests, different languages and dialects, different knowledge bases, different metaphysical knowledge and different religions, or no religion, together through provisional agreement on key principals of political pluralism (Rawls, 2005).

Marginalised groups may not feel like they belong and may be vulnerable to ideologies that give them a sense of being disconnected from community. Such a position stands as a barrier to political pluralism. When individuals of diverse, but marginalised groups cannot understand the values and behaviours of the dominant group, and their values and behaviours are different, the different groups may fear each other and believe the other will do them harm (Kakos & Palaiologou, 2014). Thus, the other moves from being 'the other' to 'the enemy' which may even be a deliberate divide and conquer strategy played out remotely by the Masters who wish to sustain their entitlement which is only possible when others entitlement is less (Taysum and Murrel-Abery, 2017[1]). The situation might be ignored in schools because developing political liberalism through evidence-informed leadership requires time, and agents need to be prepared for such identity work. However, the problem cannot be ignored if community members seek to belong with risky gangs and are vulnerable to radicalisation, which is very dangerous for them and for their communities (Khan, 2016).

Empowering others to reflect critically within an education system and talk truth to power, means hierarchical leaders need to let go of their power and control, and empower young people to engage with a standardised curriculum through pedagogical relationships that are embedded in their social contexts. Leaders, governance structures, teacher educators and teachers need to support each other, the students and the parents with their engagement with participatory philosophical inquiries to sustain moral acts in the participation of ethical democracy in education. Empowerment shifts from hierarchical teaching of standardised knowledge that is right or wrong to education system leaders empowering teachers to empower students to have confidence in themselves and in their dispositions for deep dialogue and critical self-reflection (Saran & Niesser, 2004).

Yet Mifsud (2017) investigating the turbulent situation of decentralisation and school networking in the Maltese education system found that distributed leadership is a challenge to perform at the college level; with resistance being demonstrated in overt or more subtle ways along the different hierarchies, although power does circulate. Analysis revealed differences between the leaders' narrative of distributed leadership and their performance of it. There were conflicting discourses of collegiality and isolationism, through the discourse of distributed leadership, and within the discourse of educational leadership itself. Struggles between co-leaders and middle leaders were commonplace, though not openly acknowledged. In the particular case that he studied, he found that the policy simply added more layers and new roles to the educational leadership bureaucracy.

Similarly, a study in Australia (Glen, 2009) found a range of tensions and contradictions associated with the distribution of leadership and their effect on

---

[1]There is not space to discuss the divide and conquer strategies here. For a full explanation of these strategies played out in education, please see Taysum and Murrel-Abery (2017).

leadership practice. Glen explains that the reasons for the popularity of distributed leadership in recent years included increased burden of responsibility on principals, increased accountability of all levels of school leadership, increased parent involvement in the schools and incessant reforms driven by social, political and technological changes. Glen concludes that 'in the turbulent complexity of modern schooling, effective leadership is more likely to be spread across a network of individuals rather than concentrated in the hands of one or two leaders [...] The core notion of distributed leadership suggests that school leadership does not just reside in the principal's office but requires multiple leaders, formal and informal, spread across the school community. Yet, the interesting paradox is that effective distributed leadership practice depends first and foremost on a strong, powerful, yet humble "head" or principal'.

Woods et al. (2004) asked whether interest in distributed leadership will see 'autonomy and empowerment widely spread, or the same leaders applying constraint and control in new ways' (p. 445). Other critics of distributed leadership suggest that there has been little or no change in the discourse of educational leadership, distributed leadership 'may just be the traditional model in a new guise', 'a smokescreen for the more authoritarian practices of headteachers' (Crawford, 2012, p. 617), which emerge as a response to pressure from policy-makers.

Interest has grown in distributed leadership as an approach to improving school outcomes. In the last few years research (Hallinger, 2011; Hallinger & Heck, 2010a, 2010b; Leithwood, Harris, & Hopkins, 2008; Louis, Leithwood, Wahlstrom, & Anderson, 2010) has highlighted the positive influence of leadership on organisational conditions and student achievement when it is exercised by multiple agents. This body of research also includes studies that suggested principals' distributed leadership practices are a way of enhancing schools' capacities, especially for organisational change (Hallinger, 2011) and learning (Day, Jacobson, & Johansson, 2011; Klar et al., 2016; Mifsud, 2017).

Based on the study of distributed leadership in 11 English schools, MacBeath (2005) described a three-phase model of leadership development. The findings revealed that principals first observe a school's structures, culture and history to identify people who have the requisite capacities to address existing needs, delegate responsibility to them and monitor their progress until the assigned tasks are completed. In the second stage, principals identify potential leaders and support them as they take on incrementally more complex activities. In the third stage, principals provide ongoing support from a distance as the emerging leaders become more established in their roles.

Given the research basis described previously, it would seem reasonable for principals coping with the rapid socio-economic and technological dynamics of the present era to heed the call to enhance their school's capacities to support student growth and learning by distributing leadership to other formal and informal leaders. However, one cannot assume such leaders are willing or able to assume greater leadership roles. Nor, we suggest, should it be assumed that all principals are willing or able to distribute leadership, or that doing so would be a panacea for meeting the challenges faced by their schools. Rather, we concur with Leithwood et al. (2008) who advocate for a thoughtful and purposeful approach to developing leadership for school improvement. Leithwood et al. noted, for instance, that distributing leadership might require 'intentional intervention on the part of those in formal leadership roles' (p. 279). The next chapter provides the research design that allowed us to research marginalisation in educational governance systems to inform logical, empirical, ethical and moral intervention strategies for school and college improvement.

References

Adler, M. (1941). *A dialectic of morals: Towards the foundations of political philosophy*. Notre Dame: University of Notre Dame.

Angelle, P. S. (2010). An organizational perspective of distributed leadership: A portrait of a middle school. *RMLE Online: Research in Middle Level Education*, *33*(5), 1−16.

Arar, K. (2015). Leadership for equity and social justice in Arab and Jewish schools in Israel: Leadership trajectories and pedagogical praxis. *International Journal of Multicultural Education*, *17*(1), 162−187.

Arar, K., & Massry-Herzallah, A. (2017). Progressive education and the case of bilingual Arab-Jewish co-existence school in Israel. *School Leadership and Management*, *37*(1−2), 38−60.

Arar, K., Turan, S., Barakat, M., & Oplatka, I. (2017). The characteristics of educational leadership in the Middle East: A comparative analysis of three nation-states. In D. Waite & I. Bogoch (Eds.), *International handbook of leadership in education* (pp. 355−373). Hoboken, NJ: Wiley-Blackwell.

Arnova, R. F., Torres, C. A., & Franz, S. (2013). *Comparative education: The dialectic of global and local*. Lanham, MD: Rowan & Littlefield.

Avidov-Ungar, O. (2016). A model of professional development: Teachers' perceptions of their professional development. *Teachers and Teaching: Theory and Practice*, *22*(6), 653−669.

Ball, S. (2004). *Education policy and social class: The selected works of Stephen J. Ball*. London: Routledge.

Ball, S. J. (1994). *Education reform: A critical and post-structural approach*. Buckingham: Open University Press.

Barnett, R. (2000). *Higher education a critical business*. Buckingham: SRH.

Bhaskar, R. (2013). *Reclaiming reality*. London: Routledge.

Bolden, R. (2011). Distributed leadership in organizations: A review of theory and research. *International Journal of Management Reviews*, *13*, 251−269. Retrieved from https://www.mnsu.edu/activities/leadership/distributed_leadership.pdf

Brooks, J. S., Jean-Marie, G., Normore, A. H., & Hodgins, D. W. (2007). Distributed leadership for social justice: Exploring how influence and equity are stretched over an urban high school. *Journal of School Leadership*, *17*(4), 378−408.

Brooks, J. S., & Normore, A. H. (2010). Educational leadership and globalization: Toward a global perspective. *Educational Policy*, *24*(1), 52−82.

Brown, L. (Ed.). (2009). Aristotle. In *The Nicomachean Ethics*. Oxford: Oxford World Classics.

Collins Ayanlaja, C., Brookins, W., & Taysum, A. (2017 August). Empowering superintendents in the United States to develop school communities as societal innovators for equity and renewal: Knowledge to action. *Part of a large sympo- sium European conference for educational research*, Copenhagen, Denmark.

Crawford, M. (2012). Solo and distributed leadership: Definitions and dilemmas. *Educational Management Administration and Leadership, 40*(5), 610–620.

Darling-Hammond, L., & Lieberman, A. (Eds.). (2012). *Teacher education around the world: Changing policies and practices (teacher quality and school develop- ment)*. London & New York, NY: Routledge.

Darling-Hammond, L., & Rothman, R. (Eds.). (2011). *Teacher and leader effectiveness in high-performing education systems*. Washington, DC: Alliance for Excellent Edu- cation and Stanford, CA: Stanford Center for Opportunity Policy in Education.

Day, C., Jacobson, S., & Johansson, O. (2011). Leading organisational learning and capacity building. In R. Ylimaki & S. Jacobson (Eds.), *U.S. and cross-national policies practices and preparation: Implications for successful instructional leader- ship, organizational learning, and culturally responsive practices*. Dordrecht: Springer-Kluwer.

Devos, G., Tuytens, M., & Hulpia, H. (2014). Teachers' organizational commitment: Examining the mediating effects of distributed leadership. *American Journal of Education, 120*(2), 205–231.

Dewey, J. (1897). *My pedagogic creed*. First published in The School Journal, LIV (3), 77–80 (16 January 1897). Retrieved from http://playpen.meraka.csir.co.za/ ~acdc/education/Dr_Anvind_Gupa/Learners_Library_7_March_2007/Resources/ books/readings/17.pdf. Accessed on 12 October 2018.

Dewey, J. (2016). *Democracy in education*. New York, NY: Macmillan.

Diamond, S. (2012). Beyond the Berle and Means paradigm: Private equity and the new capitalist order. In C. Williams & P. Zumbansen (Eds.), *The embedded firm: Corporate governance, labor and finance capitalism*. Cambridge: Cambridge University Press.

Donaldson, G., Marnik, G., Mackenzie, S., & Ackerman, R. (2009). What makes or breaks a principal. *Educational Leadership, 67*(2), 8–14.

Early, P., Bubb, S., Eddy-Spicer, D., Crawford, M., & James, C. (2017). Governing bodies, headteacher performance and pay: The role of external advisers. *Educational Review, 68*(3), 257–273.

Epstein, J. L., Sanders, M. G., Simon, B. S., Salinas, K. C., Jansorn, N. R., & Van Voorhis, F. L. (2002). *School, family, and community partnerships: Your handbook for action* (2nd ed). Thousand Oaks, CA: Corwin Press.

Fergusson, V. (1998). *Supervision for the self-managing school: The New Zealand experience*. Paris and New Delhi: International Institution for Educational Planning.

Gerstl-Pepin, C., & Aiken, J. (2012). *Social justice leadership for a global world*. Charlotte, NC: Information Age Publishing.

Glazer, N. (2005). *The emergence of an American ethnic pattern*. Retrieved from http://www.paperdue.com/essay/the-emergence-of-an-americanethnic-pattern- 63715. Accessed on May 1, 2017.

Glen, M. (2009). Distributed Leadership. A case study of a Queensland Secondary School. A dissertation submitted to the School of Education and Professional Studies (Brisbane, Logan), Faculty of Education, Griffith University, in fulfilment of the requirements for the degree of Doctor of Education. Retrieved from https://www120.secure.griffith.edu.au/rch/file/67dce073-8626-7282-1fed-cb4185f6e9ad/1/02Whole.pdf. Accessed on October 12, 2018.

Grogan, M., & Shakeshaft, C. (2011). *Women and educational leadership*. San Francisco, CA: Jossey-Bass.

Gronn, P. (2009). Leadership configurations. *Leadership*, *5*(3), 267–291.

Gross, S. J. (2014). Using turbulence theory to guide actions. In C. M. Branson & S. J. Gross (Eds.), *Handbook on Ethical Educational Leadership* (pp. 246–262). New York, NY: Routledge.

Gunter, H., & Forrester, G. (2008). New labour and school leadership 1997–2007. *British Journal of Educational Studies*, *56*(2), 144–162.

Grissom, J., & Anderson, S. (2012). Why superintendents turn over. *American Educational Research Journal*, *49*(6), 1147–1180.

Hallinger, P. (2011). Leadership for learning: Lessons from 40 years of empirical research. *Journal of Educational Administration*, *49*(2), 125–142.

Hallinger, P., & Heck, R. (2010a). Collaborative leadership and school improvement: Understanding the impact on school capacity and student learning. *School Leadership and Management*, *30*(2), 95–110.

Hallinger, P., & Heck, R. (2010b). Leadership for learning: Does collaborative leadership make a difference in school improvement? *Educational Management Administration and Leadership*, *38*(6), 654–678.

Harris, A. (2012). Leading system-wide improvement. *International Journal of Leadership in Education*, *15*(3), 395–401.

Harris, A. (2013). *Distributed leadership matters*. London: Corwin Press.

Harrison, K., Taysum, A., McNamara, G., & O'Hara, J. (2016). The degree to which students and teachers are involved in secondary level school processes and participation in decision-making: An Irish Case Study. *Irish Educational Studies*, *35*(2), 155–173.

Hartley, D. (2007). The emergence of distributed leadership in education: Why now? *British Journal of Sociology of Education*, *55*(2), 202–214.

Horizon 2020. (2015). *CO-CREATION-01-2017: Education and skills: Empowering Europe's young innovators*. Retrieved from https://ec.europa.eu/research/participants/portal/desktop/en/opportunities/h2020/topics/co-creation-01-2017.html. Accessed on May 30, 2017.

Institute of Educational Assessors. (2017). *Trends in international mathematics and science study*. Retrieved from http://www.iea.nl/timss. Accessed on 18 March 2018.

Ishii, S., Klopf, D., & Cooke, P. (2007). Worldview in intercultural communication: A religio-cosmological approach. In L. Samovar, R. Porter, & E. McDaniel (Eds.), *Intercultural Communication: a Reader*. Boston, MA: Wadsworth Cengage Learning.

Jackson, K. M., & Marriott, C. (2012). The interaction of principal and teacher instructional influence as a measure of leadership as an organizational quality. *Educational Administration Quarterly*, *48*(2), 230–258.

James, F., & Gordon, J. (2017 August). Turbulence in efforts at curriculum renewal for educational equity in Trinidad and Tobago part of a large symposium. *European Conference for Educational Research*, Copenhagen, Denmark.

Kahn, S. (2016). London school girl who travelled to Syria to join IS is feared dead. *BBC Radio*, August 4, 12. Retrieved from http://www.bbc.co.uk/news/uk-37053699. Accessed on August 12, 2016.

Kakos, M., & Palaiologou, D. (2014). Intercultural citizenship education in Greece: Us and them. *Italian Journal of Sociology of Education, 6*(2), 69–87.

Kesebir, P. (2014). A quiet ego quiets death anxiety: Humility as an existential anxiety buffer. *Journal of Personality and Social Psychology, 106*(4), 610–623.

Klar, H. W., Huggins, K. S., Hammonds, H. L., & Buskey, F. C. (2016). Fostering the capacity for distributed leadership: A post-heroic approach to leading school improvement. *International Journal of Leadership in Education, 19*(2), 111–137.

Leithwood, K., Harris, A., & Hopkins, D. (2008). Seven strong claims about successful school leadership. *School Leadership and Management, 28*, 27–42.

Lewin, K. (1946). Action research and minority problems. *Journal of Social Issues, 2*(4), 34–46.

Lewis, T., Rice, M., & Rice, Jr., R. (2011). Superintendents' Beliefs and Behaviors regarding Instructional Leadership Standards Reform. *International Journal of Educational Leadership Preparation, 6*(1), n1.

Louis, K. S., Leithwood, K., Wahlstrom, K., & Anderson, S. (2010). *Learning from leadership: Investigating the links to improved student learning.* New York, NY: The Wallace Foundation.

MacBeath, J. (2005). Leadership as distributed: A matter of practice. *School Leadership & Management, 25*(4), 349–366.

Marshall, C., & Gerstl-Pepin, C. I. (2005). *Re-framing educational politics for social justice.* Boston, MA: Pearson/Allyn and Bacon.

Mascall, B., Leithwood, K., Straus, T., & Sacks, R. (2008). The relationship between distributed leadership and teachers' academic optimism. *Journal of Educational Administration, 46*(2), 214–228.

McGuinness, S., Roulston, S., Bates, J., & O'Connor, U. (2017 August). Empowering school principals to overcome turbulence in school partnerships through governance systems for equity, renewal, and peace: Northern Ireland. *Part of a large symposium European conference for educational research,* Copenhagen, Denmark.

Maxfield, C. R., Wells, C. M., Keane, W., & Klocko, B. (2008). *The role of superintendents in supporting teacher leadership.* Retrieved from https://files.eric.ed.gov/fulltext/EJ1067199.pdf. Accessed on October 12, 2018.

Mifsud, M. (2017). Distributed leadership in a Maltese college: The voices of those among whom leadership is 'distributed' and who concurrently narrate themselves as leadership 'distributors'. *International Journal of Leadership in Education, 20*(2), 149–175.

Möllering, G. (2001). The nature of trust. From Georg Simmel to a theory of expectations, interpretation, and suspense. *Sociology, 35*(2), 403–420.

Moloi, K., Gravett, S., & Petersen, N. (2009). Globalization and its impact on education with specific reference to education in South Africa. *Educational Management Administration & Leadership, 37*(2), 278–297.

Organisation for Economic and Cooperation and Development. (2017). *Programme of international students assessment.* Retrieved from http://www.oecd.org/pisa/. Accessed on 18 March 2018.

Pring, R. (2007). The common school. *Journal of Philosophy of Education, 41*(4), 503–522.

Rawls, J. (1999). *A theory of justice.* Cambridge, MA: Harvard University Press.

Rawls, J. (2005). *Political liberalism.* New York, NY: Columbia University Press.

Rousseau, J. J. (1762). *The social contract.* London: Wordsworth Classics of World Literature.

Saran, R., & Niesser, B. (2004). *Inquiring minds: Socratic dialogue in education.* Stoke-on-Trent: Trentham Books Ltd.

Spillane, J. P., Halverson, R., & Diamond, J. (2001). Investigating school leadership practice: A distributed perspective. *Educational Researcher, 30*(April), 23–28. Retrieved from https://www.scholars.northwestern.edu/en/publications/investigating-school-leadership-practice-a-distributed-perspectiv

Stenhouse, L. (1975). *An introduction to curriculum research and development.* London: Heinemann.

Taysum, A. (2012a September). Convener of a large symposium in two parts: 'Globalization, policy and agency: Eight nation states working together to further understand their political sociologies of education'. *European Conference for Educational Research,* Cadiz.

Taysum, A. (2012b). 'Editorial and editor' 'Learning from international educational policies to move towards sustainable living for all' in China, England, France, Israel, Italy, Nigeria, Northern Ireland, Republic of Ireland, Russia, United States. *Italian Journal of Sociology of Education, 4*(1). Retrieved from http://ijse.padovauniversitypress.it/issue/4/1

Taysum, A. (2013 September). Convener of a large symposium in two parts: 'International boundary crossing study of teachers' and students' participation in institutional processes and practices'. *European conference for educational research,* Istanbul.

Taysum, A. (2014a). Convener of a large symposium in two parts: International boundary crossing study of higher education institutions working in partnership with schools to improve participation in processes and practices chair: Jan Heystek (Stellenbosch University) Discussant: Carole Collins Ayanlaja (Chicago, Superintendent). *European conference for educational research,* Porto.

Taysum, A. (2014b). 'Editorial and editor' Learning from international education policies to move towards education systems that facilitate sustainable full economic, cultural and political participation in Egypt, Finland, Greece, Israel (Jewish perspective), Japan, Kazakhstan, and South Korea. *Italian Journal of Sociology of Education, 6*(2). Retrieved from http://ijse.padovauniversitypress.it/issue/6/2

Taysum, A. (2014c). Convener of a large symposium in two parts: International boundary crossing study of higher education institutions working in partnership with schools to improve participation in processes and practices chair: Jan Heystek (Stellenbosch University) Discussant: Carole Collins Ayanlaja (Chicago, Superintendent). *European conference for educational research,* Porto.

Taysum, A. (2017b). 'Editorial and editor' External influences on education systems and educational leadership in Shifts in Germany Hungary, Guyana, India, Pakistan, and the US in *Italian Journal of Sociology of Education, 9*(2).

Taysum, A. (2017c). Systems theory and education: A philosophical enquiry into education systems theory. In P. Higgs & Y. Waghid (Eds.), *A reader for philosophy of education.* Cape Town: Juta.

Taysum, A. (2018). A Deweyan framework for moral training for democracy in education. In C. Lowery & P. Jenlink (Eds.), *Handbook of Dewey's educational theory and practice.* Dordrecht: Sense Publishers.

Taysum, A. (2012c). *Evidence informed leadership in education.* London: Continuum.

Taysum, A. (2016). Educational leaders' doctoral research that informed strategies to steer their organizations towards cultural alignment. *Educational Management, Administration and Leadership, 44*(2), 281–300.

Taysum, A., & Iqbal, M. (2012). What counts as meaningful and worthwhile policy analysis. *Italian Journal of Sociology of Education, 4*(1), 11–28.

Taysum, A., & Murrel-Abery, V. (2017). Shifts in education policy, administration and governance in Guyana 1831–2017. Seeking 'a political' agenda for equity and renewal. *Italian Journal of Sociology of Education, 9*(2), 55–87.

Taysum, A., & Slater, C. (2014). The Education Doctorate (Ed.D.) and educational leader dispositions and values in England and the United States. In A. Taysum & S. Rayner (Eds.), *Investing in our education? Leading, learning, researching and the doctorate.* Scarborough: Emerald.

Taysum, A. (2017a August). *Convener of a large symposium in two parts with Arar, K., Masry-Herzallah, A., Collins Ayanlaja, C., Brookins, W., McGuinness, S., ... Taysum, A. Turbulence in six international education governance-systems: Comparing knowledge to action for equity, peace and renewal. European conference for educational research,* Copenhagen, Denmark.

Taysum, A. (2015 September). *Convener of a large symposium in two parts with Arar, K., Collins-Ayanlaja, C., Harrison, K., Imam, H., Murrel-Abery, V., ... Yelbayeva, Z. A theory of young people's participation in systems and learning from international boundary crossing action-research project. Europe an conference for educational research.* Budapest, Hungary.

Taysum, A. (2016 August). *Convener of a large symposium in two parts with McNamara (Chair), Risku, M., Collins Ayanlaja, C., Iddrisu, M. T., Murrel-Abery, J. V., ... McGuinness, S. Theoretical underpinnings of an education and skills model for participation and cooperation in the youth field: Empowering Europe's young innovators. European Conference for Educational Research,* Dublin, Ireland.

Timperley, H. S. (2005). Distributed leadership: Developing theory from practice. *Journal of Curriculum Studies, 37*(4), 395–420.

UNICEF. (1948). *Universal declaration of human rights.* New York, NY: Department of Public Information.

Waghid, Y., & Smeyers, P. (2014). Re-envisioning the future: Democratic citizenship education and Islamic education. *Journal of Philosophy of Education, 48*(4), 539–558.

Wagner, T. (2010). *The global achievement gap.* New York, NY: Basic Books.

Waite, D., Rodríguez, G., & Wadende, A. (2015). Globalization and the business of educational reform. In J. Zajda (Ed.), *Second international handbook in globalization, education and policy research* (pp. 353–374). Dordrecht: Springer.

Williams, R. (2016). In S. Stephens (Ed.), After Brexit? The referendum and its discontents. Retrieved from http://www.abc.net.au/religion/articles/2016/06/24/4488874.htm. Accessed on February 11, 2017.

Woods, P., Bennett, N., & Harvey, J. (2004). Variabilities and dualities in distributed leadership: Findings from a systematic literature review. *Educational Management Administration and Leadership, 32*(4), 439–457.

Chapter 3

Epistemological Underpinnings and Methodologies for Researching Marginalised Groups in International Educational Governance Systems

Alison Taysum, Khalid Arar and Hauwa Imam

Abstract

In this chapter, we present a critical engagement with the methodology that each research team presenting a case study in this book from England, Arab Israel, Northern Ireland, Trinidad and Tobago and the United States adopted.

Education is a cultural project that consists of history, narrative and faith. The Black, Asian Minority Ethnicity (BAME) and senior leaders representing marginalised groups that we talked to in this research all stated that their faith, and religion was central to their service as an educational leader. The faiths represented in our research are Islam, Christianity, Sikhism and no faith where a humanitarian approach is taken. The chapter presents the scientific significance of what values underpin these leaders' behaviours, and to understand how their values align with legislation, education policy and the values found in Education Governance Systems.

A constructivist comparative analysis approach was adopted to address four research questions. First, how do the senior-level leaders describe and understand how school governance systems and school commissioners empower them to develop school communities as societal innovators for equity and renewal for peace in our time? Second, how do they describe and understand the role mentors, and/or advocates play to support their navigation through the governance systems? Third, to what extent do they believe a cultural change is required to empower them in school communities to Empower Young Societal Innovators for Equity and Renewal for

Turbulence, Empowerment and Marginalisation in International
Education Governance Systems, 49–77
doi:10.1108/978-1-78754-675-220181004

peace in our time? Finally, how can the findings be theorised to generate a theory of knowledge to action through impact strategies within an international comparative analysis framework?

Each of the five international cases collected the narrative biographies of up to 15 superintendents, or chief executive officers of multi-academy trusts of colour. In the Northern Ireland case, eight religiously divided key agents of change were selected as an equivalence for the governance structures in the other five case studies. The total number of senior-level leaders participating in the five case studies was 40.

Each author read their findings through Gross' (2014) Turbulence Theory and typology to categorise the level and the impact of the challenges the key agents of change need to navigate as they mediate between the governance systems. Gross (2014, p. 248) theory of turbulence is used as a metaphor and states that 'turbulence can be described as "light" with little or no movement of the craft. "Moderate" with very noticeable waves. "Severe" with strong gusts that threaten control of the aircraft. "Extreme" with forces so great that control is lost and structure damage to the craft occurs'. The chapter identifies the findings were read through the theory of turbulence to reveal the state of the Education Governance Systems and their impact on empowering cosmopolitan citizens to participate fully and freely in societal interactions and cooperation between diverse groups. The authors' chapters are subject to a comparative analysis that took place at the European Conference for Educational Research Annual Conference in two large seminars (Taysum et al., 2017) in Denmark, further developed by the editors and committed to peer-review.

Keywords: Shared world views; diversity; participatory; celebration; peace

Introduction

In the previous two chapters of this section, we have examined how our research quality is world leading in terms of originality, significance and rigour in the way we address an identified gap in the knowledge regarding issues of race, gender, religion, language and culture, socio-economic status, citizenship, migrant and refugee status within a context of colonisation. We have presented Gross (2014) theory of turbulence that we will read our data through and have conceptualised how turbulence might impact upon the empowerment of marginalised groups in International Education Governance Systems. In this chapter, we present a critical engagement with the methodology that each research team presenting a case study in this book from England, Arab Israel, Northern Ireland, Trinidad and Tobago and the United States adopted. The same methodologies were adopted so that the data collected in each case could be compared and contrasted, which optimised the quality dimensions of a comparative analysis within each case and between the five cases (Bridges, 2016; Levin, 2004; Oancea & Furlong, 2007; Pollard, 2008). The exception was the Trinidad and Tobago case study which was also located within a larger research project to describe and understand a national change in policy within education governance systems.

The objectives of the book are to present these five international cases of how governance systems empower key agents of change in school communities to Empower Young Societal Innovators for Equity and Renewal (EYSIER) for peace with a focus on marginalised communities. Our international comparative analysis compares and contrasts different world views of the turbulence in governance systems. The position of the researchers is provided to enable the reader to make judgements about the quality dimensions of the research. The quality dimensions focus on the trustworthiness of the logical, empirical ethical and moral research.

Education is a cultural project that consists of history, narrative and faith. The Black, Asian Minority Ethnicity (BAME) and senior leaders representing marginalised groups that we talked to in this research all stated that their faith, and religion was central to their service as an educational leader. The faiths represented in our research are Islam, Christianity, Sikhism and no faith where a humanitarian approach is taken. We aim to understand the scientific significance of what values underpin these leaders' behaviours and to understand how their values align with legislation, education policy and the values found in Education Governance Systems.

The policy context of the book regarding the development of education policy has been documented by international partners representing 21 nation states, including China, Egypt, England, Finland, France, Germany, Greece, Guyana, Hungary, India, the Arab perspective of Israel, the Jewish perspective of Israel, Italy, Japan, Kazakhstan, Nigeria, Northern Ireland, Pakistan, Republic of Ireland, Russia, South Korea and the United States (Taysum, 2012a, 2014a, 2014b, 2017a) using the same research design (Taysum & Iqbal, 2012). Analyses conducted with these 21 countries from five continents from the end of World War II to the present day reveals a pattern that senior-level leaders in this book are operating within. First, new performance management systems often create education governance systems where 'doing things right' (without asking questions and understanding problems) using what Adler (1941) calls intellectual virtues, is prioritised over 'doing the right thing' which Adler (1941[1]) calls primary virtues of fortitude, prudence and social justice. Evidence reveals there is a lack of alignment between the values of school leaders that underpins their educational project (Pring, 2000), and performance systems driven by quantitative data that education governance systems require them to implement.

A pragmatic consequence for pupils is that they are also trained to play the system, rather than solve societal problems together for a sustainable and

---

[1]Adler's (1941) primary virtues and secondary intellectual virtues helped theorise emergent themes from the comparative analysis of the five cases and are further explored in the 'Comparative Analysis' chapter of the book.

stable cultural, economic, political and ecological model (Taysum, 2012b, 2013, 2014a, 2014b, 2016; Taysum et al., 2015, 2016, 2017b). The book aims to understand how key leaders in Education Governance Systems in these five countries describe and understand the turbulence they face in empowering the principals, and leaders they line manage, to empower their school staff to Empower Young Societal Innovators for Equity and Renewal, particularly in marginalised communities. These senior-level leaders of Education Governance Systems include Superintendents in the US, Trinidad and Tobago and the context of the Arab education in Israel. In England, these senior-level leaders had parity of esteem with these superintendents with different titles of Chief Executive Officers(CEO) of Multi-Academy Trusts (MAT), and in Northern Ireland these senior-level leaders included principals of schools operating in a complex education system. These senior-level leaders are facing contexts of intersectionality of discrimination (Crenshaw, 1989).

Recognising intersectionality of discrimination is the first step to challenging institutional habits as identified by Glazer (1987). Institutional habits that perpetuate intersectionality of discrimination are so embedded in institutional, processes and practices that citizens may not recognise the unnatural nature of these intersectionalities of discrimination and come to take them for granted as natural (Bourdieu, 2000). The research could not be concluded in a sixth planned case study in Nigeria by Hauwa Imam, due to reluctance of most senior public officers approached to respond to questionnaires on the educational governance system. An interview with two of them revealed that intersectionalities of discrimination exist in curriculum implementation practices in the schools.

There are pragmatic consequences of the legacies of historical epochs that contain injustice revealed by intersectionalities of discrimination based on race, gender, religion, language and culture, socio-economic status, citizenship, migrant and refugee status, disability and any of the protected characteristics of the UK Equality Act (UK Government, 2010). A pragmatic consequence is that the institutions perpetuate these intersectionalities of discrimination. This may happen because the intersectionalities have not been described and documented as this book seeks to do. Or maybe because of a fear that leaders of governance systems of these institutions may lose their greater entitlement and may protect injustices in a show of fortitude driven by this fear of the other. Senior-level leaders of Education Governance Systems need what James and McCormick (2009) call policy, skills for learning to learn and what Taysum (2012c) calls Learning to Critically Analyse and Reflect for Emancipation (Learning to CARE) (Pring, 2000). Using these thinking tools, senior-level leaders can mobilise their knowledge, skills and expertise to understand problems and challenges and develop impact strategies through inclusive participatory processes of philosophical inquiry as described and critiqued in this chapter. Thus supporting senior-level leaders to develop philosophical inquiry as professionals to describe inter-sectionalities of discrimination causing marginalisation and to challenge these barriers to equity from within is important. Such an approach should be adopted rather than imposing external solutions in an hierarchical way that are disconnected from the lives of the immature citizens.

The immature citizens require education to become mature, and their education for lifelong learning may achieve this intended learning outcome by including learning experiences to help them recognise intersectionalities of discrimination as legacies of injustice and fear, with impact strategies of transformation:

(1) from injustice to justice;
(2) from acting on a survival instinct to the prudence of acting with both the functional and the aesthetic;
(3) from the fear that paralyses, to the courage that mobilises the human spirit in concert for a critical enlightenment (Lie, 2011) regardless of faith, or no faith, race, ethnicity, cultural heritage, gender, socio-economic status, language, disability, or any of the protected characteristics documented in the UK Equality Act (UK Government, 2010).

Such education is very different to the education built on standards that perpetuate institutions' customs uncritically, driven by tests and exam outcomes when there is no exam in moral training for democracy and peace in our time (Dewey, 1916).

To navigate turbulence senior-level leaders may need to develop a policy to promote learning to learn through being critical and asking good questions whilst meeting standardised curriculums and statistics to benchmark and track shifts from the unjust to the just. At the same time, Lie (2011) cautions that enlightenment and the thinking tools for reason may be taken up by the leadership of Western-educated intellectuals in struggles to counter racism, that may perpetuate marginalisation. Lie (2011, p. 251) suggests: 'Majority and minority groups often share the same language, religion and culture. The potentially contradictory claims of belonging and exclusion generate the particularities and paradoxes of minority identity'. Kant (1784) suggests that a person who is enlightened can self-legislate without the guidance of another.[2] However, education governance systems that do not empower individuals by giving them the thinking tools they need to be self-legislating will not be governing enlightening institutions in becoming. Without giving community members the opportunity to gain the thinking tools to become mature, self-legislating individuals who can make an informed choice to choose to live good lives in peace with the other and with the environment, governing systems will arguably perpetuate groups of people who will depend on the guidance of others such as a government. Taysum (2017c, p. 71) argues: 'States have lost control of the neoliberal project (Watson, 2001) and therefore cannot advocate for the rights of the child, or for human rights (United Nations, 1948, 1989/90), which are trumped by the logic of the market'. Thus, there is a real concern that groups of people are depending

---

[2]Please see Taysum (2012c, pp. 115–130) for a detailed explanation of stages citizens may travel through to become self-legislating to live a good life without the guidance of another for peace in our time.

on the guidance of others to mitigate for an education system that has not empowered them to be self-legislating. Those guiding individuals may be seeking to exploit them to increase their own entitlement such as the gambling industry targeting poor people (Hahmann & Matheson, 2018).

There is a gap in the literature regarding how Education Governance Systems empower or disempower key agents of change to deliver increased grade scores and culturally relevant curriculums to bridge marginalised communities and dominant communities within an enlightened education system hallmarked by social justice, prudence and courage. To generate new understandings of the need for cultural alignment of common values we draw on the Black-White achievement gap as a global phenomenon (Wagner, 2010). The population and sample are key agents of change within marginalised communities, and where possible these are women, because they represent traditional minorities and disempowered community members.

We wanted to understand how these senior-level leaders who interface between federal, state and district policy-makers and school boards, and school principals, staff, students, parents and community stakeholders described and understood how they could reduce achievement gaps where they existed.

Epistemological Underpinnings of the International Comparative Methods

To enable us to deliver on the objectives of the book, we adopted the same research design, epistemological approach and methodologies in each case which is a distinctive approach our team has taken over the ten years of work together. The team's outputs include a website, over 20 international peer-reviewed journal articles published and a further special edition journal in press. The policy analyses and action research conducted in partnership with Higher Education Institutions and Schools all revealed that if logical, evidence informed, ethical and moral intervention strategies were to be implemented, Education Governance Systems needed to empower senior-level leaders interfacing between federal and state policy-makers, and school principals, staff, students, parents and community stakeholders.

Each of the five international cases collected the narrative biographies of up to 15 superintendents or CEO of MATs of colour. In the Northern Ireland case, eight religiously divided key agents of change were selected as an equivalence for the governance structures in the other five case studies. The total number of senior-level leaders participating in the five case studies was 40. Implementing the same methodology in each case, allowed us to identify the roles these key senior-level leaders of change play and to categorise the kinds of 'turbulence' they experience. and navigate (Gross, 2014) as they seek to deliver their manifestos to provide professional learning, including opportunities to learn how to learn (Swaffield & MacBeath, 2009) as they mentor principals, senior leadership teams and school staff to empower students and staff to become innovators for equity and renewal. We analysed how the senior leaders articulated they navigated the turbulence. Finally, we revealed how the governance systems empower them, or disempowered them, in marginalised school communities to EYSIER for peace in our time (Dewey, 1916; Horizon 2020, 2015). Our research design, epistemology, and methodologies aim to facilitate the research teams, in partnership with the schools, to present a new theory of Empowerment in International Governance Systems. We then seek to mobilise these theories into knowledge to action as impact strategies to EYSIER, for peace in our time (Dewey, 1916).

We took a humanist approach to education where each human being has rights (United National Declaration of Human Rights, 1948) and responsibilities in their cultural, economic, and political participation in an education system. Through the analysis, we will reveal the extent to which the education system EYSIER for a democratic society (Dewey, 1916). This chapter will present the social constructivist comparative analysis approach adopted. To meet the objectives each of the five Higher Educational Institutional research teams from the five nation states asked the same four research questions for each of the cases. First, how do the senior-level leaders describe and understand how school governance systems and school commissioners empower them to develop school communities as societal innovators for equity and renewal for peace in our time? Second, how do they describe and understand the role mentors, and/or advocates play to support their navigation through the governance systems? Third, to what extent do they believe a cultural change is required to empower them in school communities to EYSIER for peace in our time? Finally, how can the findings be theorised to generate a theory of knowledge to action through impact strategies within an international comparative analysis framework?

Humanist International Comparative Analysis Approach

Each researcher will give the national context of the governance system in their respective chapter within the book, and this will be located within the Italian Journal of Sociology of Education's historiographical analyses of education policies in the 21 nation states since 1944 edited by Taysum (Angelle, 2017; Arar, 2012; Eddie-Spicer, 2012; Imam, 2012; McGuinness, 2012; Taysum, 2017a, 2014a, 2014b, 2012a). The authors then explain and critique the pertinent international, and state-level literature, or 'global' literature to shed light on the power and interests at play within the governance system. The authors then present the empirical evidence from the analysis of the key change agents' change narrative biographies that were collected using semi-structured interviews as critically discussed in the methodology provided in this chapter. Each author read their findings through Gross (2014) Turbulence Theory and typology to categorise the level and the impact of the challenges the key agents of change need to navigate as they mediate between the governance systems. Gross (2014, p. 248) theory of turbulence is used as a metaphor and states that: 'turbulence can be described as "light" with little or no movement of the craft. "Moderate" with Very noticeable waves. "Severe" with strong gusts that threaten control of the aircraft. "Extreme" with forces so great that control is lost and structure damage to the craft occurs'. The findings will be read through the theory of turbulence to reveal the state of the Education Governance Systems and their impact on empowering cosmopolitan citizens (Waghid & Smeyers, 2014) to participate fully and freely in societal interactions and cooperation between diverse groups. The authors' chapters are subject to a comparative analysis that took place at the European Conference for Educational Research Annual Conference in two large seminars (Taysum, 2017a, 2017c; Taysum et al., 2017b) in Denmark, further developed by the editors and committed to peer-review.

A theory of Empowering Governance Systems: Knowledge to Action is presented and we compare and contrast this with our International Research Team's Model: 'EYSIER for peace' as discussed in the introductory chapter. Thus, this research and the book provide further proof of concept to shore up a research proposal to implement the EYSIER Education Model with 30 nation states. International comparative analyses are important and engage with a more nuanced understanding of the fragility of marginalised groups to create an informed theoretical body of knowledge. Here fragility is understood as disempowered, marginalised humans that threaten the stability of cohesive sustainable systems (Sayed et al., 2015).

We have chosen to conduct International Comparative Education because we believe it is situated in a rich history of empowerment of marginalised human beings through knowledge mobilisation and critique. Paulston (2000) identifies Erasmus from the Renaissance period of 1467–1536 spread his research on liberal education throughout Europe using trade fairs, or as we know them today, conferences. Through his International Comparative Education studies based in Europe, he had a powerful impact on the role of education as a human's 'best hope for freedom, cooperation and possibly salvation' (Paulston, 2000, p. 357). Thus, the approach is focused on a humanistic approach with a desire to develop human beings who can fully and freely interact and cooperate with state institutions governed by overarching ethical laws, bound to a continual moral inquiry into their legitimate right to do so; based on a case by case inquiry if necessary. Paulston (2000) provides a further Renaissance example of an expert in International Comparative Education with Comenius, a Polish pedagogue and refugee. Comenius sought to teach all things to all 'men' through universal schools. His comparative education approach to mobilising knowledge crossed boundaries with the use of images in his textbook *Orbis Pictus* and his message of universal education for world peace. Perhaps like music, the image or, nowadays, the photograph can transcend the written word when there are language barriers, and high levels of illiteracy in the world. The rate varies throughout the world with developed nations having a rate of 99.2% (2013), Oceania having a rate of 71.3%; South and West Asia having a rate of 70.2% (2015) and sub-Saharan Africa having a rate of 64.0% (UNESCO, 2015). Paulston (2000, 357) identifies:

> The European Union along with the World Court, United
> Nations Educational Scientific and Cultural Organisation

(UNESCO), International Institute for Education Planning (IIEP), the International Bureau of Education (IBE) et al. have all embraced, at one time or another, his (Comenius) humanistic and scientific imaginary as their true forerunner [...] the slower and the weaker the disposition of any man, the more he needs assistance. Nor can any man be found whose intellect is so weak that it cannot be improved by culture.

Our position in this research is that we believe we need to hold a mirror up to ourselves and our thoughts and actions, as we interpret and present to you, the reader, the findings from holding up a mirror to the thoughts and actions of elements of society. We then wish to engage in dialogues about power to explore the institutional legacy of why different dispositions, including the dispositions of the marginalised, exist. We further challenge contemporary constructions of orientalism or enmity and intensification of obsession (Said, 1979) as a signifier of oppression, which became evident in the post-9/11 Islamophobic environment that targets Islam and its subjects. 'Islamophobia can be understood as the fear of Islam or its adherents, that is translated into individual ideological and systemic forms of oppression' (Zine, 2006, p. 9). For us as authors, this has meant challenging governments, and employers, and those who wish to maintain the status quo and their greater entitlement. Such critique takes courage because those with power unless committed to humanistic ideologies, may wish to remove those from office who do not agree with them. Our position in this research is that we also believe that the slower and weaker disposition of any human being means that they need more assistance within an education system if the system is to be hallmarked as socially just. This brings us back to Comenius' ideals supported by the EU, the World Court, UNESCO, IIEP, the IBE et al., who believe humans can be improved by culture open to critical analysis, reflection and a commitment to equity and renewal (Rousseau, 1762). Our response to this ideology is to meet it with prudence because we are duty bound to critically reflect carefully, upon the extent to which our research is privileging one culture above another.

We are mindful of how the research may potentially further marginalise those who have been oppressed as a legacy from particular historical epochs. Rather, our position in this research is to move slowly towards logical and evidence-informed conclusions and theories of practice within a matrix, or ethical framework guided by a moral compass that all within this research can provisionally agree on. To address ethical issues, each chapter has been internally reviewed by two reviewers from the team and externally reviewed by two reviewers from the nation state and who advocate for marginalised groups.

The irony is not lost on us that some may see such prudence as a weakness (Woodhead, 1998). Nonetheless, our position is that we will work together carefully, meaningfully, and in a worthwhile way, to ensure that we do not curb our open-mindedness to the execution of our logical, empirical, ethical and moral research and to do the right thing. Our position agrees with that of Dr Saeeda Shah's (2016, p. 4) position in her research:

> The book is embedded in my life experiences and reflects my perspectives and carries my resistance to discrimination; my rejection of all types of fanaticism; my concern over a lack of knowledge, understanding and tolerance with regard to 'others' in the case of those connected with education; my belief in human and gender equality; my insistence on social justice; my belief in humanity and my taking a firm stand for equality, even at personal costs, are all linked to my upbringing and education and have influenced my work'.

The reason for sharing this in the chapter is because our methodology is based on sharing world views within particular frameworks of trust, a search for new knowledge, and a spirit of comparing and contrasting alternative world views and their component parts. In other words, we focus on being critical and having tolerance for the other that affords the opportunity for disagreement with peace (Taysum et al., 2016). Referencing Shah's position in her research allows us to articulate clearly that we all come from different cultures, races, all faiths and none, we represent different genders and have or do not have protected characteristics documented in the UK Equality Act (UK Government, 2010). At the same time, there is a possibility to implement international comparative analyses and to find provisional, overarching, common human rights that we can agree on (United Nations, 1948). What is more, these common rights might connect with different religions. Shah (2016) identifies that the Quran, the ultimate authentic text in Islam, focuses on the holistic development of the self and society. We are interested in understanding how the metaphysical world may align with the human rights of the world in the evolution of the self and society. The human rights of the world are ideally held within institutions, and informed by individual knowledge to action and inform individual knowledge to action, such that the individual and society develop together by Learning to Critically Analyse and Reflect for Emancipation (Learning to CARE) (Taysum, 2012a, 2012b, 2012c). The interactions may draw on what Dewey (1916) calls full and free interactions and full and free cooperation and participation with a view of moving towards peace in our time. Clearly, challenges emerge when the opportunity for dialogue for democracy is reduced at the state level, which may trickle down as policy to local levels. Murray (2018) argues the US continues to increase military spending at three times the amount of all other nations states of the world and makes up more than one-third of worldwide military expenditures. Murray (2018, p. 18) continues:

> War becomes more likely simply because it is constructed to vastly exceed all other options. It evokes the old adage, when every tool is a hammer, every problem becomes a nail'. Similarly,

when all the nation-state has remaining are military options, every solution becomes a war.

Thus institutions that protect liberal diverse communities need to give and receive knowledge from which communities can co-create insights into how human beings can live together in peace in their everyday lives. Shah (2016) reveals the development of the individual and society in Islam focuses on the word *ilm* which means knowledge but transcends the English language understanding of 'knowledge' as a word because Shah (2016, p. 15) identifies that *ilm* 'has unparalleled depth of meaning, exercising a defining influence over all aspects of the Muslim civilisation'. We draw on Shah (2016, p. 15) who cites Akhtar (1997) who identifies *ilm* occurs 704 times in the Quran and *alim* 140 places and *al-ilm* in 27 places. We also cite from Shah (2016, p. 15) that Rahman (1988, 2002, p. 251) states:

> Islam is not the religion of mere dogmatic belief or ritualistic demonstration of piety, it is the religion which is more comprehensive as a guidance for human beings in every walk of life. It is something that has to be practised.

We cite from Shah (2016, p. 16) again, Hussain & Ashraf (1979, p. 10) state:

> God has bestowed on (human beings), and (human beings) alone among all the created things, ability to recognise, understand and emulate the attributes of God and realise them in practice in this life.

Shah (2016, pp. 16–17) continues:

> Al-Kindl (1974) explains three stages or steps in knowledge building: The first is acknowledge, the second is unifying knowledge by drawing on different sources and the third is seeking the progress of future knowledge and facilitating learning of younger generations. He conceptualised knowledge as an on-going endeavour towards perfection, always aimed at or striven for, and never a finished product. He also propounds the argument that knowledge of reality leads to the knowledge of the divinity and unity of God, thus linking the physical to the meta-physical and the material to the spiritual. It was this fusion of the binaries that make Douglass and Sheikh (2004) acknowledge that 'The dynamics of knowledge acquisition in early Muslim civilisation provided for a concept of Islamic education that placed no barrier between 'religious' and 'secular' learning [...] The Islamic of knowledge derives from the Quranic concepts in which seeking knowledge has been regarded as a religious activity because of the underpinning belief that knowledge should lead to God. Hussain (2010)

observes that 'seeking any kind of knowledge was seen as worship by Muslims since it meant to understand and achieve consciousness of God' (p. 239). Halstead (2004) claims that this concept of knowledge where 'knowledge is not to be accumulated for its own sake but must be put to use [...] to live in accordance with Islamic law and to fulfil the purposes of God's creation (the role of knowledge in achieving full human potential) is very different from dominant western concepts' (p. 520).

Here Halstead (2004) may refer to the opening of this chapter where we stated that our research revealed new performance management systems often create education systems where 'doing things right' is prioritised over 'doing the right thing'. In other words, one way of thinking and doing that lacks a moral compass to assure an ethical framework has colonised the other with a moral compass that assures an ethical framework (Taysum, 2017a, 2017c; Taysum et al., 2017b). Young people play the game to win in a competitive environment of neoliberal market forces underpinned by a belief that some; 'the winners and not the losers' have a greater entitlement in this life than others. The position that some deserve more than others is a barrier to achieving full human potential and stands against the values of all faiths, and none that align within the Declaration of Human Rights (United Nations, 1948).

Ilm in Islam goes beyond knowledge and needs to be practised to realise the purpose of God's creation which is all human beings achieving their full potential within the laws of Islam. Furthermore, it has been noted that Islam advocates certain timeless principles relating to education and educational leadership (Mir, 2010). In Islamic culture, an educational leader must adhere to the Qur'an and be diligent in their acts. They should attribute any successes to God and comply with a code of fairness in relation with his subordinates, forgiving them to the extent that this is in their power, encouraging others to be tolerant and discussing and sharing things with them (shora). All these are distinct recognised attributes that Islam recognises as basic criteria for an educational leader (AlSarhi, Salleh, Mohamed, & Amini, 2014; Shah, 2016). Moreover, the Islamic leader is responsible for social and religious areas including the domain of the afterlife. Thus, social and religious spheres are interrelated, while early Islamic leaders served as good models of leadership, improving their societies and creating national cohesion (AlSarhi et al., 2014).

Christians who live in the Western World and in the world can cite their own holy text; the bible which identifies the following values that shape codes of behaviour in the New International Version: 1 Corinthians 13: 13

1 If I speak in the tongues[a] of men or of angels, but do not have love, I am only a resounding gong or a clanging cymbal.
2 If I have the gift of prophecy and can fathom all mysteries

and all knowledge, and if I have a faith that can move moun-
tains, but do not have love, I am nothing. **3** If I give all
I possess to the poor and give over my body to hardship that
I may boast, but do not have love, I gain nothing.

4 Love is patient, love is kind. It does not envy, it does not boast,
it is not proud. **5** It does not dishonour others, it is not self-
seeking, it is not easily angered, and it keeps no record of wrongs.
6 Love does not delight in evil but rejoices with the truth. **7** It
always protects, always trusts, always hopes and always
perseveres.

8 Love never fails. But where there are prophecies, they will
cease; where there are tongues, they will be stilled; where there is
knowledge, it will pass away. **9** For we know in part and we
prophesy in part, **10** but when completeness comes, what is in
part disappears. **11** When I was a child, I talked like a child,
I thought like a child, I reasoned like a child. When I became a
man, I put the ways of childhood behind me. **12** For now we see
only a reflection as in a mirror; then we shall see face to face.
Now I know in part; then I shall know fully, even as I am fully
known. **13** And now these three remain: faith, hope and love. But
the greatest of these is love.

Love in the New International Version of the Holy Bible reveals that God
fully knows a human and a human shall fully know. Until Christians fully know
they have the knowledge of faith, hope and love, and the greatest of these is love
to empower them to reach their full human potential by living within the
Christian laws. This can also be seen in Islam where Hussain (2010, 239) states:
'knowledge is not to be accumulated for its own sake but must be put to use [...]
to live in accordance with Islamic law and to fulfil the purposes of God's creation (the role of knowledge in achieving full human potential). Sikhs also believe
that they should worship God, treat each other equally and be always absorbed
in meditation and prayer. Sikhs believe in making an honest income by honour-
able methods and sharing earnings and selflessly serving others (Khalsa, 2017).
These values have alignment with the Jewish faith with what Rich (2011, p. 1)
refers to within the *Pirkei Avot*, a book of Mishnah which teaches that the universe depends on three things: on Torah (law), on avodah (service) and on g'mi-
lut chasadim (usually translated as 'acts of loving kindness') (Avot 1:2), perhaps
drawing from Psalm 89:3, 'the universe is built on kindness' (more commonly
translated as 'forever is mercy built')'. The metaphysical approach connects with
Confucius who said: If your plan is for one-year plant rice. If your plan is for 10
years plant trees. If your plan is for one hundred years educate children. The
education of children needs to include induction into different world views whilst
respecting a personal faith or no faith, including

Buddhist's noble eightfold path as stated by the Dalai Lama (2014, p. 1) is:

(1) The noble eightfold path directly counteracts all fetters and defilements, releasing us from these.
(2) The noble eightfold path is the cause (hetu) for attaining all true cessations, especially that of an arahant.
(3) The noble eightfold path realises (dassana) the four truths. By realising the four truths as they are in their entirety, ariyas see what ordinary beings are unable to see. They are no longer befuddled, confused, or indecisive about what to practice and abandon.
(4) The noble eightfold path overcomes all varieties of craving and gives mastery (ādhipateyya).

Ariyas never fear to lose their attainments; they know insight wisdom and path wisdom remain firmly in their mindstreams. By practicing the three higher training, ariyas have become masters of themselves. Through having seen nibbāna, if only for some moments, they have full confidence in the Dhamma and the attainments of the Buddha and Saṅgha.

When someone fully sees with correct wisdom (*sammāpaññāya*) the three characteristics or the four attributes of true dukkha, he or she automatically understands the other twelve attributes of the four truths.

The values of Hindus connect with 'right conduct, righteousness, moral law, and duty. Anyone who makes dharma central to one's life strives to do the right thing, according to one's duty and abilities, at all times' (Srinivasan, 2017, p. 1) in the search of truth.

A comparative analysis of the values, and codes of behaviours of Islam, Christianity, Sikhism, Hinduism, Judaism, Chinese traditions, and Buddhism reveals there are connections between them in their intent to realise the purpose of humans, which is for all to achieve their individual potential within society with the divine; thus society achieves full potential.

Recent immense waves of global migration especially to Western countries have transformed states into multicultural states as they host and absorb migrants (Banks, 2017; Revel, 2012; Shah, 2016; Waghid, 2014). Two competing perceptions describe the resulting state of affairs in host societies: a meeting between different values, codes of behaviour, and different cultures (Pring, 2014), leading to a growing multicultural harmony, or a lack of meeting and dialogue which leads to a misunderstanding of the other, fear, and conflict (Bauman, 1997). Without dialogue and community cohesion (Dewey, 1916) there is a danger that non-states people who mean to cause harm can contribute to communities dividing in fear of each other leading to further conflict.

Education offers an opportunity to connect different groups of people to learn about each other's values, codes of behaviour and character and to talk about how their different values, and codes of behaviour, from all faiths and none, connect with the declaration of human rights (1948). Thus, education may underpin a movement of critical and reflective solidarity for peace in our time (Dewey, 1916).

After the World War II, which resulted in millions of brutal deaths, and millions more left homeless and starving, 50 nations assembled and wrote the United Nations Declaration of Human Rights (1948). The preamble states: 'We the peoples of the United Nations are determined to save succeeding generations from the scourge of war, which twice in our lifetime has brought untold sorrow to mankind' (United Nations, 1948, p. 1). The declaration of human rights with an overarching ethical framework with guiding moral compass states:

Article 1. All human beings are born free and equal in dignity and rights. They are endowed with reason and conscience and should act towards one another in a spirit of brotherhood.

Article 2. Everyone is entitled to all the rights and freedoms set forth in this Declaration, without distinction of any kind, such as race, colour, sex, language, religion, political or other opinion, national or social origin, property, birth or other status. Furthermore, no distinction shall be made on the basis of the political, jurisdictional or international status of the country or territory to which a person belongs, whether it is independent, trust, non-self-governing or under any other limitation of sovereignty.

Article 3. Everyone has the right to life, liberty and security of person.

Article 4. No one shall be held in slavery or servitude; slavery and the slave trade shall be prohibited in all their forms.

Article 5. No one shall be subjected to torture or to cruel, inhuman or degrading treatment or punishment.

Article 6. Everyone has the right to recognition everywhere as a person before the law.

Article 7. All are equal before the law and are entitled without any discrimination to equal protection of the law. All are entitled to equal protection against any discrimination in violation of this Declaration and against any incitement to such discrimination.

Article 8. Everyone has the right to an effective remedy by the competent national tribunals for acts violating the fundamental rights granted to them by the constitution or by law.

Article 9. No one shall be subjected to arbitrary arrest, detention or exile.

Article 10. Everyone is entitled in full equality to a fair and public hearing by an independent and impartial tribunal, in the determination of their rights and obligations and of any criminal charge against him.

To EYSIER, young people might benefit from learning about these human rights, and how they connect with the metaphysical of all faiths, and the philosophical of all faiths and none. To do this, the research design, epistemology and methodology of this book and the international comparative analysis may benefit from being brought to the centre of our education as tools that empower immature citizens to learn how to learn (Swaffield & MacBeath, 2009). All young people need the chance to gain the thinking tools and habits to learn about the 'other' with a different world view so the default position is to connect in solidarity, rather than a default position to fear and fight or run away. Such learning will not be effective if it is a bolt on curriculum subject of Religious Education, or citizenship, or philosophy, or classics such as Greek mythology. Rather, our position is that young people need to learn how to learn and do this by engaging with the values and codes of all human beings' pathologies, their causes and remedies. Such learning about the self and creating bridges to the true self, in relation to the other, or in other words the individual in relation to society through *ilm*, or love, or the divine, or human rights, needs to permeate the life of the schools as institutions characterised by social justice, prudence and courage. Such learning does not distract from important disciplines but rather excites, and motivates learners to learn maths, languages, sciences, technologies, and engineering in preparation for the labour market. This is important because marginalised students who fear the impact of their marginalisation may need to use a lot of thought to protect themselves. Such protectionism prevents them from fully engaging with their learning in class and stands as a barrier to them becoming fully developed mature human beings who can make full and free contributions to civil society.

Yet even the bolt on learning about all faiths and none is being eroded as the BBC reported in the UK (Stragwayes-Booth, 2017, p. 1):

> Among academies, which make up the majority of secondary schools, more than a third (34%) were not offering RE to 11 to 13-year-olds and almost half (44%) were not offering it to 14 to 16-year-olds [...].

The BBC (2017, p. 1) report quotes from a teacher Joe Kinnaird, and his students, Lisa, Benjamin, Luke, and Nicole who provide explanations for why they think young people need Religious Education:

> Joe said: RE in schools provides the best and the perfect opportunity to explore those issues which students see in in the wider world. RE and philosophy provide students the chance to explore fundamental questions such as what happens after we die, does God exist, how do we cope with the problem of evil? These questions are both philosophical and ethical and the RE classroom is where we can explore these issues.

Lisa, said: Not being religious myself, I think it's really interesting to learn about other religions, other cultures, I feel like it can be vital in life to understand other religions.

Benjamin, said that not being taught about religion could result in people being heavily influenced by what they find on social media.

Luke said Once you're educated about a certain religion you actually know the true meanings of it.

Nicole said better religious education could help cut the number of racially and culturally motivated crimes. Religion affects politics, so you have to think of it that way. It's really important to know the diverse cultural traditions of other people because it's really relevant today.

There is a gap between the individual and the individuals' associations with the other, the economy, and the state in terms of real knowledge, or love for the self and each other's world views (Banks, 2017) and how these connect to the Declaration of Human Rights (United Nations, 1948). Our concern is that this disconnect prevents rationalisation of different views in the search for truth, which leaves space for disagreement as Shah (2016, p. 2) identifies:

> This stresses inquiry and reflection while emphasising *shura* consultation and *Ijtihad* (rational consensus), and creates space for *Ikhtilaf* (disagreement) with regard to all. The Quran dictum 'la ikraha fi-al-din' (the Quran, 2:256) meaning 'no compulsion in religion', not only acknowledges people's right to freedom of religion but also establishes the principle of non-coercion, as supported by other ayahs in the Quran such as 'you are not one to compel them by force' (50:45) and 'Will you then compel human kind against their will to believe' (10:99). Islam as a social and ethical code places emphasis on social justice, individual freedom and social equality (Ashraf, 1987; Waghid, 2009).

The knowledge that shapes world structures is produced by powerful groups both financially and culturally and some of these groups see the world through a lens of competion for greater entitlements in a world with diminishing resources and growing populations (Banks, 2017). Philosophically, addressing these global problems by striving for greater entitlement may result in a war which could destroy all life. A second option is to co-create and innovate for equity and renewal to fully and freely interact and cooperate and plan for a sustainable world with wisdom now. The philosophical approach connects with Confucius who said:

> If your plan is for one-year plant rice. If your plan is for ten years plant trees. If your plan is for one hundred years educate children.

Increasingly, with a lack of understanding of different world views, the threat of war is real and clearly articulated by Shah (2016, p. 7) who recognises that in a post 9/11 world we may be:

> living through the threat of the tenth crusade with historical flash-backs reconstructing the images of earlier crusades and the associated hostility that escalated the tensions and challenges on education sites.

This connects with Murray (2018, p. 18) who states:

> War becomes more likely simply because it is constructed to vastly exceed all other options. It evokes the old adage, 'when every tool is a hammer, every problem becomes a nail'. Similarly, when all the nation-state has remaining are military options, every solution becomes a war.

In this chapter thus far, we have presented the comprehensive epistemological underpinnings of the international comparative analysis. We now present the socio-constructivist approach (Creswell & Poth, 2017; Robson, 2011) that has allowed us to systematically, meaningfully, and in a worthwhile way compare and contrast the different cases without privileging one world view over another.

Multicultural Dispositions to Develop Shared Cross-cultural World Views

Over the last decade in our team's work together, we have worked hard to address the findings of a rich historical examination of comparative education 'to question how our choice of ideas and forms of representation influence our views of how reality is constituted and construed, how meaning and value are created and imposed on, an otherwise unruly world' (Paulston, 2000, p. 364). Our critical cross-cultural approach to this comparative education seeks to optimise the quality dimensions of this research so the reader can make appropriate critical judgements about the warrants we present for the claims we make (Levin, 2004; Oancea & Furlong, 2007; Pollard, 2008). We therefore take a critical realist approach (Bhaskar, 2010) which we interrogate in our methodology section.

During presentations at the American Educational Research Association Annual Conferences, the European Educational Research Association Annual Conferences, and the British Educational Leadership, Management, and Administration Society Annual Conferences, we have found that members get to know one another and become more open to recognising that our world views meet, and we can play a part in working for peace or escalating conflict. We have explored the tensions that are created through these clashes and have worked hard to engage in dialogues to move beyond our own turbulence as we explore the collisions of world views from community members with different world views (Ishii,

Klopf, & Cooke, 2007). We have also worked hard to understand symbols (Helve, 1991), for example, our research colleagues from Herzen State Pedagogical University, St Petersburg, Russia, have as their University symbol a pelican that feeds its young from her own heart. As our relationships, in a state of becoming (Adler, 1941), have developed, we have come to appreciate the loyalty and love our Russian friends have for their motherland and each other, which is greatly respected. This is just one example of how we have seen symbols, but not understood their true meaning until years later after trust has developed and we have begun to talk about what matters to us for cultural, economic, political, and ecological sustainability of our world for human life. Over time, trust is built as our agency is shaped by structures such as policy, geographical boundaries, resources, and politics, which in turn have shaped our agency (Akkerman & Bakker, 2011; Arar, 2017). How the social has informed our mental models and constructs and how our constructs have informed the structures underpins our high-quality relationships that focus on philosophical inquiry that aim to ask good questions and problem-solve. Our position is that we are morally, and intellectually ambitious to empower Education Governance Systems to build relationships that focus on philosophical inquiry to problem solve, so the lessons learned from colliding world views in conference halls, may be shared and inform the community members who encounter turbulence when their world views collide in the classroom.

Rubin and Paplau (1975) suggest world views are constructed in three ways: through the education systems that transmit scientific knowledge; through the metaphysical; through the world religions, and philosophies (Chamberlain & Zika, 1992). World views, whether overtly acknowledged or not, are part of pedagogical relationships in the classrooms (Peters, 1966; Peters, 1981). Teachers and students who include inquiry in their learning, and can trust their world views are respected in a classroom are likely to build good pedagogical relationships based on respect and inclusion (Harrison, Taysum, McNamara, & O'Hara, 2016). Further, teachers and students who engage their inquiring minds to learn about the self and the other with trust are likely to learn how to learn, and are likely to apply their knowledge, skills and experience logically, empirically, ethically and morally in the construction of their lives in society (Saran & Niesser, 2004). The process of developing identity schemas (Carter, 2008) that build bridges between the self and the other, and build bridges to the true self are strengthened when sharing world views. Sharing world views needs to take place as a community participation practice, and through international comparative analyses.

The previous overview brings us to understanding the similarities and differences of their conceptualisations in education in different nation-states and in different groups in multicultural societies. Deep and comprehensive understanding of the values, contexts, competing narratives and different practices in education worldwide can build common aims and educational purposes and facilitate multi-cultural and inter-cultural education (Banks, 2017; Mir, 2010; Revel, 2012). It is hoped that the distancing of one culture from the other, which has always led to hatred, suspicion and hostility (Bauman, 1997; Nasir, 1985), can be replaced by mutual understanding and cultural tolerance (Revel, 2012). This understanding can be important for policy-makers and educational leaders in various multicultural contexts.

International Comparative Analysis; Sharing World-views to Empower Young Societal Innovators for Equity and Renewal

There are three aspects of international comparative analysis for sharing world views that we as a team need to have considered for our research to be an authentic contribution to boundary crossing, multi-disciplinary research that seeks to find provisional consensus on a logical, empirical, metaphysical, ethical and moral theory (Helve, 1991). These aspects are particularly important for the book as we seek to present a Theory of Governance for EYSIER of scientific significance.

The first is the first principles and verifiable theories that shape what Rubin and Paplau (1975) call the scientific world view. The second is people build their whole lives on what Rubin and Paplau (1975) call the metaphysical. Their lives are fulfilled by faith and their faith, by its very definition, may only be experienced and verified at an individual level, but can be understood through first principles that guide acts within the framework of a religion or philosophy. Third, that all who seek to share a cross-cultural world view need to have been inducted into the habits of generating knowledge, searching for truth, being critical and reflective, being tolerant of the other, and not compelling another what to believe as they build what Rubin and Paplau (1975) call the world religions' and philosophies' knowledge.

The authors take a multidisciplinary approach to this International Comparative Education Study referencing from educational leadership theory and practice, the philosophy of education, the history of education, world histories, critical education policy studies, the sociology of education, Critical Educators for Social Justice, teacher education, professional learning, economics, and motivation and psychology theories. Our approach draws on different purposes of comparative education that have developed over time. Our comparative education draws on Michael Sadler's approach which, in 1903, emphasised the practical application of comparative education that seeks to inform education systems' policy and practice (Higginson, 1999). Our approach also aims to empower adults and young people to renew, or reconstruct processes and practices for participation and equity. As such we also agree with Holmes' aims for comparative education in the 1950s to reconstruct education systems in the aftermath of the Second World War (Higginson, 1999). Taysum (2012b) documents the role of comparative education in this era with a focus on the United States' role in funding international reconstruction of education, which is a theme that is explored in the Japanese context by Maehara (2014) in the 2014 IJSE of international perspectives of education policy analysis. We also recognise that for refugees to return to their homelands, there will need to be a reconstruction of education infrastructures within nation states' infrastructures and this will take significant financial investments (Commission for Victims and Survivors, 2016).

We take Watson (2001) arguments very seriously that with globalisation we need to consider if the nation state is the right unit of analysis for comparative education although The World Bank, United Nations Educational, Scientific, and Cultural Organisation (UNESCO), and the Organisation for Economic and Cooperation and Development (OECD) still use the nation state as the unit of analysis.

Watson argues the role of the private sector in education is increasing. There is a lack of data on money flows (Ball, 2017) and multinationals have a higher turnover than 90 of the world's poorest countries (Watson, 2001). Overall we take Watson's following statement very seriously when he says there is a: 'weakening of central government control over planning or the running of public services such as health and education; and the growing inability of the state to control all the activities within its borders'. Such a state of affairs has significant issues for governance systems if the state wishes to assure the public's full and free interaction, cooperation and what Rousseau calls their association with governance systems, the state and the economy (Rousseau, 1762).

Our comparative education of international perspectives focuses on seeking a theory of governance for empowerment that uses a dialogic approach to the research that is conducted in partnership between those within the school and the academy. Evans and Robinson Pant (2010) call for such innovative approaches to comparative education and international perspectives. We also seek to generate new knowledge focusing on issues of power within comparative education and are mindful of how adults and young people's agency is shaped by structures that position them (Apple, 1995). We seek to understand culture, and identity and reveal through comparative education analysis the extent to which particular group's interests are marginalised and why (Arnova, Torres, & Franz, 2013). We, therefore, draw on Crossley (1999) and focus on the position of culture and policy context in our approach to this comparative educational study.

We considered Robinson-Pant and Singal (2013) regarding conflicts in shared ethical frameworks in different contexts and found the British Educational Research Association (BERA) (2011) Guidelines for Ethical Framework which England and Northern Ireland comply with, and the American Educational Research Association (2010) ethical framework which the US comply with, aligned closely with the ethical frameworks for the Israeli Ethical Framework, Trinidad and Tobago Ethical Framework, and Nigerian Ethical Framework. Each author sought ethical approval from their University Ethical Review Boards. All Ethical Review Boards approved the research. We assured our respondents anonymity, confidentiality and the right to withdraw from the research until point of publication. All respondents were invited to participate in the research and completed informed consent forms in their first language that included these assurances (please see Appendices 1 and 2 for a sample letter of invitation to the senior-level leaders and a sample informed consent form).

Population, Sample and Strategy

The sample was purposive from a population in each nation state of the senior-level leaders who were the interface between federal, state and local policy-makers and school boards, and the principals, staff, parents and students (Snoek, Enthoven, Kessels, & Volman, 2017). For the case studies in the US, Arab Israel, Trinidad and Tobago these senior-level leaders were superintendents. In England, these senior-level leaders were CEO of MATs. In Northern Ireland these senior-level leaders were principals in schools that were Catholic, Protestant and with different funding relationships with the state and with different religious institutions. We adopted a multiple case study strategy where each case aimed to examine the research questions which mapped back to the research aims and the professional challenge (Yin, 2012). The multiple case study strategy required a research team to complete. Each team collected the narrative biographies of the participants using the semi-structured interviews schedule (Denscombe 2010).

The semi-structured interview schedule allowed us to standardise the questions asked, mapped back to our research questions to enable us to compare and contrast the findings (please see Appendix 3 for the semi-structured interview schedule). As Denscombe (2010) identifies with a semi-structured interview schedule we were able to follow up each standardised question with prompts and probes. Prompts allowed us to refer the senior-level leader to particular arguments in the literature we had read to understand their perceptions on these themes. This is because participants have different priorities at different times depending on their changing work schedule, and therefore they might talk about an issue from a particular perspective at that time and in that place. A prompt allowed us to invite the leader to consider another aspect in relation to their praxis, regarding the question asked (Denscombe, 2010). The probes allowed us to ask the senior-level leaders for concrete examples to ensure we moved from the abstract descriptions and analyses of the senior-level leaders' narrative biographies to the concrete examples. Having concrete examples allowed us to compare and contrast the descriptions within the multiple cases which provided high-quality data that were grounded in the real world, rather than general recollections of senior-level leaders' praxis (Blumenfeld-Jones, 1995). After the semi-structured interview was complete, each senior-level leader received a letter of thanks (please see Appendix 4 for a sample letter of thanks). Each interview was transcribed and sent to the senior-level leader for respondent validation.

Data Analysis

When the data had been transcribed the data were organised into themes and categories (Creswell, 2009). Three themes emerged from the analyses. First, we were able to identify participants' roles and their interplay between the construction of policy as text and policy as discourse (Ball, 2006), and clashes between different values. Second, we categorised the different levels of 'turbulence' they articulated they experienced by reading the findings through Gross theory of

Turbulence (2014), and the mentors and networks they articulated helped them, or that they hoped would help them navigate the turbulence to organise education. Third, we revealed how these senior -level leaders articulated they were empowered by Education Governance Systems to implement cultural change strategies to EYSIER for peace (Horizon 2020, 2015; Taysum, 2012a, 2012b, 2012c, 2013, 2014a, 2014b, 2017a, 2017c; Taysum et al., 2015, 2016, 2017b). From the analysis of the findings in each case, and then a comparative analysis between cases, a new theory of knowledge to action is presented of Empowerment through Education Governance Systems and Impact Strategies for Knowledge to Action. Finally, we compared and contrasted this new theory of knowledge to action with the EYSIER Education Model. The aim of this stage of the project was to provide proof of concept for the research proposal: EYSIER Education Model, or to provide logical, evidence-informed, moral and ethical refinements to the EYSIER Model.

The trustworthiness of our research is underpinned by our articulated positions in the research of one committed to equity and renewal. We assure trustworthiness of our research (Oancea & Furlong, 2007) by conducting an internal review of our research where our team represents diverse cultures, races, ethnicities and genders. Our research team are also committed advocates for those with protected characteristics documented in the UK Equality Act (UK Government, 2010). All chapters have also been through external review. We invite the reader to take a critical, logical approach to the book and consider the moral compass that guided the ethical framework for our research design presented in this chapter that informs the claims we make in the following five international cases presented in the second section of the book.

The second section of the book comprises Chapters 4–9 and presents five critical International Cases of Turbulence, Empowerment, and Marginalisation in International Educational Governance Systems. First, Alison Taysum presents Chapters 4 and 5; 'The Turbulence Black, Asian, Minority Ethnicity Chief Executive Officers of Small, Medium, and Empty MATs Face In England's Education System. Chapter 4 focuses on 'the Structures' and Chapter 5 focuses on 'the agency'. In Chapter 6 Samuel McGuinness, Jessica Bates, Una O'Connor, Stephen Roulston, Catherine Quinn, Brian Waring present: 'Empowering School Principals to Overcome Turbulence in School Partnerships through Governance Systems for Equity, Renewal, and Peace: Northern Ireland'. In Chapter 7, Khalid Arar and Asmahan Masry present 'Supervisors in the Arab education system: Between governability, duality and empowerment, through a state of turbulence'. In Chapter 8, Freddy James and June George present 'Turbulence in Efforts at Curriculum Renewal for Educational Equity: A Critical Analysis of a Primary Curriculum Review Exercise in Trinidad and Tobago'. Finally, in Chapter 9, Carole Collins Ayanlaja, Warletta Brookins and Alison Taysum present 'Empowering Superintendents In the United States To Empower Societal Innovators For Equity and Renewal in the community'.

References

Adler, M. (1941). *A dialectic of morals: Towards the foundations of political philosophy*. Notre Dame, IL: University of Notre Dame.

Akhtar, S. W. (1997). 'The Islamic concept of knowledge', *Al-Tawhid. A Quarterly Journal of Islamic Thought & Culture*; *XII*(3); The Foundation of Islamic Thought, Qum, Iran. Retrieved from www.al-islam.org/al-tawhid/vol-12-no3/islamic-concept-knowledge/islamic-concept-knowledge. Accessed on May 2014.

Akkerman, S., & Bakker, A. (2011). Boundary cross and boundary objects. *Review of Educational Research, 81*(2), 132–169.

AlSarhi, N. S., Salleh, L. M., Mohamed, Z. A., & Amini, A. A. (2014). The Western and Islamic perspective of leadership. *International Affairs and Global Strategy, 18*, 42–56.

American Educational Research Association. (2010). Code of ethics. *Educational Researcher, 40*(3), 145–156.

Angelle, P. (2017). Equal educational opportunity and accountability. A review of US educational policy since World War II. *Italian Journal of Sociology, 9*(2), 126–153.

Apple, M. (1995). *Education and Power*. New York, NY: Routledge.

Arar, K. (2012). Israeli education policy since 1948 and the state of Arab education in Israel. *Italian Journal of Sociology of Education, 1*, 113–145.

Arnova, R. F., Torres, C. A., & Franz, S. (2013). *Comparative education: The dialectic of global and local*. Lanham, MD: Rowan & Littlefield.

Ashraf, S. A. (1987). Education and values: Islamic vis-a-vis the secularist approaches. *Muslim Education Quarterly, 4*(4), 4–16.

Ball, S. (2017). *Edu.net: Globalisation and education policy mobility*. London: Routledge.

Banks, J. A. (2017). *Citizenship education and global migration: Implications for theory, research and teaching*. Washington, DC: American Educational Research Association.

Bauman, Z. (1997). *Postmodernity and its discontents*. Cambridge: Polity.

Bhaskar, R. (2010). *Reclaiming reality: A critical introduction to contemporary philosophy*. London: Routledge.

Blumenfeld-Jones, D. (1995). Fidelity as a criterion for practicing and evaluating narrative enquiry. In J. Amos Hatch & R. Wisniewski (Eds.), *Life History and Narrative* (pp. 25–36). London: Falmer Press.

Bourdieu, P. (2000). *Pascalian meditations*. Cambridge: Polity Press.

Bridges, D. (2016). *Philosophy in educational research: Epistemology, ethics, politics and quality*. E-book: Springer.

British Educational Research Association. (2011). *Ethical guidelines for educational research*. London: BERA.

Carter, P. L. (2008). Teaching students fluency in multiple cultural codes. In M. Pollock (Ed.), *Everyday antiracism* (pp. 107–111). New York, NY: The New Press.

Chamberlain, K., & Zika, S. (1992). Religiosity, meaning in life, and psychological well-being. In J. F. Schumaker (Ed.), *Religion and mental health* (pp. 138–148). New York, NY: Oxford University Press.

Commission for Victims and Survivors. (2016). *To improve the lives of all victims and survivors of the conflict.* Retrieved from https://www.cvsni.org. Accessed 20 April 2018.

Crenshaw, K. (1989). *Demarginalizing the intersection of race and sex: A Black Feminist critique of antidiscrimination doctrine, feminist theory, and antiracist politics* (pp. 139–167). Chicago, IL: University of Chicago Legal Forum, 1989.

Creswell, J. W. (2009). *Research design: Qualitative, quantitative, and mixed-methods approaches.* London: Sage.

Creswell, J., & Poth, C. (2017). *Qualitative inquiry and research design: Choosing among five approaches.* London: Sage.

Crossley, M. (1999). Reconceptualising comparative and international education. *Compare a Journal of Comparative and International Education, 29*(3), 249–267.

Denscombe, M. (2010). *The good research guide second edition for small scale social research projects.* Berkshire: Open University Press.

Dewey, J. (1916). *Democracy and education.* New York, NY: Macmillan.

Douglass, S. L., & Shaikh, M. A. (2004). Defining Islamic education: Differentiation and applications. *Current Issues in Comparative Education, 7,* 5–18.

Eddie-Spicer, D. (2012). Rhetoric, reality and research: The rhetoric of systemic reform, the reality of leadership development and current trends in school leadership research in the United States. *Italian Journal of Sociology, 4*(1), 305–320.

Evans, K., & Robinson-Pant, A. (2010). Compare: Exploring a 40-year journey through comparative education and international development. *Compare: A Journal of Comparative and International Education, 40*(6), 693–710.

Glazer, N. (1987). *Affirmative discrimination ethnic inequality and public policy.* Cambridge, MA: Harvard University Press.

Gross, S. J. (2014). Using turbulence theory to guide actions. In C. M. Branson & S. J. Gross (Eds.), *Handbook on ethical educational leadership* (pp. 246–262). New York, NY: Routledge.

Hahmann, T., & Matheson, F. (2018). Problem gambling and poverty in gambling research exchange Ontario; driving knowledge into action. Retrieved from http://www.greo.ca/Modules/EvidenceCentre/files/Hahmann_and_Matheson_(2017)_Problem_gambling_and_poverty.pdf downloaded 31032018

Halstead, J. M. (2004). An Islamic concept of education. *Comparative Education, 40*(4), 517–529.

Harrison, K., Taysum, A., McNamara, G., & O'Hara, J. (2016). The degree to which students and teachers are involved in second-level school processes and participation in decision making: An *Irish Case Study. Irish Educational Studies, 35*(2), 155–173.

Helve, H. (1991). The formation of religious attitudes and worldviews: a longitudinal study of young Finns. *Social Compass, 38*(4), 373–392.

Higginson, J. (1999). The development of a discipline: Some reflections on the development of comparative education as seen through the pages of Compare. *Compare: A Journal of Comparative Education and International Perspectives, 29*(3), 341–351.

Horizon 2020. (2015). CO-CREATION-01–2017: Education and skills: Empowering Europe's young innovators. Retrieved from https://ec.europa.eu/research/participants/portal/desktop/en/opportunities/h2020/topics/co-creation-01–2017.html. Accessed on May 30, 2017.

Hussain, A. (2010). Islamic education in the west: theoretical foundations and practical implications. In K. Engebretson M. de Souza G. Durka, & L. Gearon (Eds.), *International Handbook of Inter-Religious Education (Part 4)* (pp. 235−248). London: Springer.

Hussain, S., & Ashraf, A. (1979). *Crisis in Muslim education.* Saudi Arabia: Jeddah, King Abdul Aziz University, Hodder & Stoughton.

Imam, H. (2012). Educational policy in Nigeria from the colonial era to the post-independence period. *Italian Journal of Sociology of Education, 10*(1), 181−204. Retrieved from http://www.ijse.eu/journals

Ishii, S., Klopf, D., & Cooke, P. (2007). Worldview in intercultural communication: A religio-cosmological approach. In L. Samovar R. Porter, & E. McDaniel (Eds.), *Intercultural Communication a Reader.* Boston, MA: Wadsworth Cengage Learning.

James, M., & McCormick, R. (2009). Teachers learning how to learn. *Teaching and Teacher Education, 25*(7), 973−982.

Kant, I. (1784/1970) 1991. An answer to the question: 'What is enlightenment? In Hans Reiss (Ed.), Immanuel Kant, *Political Writings* (2nd ed; trans. H. B. Nisbet). Cambridge: Cambridge University Press.

Lama, D. (2014). *The Dalai Lama on four attributes of the true path.* Wisdom Publications. Retrieved from https://www.wisdompubs.org/blog/201412/dalai-lama-four-attributes-true-path. Accessed on October 14, 2018.

Levin, B. (2004). Marking research matter more. *Education Policy Analysis Archives, 12*(56). Retrieved from https://scholarcommons.usf.edu/cgi/viewcontent.cgi?referer=https://www.google.com Accessed October 17, 2018.

Lie, J. (2011). Modern peoplehood: On race, racism, nationalism, ethnicity, and identity. UC Berkeley. Retrieved from https://escholarship.org/content/qt73c5c0cg/qt73c5c0cg.pdf. Accessed 30 March 2018.

Maehara, K. (2014). A critical historiographical analysis of Japan's educational policies from the end of the World War II to 2011. *Italian Journal of Sociology of Education, 6*(2), 114−143.

McGuinness, S. J. (2012). Education policy in northern Ireland: A review. *Italian Journal of Sociology, 4*(1), 205−237.

Mir, A. M. (2010). Leadership in Islam. *Journal of Leadership Studies, 4*(3), 69−72.

Murray, D. (2018). War without violence? Dewey's insights on modern warfare. John Dewey Society Annual Meeting, Dewey and Philosophy Panel I, Nationalism: War and Peace in American Educational Research Association, New York, April.

Nasir, S. H. (1985). *Ideals and realities of Islam.* London: George Allen and Union.

Oancea, A., & Furlong, J. (2007). Expressions of excellence and the assessment of applied and practice-based research. *Research Papers in Education, 22*(2), 119−137.

Paulston, R. (2000). Imagining comparative education: Past, present and future. *Compare: A Journal of Comparative and International Education, 30*(3), 353−367.

Peters, R. S. (1966). *Ethics and Education.* London: Allen and Unwin.

Peters, R. S. (1981). *Moral Development and Moral Education.* London: George Allen and Unwin.

Pollard, A. (2008). Quality and capacity in UK education research. Report of the first meeting of the UK's Strategic Forum for Research in Education, 16th and 17th October, Harrogate.

Pring, R. (2014). Leadership, skilled manager of virtuous professional? In A. Taysum & S. Rayner (Eds.), *Investing in our education? Leading, learning, researching and the doctorate.* Scarborough: Emerald.

Rahman, F. (1988). Islamization of knowledge: A response. *American Journal of Islamic Social Science, 5*(1), 3–11.

Rahman, F. (2002). Islam to the modern mind. In Y. Mohamed (Ed.), *Lectures in South Africa (1970–1972)* (2nd ed.). Paarl: Paarl Print.

Revel, L. (2012). *Islam and Education—The manipulation and misrepresentation of a religion.* London: Trentham Books Limited.

Robson, C. (2011). *Real world research.* Oxford: John Wiley and Sons.

Robinson-Pant, A., & Singal, N. (2013). Research ethics in comparative and international education: Reflections from anthropology and health. *Compare: A Journal of Comparative and International Education, 43*(4), 443–463.

Rousseau, J. J. (1762). *The social contract.* London: Wordsworth Classics of World Literature.

Rubin, Z., & Paplau, L. (1975). Who believes in a just world. *Journal of Social Issues, 31*(3), 65–89.

Said, A. A. (1979). Human rights in Islamic perspectives. In A. Pollis & P. Schwab (Eds.), *Human rights: Cultural and ideological perspectives* (pp. 49–71). New York, NY: Praeger.

Saran, R., & Niesser, B. (2004). *Inquiring minds; socratic dialogue in education.* Stoke-on-Trent: Trentham Books Ltd.

Shah, S. (2016). *Education, leadership and Islam.* London: Routledge.

Snoek, M., Enthoven, M., Kessels, J., & Volman, M. (2017). Increasing the impact of a Master's programme on teacher leadership and school development by means of boundary crossing. *International Journal of Leadership in Education, 20*(1), 26–56.

Srinivasan, A. (2017). Core belief of Hindus. Retrieved from https://www.dummies.com/religion/hinduism/core-beliefs-of-hindus/. Accessed on October 14, 2018.

Stragwayes-Booth, A. (2017). Schools break law on religious education, research suggests. *BBC News.* Retrieved from https://www.bbc.co.uk/news/education-41282330. Accessed on October 14, 2018.

Swaffield, S., & MacBeath, J. (2009). Leadership for learning. In J. MacBeath & N. Dempster (Eds.), *Connecting leadership and learning: Principles for practice* (pp. 32–52). Abingdon: Routledge.

Taysum, A. (2012a). *Evidence informed leadership in education.* London: Continuum.

Taysum, A. (2012b) 'Editorial and editor' 'Learning from international educational policies to move towards sustainable living for all' in China, England, France, Israel, Italy, Nigeria, Northern Ireland, Republic of Ireland, Russia, United States. *Italian Journal of Sociology of Education, 4*(1). Retrieved from http://ijse.padovauniversitypress.it/issue/4/1

Taysum, A. (2012c). *Convener of a large symposium in two parts: 'Globalization, Policy and Agency: Eight Nation states working together to Further Understand their Political Sociologies of Education'.* European Conference for Educational Research, Cadiz, September.

Taysum, A. (2013). *Convener of a large symposium in two parts; 'International Boundary Crossing Study of Teachers' and Students' Participation in Institutional Processes and Practices'*. European Conference for Educational Research. Istanbul, September.

Taysum, A. (2014a). Convener of a large symposium in two parts: 'International Boundary Crossing Study Of Higher Education Institutions working in Partnership with Schools To Improve Participation In Processes And Practices Chair: Jan Heystek (Stellenbosch University). Discussant: Carole Collins Ayanlaja (Chicago, Superintendent) *ECER, Porto.*

Taysum, A. (2014b). 'Editorial and editor ' Learning from international education policies to move towards education systems that facilitate sustainable full economic, cultural and political participation in Egypt, Finland, Greece, Israel (Jewish perspective), Japan, Kazakhstan, and South Korea in *Italian Journal of Sociology of Education, 6*(2), 1–7. Retrieved from http://ijse.padovauniversity-press.it/issue/6/2.

Taysum, A. (2015). *Convener of a large symposium in two parts: 'A Theory of Young People's Participation in Systems and Learning from International Boundary Crossing Action-Resarch Project Arar, K., Collins-Ayanlaja, C., Harrison, K., Imam, H., Murrel-Abery, V., Mynbayeva, A., Yelbayeva, Z.* European Conference for Educational Research. Budapest, Hungary. September.

Taysum, A. (2016). *Rationalising Kant with Aristotle's habits – the complexity of becoming virtuous.* Workshop presented at Almaty, Kazakhstan, November.

Taysum, A. (2016). *Convener of a large symposium in two parts: McNamara (Chair), Risku, M., Collins Ayanlaja, C., Iddrisu, M.T., Murrel-Abery, J.V., Arar, K., Masry-Herzallah, A., Imam, H., Chopra, P., McGuinness, S. Theoretical underpinnings of an education and skills model for participation and cooperation in the Youth Field; empowering Europe's young innovators.* European Conference for Educational Research, Dublin, Ireland, August.

Taysum, A. (2017a). 'Editorial and editor 'External influences on education systems and educational leadership in Shifts in Germany Hungary, Guyana, India, Pakistan, and the US. *Italian Journal of Sociology of Education, 9*(2), 1–8.

Taysum, A. (2017b). *Convener of a large symposium in two parts: Arar, K., Masry-Herzallah, A., Collins Ayanlaja, C., Brookins, W., McGuinness, S., Bates, J., Roulsten, S., O'Connor, U., James, F., and George, J., Taysum, A. Turbulence in Six International Education Governance-Systems: Comparing Knowledge to Action for Equity, Peace and Renewal.* European Conference for Educational Research, Copenhagen, Denmark, August.

Taysum, A. (2017c). Systems Theory and education: A philosophical enquiry into education systems theory. In P. Higgs & Y. Waghid (Eds.), *A reader for philosophy of education* (1st ed., vol. 1). South Africa: Juta.

Taysum, A., & Iqbal, M. (2012). What counts as meaningful and worthwhile policy analysis. *Italian Journal of Sociology of Education, 4*(1), 11–28.

UK Government. (2010). *Equality act.* London: HMSO.

United Nations. (1948). *Universal declaration of human rights* (General Assembly Resolution 217 A). Retrieved from http://www.un.org/en/universal-declaration-human-rights/. Accessed on October 14, 2018.

United Nations (UN). (1948). The universal declaration of human rights. Retrieved from http://www.un.org/en/universal-declaration-human-rights/. Accessed on February 12, 2017.

United Nations (UN). (1989/1990). Convention on the rights of the child. Retrieved from http://www.ohchr.org/EN/ProfessionalInterest/Pages/CRC.aspx. Accessed on February 12, 2017.

Waghid, Y. (2014). Islam education and cosmopolitanism: A philosophical interlude. *Studies in Philosophy of Education, 33*(3), 329−342.

Waghid, Y., & Smeyers, P. (2014). Re envisioning the future: Democratic citizenship education and Islamic education. *Journal of Philosophy of Education, 48*(4), 539−558.

Waghid, Y. (2009). Education and madrassahs in South Africa: On the possibility of preventing extremism. *British Journal of Religious Education, 31*(2), 117−128.

Wagner, T. (2010). *The global achievement gap.* New York, NY: Basic Books.

Watson, K. (2001). Introduction: Rethinking the role of comparative education. In K. Watson (Ed.), *Doing Comparative Education Research: Issues and Problems* (pp. 23−42). Oxford: Symposium Books.

Woodhead, C. (1998, March 20). Academia gone to seed. *New Statesman*, 51−52.

Yin, R. (2012). *Applications of case study research.* London: Sage.

Zine, J. (2006). Between orientalism and fundamentalism: The politics of Muslim women's feminist engagement. *Muslim World Journal of Human Rights, 3*(1), 1−24.

PART II
FIVE INTERNATIONAL CASES OF TURBULENCE, EMPOWERMENT, AND MARGINALISATION

Chapter 4

The Turbulence Black, Asian, Minority Ethnicity Chief Executive Officers of Small, Medium and Empty MATs Face in England's Education System; the Structures

Alison Taysum

Abstract

The professional challenge the chapter addresses is Black, Asian Minority Ethnic Chief Executive Officers (BAME CEOs) who lead Multi-academy Trusts (MATs) in England need to navigate turbulence to assure all schools within their MATs are high performing. In the investigation of this issue, the structures of MATs themselves emerge as causing turbulence. Evidence revealed the BAME CEOs with track records of improving failing schools to outstanding schools interviewed in this research are working in partnership with their communities. These BAME CEOs sustain their high achieving MATs and/or take on more schools that need improving and lead their change to outstanding schools with BAME communities, non-BAME communities and diverse communities. However, they were not given the opportunities to build capacity for high-performing schools by the current MAT structures. Rapid change to the organisation of Public Education Governance Systems has shifted power from local authority governance to public corporation governance without addressing any of the old problems in the change (Brighouse, 2017). The rapid change has led to a clash of cultures between those with the values of generic Public Governance Systems who have not been democratically elected by the public and do not require professional educational credentials, a track record of being ethical teachers, and a track record of leading ethical teachers in ethical communities in school

Turbulence, Empowerment and Marginalisation in International
Education Governance Systems, 81–105

improvement from 'Needs Improvement' to 'Good' or 'Outstanding'. The rapid change has been hallmarked by a lack of full and free interactions and cooperation of the public in how the change in public education is being implemented. There has been no referendum on whether parents want their schools organised by their representatives they have elected in local councils or organised by public corporations financed by Private Finance Incentive (PFI) and Private Finance 2 (PF2) and operated by public corporations like Carillion.

Keywords: Empowerment; outstanding school improvement; democracy; equity; peace

The professional challenge the chapter addresses is Black, Asian Minority Ethnic Chief Executive Officers (BAME CEOs) who lead Multi-academy Trusts (MATs) in England need to navigate turbulence to assure all schools within their MATs are high performing. In the investigation of this issue, the structures of MATs themselves began to emerge as causing turbulence. Evidence revealed the BAME CEOs with track records of improving failing schools to outstanding schools interviewed in this research are working in partnership with their communities. These BAME CEOs believe they could sustain their high achieving MATs and/or take on more schools that need improving and lead their change to outstanding schools with BAME communities, non-BAME communities and diverse communities. However, they were not given the opportunities to build capacity for high-performing schools by the current MAT structures. These BAME CEOs reported they had been told by the Department of Education (DfE) that they do not have the infrastructure they need to have more academies in their MATs. When they ask the DfE how they get the infrastructure to grow their MATs, they were told they needed more academies in their MAT to get the infrastructure to grow their MAT causing a double bind. Not being able to grow their MAT prevents them from getting recognition for their hard work supporting other schools to improve because they cannot invite them to join their MAT, and prevents them from building capacity in the system for high-performing schools.

No evidence is provided by any BAME CEO that largely BAME led schools are of clear benefit to BAME (and indeed all) students. The BAME CEOs identify that they lead their high-performing schools with BAME communities, White Communities, and Diverse Communities with a diverse staff who share one characteristic; they are high-quality educational professionals who are committed to moral, ethical, logical and evidence-informed professional standards as excellent pedagogues and classroom practitioners with British values (Pring, 2018). Their educational professional expertise enables them to meet the Educational leaders' professional values (DfE, 2017a, 2017b, 2017c) and organise education in their schools morally, ethically, logically and by taking an evidence-informed approach to mentoring their staff and building professional learning communities to optimise learning. These outstanding BAME CEOs improved schools from failing to outstanding and were supported in this culture change by other professional educational experts who offered them wisdom, and support. The change work that moved schools from extreme turbulence (Gross, 2014) and failure, to stability and outstanding, was exhausting as the BAME CEOs reached out to build bridges between their current staff, and the new staff, the parents of the new community, and students in the process of co-creating a shared multicultural world view (Darling-Hammond & Rothman, 2013; Gerstl-Pepin & Aiken, 2012; Ishii, Klopf, & Cooke, 2007). The BAME CEOs identified they had met resistance of different kinds on their new schools' journeys to realise inclusion, and evidence reveals the BAME CEOs participants in this research kept going with courage, and prudence for social justice which are primary virtues of a good character (Adler, 1941). Further, each said when they met extreme turbulence (Gross, 2014) they put their faith in God and welcomed into their schools all communities' members of all faiths and none (Pring, 2018).

However, the evidence revealed that one of the biggest obstacles to the BAME CEOs of MATs moving their newly converted schools from 'Requires Improvement' to 'Outstanding' was the destabilising changing external influences on education that distracted them from focusing on leading high-quality learning and teaching in the classrooms in partnership with parents. One fear they had was that they needed to grow their MATs or face being forced into a submissive relationship with a hierarchical, dominant larger MAT. No evidence is provided by any BAME CEO in this research that they would benefit from being taken over and becoming members of a large MAT. The BAME CEOs identified that larger MATs have no legal requirement to recognise the agency of the BAME CEO's of empty or small MATs. The fear was of a pragmatic consequence of being taken over by a large MAT; losing their job as outstanding leaders, and losing everything they had worked for all their lives. Thus, the current policy has left BAME CEOs facing real dangers of educational apartheid.

The English policy analysis from the Second World War to 2011 published in 2012 (Taysum, 2012a, 2012b), did not include an analysis of MATs because convertor academies had been introduced in 2010 but MATs had not evolved at the time of writing. Since the BAME CEOs of MATs identified that MATs were causing them extreme turbulence, I realised that I needed to describe and analyse the tensions created by the changes in structures with the introduction of MATs which I focus on in this chapter. The following chapter focuses on representing the voices of BAME CEOs of Small, Medium and Empty MATs to understand their agency within these structures to enable me to present a data-driven theory of knowledge to action.

The high performance of academies and different kinds of compulsory education institutions for children in the UK is recognised by the Office for Standards for Education (Ofsted) which inspects these institutions against a framework of performance. Ofsted is a regulatory body funded by the

Government. The School Inspection Handbook (Ofsted, 2005, p. 134) revised and re-published in October 2017 states:

> Inspectors use the following four-point scale to make all judgements, including, where applicable, judging the effectiveness of the early year's provision and the 16−19 study programmes:
>
> (1) grade 1: outstanding
> (2) grade 2: good
> (3) grade 3: requires improvement
> (4) grade 4: inadequate.

The website contains guidance for different forms of service providers to children, including 'Ofsted *inspections* of *Local Authority* arrangements for supporting school improvement'. Currently, there are *no guidance documents for inspections of MATs*. Bloom states in The Times Education Supplement reported in September (2017, p. 1) that:

> A change in the legislation would allow the watchdog (Ofsted) to inspect MATs as it inspects local authorities, by observing MAT executives, looking at centralised data and attempting to establish whether the MAT is effectively providing the services it sets out to offer. Luke Tryl, Ofsted's director of corporate strategy, said: 'There has been a huge amount of change in the structure of education, and actually inspection legislation hasn't kept pace with some of the changes. Obviously, the big one there is MATs. We want to work with the DfE to look at how we can scrutinise Multi-Academy Trusts. If decisions are being taken at a certain level of accountability, it probably makes sense to look more at that level of accountability'.

Local Authorities are Ofsted inspected whilst MATs are not. Crenshaw (1989) identifies that the intersectionalities of discrimination are revealed at the Macro level of MATs and Local Authorities thus BAME CEOS of MATS arguably need to be accountable at the Macro level, and therefore to Ofsted, and work in partnership with education governance systems to identify intersectionalities of discrimination and work for equity. Looking at centralised data (Glazer, 2005, 1987), reveals how different groups experience intersectionalities of discrimination (Dewey, 1916). If MATS are not inspected, the quality of large MATs is not transparent and accountable to the tax payer. Further, how these large public corporations are using large data sets to benchmark progress in school improvement in academies that are underperforming is not clear. At the micro level where student achievement deficits exist such as the global Black-White achievement gap (Wagner, 2010), BAME CEOs of smaller MATs are arguably closely connected to their communities and can engage with their communities. Through building strong home−school relationships (Epstein, 2015), they may be able to address the Black-White achievement gap by an high-quality education offer and enable BAME communities that are marginalised to access middle-class benefits afforded through gaining social capital for social mobility. Being absorbed into a large MAT, disconnected from local communities, may unintentionally replicate BAME community members' feelings of disempowerment and segregation (Collins-Ayanlaja & Taysum, 2016).

The disconnect may exist between the lives of the local communities and the large institutional structures that do not possess the local knowledge of the communities (Carter, 2008; Collins-Ayanlaja & Taysum, 2016; Stanton-Salazar, 2010). A principle of subsidiarity may be implemented, which moves organisation of education to the lowest possible local level where text can be most effectively described in the form of curricula, and operationalised as culturally relevant discourse with staff, parents and students who are a mature community in becoming (Harris, O'Boyle, & Warbrick, 2009; Ruşitoru, 2017). Such an impact strategy offers a margin of appreciation where legislation allows some tolerance for the legislation being organised locally to respect local values when these are carefully regulated (Berger, 2014; Harris et al., 2009; Ruşitoru, 2017). However, such opportunities for local level impact strategies are closed down because the large MATs may rapidly force a take-over of a vulnerable empty MAT which is more attractive to the large MAT if it is good or outstanding. The large MAT as identified in A House of Commons Education Committee (2017) MATs Seventh Report of Session 2016−2017 commissioned by Parliament in February 2017 states: 'There is also growing concern for 'untouchable' schools which trusts refuse to take on. The government should ensure that schools which are under-performing are not left behind by a programme which was originally designed to support such schools'. The 'untouchable' schools that are underperforming include marginalised children who are in poverty and The Guardian (2016) identifies that white working-class pupils get the worst GCSE results of all the main ethnic groups.

This research seeks to understand this disconnect, and how it causes uncertainty and turbulence (Gross, 2014) through a systematic review of the literature in this chapter. In the next chapter I examine: the perspectives of the BAME CEOs, and reveal how they navigate any turbulence; the mentoring and networks that support them in navigating the turbulence; the culture changes required to stabilise, and build capacity in the public education system to optimise learning and Empower Young Societal Innovators for Equity and Renewal[1] (Taysum, 2012a, 2012b, 2013, 2014, 2015, 2016, 2017a, 2017b).

---

[1]This framework is presented in the introductory chapter of the book, and explored in the literature review, the methodology, the international comparative analysis chapter and the conclusions.

Multi Academy Trusts, Public Corporation Models, and Educational Professionals

MATs are defined by the Government as:

> trusts that usually run more than one academy. The MAT has a single set of articles and therefore is a single legal entity accountable for a number of academies. The trust enters into a Master Funding Agreement (MFA) with the Secretary of State, and into Supplemental Funding Agreements (SFA) for each academy it operates
>
> DfE, 2016 (p. 2).

The definition of a Public Corporation Model is a large public company or group of companies authorised to act as one in law (Oxford English Dictionary), and a MAT adopts such a Public Corporation Model as a single legal entity and is registered at Company House with owners, and an Executive Board.

As a layman and philosopher Dewey (1929) wrote about the challenges of what identity meant in legal terms regarding a public corporation having an identity and a moral will. Dewey (1929) explored how public corporations consisted of many individuals with many different interests and influence, and their involvement in decision-making was at different levels. Dewey argued the moral will of these individual identities was the focus of any corporation law rather than the public corporation having a single legal identity and single moral will. Dewey (1916) identifies that recognising a public corporation is made up of many individuals with different interests and power is important in a court of law. The rationale he provides is that viewing a public corporation as a single identity, or considering the individual identities within the corporation, has implications for judgements that need to be made in a court of law. Such judgements might be about how risk was balanced with prudent planning for long-term sustainable growth underpinned by appropriate reserves (Stewart, 2012). Each academy within a MAT that adopts a public corporation model, is in a legal contract with the Department for Education and the templates for the Model Articles of Association for Academy Trusts can be found on the DfE website (DfE, 2017a, 2017b, 2017c). The MATs' position within the templates is made clear on the template (DfE, 2016, p. 1):

> Please identify any other variations from the model that apply to this academy (e.g. clauses relating to PFI, or any required because the Multi Academy Trust includes academies designated

with different religious characters, or a mixture of those designated with a religious character, and those which are not).

Here PFI refers to Private Finance Incentive where the government borrows from private incentivised investors.[2] The funding needs to pay for the
CEOs, and Mansell (2017, p. 1) identifies that Sir Daniel Moynihan, CEO of
the Harris Foundation was awarded a package last academic year that
approached £500,000 of the tax payers money. Sir Daniel runs 41 academics
that employed 2,873 staff in 2015–2016 and is paid more than the outgoing
head of the Metropolitan Police who is reported to earn £276,000 for
2016–2017, and the Head of the British Armed Forces who is reported to
have been paid £245–£249,000 in 2014–2015 for leading 197,000 people, and
the national medical director for NHS England, Professor Sir Bruce Keogh
earning £190–£195,000 last September, and the Prime Minister reported to
earn £150,402 per annum.

Nowadays, there is a debate about the need for PFI in public education systems. Richards (2017) argues no government needs to borrow because the bank
completed £435 billion of Quantitative Easing resulting in the government own-
ing nearly a quarter of its own debt. Richards continues that interest payments
could raise the additional £58 billion of Quantitative Easing to meet the capital
costs of buying the PFI contracts back into government control. Further,
Richards argues that government debt is an attractive option for those wishing
to seek a second home to invest their money in a secure savings fund. The ethics

---

[2]The National Audit Office (2018, p. 4) provide an overview of PFIs: 'More than
90% of the government's capital investment is publicly financed. Since the 1990s the
public sector has also used private finance to build assets. The PFI and its successor,
PF2, are forms of Public Private Partnerships (PPPs). In a PFI or PF2 deal, a private
finance company – a Special Purpose Vehicle (SPV) – is set up and borrows to construct a new asset such as a school, hospital or road. The taxpayer then makes payments over the contract term (typically 25–30 years), which cover debt repayment,
financing costs, maintenance and any other services provided. The government
reduced its use of PFI after the 2008 financial crisis, as the cost of private finance
increased. Parliament also became increasingly critical of the model. In 2011, HM
Treasury consulted on reform. It made some changes and relaunched the model as
PF2 a year later. So far, two departments, the Department of Health and Social
Care and the Department for Education, have used PF2. There are currently over
700 operational PFI and PF2 deals, with a capital value of around £60 billion.
Annual charges for these deals amounted to £10.3 billion in 2016–2017. Even if no
new deals are entered into, future charges which continue until the 2040s amount to
£199 billion.

of PFI cannot be the focus of this study,[3] but it is important to raise PFI in the study because it is bound tightly to MATs and their legal funding arrangements, sponsorship, and it shines a light on what Reckhow (2015) calls 'following the money' within Public Education Governance Systems.

MATs require infrastructure for a convertor academy to convert academies to improve them, or convert them because they are not financially viable or indeed convert them because they are 'empty' meaning they are made up of one academy (Children's Services Overview & Scrutiny Committee, 2015). Diamond (2012) argues public corporations return profits, but if these are deemed to be financially under-performing the public corporation could become targets for friendly or hostile leveraged takeovers from Private Equity Funds (PEF) (Diamond, 2012). Diamond (2012) argues Private Equity Funds are based on short-term exit strategies where Private Funding Investment seeks to maximise return on investments and reward those that managed the funds with high financial compensation in a short period of time before their exit (Diamond, 2012). Thus one might expect to see a pattern of friendly or hostile leveraged takeovers emerging in the English landscape of academies by MATs, and those managing these MATs may gain high financial compensation in a short period of time. There may even be evidence of CEOs of MATs deploying an early exit having gained high financial compensation, but because education is not for profit, and funded by the tax payer such a model would arguably be unethical.

Take overs are emerging with 'stand-alone academies', and MATs that are 'empty' since both of these kinds of academies may be isolated and marginalised. As stated previously, an empty MAT is a MAT that does not have the required number of academies to legitimise their status as a MAT. Both under-performing academies and outstanding stand-alone academies that are small or

---

[3]Carillion (2016) had 350 million shares in issue (Citywire Money, 2018), and for 2015 the proposed dividend per share was 18.45 pence amounting to a proposed *total payout to shareholders £64,575,000* (Carillion Annual Report and Accounts; Making Tomorrow a Better Place, 2016). About 40% of Carillion's revenue in 2016 was from construction and most of the rest was public sector contracts through PFI such as maintaining, cleaning and supplying meals for schools, prisons and hospitals (BBC, 2018a, p. 1). Carillion has now been declared bankrupt, and BBC (2018b, p. 1) report MPs as saying: 'The construction firm's annual reports were a worthless guide to its financial health and raise major questions about corporate governance'. BBC (2018c, p. 1) report: 'The chairman of trustees of Carillion's pension scheme, Robin Ellison, has suggested in a letter to a committee of MPs that there was *a funding shortfall of around £990m* with Carillion's defined benefit pension schemes by the end'. BBC (2018d, p. 1) report the National Audit Office said there had never been a "robust evaluation" of the benefits, and: 'the expected spend on one group of schools financed by PF2 were around 40% higher than the costs of a similar project financed by government borrowing. It also said Treasury Committee analysis from 2011 estimated the cost of a privately financed hospital was 70% higher than a comparative project in the public sector. The watchdog highlighted the increased cost of borrowing which it said was 2–3.75% higher for PFIs compared to state borrowing'. Further research is recommended into PFI.

medium are threatened by take-over by a MAT as a single legal entity. House of Commons Education Committee (2017) MATs Seventh Report of Session 2016–2017 identifies that there has been a shift in government policy from forcing academisation by 2022, to not forcing acadamisation which is documented in the White Paper; 'Educational Excellence Everywhere' in March 2016. The White Paper also stated most schools will join or form MATs. On 6 May the Government's withdrawal from forced acadamisation was confirmed in the Queen's speech referencing a Bill meeting the: 'foundation for a system in which all schools are academies'. The House of Commons Education Committee (2017) MATs Seventh Report of Session 2016–2017 states: 'As trusts grow in size and number we urge the Government only to promote expansion that prioritises performance'. Coles (2017) argues MATs need to have at least twenty academies to benefit from economies of scale. Such economies of scale were arguably found in the local government management of schools that was dismantled through the academisation programme. Brighouse (Times Educational Supplement, 18 August 2018, p. 1) argues:

> Multi-Academy Trusts are pooling schools' budgets and then forcing them to turn up, cap in hand – it is reminiscent of the worst of the old-style Local Education Authorities. Whoever would have thought that we would return to a day when schools were so dependent on a local authority that any budgetary decision – from staffing to loo rolls – would require sign-off from on high? And yet this incredible situation is precisely where some schools tied into Multi-Academy Trusts find themselves. E-Act, for example, is typical of the growing number of such organisations that pool individual school budgets, inviting schools to set out their wish-list for spending before deciding what they can each have (Quite what the school governors' role in the process is remains unclear – although it's worth remembering that in 2016 E-Act looked to abolish the governors' function altogether).

Coles (2017, p. 1) suggests the economies of scale with 20 academies in a MAT enables Human Resource Management, providing specialist training services, and can reduce back-office costs. On the other hand, The House of Commons Education Committee (2017) MATs Seventh Report of Session 2016–2017 cautions that the growth of MATs does not compromise raising standards and improving performance. Morgan the then Education Secretary stated in the Guardian that Academy Trusts that cannot demonstrate a 'strong track record' in improving schools will not be allowed to take on more schools (p. 1). The statement is important because in 2000 the Tony Blair New Labour Government launched academies to replace underperforming schools in struggling education authorities (Guardian, 2007). The introduction of academies was to raise standards. Ofsted cannot inspect MATs, they cannot identify if

MATs are struggling and they cannot identify MATs that include in their corporate identity underperforming academies or provide transparency for a 'strong track record' in raising standards and improving schools.

Schools Week (2016, 2017) identify that Reach, a MAT Brand of Reach2, and Reach4 have only had 16 of its 52 schools Ofsted Inspected with two of those being outstanding, seven good, and seven requiring improvement, yet the Reach brand is starting Reach South. Without the appropriate regulation of MATs in place to report on performance, the MAT policy is vulnerable. Smythe, reported in the Guardian (2017a), that as a principal of a school that is not struggling, he was concerned that one of his partner schools was struggling and faced being taken over by a MAT. He supported the improvement of the struggling school to sustain the Small to Medium community's cultural identity and good academy-community relationships, and because he did not want 10% of the partner school's budget to be top sliced for the CEO of the MAT. However, Smythe stated that the support offered the school was not funded, which excluded the school from being a sponsor, whilst at the same time improving the effectiveness of the struggling school. A House of Commons Education Committee (2017, p. 3) MATs Seventh Report of Session 2016−2017 commissioned by Parliament in February 2017 states:

> In order for the MAT model to succeed there needs to be a greater number of sponsors in the system. Certain areas of the country are struggling to attract new sponsors and small rural schools, largely in the primary sector, are at risk of becoming isolated. There is also growing concern for 'untouchable' schools which trusts refuse to take on. Government should ensure that schools which are under-performing are not left behind by a programme which was originally designed to support such schools.
>
> High performing trusts have a role in sharing their best practice and we recommend the Government creates structures to enable this. Finally, in order to support future expansion the Government should commission and publish independent, robust research on the structures and practices of the highest performing MATs.

High-performing trusts have a role in sharing their best practice and we recommend the Government creates structures to enable this. Finally, in order to support future expansion, the Government should commission and publish independent, robust research on the structures and practices of the highest performing MATs.

The rapid expansion of the Wakefield City MAT which ran 21 schools identified it was pulling out in the first week of the new 2017−2018 term because it was unable to:

> facilitate the rapid improvement our academies need, and students deserve [...] The Department for Education (DfE) said

many of the schools within the trust were performing below the
national average [...] The Trust said the decision was in the 'best
interests' of the students [...] The trust had paid its then Chief
Executive Officer £82,000 for 15 weeks work

BBC News (2017, p. 1).

The Guardian (2017b) provided evidence that the collapsing academy trust
asset stripped the schools of millions of Great British Pounds of the tax payers'
money. The CEO of Wakefield City MAT is exiting from the Public
Corporation without improving performance, but taking large financial compensation. Which raises a question; to what extent has this MAT acted in a similar
way to a Private Equity Fund (Diamond, 2012) as identified previously?
Further, what systems of accountability are in place to identify such behaviour
and prevent it happening in the future? If the intention is to provide financial
rewards for managing MATs, the threatened takeover of outstanding and good
academies that are empty MATs or stand-alone academies are more attractive
than what the House of Commons Education Committee (2017, p. 27 call:
'untouchable' underperforming academies in the MATs Seventh Report of
Session 2016–2017.

MAT CEOs arguably need to adopt a predatory, or even 'colonising'
approach to taking over high-performing academies so that their MAT has three
academies and relative safety from any takeover bid, and preferably at least 20
MATs to assure economies of scale. Such a colonising approach may be in conflict with a desire to work with outstanding schools in partnership with each
other, and with their local communities who have the chance to stand for and be
elected directors on the Board of their local school. MATs are registered as limited companies at Companies House (gov.uk, 2015). Companies are run by a
board of directors who appoint a CEO. This means that there is no apparent
reason why a trust could not be run by directors from the community. However,
in the case of MATS, it is the CEO who appoints the directors within the overarching structures of accountability which include the unelected Regional
Schools Commissioners (RSCs) who are appointed by the Department for
Education (Schools Commissioners Group, 2018). An unintended consequence
of the growth of MATs is that headteachers who have the potential to work
closely together to raise standards in their region, and mentor future leaders for
succession planning, are instead competing with each other to grow their MATs.
Such competition between senior-level leaders may unintentionally create a
'divide and conquer' approach that Taysum and Murrel-Abery (2017) have identified was a strategy of colonisation. A divide and conquer strategy creates competition between groups for entitlement to the goods and their means of
production for a good life, which creates disconnects within communities.

Arguably, MATs that do not grow face being taken over themselves, and
MATs that do grow, face building conflict and dividing their local communities
as they force takeovers with neighbouring schools. Smythe Guardian (2017a)
identifies forced take overs can damage relationships between the local school
and the local community. Such a divide and conquer approach to headteachers

who find themselves positioned to work against each other to secure their own autonomy through a growing MAT builds high levels of turbulence in Public Education Governance Systems and within the educational professional body.

Small, Medium and Empty MATs compete with each other, rather than critically analysing who is missing from the competition between Small, Medium and Empty MATs, and how these invisible characters may be intentionally or unintentionally creating the competitive structures that protect their own interests, rather than serving the interests of the tax payer. In other words, the Small, Medium and Empty MATs and principals of schools in local communities are competing with each other for survival, and are potentially overwhelmed by the rapid changes in structures that may distract them from challenging the colonisation process. At the same time large MATs that are not part of the competition between Small, Medium and Empty MATs can pick and choose who to colonise which may, or may not be based on the purpose of creating convertor academies to convert failing schools to raise standards. The pragmatic consequence is that 'untouchable' schools are created that fails the children, the parents, the tax payer and society.

The evidence reveals that rapid change to the organisation of Public Education Governance Systems has shifted power from local authority governance to public corporation governance without addressing any of the old problems in the change (Brighouse, 2017). The rapid change has led to a clash of cultures between those with the values of generic Public Governance Systems who have not been democratically elected by the public, and do not need professional educational credentials, and those with the values of Educational Executive Leaders who have professional credentials, a track record of being ethical teachers, and a track record of leading ethical teachers in ethical communities in school improvement from 'Needs Improvement' to 'Good' or 'Outstanding'.

The rapid change has been hallmarked by a lack of full and free interactions and cooperation of the public in how the change in public education is being implemented, and certainly there has been no referendum on whether parents want their schools organised by their representatives they have elected in local councils, or organised by public corporations financed by PFI and PF2. In the Guardian (2016, p. 1) Morgan states: 'the public were unlikely to have strong feelings about changes to school governance, including plans to scrap the right of parents to have representatives on schools' boards of governors'. The statement from Morgan is justification for by-passing the public having a chance to state whether they want to have a say in how their children's schools are organised, or not, and whether they, as parents, want to be represented. Morgan's statement undermines democracy because it reveals all citizens are determined by the government to not have strong feelings about having full and free participation in the organisation of the institution of public education. Further clarity is required regarding how the Minister of Education identifies that all citizens have enjoyed an education that has equipped them with the philosophical/cultural, political and economical knowledge, skills and experience they need to become mature citizens to fully and freely interact and cooperate with their society's institutions and identify whether they have strong feelings or not about how their children's education is organised (Dewey, 1916).

The rapid execution of education reforms with an assumption that the public do not want to be involved is happening at the same time as a clash of different values systems between two kinds of experts within the organisation of education. On the one hand are the values of generic Public Corporation Governance Systems, and on the other hand are the values of the expert Educational Executive Leaders with professional education credentials as members of the teaching profession, and who have track records of high-quality teaching, and track records of moving schools from failing to outstanding through high-quality leadership of learning and teaching.

There is a gap in the literature on how the MATs' Chief Executive Officers engage the Governance of Public Services, and the public, and seek alignment between different sets of principles in a Memorandum of Cooperation or Articles of Association. Further, there is no literature regarding how BAME CEOs of MATs, engage with these different cultures in their professional work for equity and renewal.

The Principles of Good Governance of public services was created by The Independent Commission on Good Governance in Public Services in 2004 (ICGGPS, 2004). The Commission was established by the Office for Public Management, the Chartered Institute of Public Finance and Accountancy, and Joseph Rowntree Foundation. The aim was to deliver stable public governance systems that empower, underpinned by professional values. The Principles of Good Governance (ICGGPS, 2004, p. iii) start with *'focusing on the organisation's purpose and on outcomes for citizens and service users'*. The purpose and the outcomes for citizens and service users in education are complex because there are different interests being served in education (Dewey, 1916). Potentially one of the priorities for the governance system of an education system is to establish the desirable characteristics of a mature citizen. The next step is to identify the thinking tools immature citizens need to gain the characteristics of a mature citizen. In other words, a priority is to identify the Intended Learning Outcomes that need to be met to enable a person to become mature. The next step is to identify how an immature citizen can acquire the knowledge, skills, experience and wisdom to attain the Intended Learning Outcomes they need to transition from an immature citizen to a mature citizen. John Dewey (1916) identifies mature citizens have a finite lifespan and therefore need to pass on their knowledge skills, and experience to the immature. At the same time, some mature people may feel threatened and view the younger generation as competition and may seek to sustain their own power and resources to sustain their own supremacy. This kind of 'threatened mature' folk may use cunning, experience, or financial resources to control the younger generation and limit opportunities for the growth of communities to work for equity and renewal to reduce the competition for their own supremacy and greater entitlement. Arguably governance systems of education need to be on their guard to ensure the structures and the agents of an education system are empowered to empower every student to be the best they can be.

A clash in culture between being 'senior' and being 'mature' emerges when a senior person may behave in immature ways that do not serve the good of the community, or education governance systems. Such behaviour, rooted in the fear of losing power, may prevent clear succession planning and passing on wisdom to the immature, and instead, 'senior' people may spend their energies maintaining their supremacy. With such conditions, those who will have to take over from these senior citizens will not have had the preparation to do so through professional learning, or access to networks of wise leaders because they may have been seen as a threat to seniors rather than as future leaders.

Preparing future professional leaders needs to be a role of a professional body that has ethical policies guided by a moral compass with knowledge of the logics of the field informed by evidence of the best that has been thought and said throughout the epochs of the Earth. Such a professional body is equipped to engage with succession planning. A clash of cultures emerges when a professional body is undermined by individuals who do not have professional knowledge, skills, experience, and wisdom or the processes and practices in place to empower a professional body to pass on professional knowledge, skills, experience and wisdom (Hodgson & Spours, 2006; Taysum & Iqbal, 2012). Thus, a professional body will consist of mature professionals who seek to induct the immature professionals on a pathway to maturity based on merit, to assure moral and ethical succession planning for the profession that is open to critique, reflection and transparency and who want to do the right thing. A professional body is undermined by those who do not have the principles, values behaviours, or track records of school improvement, but seek to govern it with the values of assuring their own supremacy and greater entitlement, and want to do things right. The argument is summed up by Plato (2017) some 2000 years ago in *Timaeus* in p. 16376:

> Thereupon one of the priests, who was of a very great age, said: O Solon, Solon, you Hellenes are never anything but children, and there is not an old man among you. Solon in return asked him what he meant. I mean to say, he replied, that in mind you are all young; there is no old opinion handed down among you by ancient tradition, nor any science which is hoary with age...

And by Plato (2018) in Critias, p. 17765:

> By such reflections and by the continuance in them of a divine nature, Like the qualities which we have described grew and increased among them; but when the divine portion began to fade away, and became diluted too often and too much with the mortal admixture, and the human nature got the upper hand, they then, being unable to bear their fortune, behaved unseemly, and to him who had an eye to see grew visibly debased, for they were losing the fairest of their precious gifts (their virtue); but to

those who had no eye to see the true happiness (found through right), they appeared glorious and blessed at the very time when they were full of avarice and unrighteous power.

Education Governance Systems and the CEOs who are the interface between the Education Governance Systems and headteachers, teachers, parents and students arguably need to describe the characteristics of a mature citizen in becoming that Plato identifies are hallmarked by 'their precious gifts' those of virtue found through right. These characteristics connect with the community's understanding of a mature citizen and draw from all cultures, faiths, and none to arrive at an overarching set of characteristics of a shared world view of a good citizen and a good life (Taysum, forthcoming). The characteristics need to be extracted from the best that has been thought and said from all cultural heritages, all faiths and none over the epochs of time, to enable an old opinion to be handed down. These old opinions may be found in the codes of human behaviour which exist or have existed in the past that are held in the holy books of all faiths and the books that represent no faiths, the philosophical books of different traditional classical texts such as the Greek myths, the books of science, mathematics and technologies, including socio-histographical books, the art, music and architecture and in the United Nations Declaration of Human Rights (1948).

The mature may benefit from inducting the immature into values, habits and behaviours with a commitment to the critique of undesirable values and acts, such that a provisional consensus may be agreed upon in a space of tolerance for different views (Shah, 2016). Any CEOs that are committed to knowing the self, in a relationship with the others (Socrates edited by Beck, 2003) may benefit from being able to deeply listen to the narratives of the other (Leal & Saran, 2004). Mature citizens are self-aware, have self-control and are able to regulate the self based on self-evaluation and reflection which Kesebir (2014) identifies are important characteristics for a quiet ego and for establishing and attaining realistic goals. CEOs wishing to empower others to engage in this moral training for democracy in education (Taysum, forthcoming) need to provide them with the thinking tools to prevent them from being manipulated by people who wish to rush them into new ways of thinking and doing. These kinds of people, who manipulate people by rushing in new ways of thinking and doing, may have the characteristics of being senior citizens but are self-seeking and only wish to secure their own supremacy and greater entitlement.

Change requires giving mature citizens the time and space to think things through by: asking good questions about the current state and the proposed change; critiquing the evidence underpinning the change; inquiring into the logic of the change; holding a moral compass up to the change to check the direction steers a sure and steady ethical course. Without this kind of empirical, logical, moral and ethical approach to change, the chance to 'hand down old opinion by ancient tradition', balanced by prudent, moral, democratic innovatory strategies from intergenerational communities for equity and renewal, is lost. These are the thinking tools found in the study by Taysum (2012a, 2012b) Learning to Critically Analyse and Reflect for Emancipation, or Enlightenment (CARE) and in a synthesis of John Dewey's framework Moral Training for Democracy in Education (Taysum, 2017b).[4]

Sharing different traditions and world views underpin description of intersectionalities of different values' systems, and possibly intersectionalities of discrimination. Critically analysing and reflecting on these descriptions may offer opportunities to develop curricula and pedagogies for emancipation by adopting 'Learning to CARE'. Therefore, curricula and pedagogies may provide opportunities to reach provisional consensus on the kinds of values, and characteristics required to form habits, and behaviours that respect the human dignity of all as a 'mature' community in becoming. Thus, the ethical framework of the educational profession needs to be clear (Gluchmanova, 2015), and the mature educational leaders of the educational profession need to act as gatekeepers who provide ethical leadership and prevent colonisation of Educaitonal Governance Systems by senior leaders who are self-seeking and only wish to secure their own supremacy and greater entitlement. Gatekeepers of the education profession are people who control access to the education profession and hold a moral compass that assures the ethical framework of the principles, and standards of the education profession. The gatekeepers pass on the wisdom of the education profession to future generations that draw on the best that has been thought and said throughout the epochs of time, and interrogates the logic, and empirical evidence of any innovations that evolve with new knowledge, skills and experiences of new ages and the technologies they bring. Such an education profession, with professional values, is open to full accountability by an independent body such as the Office of the Ombudsman. Such a professional body works like other professions such as architects, accountants, medics, lawyers, with an elected government who represent the will of the people, and with all stakeholders (Tomlinson, 2004). Such an approach provides an antithesis to the thesis from Plato's Critias: 'those who had no eye to see the true happiness (found through right), appeared glorious and blessed at the very time when they were full of avarice and unrighteous power'.

A new synthesis may bridge cultures (Carter, 2008; Stanton-Salazar, 2010) and CEOs might work for the best outcome for all young people, empower educational professionals and their professional body, and not fear, or label underperforming institutions, often with communities that are in poverty, as 'untouchable' (Government Report on MATs, 2017). Such an approach is different to that of Private Equity Funds (PEFs) that seek to gain the highest returns on investment and then execute a swift withdrawal when they have got what they wanted (Diamond, 2012).

---

[4]There is not scope to describe and analyse the Learning to CARE framework here, and the reader is invited to read Taysum, A. (2012a, 2012b) *Evidence informed leadership in education*. London: Continuum for a full explanation.

Educational Executive Leaders' professional values from the Department for Education mapped to the National Professional Qualification for Executive Leaders' behaviours (DfE, 2017a, 2017b, 2017c, pp. 33–36) tie in very closely to the characteristics of a mature citizen mentioned above and identify educational executive leaders:

> Use school-to-school partnerships and collaboration to drive improvement in a range of different areas, manage risk and are committed to their pupils and understand the power of world-class teaching to improve social mobility, wellbeing and produc-tivity [...] engage with collaboration [...] remain courageous and positive in challenging, adverse or uncertain circumstances [...] will know themselves and their teams, continually reflect on their own and others' practices, and understand how best to approach difficult or sensitive issues [...] respect the rights, views, beliefs and faiths of pupils, colleagues and stakeholders [...] act with honesty, transparency and always in the interests of the school and its pupils.

Comparing the professional values of the Educational Executive Leaders (DfE, 2017a, 2017b, 2017c) and the professional value of the Independent Commission on Good Governance in Public Services (2004, p. iii): 'focusing on the organisational purpose and on outcomes for citizens and service users', two key difference can be identified. First, the Educational Executive Leaders focus on social mobility and social justice, collaboration and partnership, prudence in embracing risk and innovation and having the courage to achieve the best out-comes for social justice for the community. The Public Governance values are more generic because they do not have a professional educational focus, and they do not include the need for a track record in school improvement. Second, Educational Executive Leaders have professional educational credentials. Public governors do not need educational professional credentials, and can only tell others who do have the educational professional credentials and a track record in school improvement to improve schools.

The Public Governance Systems arguably need to work with the Chief Executive Officers (CEOs) to produce a Memorandum of Cooperation, or Articles of Association that focus on how, step by step, CEOs with educational professional credentials have moved a school from 'requires improvement' to 'good' or 'outstanding', and what infrastructure, support for agency, and culture change is required to move all schools from 'requires improvement' to 'good' or 'outstanding'. The Public Governance Systems need to ensure as McGuinness et al. identify in their chapter in this book that governors do not confuse their strategic responsibilities with the leadership and management responsibilities of the professional educational leaders with a track record of school improvement to empower their professional teachers with professional educational credentials, to raise educational standards.

The principles of such Articles of Association potentially need to be agreed to include a forum where the intersectionalities of different principles can be presented, and described, questioned, critiqued, and logical, empirical, moral, and ethical provisional principles agreed. The first principle might focus on describing the characteristics of a mature, good citizen, and what it means to live a good life of virtue in a diverse community (Adler, 1941), and how this is embedded in the school curriculum, rather than bolted on in isolated subjects such as religious education, or citizenship.

The documents and their legislation and characteristics can only be fully and freely debated if the community members have the knowledge, skills and experience to engage in such a debate (EU, 2009, Taysum, 2012, 2016). Critical analysis and reflection, as one of the characteristics of a mature citizen, can be deployed to empower mature communities to reach a provisional consensus on the desirable characteristics that will underpin interaction and cooperation with all institutions (Dewey, 1916). All democratic institutions need to be organised by representatives for the community who have been appointed because of their professional expertise and track record in school improvement, and/or elected by the community based on their manifestos that detail their track record, and professional credentials for organising particular institutions, in this case the institution of public education. Such democracy in education focuses on the community, and the quality of the communities' associations with the self, with the other, with the institutions and with the diverse governance systems.

The Educational Executive Leaders DfE (2017a, 2017b, 2017c, p. 36) state that the leaders need to: 'respect the rights of others'. The Public Governance Values created by The Independent Commission on Good Governance in Public Services (2004, p. iii) state they need to: 'be clear about relationships between governors and the public'. Here The Education Executive Leadership values focus on personal relationships and the quality of those relationships and that these educational leaders have a track record of optimising students' learning by building relationships of trust. The public governance values focus on more general statements about relationships that have no clarity about how to create a participatory approach to connect the Governance representatives, the educational leaders, the educational staff and the public. The public governance role is reduced to telling others how to optimise learning because the role does not require a proven track record for school improvement. This is further exemplified with The Public Governance Values' (The Independent Commission on Good Governance in Public Services, 2004, p. iii) that state: 'Taking an active and planned approach to dialogue with, and accountability to the public'. How Public Governance Systems in MATs with ideal infrastructures of 20 academies or more achieve this by connecting the different stakeholders in each academy's local community is not standardised. The DfE (2017a, 2017b, 2017c, pp. 32–50) have a much more specific value for Educational Executive Leaders:

> Motivate and unite a wide range of people, Assess and improve
> teaching quality, pupil progress and attainment in a range of

different contexts, including for disadvantaged pupils or those with particular needs (for example, including Pupil Premium, Special Educational Needs and Disability (SEND), English as an Additional Language (ASL) or the most able pupils) [...] increase capacity with high quality professional development [...] Analyse their own motivations and moral purpose and integrate these in own design, communication, and leadership of plans;

The Educational Executive Leaders' values and behaviours (DfE, 2017a, 2017b, 2017c) focus on what expertise is required to improve effective schools and how to do it, and The Principles of Good Governance of Public Services, created by The Independent Commission on Good Governance in Public Services (2004) focus on what needs to be done to improve effective schools but does not state how.

There is a gap in the literature of how CEOs and BAME CEOs address deficits of the achievement gap based on race (Wagner, 2010) within systems that may have institutionalised racism (Collins-Ayanlaja & Taysum, 2016). There is a gap in the literature focusing on how CEOs of MATs have identified levels of turbulence in education systems and how they have navigated this turbulence to improve the performance of underperforming academies/schools in a step by step way. However, it is possible to argue that forced takeovers of high-performing schools that are no longer financially viable because their MAT is empty can be described as experiencing extreme turbulence which Gross (2014, p. 248) identifies with his typology of turbulence as: 'Extreme, with forces so great that control of the (academy) is lost'.

Different groups who are outside the large MAT infrastructures, who are seeking to grow their MAT, may have different access to the knowledge, skills, experience, and infrastructure they need to grow their MAT which may create the conditions of colonialism achieved by what Taysum and Murrel-Abery (2017) call a divide and conquer strategy. Taysum and Murrel-Abery (2017) document a colonialism strategy of divide and conquer in Guyana where White people had dominance over AmerIndians, who had dominance over Black people who were brought to Guyana as slaves. Once the Black slaves were freed, they had dominance over the indentured Indian people who had been brought to Guyana to do the work the Black people did when they were slaves. The different groups experienced what Dewey (1916) and Crenshaw (1989) call different intersectionalities of discrimination. The intersectionalities of discrimination were rooted in race, different education offers, and different levels of influence in governance systems (Taysum & Murrel-Abery, 2017). Sustaining these different levels of entitlement in governance systems between different groups sustained the conflict between them. Sustaining the conflict between different groups sustained their different levels of entitlement, which prevented different groups from identifying, describing, questioning, and critiquing their different levels of entitlement. Preventing the different groups from working together to describe the different levels of entitlement and engaging in a philosophical inquiry into the different levels of entitlement, prevented them from developing evidence-informed, logical, moral and ethical impact strategies that Empower Young Societal Innovators for Equity, Renewal (EYSIER) and peace in our time.

Smith's (1776) economic liberalism as a framework has the potential to enable people who work hard to have fair and equitable financial compensation for labour. Competition arguably prevents feudalism and master-slave relationships that stimulate innovation and protects citizens' rights (Smith, 1776). Balancing liberalism with a welfarist approach to societal associations may prevent elites developing pseudo-master−slave relationships that *excludes citizens', causes conflict by dividing groups and giving different groups different levels of entitlement, and de-regulates accountability structures.*

In the UK earnings are still not at the level they were at in 2007 (BBC, 2017). The BBC report argues capitalism is currently amplifying the distribution of labour, and the profits from the labour are being redistributed to a small number of shareholders of public corporations, and not the labour force. Thus, the current economic framework is one of neo-liberal market forces (Ball, 2004) that are not rewarding hard work and this differs significantly from Adam Smith's economic liberalism. Larger differences between the average wage of an employee and the income of the CEO are emerging. Parker (2017, p. 1) in *The Financial Times* identifies that the UK Prime Minister Theresa May: 'will attempt to put downward pressure on boardroom pay next week with plans that would force listed companies to publish the ratio between the total remuneration of their chief executive and their average worker'. The move is important because Parker identifies that true capitalism builds infrastructure and regulations to allow those who work hard to be invested in longer term steady and sustainable growth *in their Small and Medium enterprises* and in their *local communities* that they are *connected* to. Liberalism is not about the quick financial gratification of those forcing a takeover, with no connection or care for the people of the organisation they are colonising, or leaving as 'untouchable'. Parker identifies that the lack of commitment to true capitalism in the Corporate Public Multinationals has prevented citizens from being fairly financially compensated for their hard work. The relationship between large pay gaps between CEOs and the average worker, and the tyranny of feudalism, begs the question to what extent have corporate public governance systems become characterised by fear, instability caused by rushing into 'shoot from the hip' rapid change that causes turbulence, a lack of prudence, a lack of social justice which is manifested in hard work not being rewarded, a lack of courage to build bridges and shared world views that are inclusionary and connect Corporate Public Governance Systems with their communities and that work for equity, renewal and peace in our communities? Further, to what extent do Public Education Governance Systems of large MATs have these characteristics, and to what extent do they EYSIER?

The context of the MATs explored in this chapter underpins the focus of the next chapter regarding how BAME CEOs of Small, Medium and Empty MATs navigate turbulence in Education Governance Systems, and mobilise their track records of school improvement to systematically transform failing schools to outstanding schools, as they slowly grow their MATs in England to optimise students' learning for social mobility, equity and renewal.

References

Adler, M. (1941). *A dialectic of morals: Towards the foundations of political philosophy*. Notre Dame: University of Notre Dame.

Ball, S. (2004). *Education policy and social class: The selected works of Stephen J. Ball*. London: Routledge.

Barnett, R. (2000). *Higher Education: A critical business*. Buckingham: SRH.

BBC. (2018a). *Mapping Carilliion's biggest construction projects*. Retrieved from http://www.bbc.co.uk/news/business-42717735. Accessed on 18 February 2018.

BBC. (2018b). Carillion investors were 'fleeing for the hills'. Retrieved from http://www.bbc.co.uk/news/business-43107500. Accessed on 18 February 2018.

BBC. (2018c). Carillion: Are pensions on the brink? Retrieved from http://www.bbc.co.uk/news/business-42705641. Accessed on 18 February 2018.

BBC. (2018d). PFI Deals costing taxpayers millions. Retrieved from http://www.bbc.co.uk/news/business-42724939. Accessed on 18 February 2018.

BBC News. (2017). *Wakefield City academies trust pulls out of 21 schools*. Retrieved from http://www.bbc.co.uk/news/uk-england-leeds-41198403. Accessed on 22nd December 2017.

Berger, Z. (2014). Negotiating Between equality and choice – A dilemma of Israeli educational policy in historical context. *Italian Journal of Sociology of Education*, 6(2), 88–114.

Brighouse, T. (2017). Mats are taking us back to the bad old days. In Times Education Supplement 18th August 2017. Retrieved from https://www.tes.com/news/school-news/breaking-views/mats-are-taking-us-back-bad-old-days. Accessed on 22 December 2017.

Carillion. (2016). Carillion annual report and accounts; making tomorrow a better place. Retrieved from http://www.annualreports.co.uk/HostedData/AnnualReports/PDF/LSE_CLLN_2016.pdf. Accessed on 18 February 2018.

Carter, P. L. (2008). Teaching students fluency in multiple cultural codes. In M. Pollock (Ed.), *Everyday antiracism* (pp. 107–112). New York, NY: The New Press.

Children's Services Overview and Scrutiny Committee. (2015). Multi academy trust relationships. Retrieved from http://democracy.thurrock.gov.uk/documents/s5955/ITEM%206%20-A%20OS%20Report%20Multi%20Academy%20Trust%20Relationshipsi%20v3.pdf. Accessed on 2 May 2018.

Citywire Money. (2018). Carillion PLC fact sheet. Retrieved from http://citywire.co.uk/money/share-prices-and-performance/share-factsheet.aspx?InstrumentID=87227. Accessed on 18 February 2018.

Coles, J. (2017). Twenty schools is too small for a multi academy trust in schools week 03 July 2017. Retrieved from https://schoolsweek.co.uk/academy-boss-20-schools-is-too-small-for-a-multi-academy-trust/. Accessed on 22 December 2017.

Collins-Ayanlaja, C., & Taysum, A. (2016). A Bourdieusian analysis of institutionalised racism. World Educational Research Association, April, Washington.

Crenshaw, K. (1989). Demarginalizing the intersection of race and sex: A Black feminist critique of antidiscrimination doctrine, feminist theory, and antiracist politics, University of Chicago Legal Forum, *69*(Article 8), 139–167. Retrieved from https://chicagounbound.uchicago.edu/uclf/vol1989/iss1/8. Accessed October 20, 2018.

Darling-Hammond, L., & Rothman, R. (2013). *Teacher and leader effectiveness in high performing education systems*. Stanford, CA: SCOPE.

Department for Education. (2016). Template documents with standard articles of association for different types of academy trust. Retrieved from https://www.gov.uk/government/publications/academy-model-memorandum-and-articles-of-association. Accessed November 11, 2017.

Department for Education. (2017a). Academy trust survey July 2017. Retrieved from https://www.gov.uk/government/uploads/system/uploads/attachment_data/file/629779/Academy_Trust_Survey_2017.pdf. Accessed on 23 December 2017.

Department for Education. (2017b). *Model articles of association for academy trusts*. Retrieved from https://www.gov.uk/government/publications/academy-model-memorandum-and-articles-of-association#history. Accessed on 22 December 2017.

Department for Education. (2017c). National professional qualifications (NPQ) content and assessment framework. Retrieved from https://www.gov.uk/government/uploads/system/uploads/attachment_data/file/653046/NPQ_Content_and_Assessment_Framework.pdf. Accessed on 25 February 2018.

Dewey, J. (1916). *Democracy and education*. New York, NY: Macmillan.

Dewey, J. (1929). *Experience and nature*. Kindle Edition.

Diamond, S. (2012). Beyond the Berle and means paradigm: Private equity and the new capitalist order. In C. Williams & P. Zumbansen (Eds.), *The embedded firm: Corporate governance, labor and finance capitalism* (pp. 151–176). Cambridge: Cambridge University Press.

Epstein, J. (2015). *School, family, and community partnerships, student economy edition: preparing educators and improving schools*. London: Westview Press.

European Union. (2009). Council Resolution of 27 November 2009 on a renewed framework for European cooperation in the youth field (2010 2018) 2009/C 311/01. Retrieved from http://eur-lex.europa.eu/legal-content/EN/TXT/?qid=1513983478783&uri=CELEX:32009G1219(01). Accessed on December 22, 2017.

Gerstl-Pepin, C., & Aiken, J. (2012). *Social justice leadership for a global world*. Charlotte, NC: Information Age Publishing.

Glazer, N. (1987). *Affirmative discrimination ethnic inequality and public policy*. Harvard: Harvard University Press.

Glazer, N. (2005). *The emergence of an American ethnic pattern*. Retrieved from http://www.paperdue.com/essay/the-emergence-of-an-americanethnic-pattern-63715. Accessed on 01 May 2017.

Gluchmanova, M. (2015). The importance of ethics in the teaching profession. *Procedia – Social and Behavioural Sciences, 176*, 509–513.

Gov.UK. (2015). Companies house. Retrieved from https://www.gov.uk/government/organisations/companies-house. Accessed on 22 February 2018.

Gross, S. J. (2014). Using turbulence theory to guide actions. In C. M. Branson & S. J. Gross (Eds.), *Handbook on Ethical Educational Leadership* (pp. 246–262). New York, NY: Routledge.

Harris, D., O'Boyle, M., & Warbrick, C. (2009). *Law of the European convention on human rights*. Oxford: Oxford University Press.

Hodgson, A., & Spours, K. (2006). An analytical framework for policy engagement: the contested case of 14-19 reforms in England. *Journal of Education Policy*, *21*(6), 679–696.

House of Commons Education Committee. (2017). Multi academy trusts seventh report of session 2016-17. Retrieved from https://publications.parliament.uk/pa/cm201617/cmselect/cmeduc/204/204.pdf. Accessed on 23 December 2017.

Ishii, S., Klopf, D., & Cooke, P. (2007). Worldview in intercultural communication: A religio-cosmological approach. In L. Samovar, R. Porter, & F. McDaniel (Eds.), *Intercultural Communication A Reader* pp. 28–35. Boston, MA: Wadsworth Cengage Learning.

Kesebir, P. (2014). A quiet ego quiets death anxiety: Humility as an existential anxiety buffer, personality processes and individual differences. *American Psychological Association*, *106*(4), 610–623.

Leal, F., & Saran, R. (2004). A dialogue on the socratic dialogue, Act Two in P. Shipley (Ed.), *Occasional Working Papers in Ethical and Critical Philosophy* 3.

Mansell, W. (16 March 2017). Time for a pay cap for Academy CEOs. Retrieved from https://www.moderngovernor.com/time-for-a-pay-cap-for-academy-ceos/. Accessed on 23 December 2017.

National Audit Office. (2018). *Report by the comptroller and audit general on PFI and PF2*. HM Treasury. Retrieved from https://schoolsweek.co.uk/wp-content/uploads/2018/01/NAO-PFI-AND-PFI-2-2018.pdf. Accessed on 2 May 2018.

Ofsted. (2005). *The school inspection handbook*. Published in October 2017. Retrieved from https://www.gov.uk/government/publications/school-inspection-handbook-from-september-2015. Accessed on 23 December 2017.

Parker, G. (2017). 'Theresa May to force reporting of pay gap between bosses and workers. In Financial Times' 24th August 2017, in *Financial Times*. Retrieved from https://www.ft.com/content/c45e19c4-8905-11e7-8bb1-5ba57d47eff7. Accessed on 22 December 2017.

Plato reprinted. (2017). *Timaeu/Crilas*. London: CreateSpace Independent Publishing Platform.

Pring, R. (2018). *The future of publicly funded faith schools; a critical perspective*. London: Routledge.

Reckhow. (2015). *Follow the money: How foundation dollars change public school politics*. Oxford: Oxford University Press.

Richards. (2017). *The PFI contracts that keep costing the taxpayer* 26 September 2017. Retrieved from https://www.theguardian.com/politics/2017/sep/26/the-pfi-contracts-that-keep-costing-the-taxpayer. Accessed on 23 December 2017.

Ruşşitoru, M.-V. (2017). *Le droit à l'éducation et les politiques éducatives*. Union européenne et Roumanie. Paris: Harmattan.

Schools Commissioners Group. (2018). The National Schools Commissioner and regional schools commissioners work with school leaders to take action in under-performing schools. Retrieved from https://www.gov.uk/government/organisations/schools-commissioners-group/about. Accessed on 2 May 2018.

Schools Week. (2016). *Morgan: Academy trusts without 'strong track record' can't have more schools*. Retrieved from https://schoolsweek.co.uk/morgan-academy-trusts-without-strong-track-record-cant-have-more-schools/. Accessed on 22 February 2018.

Schools Week. (2017). *REACH academy chain creates third arm to sponsor 15 schools* 23 May 2016. Retrieved from https://schoolsweek.co.uk/reach-academy-chain-creates-third-arm-to-sponsor-15-schools/. Accessed on 23 December 2017.

Shah, S. (2016). *Education, leadership and Islam*. London: Routledge.

Smith, A. (1776). Wealth of nations. Kindle Edition.

Stanton-Salazar, D. (2010). A social capital framework for the study of institutional agents and their role in the empowerment of low status students and youth. *Youth and Society, 43*(3), 1066–1109.

Stewart, F. Jr. (2012). The primacy of Delaware and the embeddedness of the firm. In C. Williams & P. Zumbansen (Eds.), *The embedded firm corporate governance, labor, and finance capitalism* (pp. 104–118) Cambridge: Cambridge University Press.

Taysum, A. (2012a). *Evidence informed leadership in Education*. London: Continuum.

Taysum, A. (2012b). *Convener of a large symposium in two parts: 'Globalization, Policy and Agency: Eight Nation states working together to Further Understand their Political Sociologies of Education'*. European Conference for Educational Research, Cadiz, September.

Taysum, A. (2013). *Convener of a large symposium in two parts; 'International Boundary Crossing Study of Teachers' and Students' Participation in Institutional Processes and Practices"*. European Conference for Educational Research. Istanbul, September.

Taysum, A. (2014). *Convener of a large symposium in two parts: 'International Boundary Crossing Study Of Higher Education Institutions working in Partnership with Schools To Improve Participation In Processes And Practices Chair: Jan Heystek (Stellenbosch University) Discussant: Carole Collins Ayanlaja (Chicago, Superintendent)*. ECER, Porto.

Taysum, A. (2015). *Convener of a large symposium in two parts: 'A Theory of Young People's Participation in Systems and Learning from International Boundary Crossing Action-Resarch Project Arar, K., Collins-Ayanlaja, C., Harrison, K., Imam, H., Murrel-Abery, V., Mynbayeva, A., Yelbayeva, Z.* European Conference for Educational Research. Budapest, Hungary. September.

Taysum, A. (2016). *Convener of a large symposium in two parts: McNamara (Chair), Risku, M., Collins Ayanlaja, C., Iddrisu, M.T., Murrel-Abery, J.V., Arar, K., Masry-Herzallah, A., Imam, H., Chopra, P., McGuinness, S. Theoretical underpinnings of an education and skills model for participation and cooperation in the Youth Field; empowering Europe's young innovators*. European Conference for Educational Research, Dublin, Ireland, August.

Taysum, A. (2017a). A Deweyan blueprint for moral training for Democracy in Education presentation Oxford University Symposium, April.

Taysum, A. (2017b). *Convener of a large symposium in two parts: Arar, K., Masry-Herzallah, A., Collins Ayanlaja, C., Brookins, W., McGuinness, S., Bates, J., Roulsten, S., O'Connor, U., James, F., and George, J., Taysum, A. Turbulence in Six International Education Governance-Systems: Comparing Knowledge to Action for Equity, Peace and Renewal*. European Conference for Educational Research, Copenhagen, Denmark, August.

Taysum, A., & Iqbal, M. (2012). What counts as meaningful and worthwhile policy analysis. *Italian Journal of Sociology of Education, 4*(1), 11–28.

Taysum, A., & Murrel-Abery, V. (2017). Shifts in education policy, administration and governance in Guyana 1831—2017. *Seeking 'A-Political' Agenda for Equity and Renewal In Italian Journal of Sociology of Education*, *9*(2), 55—87.

The Guardian. (13 November 2007). What are academy schools? Retrieved from https://www.theguardian.com/education/2007/nov/13/newschools.schools. Accessed on 23 December 2017.

The Guardian. (2016). Ofsted chief criticises academy chains 10 March 2016. Retrieved from https://www.theguardian.com/education/2016/mar/10/academy-chains-come under-fire-from-ofsted-chief. Accessed on 22 December 2017.

The Guardian. (2017a). Joining a multi-academy trust is like marriage without divorce. Retrieved from https://www.theguardian.com/teacher-network/2016/jun/01/process-becoming-an-academy-experiences. Accessed on 22 February 2018.

The Guardian. (2017b). Collapsing academy trust 'asset-stripped its schools of millions' October 21 2017. Retrieved from https://www.theguardian.com/education/2017/oct/21/collapsing-wakefield-city-academies-trust-asset-stripped-schools-millions-say-furious-parents. Accessed on 22 December 2017.

The Independent Commission on Good Governance in Public Services (ICGGPS). (2004). The good governance standards for public services. Retrieved from https://www.jrf.org.uk/sites/default/files/jrf/migrated/files/1898531862.pdf. Accessed on 22 December 2017.

Times Educational Supplement. (2018). DfE can't say what £31m regional schools commissioners budget pays for. Retrieved from https://www.tes.com/news/school-news/breaking-news/exclusive-dfe-cant-say-what-ps31m-regional-schools-commissioners. Accessed on 22 February 2018.

Tomlinson, H. (2004). *Educational leadership: Personal growth for professional development (published in association with the british educational leadership and management society)*. London: Sage.

United Nations. (1948). *Universal declaration of human rights* (General Assembly Resolution 217 A). Retrieved from http://www.un.org/en/universal-declaration-human-rights/. Accessed on 29 April 2018.

Wagner, T. (2010). *The global achievement gap*. New York, NY: Basic Books.

White Paper. (March 2016). Educational excellence everywhere in. Retrieved from https://www.gov.uk/government/uploads/system/uploads/attachment_data/file/508447/Educational_Excellence_Everywhere.pdf. Accessed on 25 February 2018.

Chapter 5

The Turbulence Black, Asian, Minority Ethnicity Chief Executive Officers of Small, Medium and Empty MATs Face in England's Education System; the Agency

Alison Taysum

Abstract

This chapter addresses how Black, Asian Minority Ethnic (BAME) Chief Executive Officers (CEOs) of Multi-academy Trusts (MATs) with track records of outstanding school improvement navigate turbulence when leading school improvement to optimise students' learning. There are different ideas of what it means to have equitable access and equitable outcomes in education systems, and beyond, and how to live a good life on the journey to both. These different ideas and values' systems have different intersectionalities of recognition by 'the other' in societies. Crenshaw argues, once these intersectionalities of discrimination have been identified, it will be possible to understand what Dewey calls their intrinsic nature and to seek ways to reconnect the isolated, and marginalised that are subjects of discrimination. The BAME CEOs articulate the current Public Governance of Education Systems that induces fear of forced takeovers and job insecurity creates a kind of divide and conquer approach of colonialism and intersectionalities of discrimination. The chapter identifies BAME CEOs want to create cultures where they can make a commitment to take the time to know the self, in relationship with the other, and build bridges between different groups in society for equity, renewal, trust, and peace in our time. The BAME CEOs wishing to empower others to engage in this moral training for democracy in education need to have and share the thinking tools to prevent community members from being manipulated by people who wish to rush them into new ways of thinking and doing. Change requires giving mature citizens the time and space to think things through by: asking good questions, critiquing the evidence underpinning the change, inquiring

Turbulence, Empowerment and Marginalisation in International
Education Governance Systems, 107–135
doi:10.1108/978-1-78754-675-220181006

into the logic of the change and holding the moral compass of the change to check the direction steers a sure and steady ethical course with what Adler calls the primary virtues of social justice, prudently and with courage.

Keywords: Empowerment; outstanding school improvement; democracy; equity; peace

Introduction

In the previous chapter, I explored the context of the Multi-academy Trusts (MATs) in England which has developed since I wrote the project's underpinning socio-historiographical education policy history of England (Taysum, 2012a, 2012b). Critiquing the context of the MATs has been important to understand the professional challenge of the research: How Black, Asian Minority Ethnic (BAME) Chief Executive Officers (CEOs) of MATs navigate the turbulence when leading school improvement to optimise students' learning. The BAME people in England are categorised as belonging to marginalised groups. Marginalised groups include children living in poverty in England who are more likely to be in poor health, overweight, obese, suffer from asthma, have poorly managed diabetes, experience mental health problems and die early (Boseley, 2017). About 4.1 million children in the UK, or 30% of children, were living in poverty in 2016–2017 which is 9 out of every class of 30 children (Child Poverty Action Group, 2018). The Guardian (2017, p. 1) identifies the Prime Minister, Theresa May, has stated that the findings of a Government race audit finds BAME women are hardest hit by austerity where: 'Asian households have faced the biggest drop in living standards, of 19.2% and 20.1% respectively. That amounts to a real-terms average annual loss of £8,407 and £11,678'. The report as a whole has illuminated huge differences between the experiences of BAME marginalised groups in Britain in education, hospitals, the workplace, and the judicial system. The Prime Minister states she wants to reveal:

> uncomfortable truths [...] People who have lived with discrimination do not need a government audit to make them aware of the scale of the challenge. But this audit means that for society as a whole – for government, for our public services – there is nowhere to hide. These issues are now out in the open. And the message is very simple: if these disparities cannot be explained then they must be changed.
>
> Guardian (2017, p. 1).

Four aims address the professional challenge: first, to reveal what turbulence these BAME CEOs navigate and how they navigate it to mobilise their track records of school improvement; second, to establish who helps them navigate the turbulence; and third, to describe and understand what kinds of cultural change the BAME CEOs of MATs articulate is needed to navigate or remove any turbulence to assure all students' learning, including marginalised groups, is optimised in all schools within their MATs; and finally, to theorise the evidence to present impact strategies of knowledge to action, empowering BAME CEOs to empower their staff and young societal innovators for equity and renewal.

The narrative biographies of five BAME CEOs of MATs from a population of seventeen BAME CEOs of small and empty MATs are presented. All seventeen of these BAME CEOs were invited by letter to take part in the research and five contacted me and participated. At the time of the research there were no BAME CEOs of large MATs. The findings were read through Gross (2014) Turbulence Theory. Gross (2014, p. 248) Turbulence Theory states that 'turbulence can be described as 'light' with little or no movement of the craft. 'Moderate with Very noticeable waves. 'Severe' with strong gusts that threaten control of the aircraft. 'Extreme' with forces so great that control is lost and structure damage to the craft occurs'. The Turbulence Theory or typology aims to categorise the level and the impact of the turbulence the BAME CEOs, as key agents of change need to navigate as they mediate between governance systems, and the academy, school leadership teachers, parents and students. The research also presents the mentors, networks and legislation that the BAME CEOs of MATs identify support them in this work. The Cultural changes the BAME CEOs of MATs articulate are required for this work are also presented.

Four questions address the aims of the research. First, how do the BAME CEOs leading small, medium and empty (SMEs) MATs describe and understand how Education Governance Systems and School Regional Commissioners empower or disempower them to develop school communities as societal innovators for equity, and renewal? Second, how do the BAME CEOs describe and understand the role mentors, and/or advocates play to support their navigation through the turbulence? Third, to what extent do the BAME CEOs believe a cultural change is required to empower them in school communities to Empower Young Societal Innovators for Equity and Renewal (EYSIER)? Finally, what impact strategies of knowledge to action emerge regarding how BAME CEOs of MATs might successfully navigate turbulence to empower marginalised groups in Public Corporate Education Governance Systems?

Critical Review of the Literature to Shed Light on the Research Questions

Empowering Educational System Leadership through Public Governance in England

There is very little literature available on the lived experiences of BAME CEOs of MATs, or indeed of any CEOs of MATs. A critique of the literature that addresses the first research question was presented in the previous chapter. The critical review explored the impact of intersectionalities of different cultures in Education Governance Systems. The chapter considered how a clash of cultures empowers or disempowers educational system leadership through Public Education Governance Systems in England in the context of MATs. The review of literature that addresses the second research question is presented in this chapter, and considers the role of mentors, and/or advocates in supporting BAME CEOs of MATs navigate the turbulence of the rapidly changing Public Education Governance Systems. The review of literature that sheds light on the third research question focuses on how to bridge different cultures in Public Education Governance Systems in England. Bridging different cultures includes dominant groups and groups who may experience marginalisation based on their race, gender, cultural heritage, class, language, their faith, or having no faith, being Gay, Lesbian, Bisexual, Queer, Transgender, those recognised as disabled by society and all those with protected characteristics in the UK Equality Act (UK Government, 2010). The critical engagement with the literature considers how to empower diverse community members with the knowledge, skills, and experience they require, as mature societal innovators in becoming, to develop the virtues they require to co-create democracy in education for equity and renewal (Dewey, 1916).

Mentors, and/or Advocates Supporting BAME CEOs of MATs

There are different ideas of what it means to have equitable access, and equitable outcomes in education systems, and beyond, and how to live a good life on the journey to both (Adler, 1941). These different ideas and values' systems have different intersectionalities of recognition by 'the other' in societies. Crenshaw (1989) argues, once these intersectionalities of discrimination have been identified, it will be possible to understand what Dewey (1916) calls their intrinsic nature and to seek ways to reconnect the isolated, and marginalised, that are subjects of discrimination. A disconnect between Public Corporate Education Governance Systems' CEOs of MATs with professional educational credentials, and those without professional educational credentials, education system headteachers, staff, parents, students and the wider general public, may be addressed by wise professional mentors with track records of school improvement. Such mentors may play a vital role in providing wise counsel and support to those developing essential institutional structures that reconnect these different groups by building what Takyi-Amoako (2014) calls networks. Networks have the potential to mobilise impact strategies of knowledge to action, and critically evaluate their pragmatic consequences to inform future improvement. Networks might include knowledge to action on how to build infrastructure to grow an empty or small MAT, and/or strengthen connections between parents of children with school staff to work together (Epstein, 2015) whilst respecting the dignity and autonomy of 'the self and the other' (Kesebir, 2014).

Dewey (1929) suggests that reconnecting different groups of people has been challenging because scientific knowledge has denied the instruments of social interactions and social cooperations. Consequently, Dewey argues there is a disconnect between people of different groups including those of different faiths and none in the communities they live in, and the development of meaning related to the development of character, virtues, and shared cultures that over-come potential clashes of values, entitlement and conflict for community cohesion and peace. Without opportunities to reconcile what Shook and Good (2010) cite as Hegel's thesis and antithesis, it will not be possible to reach a provisional consensus, or synthesis, for community cohesion and peace (Shook & Good, 2010). Dewey (1929, pp. 13–14) identifies:

> Ability to respond to meanings and to employ them, instead of reacting merely to physical contacts, makes the difference between humans and other animals, it is the agency for elevating humans into the realm of what is usually called the ideal and spiritual.

Dewey (1916) suggests the foundations of our conception of an ideal society and the development of a good character and virtues need to have existed over the epochs of time. Communities need to define those desirable rules or right acts of society that have existed in previous epochs and use the definitions to critique undesirable rules and wrong acts, or clashes of cultures, values and different entitlements that exist in society today. Mentors can support key agents of change to know the self, and help their communities know the self, and together develop desirable rules or right acts that shape good character and virtue. The potential 'good' society, right rules, right acts, and right order of products and instruments of production (Adler, 1941) will have proof of concept because they have previously existed, and they can be mapped to legislation today. Perhaps the proof of concept in history might be represented by a teacher or leader of virtue and good character from past cultures, all faiths and none. Taysum (2017a, 2017b, 2017c, 2018) suggests leaders may benefit from engaging with practitioner inquiry by engaging with moral training to develop their virtuous acts as habits (ethos) from reasoned empirical evidence (pathos) and logical (logos) dispositions, drawing from leaders and teachers of all faiths and none, and their associated cultural heritages. Core virtues may be identified and tested. Aristotle, in *The Art of Rhetoric* translated by Freese (1926), provides the following virtues: kindness, politeness, integrity, effort, courage, resilience, gratitude, and faith which fall under the umbrella of 'love'.

Virtues may be critiqued as identified in the methodology chapter of this book, to seek to understand what might be required to develop shared world views in communities hall marked by clashes: of cultures; of faiths and none; of values; of different entitlements that may lead to conflict. Dewey (1909) includes virtues as prudence, fortitude, justice, circumspection, and a desire to foresee future events as knowledge to action and to define, and avert that which is harmful, and that which we fear. The virtues may be rationalised in the classroom to bridge shared worlds views taking a Kant (1803) approach to a dialogue. Such dialogues occur with trust, respect for the self and the other, agreeing to disagree, and recognising diversity through inclusive practices (Barnett, 2000; Möllering, 2001; Taysum, 2017a, 2017b, 2017c; Wagner, 2010).

As such Dewey (1916, p. 1920) suggests:

> We must depend upon the efforts of *enlightened humans* in their
> private capacity [...] The full development of private personality is
> identified with the aims of humanity as a whole and with the idea
> of progress [...] and the very idea of education as a freeing of indi-
> vidual capacity in a progressive growth directed to social aims.

The role of enlightened human beings organising education, mentoring
others, and assuring succession planning to pass on wisdom and expertise from
the immature to the mature, from one generation to the next, is therefore very
important as identified by Plato (reprinted; 2017). Such knowledge to action is
key to cultural changes, to connect Educational Governance Systems, the academy, school leaders, school staff and different groups of parents and students in
the community at a personal relational and empathetic level and to work with
different groups of parents to empower mature communities in becoming.

Cultural Change to Empower Young Societal Innovators for Equity and Renewal

The kinds of cultural change that are required, to synthesise the thesis and
antithesis of different world views to move to shared world views may be operationalised by engaging with philosophical inquiry that provides moral training
for democracy in education (Taysum, 2017b). To do this the cultural change
needs to do two things:

(1) Educational leaders develop strategies to mobilise knowledge to action to
    empower staff and parents to EYSIER to co-create and renew institutional
    customs, rules, and responsibilities as a cultural project;
(2) Educational leaders with track records of school improvement work with
    the academy to develop strategies to mobilise knowledge to action to
    empower staff and parents to empower young people to understand the
    codes of human habits and behaviours, and the vision, values, and strategies
    that underpin those codes, in age appropriate ways. Such knowledge may
    enlighten them and be applied in their lives to emancipate them from fear
    (Taysum, 2017b). The fear includes what De Gruy (2005) identifies as
    humans not being able to protect their families because they are dominated
    by other cultures which do not recognise them (Payne, 2008). Renewal of
    participatory institutions for equity enables all citizens to have the knowl-
    edge, skills and experience they require as mature citizens to fully and freely
    cooperate, and interact with those who create the institutional legislation, or
    education policy (Dewey, 1916). The dominant cultures may maintain a sta-
    tus quo unnaturally privileging themselves through institutional customs
    located in historical epochs regulated by geographical borders and statistics
    that are so entrenched the unnatural, and socially constructed privilege and
    extra entitlement, may appear natural (Bourdieu, 2000; De Gruy, 2005;

Dewey, 1916). Evidence of privilege in society today is that eight men have the same wealth as 50% of the world's poorest people (Oxfam, 2017).

A marginalised community requires resources and conditions conducive to building: 'respect for the rights of others' (DfE, 2014, 2017a, 2017b, 2017c, p. 36) as community members share their world views with other community members including their virtues, ideals, spirituality, and knowledge. Resources include thinking tools to help them arrive at a provisional consensus. The provisional consensus on the synthesis between thesis and antithesis needs to occur without coercion, or radicalisation to work towards community cohesion, peace and economic, cultural and political prosperity. Such development allows people to work hard together, and their hard work may contribute to building their personal wealth in the realisation of true economic liberalism where hard work is rewarded (Smith, 1776) in balance with welfarism. The culture change may need to focus on understanding and participating in the governance, and regulation of institutions, the goods, the instruments of production, and the rules related to human rights (Adler, 1941). The cultural change that CEOs may need to effect needs to assure that all stakeholders have equitable rights to develop their ideals, spirituality, virtues and prioritisation of goods and their instruments of production (Adler, 1941). Here goods and their instruments of production are those required for health, and wealth, activities, and habits, where their prioritisation reveals a good life in becoming that can only be fully realised as a life that was worth living as an end outcome (Adler, 1941).[1]

Nowadays we are living with the legacy of institutions that have their roots in histories that have not advocated equity and renewal as discussed in the introductory chapter with reference to colonising, and Karpman's (1968) Triangle of shifting roles of oppressors, victims and rescuers in the colonisation process. CEOs who interface between different values systems need the opportunity to work with Regional Schools Commissioners (RSC), School Boards, policy-makers and stakeholders to renew constitutions or policies/legislation that assure democratic processes and practices have been constructed (Collins-Ayanlaja, Taysum, & Brookins, 2017). However, The Times Educational Supplement (2018, p. 1) states:

> The rise of the RSCs has come amid growing concerns about an overlap between their work, and that of Ofsted. The RSCs use of education advisers to visit schools and report privately to RSCs on how they are performing has led to fears they are operating a 'shadow inspection regime'. Last week, Sir David Carter, who oversees the RSCs in his role as national schools commissioner, acknowledged duplication with Ofsted, and said he would scale back school visits commissioned by RSCs. And according to Ofsted's board minutes for November 2017, Paul Kett, the DfE's

---

[1]There is not scope to critically engage with the goods and their instruments of production here, and this is in development by Taysum (2018).

director general, education standards, acknowledged an overlap between the RSCs and the inspectorate's regional directors, saying 'the value for money issue this could present is part of active business planning discussions at the DfE'.

The RSCs are unelected and appointed by the Schools' Minister and by-pass the real, elected representatives of the people; the local councils. Further the TES (2018) identify that the DfE cannot say what the £31million pounds of tax payers' money, allocated to RSCs pays for. Perhaps a more democratic approach would be to develop institutions where citizens elect their representatives in education governance systems as they used to elect councils, with the opportunity for community members to also stand for election. Community members' participation in institutions demonstrated by behaviours of full and free interactions and cooperation with education systems (Dewey, 1916) gives communities the chance to co-create and renew the rules and responsibilities within their institutions through a social contract (Rousseau, 1762; Taysum, 2017b).

Cultural changes may need to transcend 'school reform' that Payne (2008) identifies has not had any impact on equity. Rather the focus needs to be on developing a logical, empirical and shared moral compass that assures an ethical Education Governance System for all (Taysum, 2017a, 2017b, 2017c). This kind of cultural change may provide opportunities for community members to identify intersectionalities of discrimination connected with the global phenomenon of the Black-White achievement gap (Crenshaw, 1989; Glazer, 2005; Wagner, 2010). The intersectionalities of discrimination may then be reconciled working through opposing arguments (both thesis and antithesis) to try to reach a provisional consensus within groups, and between groups for democracy for social justice (Adler, 1941; Dewey, 1908, 1916).

The co-creation and renewal of participatory institutions such as the legal system, the governance systems including Education Governance Systems, and the economy would benefit from citizens seeing people who 'look like me' leading these institutions to believe they will be respected in truth (Sleeter and Carmona, 2017). The people who 'look like me', including BAME people, need to participate in leading these institutions as role models with track record of moral and ethical success, who have succeeded in making their dreams, ideals and spiritual longings a reality (Gordon, 1993). Further, the cultural change may benefit from describing discrimination (Glazer, 1987) to deepen understandings of how some have greater entitlement than others in a divide and conquer context (Taysum and Murrel-Abery, 2017) resulting in White privilege (McIntosh, 1997). A dominant group may gain new insights and understand the institutions that reproduce the 'unnatural supremacy' of the dominant group that appears 'natural'. The insights may emerge from asking good questions about the inequities that reveal careful description of the inequities, and then critically analysing, and reflecting upon closed reproductive systems of culture that replicate inequity. Such philosophical inquiry may underpin a cultural change to open networks and systems of informed consent, underpinned by the

Empowerment of Young Societal Innovators for Equity and Renewal. The CEOs interacting and cooperating with Corporate Public Education Governance Systems, academies, and the headteachers, staff, parents and students may benefit from connecting communities together through engagement with the knowledge, skills and experience required for democracy in education.

Education policy can empower CEOs of small, medium and empty (SME) MATs to do this. The physical scientific knowledge may be connected with the spiritual understandings of social interactions and social cooperation, with the self, the other, the community, and the states people who pen the rules (Dewey, 1929; Shook and Good, 2010). Thus, those organising education systems would role model what it means to overcome clashes in prime principles of different cultures, and share this way of thinking and doing with their communities. This kind of capacity building empowers mature communities with the knowledge, skills and experiences they need to participate in full and free interactions and cooperation with societal institutions (Dewey, 1916).

The academy, who have become experts in this field, including the authors in this book, may play a role as critical friends who can facilitate knowledge mobilisation, knowledge gatekeeping, and passing on of ancient traditions through networks (Takyi-Amoako, 2014). The academy through philosophical inquiry can operationalise a logical and critical reflection of the ancient traditions with the modern, using a moral compass that assures an ethical framework. The philosophical inquiry focuses on the thesis and antithesis of different values systems from different groups of society. These different groups include those from Corporate Public Education Governance Systems and those from the Education Profession and all those who are part of very large or small, medium or empty MATs who are all part of small and medium local communities located within a wider society in a globalised context. The CEOs who have benefited from the advice and support of their wise networked mentors located in a professional body may, supported by the academy, mentor their headteachers to navigate turbulence and build capacity for the headteachers to go on to mentor staff. These staff may then mentor the parents and students such that meaningful, worthwhile, rigorous, epistemic and methodological cultural change that Empowers Young Societal Innovators for Equity and Renewal may be realised, step by step (Taysum, 2012a, 2012b, 2013, 2014, 2015, 2017a, 2017b, 2017c; Taysum, Collins-Ayanlaja, & Popat, 2016; Taysum and Collins-Ayanlaja, 2018).

Research Design

The research design is discussed in depth in the methodology chapter of this book. The research takes a social/structural constructivist approach (Bourdieu, 2000). Real-world ontological structures such as legislation and policy, shape what a human being can and cannot think and do, in other words their constructs. Depending on the knowledge the human beings access and apply, they may be able to critique the logic and the extent to which the structures are evidence informed and use traditional ancient wisdom and modern knowledge.

Human beings can ask good questions and engage in philosophical inquiry into the intersectionalities of discrimination that reveal how different groups' are recognised and/or marginalised within the structures. Human beings can ask good questions and engage in philosophical inquiry about the quantity and quality of different groups' interactions and cooperations with the structures (Dewey, 1916). The philosophical inquiry may be optimised when using an explicit moral compass that assures an ethical framework in a search for truth. Human beings may then develop impact strategies to change the structures, which in turn changes what human beings can and cannot think and do. Thus institutions and their structures shape human beings' principles, values, virtues, habits and behaviours, or their codes of behaviour, and they shape the interactions and cooperation human beings have to shape the institutions' structures. In an iterative process human beings shape the structures that shape their agency that can perpetuate the status quo and marginalisation, or work inclusively together for equity and renewal in the democratisation of knowledge (Delanty, 2001) put to work as knowledge to action.

The principles of the social or structural constructivism need to be revealed through an overt methodology, or articles of association, or business plan so that human beings can fully understand how their constructs are formed and how they can influence how their constructs are formed through closed hierarchical systems or open participatory systems (Bourdieu, 1994, 2000, 2004).

The research strategy is a qualitative case study (Yin, 2008) where the full population of 17 BAME CEOs of small, medium or empty MATs were invited by letter to participate in semi-structured interviews, and five agreed (Mertens, 1998). Two of the BAME CEOs are Christian, two are Muslim, one is Sikh, and each BAME CEO has between five and two academies in each MAT. However, at the time the invitations to interview were issued, one BAME CEO's MAT was empty. To safeguard anonymity and confidentiality, it is not possible to state how many academies each BAME CEO's converter academy had converted into their MAT. All five BAME CEOs are professional educationals with professional credentials. All five have outstanding track records as professional teachers and outstanding track records as professional educational leaders who have led schools from 'Requires Improvement' to 'Outstanding'. The sample includes participants who have been publicly recognised for services to educational leadership.

The transcripts from the semi-structured interviews were sent to the participants for respondent validation. All respondents had the right to withdraw from the research up until the time of publication and gave written informed consent to participate in the research. All participants were assured anonymity and confidentiality as per the British Educational Research Association ethical guidelines (BERA, 2011) and the University of Leicester Research Ethics Board. The rich qualitative data were analysed using axial coding and pattern matching. To assure the quality dimensions of the research, each quote can be tracked back to the large analysis tables which held the coding, and these can be mapped back to the transcripts. The analysis also faithfully represents what the participants said and is true to the narratives they provided and the order in which they stated events occurred (Blumenfeld-Jones, 1995). The qualitative data provide rich understandings of the biographical narratives of these BAME CEOs and cannot be generalised. The theories of knowledge to action that emerge may have leverage for others. Further, the knowledge to action is amplified through the comparative analysis of the five international cases presented in this book regarding how senior leaders of Education Governance Systems are empowered to 'Empower Young Society Innovators for Equity and Renewal', how they are mentored to do this, and the cultural changes required for developing moral virtues to move from marginalisation of groups of people to democracy in education for all.

Findings

Empowering Educational System Leadership through Public Governance in England

All five BAME CEOs identified that they were motivated to improve failing schools as a commitment to the children that were being failed. All five BAME CEOs identified a clash in their values and the values of others in the public Education Governance System who were interested in securing large financial rewards for themselves from tax payers' hard-earned money within new cultures of performance management and in the form of PFIs. Luke, a BAME CEO of a MAT states:

> It is a general issue that I have not been involved in running the PFI of schools, but I have seen a few of them and as I have visited them the people who own the school have been able to use it as a cash cow for their businesses. I will give you a little example that someone told me that was quite funny. When they fitted out the toilets in one of these PFI buildings, they deliberately put the soap dispenser and the hand dryer in the wrong places because they knew it would increase the likelihood for the need for repairs and it would increase the likelihood of failure of those components which in turn would mean the service contractors would always have something to do.

Hema states:

> Now that I am CEO of a MAT my salary is agreed by my governors and I think it is reasonable because at this school my salary is circa £65K the out going head's salary of my new school was circa £75K so if you add it together that is £140K. Now I am CEO I act as head teacher for both schools and my combined salary is circa £85K ... that is not what some CEOs out there are getting. I have said to my governors my salary will not go over £93K however many schools I get.

The findings connect with the values of a Private Equity Fund manager (Diamond, 2012) that seeks to make as much money before making a swift withdrawal or exit with no responsibility for duty of care and the rights of the human-beings left behind (BBC News, 2017). Without financial decisions being made drawing on policy memory (Hodgson and Spours, 2006) that are empirical, logical, moral and ethical, and regulated by a professional body of independent experts acting as gatekeepers for the profession, along with Ofsted acting as regulators, there is no opportunity to 'hand down old opinion by ancient tradition'. Plato (2018) (reprinted; 2017) identifies such gatekeepers of knowledge are vital in 'Timaeu and Crilas'. Taysum (2017a, 2017b, 2017c) suggests engaging with decision-making with ethos, pathos and logos is possible when applying the thinking tools found in Taysum (2012a, 2012b) Learning to Critically Analyse and Reflect for Emancipation, or Enlightenment (CARE). These tools are also applied in Taysum's (2017b) synthesis of John Dewey's framework Moral Training for Democracy in Education (Dewey, 1908, 1916) that seeks to identify injustice in a system and eradicate it (May, 2017). There are parallels here with the Programme of International Students Assessment (Organisation for Economic and Cooperation and Development, 2017) and Trends in International Mathematical and Science Study (TIMSS) (International Education Assessors, 2017), and Progress in International Reading Literacy Study (PIRLS) (IEA, 2017). These quantitative educational assessors examine the output of national education systems through a global lens and always have something to do that generates them income in a system that is, like Luke's example of the soap-dispenser and hand-dryer, set up to fail for some nation states that are not cash rich, and do not have the resources of other cash rich nation states, at the cost of the same nation states' tax payer. Perhaps it is time for these educational assessors to assess: the socio-economic, and political context that shape the values and acts of particular legislation, and economic policy and infrastructure that sets up groups of people to become marginalised. The empirical evidence connects with a pattern of intellectual, cultural and economic colonisation that arguably lacks moral and ethical frameworks (Adler, 1941).

Four of the BAME CEOs identified that turning around a failing school was exhausting work, and required all their many years of professional expertise as leaders of learning and teaching, and working in schools that moved from 'Requires Improvement' to 'Outstanding'. BAME CEO Mohammad states:

> Just simply when we first went into the first school that we eventually took on....What quickly unravels is a situation of a school that actually should probably have been closed down. There are huge safe guarding issues. And then the sort of moral purpose kicks in and you think, okay (circa 500) kids who are being systematically failed and have been for a long time. We need to do something about this. I am physically ill from what I have had to do at that school (to improve the leadership, and the learning and

teaching and the relationships in the community)...I would not have survived, but it was only because I had people here to call upon, of headteacher colleagues to come in and give me support when I needed them. Then there was a fight when we were putting this much into this school putting our own school at risk, and then you are going to give it to somebody who is inexperienced and six months later it is back in the same state.

The BAME CEO Victoria also transformed a failed school and stated 'I worked with the DFE on improving schools out of special measures'.

Another BAME CEO Ranjit states:

Nobody wanted to take the headship (of the school), and (I was told) the staff would rather have you as a fall-back person, if you know what I mean...and God smiled on me, we were one of the few schools that got a good report.

BAME CEO Hema states:

Here, when we have challenges at our second school the first thing I say to my staff is what is it that we are doing well in the first school, and how are we transferring it to the second. So that depends on your staff doesn't it? That depends on your senior leaders. It depends how you are managing and supporting them to support others. Pressure can make you behave in different ways... So when you look at children's assessment for learning and what Dweck says about raising their resilience, making them feel that they can do it, positivity, that applies to teachers as well. So we shouldn't be in our leadership positions thinking 'tell them and they will do it'.... My White CEO counterparts at MAT CEO meetings have said to me 'oh no, no, no, you are not strategic'. I don't think they are there for the moral compass, they are there to see 'how can I grow my MAT? What is going on? How am I going to get my second and third school?'....Every one is ringing their Regional School's Commissioner; 'how do I get another school? How do I get another school? Getting another school is an increase in salary, correct? So where is that drive that still holds us accountable about what is going on in our schools? I go to my classroom I go to my other school, I go to my class rooms, I meet with my leaders. I do manage what my leaders do in their non- contact time. I am then assessing the leaders in the first school, and the leaders in the second school....The leadership isn't by email messages. My personal view is the government started the academies programme in a drive to do something about failing schools. So why would I want to go to a good school and ask them to join our MAT?

Now you have got groups of schools in competition. CEOs now, of academies they don't want to work together really. I asked Name what is the criteria for getting a third school because I think we are ready for a third school, but so are other people out there, so are empty MATs so are single MATs so the moral compass really is, why is my colleague down the road sitting with an empty MAT when the Government don't want them to do that, but how have they created the conditions for them to have academies in their MAT? They are not there, so if I am offered a third school I will be thinking of my colleague down the road - maybe they should have my school and I won't have a third school yet.

We must never lose sight of individuals make society, whichever kind of individuals we have. So the BAME issue, it is very potent. The civil servants rely on certain people to give them information that feeds into policy some how. I don't know, maybe they should come and sit and talk to me. If people do not have opportunities to be stakeholders in society, they choose to back out and they do other things whatever you want to call it.

Where do we look at the impact of policy? It is too much isn't it? It is too much....We have taken on schools in special measures, we are outstanding. My forte lies with moving schools from special measures, and requires improvement (to outstanding)....
I personally believe CEOs and head teachers must not become company directors they must stay at the heart of what the school is for. How are you going to empower your staff if you don't connect with them?

Policy is a bit out of control now. A lot of MAT CEOs are saying; 'but we go in, we give support, and at the end of it, they don't want to come to us. Then they say it is about visions, values and ethos, but it is not just about that is it though? It is about; 'you want to come in and take us over'.

You can't have another school unless you have got the infrastructure, and you can't have the infrastructures unless you have got a few more schools. The government is then saying; 'you can't function as an empty MAT'. So people have got all these issues haven't they? I don't know who is going to sort the mess out from five schools, ten schools, three schools? Now, what am I going to do, try and find five schools? I am very measured, I won't take on a school if I feel I haven't got the capacity, but how are we measuring (who has the capacity)?

The findings reveal that BAME CEOs of MATs who have a track record of improving schools from 'Requires Improvement' to 'Outstanding' are facing barriers to growing their MATs because they do not have the infrastructure. Without an infrastructure, their professional expertise as key agents of change, to develop Dewey's (1916) desirable rules or right acts that shape good character and virtue are prevented from flourishing (Adler, 1941). The BAME CEOs are also concerned that if they take on an additional school, they may leave their colleague's good or outstanding school down the road, vulnerable to a rapid forced takeover, or colonisation from a large MAT. They are also concerned that if academies were developed to raise standards, why would a MAT want their converter academy to convert a good or outstanding academy that already has high standards.

The pragmatic consequence of takeovers may be the connections between the community, parents, students, school staff and CEOs will be lost, along with the chances to debate what it is to lead a good life with the other and become mature citizens together. The BAME CEOs state they want to move slowly when growing their MATs, and want to convert failing academies and mobilise their track record for school improvement and move the failing schools to out-standing. The BAME CEOs want to ensure that all their academies in their MATs are 100% 'Good' or 'Outstanding' before building capacity and taking on more failing schools to improve them. The BAME CEOs articulated that the current policy puts one BAME CEO against another BAME CEO as they fight to fill their empty MATs, or grow their MATs to protect their survival. The fighting for survival distracts the BAME CEOs from addressing a clash in cul-tures between those in education governance systems who are motivated by serv-ing the community and those that have come into education through PFI and/or have joined Public Corporate Education Governance Systems to make money from the tax payers' hard earned cash. The motivation to make money rather than serve the children was demonstrated by the Wakefield City Multi-academy Trust which ran 21 schools and identified it was pulling out in the first week of the new 2017–2018 term because it was unable to:

> facilitate the rapid improvement our academies need, and stu-dents deserve...The Department for Education (DfE) said many of the schools within the trust were performing below the national average...The Trust said the decision was in the 'best interests' of the students...The trust had paid its then Chief Executive Officer £82,000 for 15 weeks work. BBC News (2017, p. 1).

The clash of values between educational professionals with track records of school improvement and who are motivated to optimise students' learning and those entering public Education Governance Systems to make large financial gains is causing extreme turbulence. Further the Government policy of rapid forced takeovers in schools has caused fear in the system which again has caused extreme turbulence. These BAME CEOs professional educational leaders want support from the Government to allow them to mobilise their excellent track record of school improvement to raise standards and build capacity for outstanding schools. These BAME CEOs who are leading 'Good' and 'Outstanding' schools do not want to waste their time fighting for survival in an Education Governance System that does not recognise their professional wisdom and does not recognise their 'strong track record' in improving schools (Guardian, 2016a, 2016b). The BAME CEOs want to spend their time applying their track records of outstanding school improvement to improve more schools from failing to outstanding. The BAME CEOs articulated currently policy is preventing them from doing this.

The Role of Mentors, and/or Advocates in Supporting BAME CEOs of MATs to Navigate Governance Systems

All five BAME CEOs identified their faith including Islam, Christianity and Sikhism helped them develop their character, virtues, habits and behaviours that aligned with the principles of the education profession, and helped them navigate the turbulence of the organisation of education in flux. Four identified that individuals supported them, but none identified formal mentors, formal networks or formal advocates outside of their faith supported their navigation through the Education Governance Systems. When asked about the role of mentors or advocates in their lives, the BAME CEOs responded as follows.

Luke identified:

> I don't think I could identify a single individual. I will say that my faith, and being brought up in a Christian family, attending church schools myself, all of the journey I have gone through over the last five decades means that that's why I believe these (values) are important, that's why I put them as a high priority.

Victoria stated:

> I have been really lucky that in the past I have worked with people who are both indigenous White friends like Name, and also people like Name who is Caribbean heritage working in Jamaica at the moment, who support me. But also along the way Teaching Assistants who mention things or a parent (support me).

Mohammad stated:

> The moral and emotional support from people here (convertor academy), every so often I would just walk into the building and sit down, and it was almost like someone rescuing me from disaster, putting the foil blanket round me and giving me a cup of tea

and then I would go back into it, taking various people with me. So those first eighteen months were a real example of people coming together with a common cause to turn this failing school round and now it is a fantastic school and doing really well, and you would not know if you walk round that it was in that situation.

Hema identified that previously:

Section 11 was BAME, dealing with EAL, home school liaison, so I spent a number of years working in section 11 and I got more experience of working in schools, after that I went to a primary school where the headteacher recognised something in me and gave me more responsibility.

Ranjit states:

At the lowest point in my life our Chair would say to us, look at the time of our Guru's and look at what they went through, we are not suffering 1% of it.... When the Golden Temple for example was being built, they sometimes did not have anything there to eat....We are not suffering 1% of that are we? That inspired you. And that is what kept us going.

Those that supported the BAME CEOs passed on wisdom and traditions from their faith and the divine, passing on traditional knowledge that has sustained over epochs (Plato, 2018). No BAME CEOs reported that a formal educational professional network systematically supported them to navigate turbulence created by the clash of cultures between educational professionals' values found in their Small, Medium and Empty (SME) MATs, and the Public Corporate Educational Governance System values found, in what they described as, the large MATs.

Cultural Change to Empower Young Societal Innovators for Equity and Renewal

All BAME CEOs identify that their academies are committed to bridging different cultures to enable all in the community to share world views, and to respect the self and each other. Victoria states:

bridging cultures and seeking equity in entitlement: It is all about social mobility [...] I want them to go to the ballet, to the theatre, and the best restaurants I want them to feel they should be there, it is as simple as that. It is about an entitlement. The fact that we do dance, and it is ballroom dancing it is calypso it is bangra it is gymnastics it is Spanish, we have Year 6 boys and girls dancing together holding each other in Salsa. To me it is one of our successes. It is a cultural mix, so you have got Caribbean boys dressed up in Asian costumes, Asian boys doing Caribbean dance, Asian boys and Asian girls dancing, and in schools the Asian heritage children don't dance because they say; 'oh no, we can't do that'. Our parents know if they come to our school its what you do, and we have got it all the way through school from Nursery. And it is a message about us, about community; a seamless blend of culture […]. And it is a message about the staff, and about me, and the children and about the parents. What we should be working on is having governors who are open minded to different cultures and ethnicities and can see the value, rather than Name and Name perpetuating the imagery they have already. We say the Lord's prayer because it's a Church of England school, we say a Muslim prayer in home language, we say a Sikh prayer in home language we say a Hindu prayer in home language and people say how have you managed to do that, and I say that is what the children need and that is what they told me they wanted. Therefore we have produced it for them. So it is about believing in improving. It is about them feeling valued and us demonstrating that we are valuing them. It is about finding the things that aren't the same, the things that are different.

Mohammad states:

I have had that conversation with a Cambridge graduate a few years ago, a White lady. Her expectations for our (BAME) children were different to the expectations that perhaps her parents had for her, and perhaps she would have for her own children. We are uncompromising in how we communicate that with people whose expectations may be different and we are happy to say; 'this is not the place for you, it is not going to work'.

Victoria also identifies institutionalised racism when governors have said to her she has been asked to present because she is Black and not because she is good, and when an early years, teacher said the 'Angel in the Christmas production needed to be White because Angels are not Black'. Victoria identifies when people have got racism, for example, stating Angels are not Black, it needs to be addressed. She provides another example when she states:

The whole scenario of the thing made me realise that (Name) had got racism […] I suppose it is a bit like the plantation, and the plantation owner who has one of those Black people who whip the others, and (they thought) I must have been one of those, and that is how (they) saw it and it is as simple as that.

The empirical evidence reveals that fear is being created in a system by marginalisation and one group is set against another group through racism to ensure they do not become marginalised, or they do not become the most marginalised group. Drawing on the introductory chapter this may be theorised using Karpman's Triangle (1968) where people or groups play a role as a victim, or oppressor, or a rescuer, or shift roles on the triangle. A victim may become an oppressor to regain a sense of power and to escape their fear (De Gruy, 2005). Those who wish to maintain their additional entitlement in a system, such as the 'lady from Cambridge' may create strategies of divide and conquer that assure different groups have different levels of access leading to different levels of entitlement to assure the success of their colonisation (Taysum and Murrel-Abery (2017). When groups are fighting for survival to protect themselves, they do not have the time or the energy to ask good questions and problem solve why the system has oppressors, or bullies, victims and rescuers, and what needs to be done to gain enlightenment and put that wisdom to good use to get off the cycle of replicating fear in a system through marginalisation.

Marginalisation is an issue that the current Prime Minister is taking very seriously and has identified needs to be changed (Guardian, 2017). The divide and conquer approach, similar to what Victoria calls: 'making one of those Black people whip the other Black people' creates fear, a sense of learned helplessness, and is not conducive to building peace in our time (Dewey, 1916) in local small and medium communities.

The culture change the BAME CEOs empower in their SME MATs enables all community members to engage physically through dance, scientifically through the curriculum, philosophically through the thinking tools of Learning to CARE focusing on ethos, logos and pathos (Taysum, 2012a, 2012b; Taysum, 2017a, 2017b, 2017c), and spiritually as they explore all faiths and none in a safe place together (Shah, 2016). The young people are able to talk about, in the classic method, the best that has been thought and said about different cultural heritages represented in the classroom (Carter, 2008; Stanton-Salazar, 2010). The evidence reveals these BAME CEOs enable their communities to fully and freely cooperate, and interact with those who create the institutional legislation, or education policy at the school level (Dewey, 1916; Harris, O'Boyle, & Warbrick, 2009; Ruşitoru, 2017). Empowering communities to engage with the institutional level and government level, adopting the principle of subsidiarity with all proper regulatory processes and practices (Harris et al., 2009; Ruşitoru, 2017) are next steps in developing impact strategies to put knowledge to action. The knowledge to action builds capacity to raise up children from marginalised groups including those who are discriminated against because they are BAME, those who are discriminated against because they are in poverty, and/or those who experience intersectionalities of discrimination because they are BAME and in poverty.

Concluding Comments and Recommendations for Knowledge to Action

BAME CEOs identify that turbulence in the public Education Governance Systems is extreme (Gross, 2014) and the structure of good organisation of education by enlightened professional educational leaders with track records of school improvement is put at risk through forced takeovers, or colonisation by large MATs. At the same time, some failing schools are deemed 'untouchable'. These untouchable schools are the ones the BAME CEOs in this research have told me they have converted and improved from failing to outstanding, and would like to take on more failing schools, one at a time, and support them. However, the BAME CEOs informed me they are told they cannot mobilise their track records for school improvement because they have been told they do not have the infrastructure to grow their MATs. They have been told that they need to have large MATs to gain the infrastructure to grow their MATs.

The BAME CEOs identify a disconnect from their participation in the rapid change happening through new systems of Public Education Governance Systems. The BAME CEOs articulated their voices are not listened to, and they cannot protect themselves, and that which they care about citing an opaque process of PFIs, and/or how to get an infrastructure to grow an empty MAT. The BAME CEOs articulate when they are successful in moving a failing school to good or outstanding, they are at risk of not keeping the school in their MAT because they are told they do not have the infrastructure to grow their MAT. They are concerned that a large MAT will take over the school, and that the school will be back in the same place within six months. At the same time, they state they are told they cannot have an infrastructure until they grow their MAT with more academies.

There is currently no advice or mentoring on how to navigate this extreme turbulence, and how to grow a MAT to assure local small- and medium community schools that are outstanding are allowed to continue to flourish in a liberal framework. There is no advice or mentoring on how successful leadership teams are allowed to grow their MATs slowly by taking on one failing academy at a time. The BAME CEOs identify that their track record of improving failing schools to outstanding is not recognised in the current Public Education Governance System, and there is little support to help them protect their SME MATs, their jobs and their pensions. These BAME CEOs identify that there is fear in the system that CEOs with empty MATs will not be able to protect their communities from a forced takeover, and will not be able to protect their careers hallmarked by outstanding track records of school improvement, or protect the future welfare of their families. De Gruy (2005) identifies humans feel fear when they do not perceive they are able to protect that which they care about, be that their schools, other schools in their communities, their communities, their staff, their students, their families and their careers. The BAME CEOs risk losing their jobs and their pensions, and security for their family if their good or outstanding academies are part of a forced takeover or colonisation by a large MAT.

There is a danger that high-quality CEOs of SME MATs may take consultancy roles within large MATs during a takeover to protect their future. Moving committed successful professional educational leaders with track records of school improvement from the education system into consultancy roles, as a consequence of competition to grow a MAT for survival, produced extreme turbulence. Increasing consultants in a system arguably reduces loyalty and commitment of those individuals to the system (Gunter, Hall, and Mills, 2015), and limits the opportunity for wise enlightened mature organisers of education to become gatekeepers of logical, empirical, moral, and ethical traditional knowledge who can pass on the principles of the education profession to the next generation of good organisers of education. The negative impact on high-quality succession planning is a pragmatic consequence.

In summary, evidence reveals that fast moving mergers through forced take-overs by large MATs prevent both quality succession planning and the chance to 'hand down old opinion by ancient tradition' (Plato, 2018), balanced by inno-vation for equity and renewal. There is a danger that the current system depends upon the efforts of *enlightened humans* in their private capacity (Dewey, 1916), rather than having legislation that supports high-quality professional educa-tional leaders with the professional credentials, track record of, and appetite for, the transformation of failing schools to 'Outstanding' one school at a time.

The BAME CEOs articulate the current Public Governance of Education Systems that induces fear of forced takeovers and job insecurity creates a kind of divide and conquer approach of colonialism (Taysum and Murrel-Abery, 2017). The BAME CEOs want to create cultures where they can make a com-mitment to take the time to know the self, in relationship with the other (Socrates edited by Brown, 2003, 2009). Such an approach builds bridges between different groups in society for equity, renewal, trust and peace in our time (Dewey, 1916). The BAME CEOs who cannot provide opportunities to develop self-knowledge cannot build opportunities for their staff through profes-sional learning, or their community members of parents and students to build such self-knowledge by deeply listening to the narratives of the other (Leal and Saran, 2004). Being self-aware, having self-control and being able to regulate the self based on self-evaluation and reflection are important characteristics for a quiet ego and for establishing and attaining realistic goals (Kesebir, 2014). The BAME CEOs wishing to empower others to engage in this moral training for democracy in education need to have, and share the thinking tools to prevent community members from being manipulated by people who wish to rush them into new ways of thinking and doing (Taysum, 2017a, 2017c, 2017b). Change requires giving mature citizens the time and space to think things through by:

(1) asking good questions;
(2) critiquing the evidence underpinning the change;
(3) inquiring into the logic of the change;
(4) holding the moral compass of the change to check the direction steers a sure and steady ethical course for social justice, prudently and with courage (Adler, 1941).

The evidence reveals the Public Education Governance System is presenting opportunities for mirroring public corporations which return profits. Public cor-porations that are financially under-performing become targets for friendly or hostile leveraged takeovers from Private Equity Funds (PEF) (Diamond, 2012).

The evidence reveals SME MATs that do not benefit from the economies of scale of a large MAT (of at least 20 academies (Coles, 2017)) are targets for a forced takeover, or colonisation. However Academies were set up to raise standards, not to create economies of scale.

When community members see this kind of extreme turbulence affect their children's education and lives, it may create strong feelings of disconnection from the education system. These strong feelings of disempowerment may induce fear, particularly when communities cannot protect their school from a hostile takeover, or colonisation (De Gruy, 2005). Fear amplifies the clash of cultures which is a barrier to bridging differences. The fear is further amplified when community members see PFIs fail.

The evidence reveals state behaviour needs to model good, slow, socially just, prudent, and courageous organisation of change. The change in schools needs to focus on social inclusion in a liberal economy that facilitates equity of opportunity for social mobility with logos, pathos and ethos (Taysum, 2016). Such state behaviour might be possible with the principle of subsidiarity and margins of appreciation enabling individuals to have full and free participation in institutions. Courage is required because government's role modelling such state behaviour needs to bridge between themselves and the opposition. Moving from demonising the opposition, or even members of the same party as disloyal, or mad, to a position of respecting and seeking balance in the organisation of state affairs will potentially take considerable courage (Jenkins 2012). However, such a courageous approach might earn the public's trust and the public's vote in an election. Arguably, the problem of clashes is amplified when parties clash within themselves publicly, rather than diplomatically working to deliver their manifesto. Clashes of culture within a party are state behaviours that are potentially confusing for citizens who have voted for a manifesto and do not understand how the implementation of a manifesto can cause so many clashes for their elected representatives.

Limitations of the Research

I was unable to interview a BAME CEO of a large MAT because there is no current BAME CEO of a large MAT. Whilst this research focuses on the extensive narrative biographies of a third of all BAME CEOs, it is acknowledged the research is limited. A full and comprehensive survey of all CEOs of all MATs is recommended to establish how many MATs have more than one failing school within them, and how this problem will be addressed by the good organisation of education that assures no MAT has more than one failing school being transformed to good or outstanding at a time. The survey needs to be anonymous and independent and needs to clarify who is representing MATs when responding to the survey. The Academy Trust Survey (DfE, 2017a, 2017b, 2017c, p. 22) begins to meet this need and finds:

> The vast majority (96 per cent) of MATs with two or more academies believe that their structure has facilitated collaboration and

that academies within their MAT regularly collaborate in a number of areas that lead to financial savings.

The report also states on p. 6: 'The vast majority (87%) of Single Academy Trusts (SATs) support other schools'. The report does not state how many of these MATs and SATs have been mentored to develop an infrastructure to grow a MAT and avoid a forced takeover. Neither does the report state how these MATs and SATs describe and understand how growth to avoid a forced take-over, or a takeover will foster collaboration, or induce competition for survival. Thus, this research recommends a further full survey is conducted in consultation with BAME CEOs, and CEOs of large MATs, SME MATs and SATs to develop survey questions that will describe the current situation (Glazer, 1987). When these have been defined, they can be critiqued and mentors can support key agents of change to develop desirable rules or right acts that shape good character and virtue within the Public Education Governance Systems. The potential 'good' society, right rules, right acts and right order of products and instruments of production will have proof of concept because they will have previously existed (Adler, 1941; Dewey, 1916, Plato, 2018).

Recommendations: Knowledge to Action to Empower Young Societal Innovators for Equity and Renewal (EYSIER)

First, BAME CEOs with professional education credentials and with DfE (2017a, 2017b, 2017c) values, with a track record for improving schools to good and outstanding, need to be supported by legislation. The legislation needs to allow BAME CEOs of SME MATs to grow their MATs slowly, moving one failing school to 'Good' or 'Outstanding' at a time. Evidence reveals no CEOs of any size MAT should take on a new failing school to improve it, until all their current schools are 'Good' or 'Outstanding'. 'Good' and 'Outstanding' schools need to build high-quality relationships within communities (DfE, 2017a, 2017b, 2017c) to bridge cultural differences within communities to EYSIER (Taysum et al, 2016; Taysum, 2012a, 2012b, 2013, 2014, 2015, 2017a, 2017b, 2017c).

Second, an 'A' political educational professional body needs to be developed with wise, enlightened educational professionals with track records of school improvement to act as gatekeepers for professional learning networks connected between the Academy and schools. The professional body needs to represent the profession in the co-construction of education policy.

Third, all BAME CEOs of MATs need to be invited to be mentored by enlightened professionals they trust within an educational professional body. These enlightened professionals need to organise education as gatekeepers of wisdom, traditional knowledge, and innovation through educational professional constructive networks underpinned by ethos, pathos and logos. The mentoring needs to support decision-making that connects individuals to each other and their communities to build peace, and optimise learning, social mobility, access to middle class benefits and support transitions from immaturity to maturity. Mentors need to have educational professional credentials and DfE (2017a, 2017b, 2017c) values of educational leaders. Mentors and wise enlightened leaders should not be squeezed out of full-time permanent employment with a pension by a large MAT through a forced take over, or colonisation, and then be re-employed by the large MAT as a temporary consultant with no job security, and no long-term formal contractual connection to the school and MAT.

Fourth, the role of Corporate Public Education Governance Systems' CEOs of MATs, without professional educational credentials, and unelected, who can only tell experts to improve schools because they do not know how to do it themselves, need to empower the enlightened educational professional experts, with track records of school improvement, to organise education.

Fifth, all MATs need to be regulated, regulation is currently operationalised by Ofsted.

Sixth, a cultural change is required that will bridge the clashes between different cultures within education governance in England. The cultural change needs to be fully integrated from Initial Teacher Education to professional learning for experts to assure all stakeholders have equitable rights, and freedoms to develop their ideals, spirituality, virtues and prioritisation of goods and their instruments of production that do no harm to others (Adler, 1941). Here, goods and their instruments of production are those required for health, and wealth, activities, and habits, where their prioritisation reveals a good life in becoming that can only be fully realised as a life that was worth living as an end outcome (Adler, 1941). The characteristics need to be extracted from the best that has been thought and said from all cultural heritages, all faiths, and none to enable what Plato (reprinted, 2017) described as old opinion to be handed down. These old opinions may be found in the codes of human behaviour held in the holy books of all faiths, the books of no faith, and the philosophical books of different traditions, and classical texts such as the Greek or Chinese, or Japanese myths, and legends, and in the United National Declaration of Human Rights (1948). These codes need to exist now or in the past.

Impact Strategies for bridging Knowledge to Action need to be presented to BAME CEOs and CEOs for review, feedback, and improvement. Policy needs to support the strategies so that they are part of the curriculum and not bolted on. Enlightened professional educationals need to organise education, be mentors and build supportive networks to build capacity for school improvement. All discrimination needs to be identified, and addressed through cultural change with BAME CEOs being empowered to empower staff and parents to replace fear of a system to Empowering Young Societal Innovators for Equity and Renewal (EYSIER) to co-create systems, and institutions characterised by social justice, prudence and courage (Taysum, 2018). These kind of impact strategies aim to overcome clashes of all kinds peacefully and to build sustainable Education Governance Systems that facilitate the transition of immature citizens to mature citizens who can fully and freely participate in society's cultural, economic and political systems.

References

Adler, M. (1941). *A dialectic of morals: Towards the foundations of political philosophy.* Notre Dame: University of Notre Dame.

Aristotle. (1926). The Art of Rhetoric (Freese, J. Trans.). London: William Heinemann.

Barnett, R. (2000). *Higher Education: A Critical Business.* Buckingham: SRH.

BBC News. (2017). *Wakefield City Academies Trust pulls out of 21 schools.* Retrieved from http://www.bbc.co.uk/news/uk-england-leeds-41198403. Accessed on 22 December 2017.

Blumenfeld-Jones, D. (1995). Fidelity as a criterion for practicing and evaluating narrative enquiry. In J. Amos Hatch & R. Wisniewski (Eds.), *Life history and narrative* (pp. 25–36). London: Falmer Press.

Boseley, S. (2017). Poverty in the UK jeopardising children's health, warns landmark report. *The Guardian.* Retrieved from https://www.theguardian.com/society/2017/jan/25/poverty-in-the-uk-jeopardising-childrens-health-warns-landmark-report. Accessed on 23 April 2017.

Bourdieu, P. (1994). *The field of cultural production.* Cambridge: Polity Press.

Bourdieu, P. (2000). *Pascalian meditations.* Cambridge: Polity Press.

Bourdieu, P. (2004). *The field of cultural production.* Cambridge: Polity Press.

British Educational Research Association. (2011). Ethical guidelines for educational research. London: BERA.

Brown, S. (2003). *Socrates know thyself.* Retrieved from http://1worldpeace.org/san.beck.org/SOC1-KnowYourself.html. Accessed on 23 December 2017.

Brown, L. (Ed.) (2009). Aristotle. In *The Nicomachean ethics.* Oxford: Oxford World Classics.

Carter, P. L. (2008). Teaching students fluency in multiple cultural codes. In M. Pollock (Eds.), *Everyday antiracism* (pp. 107–112). New York, NY: The New Press.

Child Poverty Action Group. (2018). *Child poverty facts and figures.* Retrieved from http://www.cpag.org.uk/content/child-poverty-facts-and-figures. Accessed on October 20, 2018.

Coles, J. (2017). Twenty schools is too small for a multi academy trust in schools week 03 July 2017. Retrieved from https://schoolsweek.co.uk/academy-boss-20-schools-is-too-small-for-a-multi-academy-trust/. Accessed on 22 December 2017.

Collins-Ayanlaja, C., Taysum, A., & Brookins, W. (2017). Empowering superintendents in the United States to develop school communities as societal innovators for equity and renewal; knowledge to action in Taysum, A (Convener) turbulence in six international education governance-systems; comparing knowledge to action for equity, peace and renewal (in two parts). Copenhagen, Denmark: ECER.

Crenshaw, K. (1989). Demarginalizing the intersection of race and sex: A Black Feminist critique of antidiscrimination doctrine, feminist theory, and antiracist politics, University of Chicago Legal Forum, 1989, 139–167.

De Gruy, J. (2005). *Post traumatic slave syndrome.* Portland: Joy De Gruy Publications Inc.

Delanty, G. (2001). *Challenging knowledge: The university in the knowledge society.* Buckingham: SRHE and Open University Press.

Department for Education. (2017a). National professional qualifications (NPQ) Content and assessment framework. Retrieved from https://www.gov.uk/government/uploads/system/uploads/attachment_data/file/653046/NPQ_Content_and_Assessment_Framework.pdf. Accessed on 25 February 2018.

Department for Education. (2017b). Academy trust survey July 2017. Retrieved from https://www.gov.uk/government/uploads/system/uploads/attachment_data/file/629779/Academy_Trust_Survey_2017.pdf. Accessed on 23 December 2017.

Department for Education. (2017c). *Model articles of association for academy trusts.* Retrieved from https://www.gov.uk/government/publications/academy-model-memorandum-and-articles-of-association#history. Accessed on 22 December 2017.

Department for Education (DfE). (2014). Professional values of educational leaders.

Dewey, J. (1908). *The collected works of John Dewey: 1908, Ethics Volume 5: the middle works, 1899–1924.* Carbondale: Southern Illinois University Press.

Dewey, J. (1909). *Moral principles in education.* New York, NY: The Riverside Press Cambridge.

Dewey, J. (1916). *Democracy and education.* New York: Macmillan.

Dewey, J. (1929). *Experience and nature.* Kindle Edition.

Diamond, S. (2012). Beyond the Berle and means paradigm: Private equity and the new capitalist order. In C. Williams & P. Zumbansen (Eds.), *The embedded firm: corporate governance, labor and finance capitalism.* Cambridge: Cambridge University Press.

Epstein, J. (2015). *School, family, and community partnerships, student economy edition: Preparing educators and improving Schools.* London: Westview Press.

Glazer, N. (1987). *Affirmative discrimination ethnic inequality and public policy.* Harvard: Harvard University Press.

Glazer, N. (2005). *The emergence of an American ethnic pattern.* Retrieved from http://www.paperdue.com/essay/the-emergence-of-an-americanethnic-pattern-63715. Accessed on 01 May 2017.

Gordon, J. (1993). If not you, *then who? Are teachers of colour recommending teaching as a profession?* Retrieved from https://eric.ed.gov/?id=ED383648. Accessed on 22 December 2017.

Gross, S. J. (2014). Using turbulence theory to guide actions. In C. M. Branson & S. J. Gross (Eds.), *Handbook on ethical educational leadership* (pp. 246–262). New York, NY: Routledge.

Gunter, H., Hall, D., & Mills, C. (2015). Consultants, consultancy and consultocracy in education policymaking in England. *Journal of Education Policy*, *30*(4), 518–539.

Harris, D., O'Boyle, M., & Warbrick, C. (2009). *Law of the European convention on human rights.* Oxford: Oxford University Press.

Hodgson, A., & Spours, K. (2006). An analytical framework for policy engagement: the contested case of 14–19 reforms in England. *Journal of Education Policy*, *21*(6), 679–696.

Institute of Education Assessors. (2017). *Trends in international mathematics and science study.* Retrieved from http://www.iea.nl/timss. Accessed on March 18, 2018.

Jenkins, R. (2012). Home thoughts from abroad (1979). In B. MacArthur (Ed.), *The Penguin book of modern speeches.* London: Penguin.

Kant, I. (1803). On education. E-Book. The Online Library of Liberty, Liberty Fund, Inc. Retrieved from http://oll.libertyfund.org/index.php?option=com_staticxt&staticfile=show.php%3Ftitle=356&Itemid=28. Accessed on 22 December 2017.

Karpman, S. (1968). Fairy tales and script drama analysis. *Transactional Analysis Bulletin, 7*(26), 39−43.

Kesebir, P. (2014). A quiet ego quiets death anxiety: Humility as an existential anxiety buffer, personality processes and individual differences. *American Psychological Association, 106*(4), 610−623.

Leal, F., & Saran, R. (2004). A dialogue on the socratic dialogue, Act Two in P. Shipley (Ed.) *Occasional Working Papers in Ethical and Critical Philosophy* 3.

McIntosh, P. (1997). White privilege and male privilege: A personal account coming to see correspondences through work in Women's Studies. In R. Delgado & J. Stefancic (Eds.), *Critical White studies: looking behind the mirror* (pp. 291−299). Philadelphia, PA: Temple University Press.

Mertens, D. (1998). *Research methods in education and psychology*. London: Sage.

Möllering, G. (2001). The nature of trust. From Georg Simmel to a theory of expectations, interpretation, and suspence. *Sociology, 35*(2), 403−420.

Organisation for Economic and Cooperation and Development. (2017). *Programme of international students assessment*. Retrieved from http://www.oecd.org/pisa/. Accessed on March 18, 2018.

Oxfam. (2017). *Just eight men own the same wealth as half the world*. 16 January 2017. Retrieved from https://www.oxfam.org/en/pressroom/pressreleases/2017-01-16/just-8-men-own-same-wealth-half-world. Accessed on 23 December 2017.

Payne, C. (2008). *So much reform, so little change: The persistence of failure in urban schools*. Harvard: Harvard Education Press.

Plato, Jowett, B. (Ed.) (2018). *Timaeus and Critias in The Complete Works of Plato*. London: CreateSpace Independent Publishing Platform.

Pring, R. (2008). *John Dewey: A philosopher of education for our time?* London: Bloomsbury.

Rousseau, J. J. (1762). *The social contract*. London: Wordsworth Classics of World Literature.

Ruşitoru, M.-V. (2017).*Le droit à l'éducation et les politiques éducatives. Union européenne et Roumanie*. Paris: Harmattan. 264 pages.

Shah, S. (2016). *Education, leadership and Islam*. London: Routledge.

Shook, J., & Good, J. (2010). *John Dewey's philosophy of spirit, with the 1897 Lecture on Hegel*. New York, NY: Fordham University Press.

Sleeter, C., & Carmona, J. (2017). *Un-standardizing curriculum: Multicultural teaching in the standards-based classroom (multicultural education series)*. New York, NY: Teachers College Press.

Smith, A. (1776). Wealth of Nations. Kindle Edition.

Stanton-Salazar, D.. (2010). A social capital framework for the study of institutional agents and their role in the empowerment of low status students and youth. *Youth and Society, 43*(3), 1066−1109. first published online then in 2011.

Takyi-Amoako, E. (2014). Developing nodes in leading networks of knowledge for leader and leadership development: Some African students' perspectives on their experience of doctoral education. In A. Taysum & S. Rayner (Eds.), *Investing in* our education: Leading, learning, researching and the doctorate (international perspectives on higher education research). Scarborough: Emerald.

Taysum, A. (2012a). *Evidence informed leadership in Education.* London: Continuum.

Taysum, A. (2012b). *Convener of a large symposium in two parts: 'Globalization, Policy and Agency: Eight Nation states working together to Further Understand their Political Sociologies of Education'.* European Conference for Educational Research, Cadiz, September.

Taysum, A. (2013). *Convener of a large symposium in two parts; 'International Boundary Crossing Study of Teachers' and Students' Participation in Institutional Processes and Practices".* European Conference for Educational Research. Istanbul, September.

Taysum, A. (2014). *Convener of a large symposium in two parts: 'International Boundary Crossing Study Of Higher Education Institutions working in Partnership with Schools To Improve Participation In Processes And Practices Chair: Jan Heystek (Stellenbosch University) Discussant: Carole Collins Ayanlaja (Chicago, Superintendent).* ECER, Porto.

Taysum, A. (2015). *Convener of a large symposium in two parts: 'A Theory of Young People's Participation in Systems and Learning from International Boundary Crossing Action-Resarch Project Arar, K., Collins-Ayanlaja, C., Harrison, K., Imam, H., Murrel-Abery, V., Mynbayeva, A., Yelbayeva, Z.* European Conference for Educational Research. Budapest, Hungary. September.

Taysum, A. (2016). *Convener of a large symposium in two parts: McNamara (Chair), Risku, M., Collins Ayanlaja, C., Iddrisu, M.T., Murrel-Abery, J.V., Arar, K., Masry-Herzallah, A., Imam, H., Chopra, P., McGuinness, S. Theoretical underpinnings of an education and skills model for participation and cooperation in the Youth Field; empowering Europe's young innovators.* European Conference for Educational Research, Dublin, Ireland, August.

Taysum, A. (2017a). Systems theory and education: A philosophical enquiry into education systems theory. In P. Higgs & Y. Waghid (Eds.), *A reader for philosophy of education* (Vol. 1, p. 1). South Africa: Juta.

Taysum, A. (2017b). A Deweyan blueprint for moral training for Democracy in Education presentation Oxford University Symposium, April.

Taysum, A. (2017c). Convener of a large symposium in two parts: Arar, K., Masry-Herzallah, A., Collins Ayanlaja, C., Brookins, W., McGuinness, S., Bates, J., Roulsten, S., O'Connor, U., James, F., and George, J., Taysum, A. Turbulence in Six International Education Governance-Systems: Comparing Knowledge to Action for Equity, Peace and Renewal. *European Conference for Educational Research, Copenhagen, Denmark, August.*

Taysum, A. (2018). A Deweyan framework for moral training for democracy in education. In C. Lowery & P. Jenlink (Eds.), *Handbook of Dewey's educational theory and practice.* Dordrecht: Sense Publishers.

Taysum, A., & Collins-Ayanlaja, C. (2018 August). Parents' authentic participation in a United States public school to advocate for their Black children's education success. Presented at World Education Research Association, Cape Town South Africa.

Taysum, A., Collins-Ayanlaja, C., & Popat, S. (2017). *Developing school leaders' characters as critical educators for social justice through a lens of Agape in T.*

Fawssett The Feast (Chair) Community Cohesion Symposium, Brahma Kumaris World Spiritual University, Leicester.

Taysum, A., & Murrel-Abery, V. (2017). Shifts in education policy, administration and governance in Guyana 1831–2017. Seeking 'A Political' agenda for equity and renewal. *Italian Journal of Sociology of Education*, 9(2), 55–87.

The Guardian. (2016a). Ofsted chief criticises academy chains 10 March 2016. Retrieved from https://www.theguardian.com/education/2016/mar/10/academy-chains-come-under-fire-from-ofsted chief. Accessed on 22 December 2017.

The Guardian. (2016b). *Schools must focus on struggling White Working Class Pupils says UK Charity*. Retrieved from https://www.theguardian.com/education/2016/nov/10/schools-focus-struggling-white-working-class-pupils-uk. Accessed on 25 February 2018.

The Guardian. (2017). Audit lays bare racial disparities in UK Schools, courts and workplaces. 09 October 2017. Retrieved from https://www.theguardian.com/uk-news/2017/oct/09/audit-lays-bare-racial-disparities-in-uk-schools-courts-and-work-places. Accessed on 22 December 2017.

Times Educational Supplement. (2018). DfE can't say what £31m regional schools commissioners budget pays for. Retrieved from https://www.tes.com/news/exclusive-dfe-cant-say-what-ps31m-regional-schools-commissioners-budget-pays. Accessed on 22 February 2018.

UK Government. (2010). *Equality act protected characteristics*. Retrieved from https://www.equalityhumanrights.com/en/equality-act/protected-characteristics. Accessed on 22 March 2017.

United Nations. (1948). *Universal Declaration of Human Rights* (General Assembly Resolution 217 A). Retrieved from http://www.un.org/en/universal-declaration-human-rights/. Accessed on October 14, 2018.

Wagner, T. (2010). *The global achievement gap*. New York, NY: Basic Books.

Yin, R. (2008). *Case study research: Design and methods (applied social research methods)*. London: Sage.

Chapter 6

Empowering School Principals to Overcome Turbulence in School Partnerships through Governance Systems for Equity, Renewal and Peace: Northern Ireland

*Samuel McGuinness, Jessica Bates, Stephen Roulston,
Una O'Connor, Catherine Quinn and Brian Waring*

Abstract

This chapter explores the topic of supporting young people to become innovators for societal change in terms of equity and renewal from the perspective of school principals in Northern Ireland, a post-conflict society. We examine how school principals can be empowered in their role in providing this support and the challenges and turbulence that they face in their work. The chapter provides contextual information about education in what is still largely a divided society in Northern Ireland. The principals who were interviewed as part of this research were working within school partnerships as part of 'shared education' projects. In Northern Ireland, the Shared Education Act (2016) provides a legislative basis for two or more local schools from different educational sectors to work in partnership to provide an opportunity for sustained shared learning activities with the aim of improving both educational and reconciliation outcomes for young people. The challenges for school leadership of working in partnership in societies emerging from conflict has not been given the attention it deserves in the literature, so this work is significant in that it brings together a focus on school leadership in a 'shared education' context, drawing on theories of collaboration and turbulence to examine how principals can best be empowered to be agents of change, so that pupils in Northern Ireland can also become empowered to make society there more equitable and peaceful.

Turbulence, Empowerment and Marginalisation in International
Education Governance Systems, 137–157
doi:10.1108/978-1-78754-675-220181008

While the focus is on Northern Ireland, the learnings from this study will be of wider interest and significance as similar challenges are faced by school leaders internationally.

Keywords: Schools; school principals; Northern Ireland; turbulence theory; social change

Introduction

The aim of this research is to generate new understandings of the potential turbulence that school principals encounter as they seek to empower themselves and their staff to empower young people to be societal innovators for equity, peace and renewal.

Northern Ireland (NI) is a society, emerging from recent conflict, which continues to display considerable division. The case study, which forms this chapter, was undertaken within the context of school partnerships and shared campuses forged through the shared education programme in Northern Ireland. Eight school principals were interviewed to explore the manner in which they undertook their roles and categorise the kinds of 'turbulence' they experience – for example, in terms of strength and whether turbulence is light, moderate, severe or extreme (Gross, 2016). We analysed how they navigated the turbulence. We examined how the governance systems sanction them to empower school communities to become societal innovators for equity, peace and renewal. It is hoped that from the five country/regional case studies, a new theory of Empowerment through Governance Systems for equity, peace and renewal can be developed as knowledge to action.

The Northern Ireland Context

Northern Ireland has a long history of political conflict, sectarianism and terrorism.

More than 3,600 people were killed and 30,000 injured as part of a period of ethno-sectarian violence known colloquially as 'the Troubles' and over half of these deaths were civilians (Worden & Smith, 2017). Lasting between 1968 and 1998, 'the Troubles' refers to a period of cross-community tensions and violence in Northern Ireland, and occasionally Britain and beyond. Since 1998 and the signing of the Belfast (Good Friday) Agreement a power-sharing government was established (although there have been periods of direct rule from Westminster when the power-sharing assembly has collapsed). Whilst Northern Ireland has been considered a post-conflict society, it remains heavily segregated in terms of its political institutions as well as in housing and education (Niens, O'Connor, & Smith, 2013). Segregation can have a lasting impact on society, and in particular, on young people (Roulston, Hansson, Cook, & McKenzie, 2016). The Northern Ireland *Strategy for Victims and Survivors* (OFMDFM, 2009) 'recognises the impact of the Troubles/Conflict on Children and Young People' (Commission for Victims & Survivors, 2016) and states:

> An important area to be addressed is likely to be the inter-generational impact of the troubles on children and young people and the need to promote cross-community work with children and young people.
>
> OFMDFM (2009, p. 12)

The commitment to develop common shared spaces in education, housing and society in general is highlighted in the Programme for Government as essential for the development of a tolerant, respectful and equitable Northern Ireland (NIE, 2016). In particular, the enduring gap in educational and social outcomes for some pupils is a key challenge for government and policy-makers (Harland & McCready, 2012; Nolan, 2013). This inequity has strong historical roots in the conflict of Northern Ireland; the geography of its worst extremes is closely aligned to those areas where social disadvantage and marginalisation were most prevalent, so that poverty, poor housing, limited social and educational opportunities and unemployment co-existed with entrenched views of the 'other' community (Deloitte, 2007). Whilst some communities have flourished more than others, an inter-generational pattern of poor educational outcomes and reduced social opportunity has tended to prevail in spite of successive community and education-based initiatives (MacInnes, Aldridge, Parekh, & Kenway, 2012; Purvis, 2011).

The Education Context

The Education (NI) Act of 1947, drawing from the Butler Act (Taysum, 2012), introduced a system of free secondary (termed 'post-primary' in NI) education into Northern Ireland that operated on 'the principle of academic selection for grammar, intermediate and technical schools according to ability, aptitude and parental choice' (Oliver, 1994, p. 108). In the decades that followed, while Britain adopted a more comprehensive education system, NI largely retained academic selection at age eleven with pupils proceeding to a grammar or a non-grammar school.[1] These schools are 'controlled' (predominantly Protestant), or 'maintained' (predominantly Catholic). In addition, there are several 'Voluntary' grammar schools, some Protestant, others Catholic, which are allowed considerable autonomy; Integrated schools, whose primary focus is to provide a religiously mixed environment capable of attracting reasonable numbers of both Catholic and Protestant pupils; a small number of Irish-language schools, where all teaching is done through the medium of the Irish language; and a small

---

[1]Academic selection was formally abolished in 2008 but in 2016, the new Education Minister produced revised guidance that authorises schools to facilitate transfer testing unregulated by the Department.

number of independent Christian schools associated with the Free Presbyterian Church, which do not receive government funds.[2]

Reflecting the segregated nature of most schools, figures for 2016/2017[3] show that:

- only 11% of Catholic children attended controlled primary schools and less than 1% of Protestant children attended Catholic maintained primary schools;
- only 5% of Catholic children attended controlled post-primary schools and only 2% of Protestant children attended Catholic maintained post-primary schools;
- Catholic children make up 13% of the controlled grammar schools population and Protestant children make up 1% of the voluntary Catholic grammar school population;
- 4% of Catholic children and 6% of Protestant children attended an integrated primary school; and
- about 6% of Catholic children and 10% of Protestant children attended an integrated post-primary school.

The complex set of arrangements regarding education in Northern Ireland puts extreme pressure on those involved in school governance and creates an environment where turbulent conditions can develop and ferment.

Educational Collaboration

Hughes and Loader (2015), among others, contend there is broad agreement that interaction between schools can facilitate positive intergroup relations. Over the past thirty years in Northern Ireland, there has been a drive to encourage schools of all sectors and types to form learning communities. This is particularly evident through the formation of formal partnerships at a local level in area learning communities (ALCs). In Northern Ireland, every post-primary school is part of an ALC which can also involve colleges of Further Education, in order to 'maximise(s) the opportunity to meet the needs of pupils across the [given] area'. McGuinness (2012) states:

> Where schools once competed with each other, they increasingly collaborate through the growth of Area Learning Communities (ALCs) [...], it is with these ALCs that our greatest hope may lie (2012, p. 232).

---

[2]Further information about school types in Northern Ireland can be found at: https://www.education-ni.gov.uk/articles/information-school-types-northern-ireland
[3]See Department of Education, School enrolments – Northern Ireland Summary Data. Pupil religion by school management type 2000/2001 to 2016/2017, https://www.education-ni.gov.uk/publications/school-enrolments-northern-ireland-summary-data

Over the last thirty years, a range of formal and informal initiatives such as the Schools Community Relations Programme, Education for Mutual Understanding (EMU), Cultural Heritage and Local and Global Citizenship have been introduced. These have been primarily designed to facilitate contact and improve relationships between pupils from the controlled (de facto Protestant) and Catholic maintained sectors. Whilst the intention behind them has been generally welcomed and has enabled some meaningful engagement, there have also been concerns that partial and tokenistic delivery has limited the opportunity for proper integration and knowledge sharing between pupils from diverse backgrounds (O'Connor, Beattie, & Niens, 2009; Wardlow, 2003). Since 1989, the Department for Education has a statutory duty 'to encourage and facilitate integrated education' (through The Education Reform (Northern Ireland) Order 1989) and the growth of integrated schooling has taken place in parallel to these initiatives. There are currently 66 integrated schools in NI, representing seven per cent of the pupil population (Bates, O'Connor Bones, & Milliken, 2017). More recently, shared education, where two or more schools from different sectors work in collaboration with the aim of delivering educational benefits to all learners, has been promoted as a:

> curriculum-based interaction between pupils attending all school types, aimed at promoting the type of contact likely to reduce negative social attitudes and ultimately contribute to social harmony
>
> Hughes & Loader (2015, p. 1).

According to the Department of Education, NI (2016), the purpose of shared education is to:

- deliver educational benefits to children and young persons;
- promote the efficient and effective use of resources;
- promote equality of opportunity;
- promote good relations; and
- promote respect for identity, diversity and community cohesion.

The Shared Education Act (Northern Ireland) 2016[4] provides the legislative framework for shared education in Northern Ireland and builds upon the government's shared education policy, 'Sharing Works – A Policy for Shared Education' (2015).[5]

---

[4]http://www.legislation.gov.uk/nia/2016/20/section/1
[5]https://www.education-ni.gov.uk/publications/sharing-works-policy-shared-education

Governance

Governance, in all its forms, involves a complex milieu of inter-relationships between inter-dependent groups and individuals (Balarin, Brammer, James, & McCormack, 2008; Lewis & Naidoo, 2004). School governors play a vital role in school development and improvement, particularly in Northern Ireland where they provide strategic direction to school leaders, and changes in education policy have had implications for their role. For example, the Education Reform Order (1989)[6] introduced autonomous self-managed schools with significant changes in curriculum, budget formula allocations and the emergence of various government educational policies and initiatives. This transition reflected challenges elsewhere – for school leaders who were resistant to engaging with a more scrutinising form of governance (Blase, 1997; Harrison, 1998) and for governors who could potentially confuse their strategic responsibilities with the management responsibilities of the head teacher and senior leaders (Allen & Mintrom, 2010). More recently, a new single statutory support agency across Northern Ireland (the Education Authority) was established to provide a more cost-effective model for the delivery of education services, although the current economic situation presents funding challenges creating further turbulence for governing bodies (Shapiro & Gross, 2013).

The Department of Education states that all schools should have a dynamic governing body, where responsibilities are understood within a robust system of accountability (DE, 2017). Schools each have individual Boards of Management, although new governance models have been suggested (Perry, 2011) – for example, a federation model, where a group of schools share a single governing body, and a similar collaborative model, where schools have an advisory council feeding into one overarching governing board.

The Northern Ireland Department of Education states that the core strategic role of the board of governors of a grant-aided school is to fulfil its functions in terms of 'promoting the achievement of high standards of educational attainment' (DE, 2017, p. 36) and encourages governors to be cognisant of institutional performance by publishing challenging 'Public Service Agreement Targets'. Similarly, the Education and Training Inspectorate invites stakeholders to assess 'how effective the leadership of the school is in providing strategic leadership' (ETI, 2015) in a process of self-evaluation. These are challenging requirements which carry considerable individual responsibility, and evidence elsewhere suggests that, if governors are to fully understand the terminology and associated responsibilities of their role, mandatory induction training is essential (Creese & Earley, 2005; National Governors' Association Manifesto, 2014, p. 8).

Within the educational context of Northern Ireland, one of the key issues for principals and governors in the past decade has been to address the possibilities for liaising and collaborating with schools of different cultures and value sets. In building these shared learning communities, it is inevitable there may be tensions

---

[6]http://www.legislation.gov.uk/nisi/1989/2406/contents

between the schools, school population, parents and wider community. Concepts of community and individual rights come from widely divergent sources. Tutu (2004) explains the community concept of Ubuntu, the Nguni Bantu term meaning 'humanity towards others', in this way: 'In the end, our purpose is social and communal harmony and well-being. Ubuntu does not say, "I think therefore I am." It says rather: 'I am human because I belong. I participate. I share.'" (p. 27). Kept in balance, the forces of community standards and individual rights can complement one another and make a relatively free society feasible. The same pursuit of harmony between community and the individual can be found in the history of education and, it is hoped, in Northern Irish schools.

Definition of Turbulence Theory to Contextualise

> [...] the only sure way to avoid turbulence is to stay on the ground. Those who journey into the sky must be prepared.
>
> Gross (1998, p. 140)

Since the late 1990s, Gross has been using the metaphor of turbulence during flight as a typology by which school leadership in different contexts can best be understood. In his 1998 text on curriculum leadership he writes that 'Turbulence is a normal part of flying and a normal part of curriculum leadership that can be studied and understood' (Gross, 1998, p. 113). He comments on how the case studies he examined 'responded successfully to the rough air they encountered [...] [and] often spoke of becoming stronger as a result' (Gross, 1998, p. 113). Turbulence theory has the potential to help us understand school leadership in the shared education context in Northern Ireland. Turbulence theory is essentially concerned with opposition and/or reactions to change, and as such is particularly relevant to a society moving out of the conflict. This definition does not presume turbulence solely as a negative construct 'that leaders need to defend against' (Gross, 2014, p. 251) but also as a mechanism for positive change. Turbulence therefore can be experienced differently by individuals and is often shaped by their various identities – or positions – such as social class and professional standing (Kezar, 2000). In this work, we are focused on the extent to which a turbulence framework can contribute to understanding the leadership challenges that school principals involved in Shared Education projects and initiatives in Northern Ireland might face. What level of turbulence, if any, did school principals face? In what contexts? How did they deal with turbulence? What support did they have from mentors? What leadership characteristics can be determined from their behaviour? Gross (2016) outlines the variance in the turbulence that may be experienced in his typology or 'turbulence gauge'. Light turbulence is where 'little or no disruption' is experienced; moderate turbulence occurs where there is 'widespread awareness of the issue'; severe turbulence is where there is a 'sense of crisis'; and extreme turbulence can be determined where there is 'structural damage to [the] institution'. In the context of this study, school principals used a variety of leadership intelligences to overcome approaching different levels of turbulence in the typology. How school leaders navigate turbulence is central to the development of governance systems for equity, peace and renewal in society and for the extent to which they can empower young people to become societal innovators for equity, peace and renewal in their communities.

Research Methodology

The approach was social constructivist as explained in the methodology chapter, and was a qualitative study aimed at gaining insight into the experiences of school principals in Northern Ireland in terms of how they navigate turbulence within educational governance systems. The challenges for school leadership of working in partnership in contexts of shared education has often been over-looked in the literature, so this study was exploratory in nature. Fieldwork involved carrying out interviews with school principals in Northern Ireland. The research findings are framed by Gross (2014) typology of different levels of tur-bulence, which is used to categorise the level and the impact of the challenges that the key agents of change (school principals) need to navigate within gover-nance systems of shared educational contexts. In this study we were concerned first with the positive experiences that principals had in relation to school leader-ship and working with governance systems and structures, and second how inter-viewees defined opportunities and challenges to work for equity and renewal within education governance systems. Third, we wished to investigate how school principals understand the role that mentors, and/or advocates play to support their navigation through the governance structures. Finally, we deter-mined to investigate to what extent principals believe that cultural change is required within existing governance systems to sanction them to empower school communities to become societal innovators for equity, peace and renewal and how they would like use governance systems to empower students to be societal innovators for equity and renewal.

In-depth interviews were undertaken with eight school principals in Northern Ireland. Two were from primary schools and six from post-primary schools, and all had experience of working in formal or informal partnership with schools from different sectors to their own and in working across community divides in Northern Ireland. Principals from both rural and urban schools were included, and the main school sectors were represented (controlled, maintained, voluntary grammar and integrated). Schools ranged in size from less than 100 pupils to over 1,300. Half of the schools had 40% or more pupils in receipt of free school meals, which is typically used as an indicator of deprivation. There were four male and four female interviewees, and their experience of being a school princi-pal ranged from one to over 25 years (Table 1).

The interview structure followed the template that was adopted by each of the case studies undertaken as part of the overall project, mapped back to the key research questions and included prompts and probes (see Methodology chapter). In a small number of instances, the wording was slightly altered to

Table 1. Profile of Study Participants.

	Gender	Years as Principal	Primary/Post-primary	School Sector	Rural /Urban	No. of Pupils	% Pupils on FSM
Interviewee A	Female	10+	Primary	Maintained	Rural	<100	60–70
Interviewee B	Male	0–4	Primary	Maintained	Rural	<100	10–20
Interviewee C	Male	5–9	Post-primary	Controlled	Urban	300–400	30–40
Interviewee D	Male	10+	Post-primary	Integrated	Urban	600–700	40–50
Interviewee E	Male	10+	Post-primary	Voluntary Grammar	Urban	900–1000	20–30
Interviewee F	Female	0–4	Post-primary	Maintained	Urban	700–800	40–50
Interviewee G	Female	10+	Post-primary	Maintained	Urban	800–900	50–60
Interviewee H	Female	5–9	Post-primary	Voluntary Grammar	Rural	1300–1400	20–30

Source: Data on schools from 2016–17 Department of Education NI school statistics. https://www.education-ni.gov.uk/publcations/school-enrolments-school-level-data-201617.
Note: FSM, free school meals.

ensure the questions and topics covered were meaningful within a Northern Ireland context.

Each of the eight interviews was fully transcribed, with inter-rating checking, to enable thematic analysis (see methodology chapter).

Findings

Positive Aspects of Being a School Leader

We found that those principals who demonstrated passion in their work and articulated clarity in terms of their vision for building relationships with community were able to handle challenges and minimise any negative impact of turbulence. Having support from the governing body, from colleagues and from the wider school community was highlighted as being critical to having a positive experience of leading a school.

Representative quotes of this position include one from a post-primary principal who commented on the challenge needed to be an effective school leader in terms of trust-building, working alongside the governing body, saying:

> [...] as Principal [...] first of all I need them to trust me [...] they've employed me to run the school and to let me develop a vision that I believe in passionately (Interviewee D).

Another post-primary principal, in a large city school, emphasised the importance of building relationships with the community in terms of her affirmation as a principal. She spoke of the challenges involved in moving site (in which there would be potential for severe turbulence), and that the support of the community continued through that difficult process:

> [...] I enjoyed that support and that rapport we have with the wider community (Interviewee G).

Interviewee A, who is principal of a small rural primary school, emphasised that working in close partnership with her counterpoint in the school she was in a shared education project with, had made her job *less lonely* and *it just makes me feel like I've got some sort of support there as well, you know I'm just not by myself all the time.*

Professional collaboration was identified as a positive aspect of being a school leader by Interviewee B: *the most enjoyable thing within our context here is that sort of professional collaboration with our colleagues in (name of school)].*

Overall, what we found was that the most positive aspects of school leadership concerned positive relationships with others, be that the pupils and school community, the wider community in which the school is located, or relationships with other school principals through shared education and other partnerships. Leadership clearly does not operate in a vacuum. Of course, inter-personal relationships – our relationships with others – also have the potential to create grounds for turbulence. However, as the next section shows, challenges that school principals faced in relation to empowering their school communities and young people tended to be more structural or cultural in nature, although the timing and content of external communications was also cited as causing turbulence. Positive encouragement (of pupils and staff), by sharing knowing and sharing power through distributed leadership for democracy in education and sharing a vision a better future were employed by some of the school principals as ways of optimising opportunities for empowerment in relation to equity, renewal, and peace. Change does not come about when the status quo is maintained and as the next section shows, one of the study participants confessed to overtly creating turbulence in order to equip staff to help facilitate and lead change in their environment. Just as inter-personal relationships featured strongly in positive experiences of school leadership for our participants, relationships with others, as the next section demonstrates, are key to dealing with turbulence.

Challenges and Opportunities School Principals Face in Empowering School Communities to Empower Students to be Agents of Social Change

It is clear that communities in Northern Ireland could benefit from movements towards equity, renewal, and peace, and it would appear that schools are places where students can be empowered to encourage change to happen (Hughes & Loader, 2015). It is equally apparent that empowering school communities can be a challenge for principals and a source of turbulence.

One principal was pursuing a merger with another, to make each school sustainable in terms of numbers. This merger had the additional complexity that one school was predominantly Catholic and the other predominantly Protestant. Parents initially voiced objections:

> [...] (the news) went out too early on the television, so that afternoon [...] I had parents shooting daggers at me because they [...] interpreted the television thing wrongly. They assumed that we were closing and all the children were going to (attend the other school)' [...] but, following a hastily arranged meeting [...], '[...] we managed to convince them that this isn't what we are doing [...] we had practically all our parents came to that open meeting (Interviewee A).

Proactive invitational communication was key to overcoming this potential turbulence, keeping it in the 'mild' domain.

The principal expanded on the rationale for the merger, emphasising that the vision of the merger was aimed at community construction: [...] *when we started this* [...] *you know it wasn't doing it with the plan of becoming a new school, it was just doing it because it was a very divided community, the schools have never been divided so why not try and bring the children together because if it doesn't start there where is it going to start?* (Interviewee A). This indicates a recognition of the potential power of students in effecting social change. It was clear that the principal saw the value of envisioning as a first step to planning, in order to avoid severe turbulence later on the journey to change. This approach is emphasised by Maulding Green and Leonard (2016).

In terms of empowerment towards societal change, Interviewee B described the pupils as his main advocates; they were very open to change; he described telling them that *what you are doing here is ground-breaking.*

A further interview was with a principal who led an integrated school. Due to the nature of the school, sharing across the community is already embedded in the culture. Nonetheless, this principal proffered that societal challenges unique to Northern Ireland were experienced on a regular basis. For example, he described 'mild turbulence' around 'Remembrance Day', when those who died in WW1 are remembered, involving the wearing of red poppies, and which has traditionally been perceived as a Protestant event. Similar turbulence was reported on religious ceremonies such as on Ash Wednesday, in that case an event traditionally associated with Catholics. Regarding Remembrance Day, he said that: *I am encouraging these youngsters to play their part in creating that better world. I've even once or twice apologised on behalf of my generation, that we haven't done a better job. And I have said you guys need to do better than we have done, and then at the end of the assembly we give them choice, would they like to wear a poppy or would they not?* (Interviewee D). He went on to describe the genesis of the issue of Remembrance Day and the wearing of poppies: *our approach to Remembrance was forged out of the difficulty, of a child coming along holding his poppy years ago, and some other guys in the corridor had coloured it in orange and white and green* [the colour of the Irish flag, associated with a Catholic/ Nationalist tradition in Northern Ireland] [...] *and given it back to him. And we learnt then, right; let's address this; we need a strategic approach.*

Another principal articulated his vision to develop leadership potential in the young students in his all-boys faith school, but identified the impediments to success as 'finance' and 'time'. He overcame these sources of turbulence through an optimistic leadership style. He praised the talents of the pupils, describing them as *highly skilled, highly talented,* [with] *huge energy* (Interviewee E), and yet he displayed modesty as he commented that the school is 'only scraping the surface' in what is being done. He described how he had negotiated with external groups for assistance, some of this negotiation resulting in finance for developing leadership training, with parallel leadership development for some of his teaching staff. This, along with his overtly distributed approach to leadership, was empowering to his colleagues.

One strategy that this individual displayed in terms of dealing with turbulence was to proactively create his own turbulence. While this might seem a counterintuitive approach, the outcome was that his colleagues were caught up and taken along by the white-water maelstrom of his making. His leadership style was so empowering and facilitating that, rather than be confused or demotivated, they learned to 'ride the wave'.

The principal was very open about the culture of the faith school as a potential source of turbulence in terms of the development of shared education. He pragmatically commented: *we will be a Catholic school, we will have our traditions, our culture, our history* and, referring to a neighbouring school with a different culture, *'the two of us would agree to respect each other, (ok) we are different but in terms of shared education we will share for the benefit of the youngsters but we respect that we are different'* (Interviewee E). This principal demonstrated a blend of leadership skills and intelligences, exhibiting passion in regard to setting vision and direction, merged with pragmatism when dealing with potential turbulence.

With regard to collaboration, another principal identified severe turbulence as a consequence of operating in a challenging competitive climate where there is a significant demographic downturn. [...] *you are asked to collaborate and work together with schools often when you are competing with them and the reason you're competing with them is because there's fewer pupils and pupils mean money, and money means security in terms of curriculum offer [...] it's mad [...] there's a system that is based on competition that is telling you to collaborate* (Interviewee G). However, this principal also conceded that the school's current collaborative arrangements through the area learning community were extremely beneficial to the school and its constituency as it brought [...] *principals together in a structured way.* It was apparent that her strategy for coping with either source of turbulence was a pragmatic one. She used her skill set and her experience of over ten years to help her to cope.

Interviewee H's strategy for reducing turbulence was evident in her emphasis on the development of the teams around her in terms of their leadership skills and competences. She described her senior leadership team as complementing each other's skills and attributes, describing the use she had made of training agencies. Strong leadership and management intelligences were apparent, particularly in regard to an understanding of what network routines need to be in place to facilitate effective action. There was an implicit appreciation of the importance of effective structures and of coordination of message. The principal demonstrated that she had a robust appreciation of the importance of strategic alignment of her team when she contended that [...] *we would sit down as a leadership team and look at how we are going to drive this or that initiative forward, [...] it's your middle leaders who are on the real frontline and they are leading departments of maybe eight people in a school as big as this [...] so, they're the people that you really need on board* (Interviewee H). This might suggest where the drivers may lie in achieving the empowerment of the school community.

Another principal was open about the severe turbulence he had encountered in taking on his role six years previously. Speaking of his steep learning curve and of the coping mechanisms he had used to address this, he emphasised the strong team ethos he had developed, suggesting that he was 'fortunate' to have people around him with a skill-set complementary to that of him. He spoke of the empowerment which had emerged as part of this team growth and was full of praise for his colleagues, describing them as: *very strategic thinkers in terms of the way forward so I suppose the synergy if you like of combining that all together, that is positive* (Interviewee C).

His school was part of a very successful and well-established area learning community, established before the start of his tenure in post, but clearly nurtured by him. He spoke eloquently about the relationship with his neighbouring school principal, emphasising the need to engender social capital: *I mean you are very much hand in glove with your neighbour [name of other local school] and that has been, that has immense strengths for this school [...] not only from a practical point of view [...] but just the professional development that goes on when two colleagues are working so closely together.*

Just as inter-personal relationships featured strongly in positive experiences of school leadership for our participants, relationships with others, as articulated previously, are key to dealing with turbulence. But how are school principals supported in the work they do? The next section continues the theme of inter-personal professional relationships and focuses on who school leaders draw on for support and mentorship, either at a formal or informal level.

The Engagement of Principals with Mentors and Advocates in the Context of Navigation through Turbulence Experienced through Governance Structures

Successful principals utilised mentors and advocates to build clarity of purpose, and to combat the potential for loneliness of leadership.

One example of this can be seen in a partnership between two rural primary schools. The first principal described working closely with the other principal in the partnership and felt their skills complemented their own. This 'mentor' happened to be younger than Interviewee A:

> He has got a lot of younger ideas than I have [...] I just think it's very good for me from that point of view that I've got somebody else there who's got all, just newer ideas, he's got the technology, stuff like that, that I haven't got. It's not as lonely [...] (Interviewee A)

The final phrase in this alludes to the loneliness of leadership, and implies the necessity for interaction and dialogue with a trusted colleague, in order to construct meaning, and address or avert turbulence in governance. In this example, the mentor was not from the same school as the principal; such distance provides detachment and consequent openness and trust in exchanges.

This was replicated when we interviewed the second principal in the partnership, who acknowledged that he relied closely on the sustained support from the principal of the other school.

> [She] has been a great source of comfort to me [...] she's been a real leader [...] through her time here with all the different principals that have come and gone. (Interviewee B)

Interviewee D singled out the school governors for their support and advocacy, commenting that '[...] *we have strategically and carefully built up our Board of Governors, not only for their expertise but their hearts and that's working well for us'.* He went further to highlight the role of the formally constituted principal support network, specific to the school sector. This body comprises principals from other schools not in the same neighbourhood, so there is no competition between them, and he felt that such an arrangement fosters collaboration:

> [...] it's a much more open network to share and equally to draw strength from each other.

Another principal described close relationships with his governors, including one who is a [...] *designated governor who* [...] *rides shotgun with me and provides support, and I can contact her at any stage'* (Interviewee E). Additionally, this Board of Governors has a former principal of a large school who is '[...] *a real treasure to me as well.* This principal also commented on the range of skills and professional backgrounds among the governors, including a solicitor, a top civil servant and an accountant, each of whom brought their professional expertise to support the principal and the governors in their decision-making.

A principal of a large city school commented on the role of staff, including the senior leadership team, in providing support for her. She also talked about the area learning community and the meetings between principals of schools in that group also provided significant levels of support and mentorship. The role of the wider school community, particularly parents of children attending the school, was also discussed, as well as [...] *civic leaders in society who endorse and support you, [and] send you a little text message 'well done'* (Interviewee G). The use of social media such as Twitter was also seen as a supportive medium. *'We're very active on Twitter and people I haven't really met, we follow each other we watch what we are doing and we can endorse each other, with an affirmative retweet or something like that, that's just people you know, that are they're look-ing in at you'*, she stated (Interviewee G).

The team of people working in the school around the principal were identified as the first line in mentorship and support by another principal. The Board of Governors were also acknowledged as having an important role, and two formal groupings of principals: the area learning community and a national body, were identified as having a role in mentorship.

> in terms of the kind of macro level, it would be the [national body] that I would [use] [...] we meet three or four times a year. What we would be in email contact, every other week [...] from basic things like 'does anybody know a sub for [...]' to the bigger questions 'what are you doing about [...]' or 'I've come across this staff development, it might be of interest to you' so it's a gen-uine sharing group. (Interviewee H)

A principal working alongside another school from a different community background described the mutual mentorship with the neighbouring principal. As these schools were serving different communities, there was arguably no competition between them and this was identified as an important factor allowing that mentorship to establish and flourish. He commented

> I wouldn't think there's many schools whereby you have a neighbouring Post Primary school with a Principal that you can openly talk to without any hesitation or fear because we're not competitive [...] we are truly collaborative [...] there is a mentoring role comes in there which is been very, very good. (Interviewee C)

This principal also highlighted the contribution from an experienced Board of Governors and from faith leaders in the community who were identified as *'pastorally very supportive and they get the pressure you are under and [...] you know you just need to off-load to somebody and that's it [...] it's almost like a counselling type thing but I mean it's your job and you are just going to have to do it'.* (Interviewee C)

In summary, the school principals in our study were able to draw on a range of sources, internal and external to the school, for support. We also asked them about how they would like to be supported going forward in their work to effect change and empower young people.

How Principals Would Like to be Supported and Empowered in Order to Effect Change and Empower Young People

Most of the school principals mentioned the importance of having support from colleagues within the school and from their Board of Governors in relation to their role and the role of the school in empowering their young people to be drivers for social change in Northern Ireland. One principal also mentioned the need for middle leadership training, as this would help develop better support structures within the school as well as helping develop relationships with others in school leadership roles across Northern Ireland, which would also extend the support network. Another school principal referred to being able to discuss ideas with and have the support of local religious leaders and that this was invaluable in terms of support for empowering young people.

However, interviewees also emphasised that, with shrinking school budgets, it was becoming increasingly unrealistic to do all the work they would like to do. Considering that they believe that it is important to support and empower young people to become societal innovators for social change, they were frustrated by this. For example: *'our biggest enemy now is the shrinking budget, I just don't have the resources I need'.* (Interviewee D)

One interviewee emphasised that an inner resilience was needed, particularly in a context of limited resources, and she used the VUCA Prime[7] model (which she had learned about at a recent seminar) to illustrate this:

---

[7]https://iduniversity.wordpress.com/2009/11/05/futurist-bob-johansen-leadership-vuca-world/

instead of volatility you need vision, and instead of uncertainty you need understanding, instead of complexity you need clarity, and instead of ambiguity you need agility. In other words, as an organisation we must develop our own strength, our ability to fulfil our own vision, to be very clear on what it is we trying to achieve because we have limited resources. (Interviewee D)

In the context of the Northern Ireland interviews, one way forward to create an empowering environment that was highlighted by several school principals (who were advocates for shared education programmes) was through the continuation and strengthening of shared education which can allow individual schools to maintain their own religious ethos while enabling pupils from different backgrounds more opportunities to learn together and to access a broader curriculum. In relation to shared education, one of the school principals emphasised the need to avoid having too rigid a structure and a 'one-size-fits-all' approach as there would be variation in terms of best approaches to shared education across Northern Ireland depending on the locality and particular local contexts.

The need for structural change was also identified, for example:

I just think we need a different language, to be more inclusive, to be more respectful and it is about equity and it is about equity in terms of recognising the progress that our children have made, recognising stages of progression and recognising progression rather than recognising these landmark ages, when we expect them all to have got this standard. (Interviewee G)

Discussion and Conclusion

It is clear that the principals themselves felt empowered by those around them as inter-personal relationships tended to dominate discussions around the positive aspects of being a school leader. Trust as a foundation for strong, positive relationships was a keystone. Establishing trust in a post-conflict society can be challenging. As Tschannen-Moran and Gareis (2015) recognise 'trust becomes salient when people enter into relationships of interdependence, where the outcomes one desires cannot be met without the involvement and contribution of others'.

Different examples of turbulence were articulated which ranged from light turbulence, for example, resulting from a poorly managed media announcement which caused a disturbance within the school community – what kept this within the mild domain was how the school principal managed and responded to it by immediately opening up communication directly with the school community, to more severe turbulence caused by austerity and a lack of adequate resources. Strong relationships, resilience and collaboration were viewed as ways out of turbulence. However, the issue of collaboration, which is at the heart of shared education, is a complex one. As one of the interviewees explicitly acknowledged, a school may well be in competition with other neighbouring small schools for pupil enrolment, yet through shared education are expected to work together. In addition to collaboration through shared education, other networks which proved fruitful for participants included a school leader/principal network within their school sector, and relationships developed through the area learning community.

The role and support of mentors and advocates was clearly important for the principals and also helped equip them to deal with turbulence. Gross (2014) emphasises the value of strong relationships with or between mentors and this was found to be the case in our study. Relationships varied in terms of the formality of the relationship and principals would appear to value both formal and informal mentor relationships as part of their wider support network.

We found that those principals who demonstrated passion in their work and articulated clarity in terms of their vision for building relationships with community were able to handle the challenges and minimise any potential negative impact of significant turbulence. Successful principals relied heavily on mentors and advocates sensitively to build clarity of purpose and to combat the potential for loneliness of leadership. The interviews demonstrated that those principals who acted openly, intentionally and invitingly in their communication with communities and students were most successful in addressing possible sources of turbulence and consequently in empowering these groups for equity and renewal. Building support from colleagues within the school, from their school governors and from the wider school community was empowering for the principals, staff and pupils and a requisite for empowering their young people to be drivers for social change. Leadership training was also regarded as helping to develop better support structures within the school as well as helping to foster relationships with others in school leadership roles across Northern Ireland, extending the support network.

Shapiro and Gross (2013) contend that the underlying dynamics of turbulence may be described as positionality, cascading and stability. Positionality challenges us to use a multi-dimensional approach to the relative situation of individuals in the organisation, keeping in mind that different players will experience turbulence differently. A further study would ask where the different groupings are and, depending on their perception, how they might be affected by examples of turbulence and how this perception is affected by their position in the organisation. Cascading describes the cumulative impact of turbulent forces, and uses the metaphor of a white-water rafting experience, as individuals are buffeted by one incident after another producing a cumulative pummelling effect. School principals in Northern Ireland experience such pummelling as their lived experience involves innovations, inspections and financial stringency. Such cascading was evident in the responses of the school principals interviewed. Stability, the third dynamic, was evident in the responses of those principals who knew their context well, and who used a pragmatic approach to address turbulence in whatever form it presented. They had an assurance in their long history of addressing the aspirations of their staff, the pupils, their parents and the community, and this assurance gave them the stability they needed to succeed on a daily basis.

Turbulence theory provides a useful lens through which to examine the experiences of school leaders working in divided societies or communities. Focusing on how turbulence can best be managed is vital for enabling school leaders to be empowered so that they in turn can empower their staff and young people in their communities to be innovators in their communities and help build a society based on equity where they are key agents of change. In the Northern Ireland context, turbulence theory must be considered as part of the current discourse in education that assumes the majority of children will continue to be educated in separate schools for the foreseeable future in a context, at least at present, where the political will to integrate schools has until now been largely absent (although this may change with the publication of the Department of Education report *Integration Works. Transforming Your School*, in December 2017).

In terms of 'shared' education, Northern Ireland has many years' experience of cross-community contact and movement of pupils between schools but in recent years the Department of Education has reduced its financial commitment to these activities. Whilst current initiatives on shared education are supported by more than £25 million (with funding from philanthropy, the Office of the First Minister and Deputy First Minister (OFMDFM) and the Department of Education), extending arrangements to the whole system would cost significantly more. Thus, there is a challenge to sustain sharing policies – including empowering principals – once current sources of funding disappear.

In this chapter, we have focused on Northern Ireland, a society which is emerging from over thirty years of conflict (in terms of recent history), and where inter-community tensions can remain high. Education systems have the potential to help develop a more stable society. School leaders, and how they engage with governance systems, are in a pivotal position to drive positive change. This chapter has shown the challenges, opportunities and supports needed for this to happen.

References

Allen, A., & Mintrom, M. (2010). Responsibility and school governance. *Educational Policy, 24*(3), 439–464.

Balarin, M., Brammer, S., James, C., & McCormack, M. (2008). *The School Governance Study*. London: Business in the Community.

Bates, J., O'Connor Bones, U., & Milliken, M. (2017). *Community audit: Views on education provision in Augher, Clogher and Fivemiletown, Co Tyrone*. Belfast: Integrated Education Fund.

Blase, J. (1997). *The fire is back!: Principals sharing school governance*. Corwin Pr.

Commission for Victims and Survivors. (2016). *Children and young people engagement project. Research Report March 2016*. Retrieved from https://www.cvsni.org/media/1617/cvs-cyp-final-report-26-april-2016.pdf

Creese, M., & Earley, P. (2005). *Improving schools and governing bodies: Making a difference*. London: Routledge.

Deloitte. (2007). *Research into the financial cost of the Northern Ireland divide.* Belfast: Deloitte.

Department of Education, NI. (2016). *Shared Education.* Retrieved from https://www.education-ni.gov.uk/articles/what-shared-education

Department of Education, NI. (2017). *Governor Guide 2017.* Retrieved from https://www.education-ni.gov.uk/publications/guide-governor-roles-and-responsibilities

Education and Training Inspectorate. (2015). *Together Towards Improvement: A Process For Self-Evaluation.* Retrieved from http://www.etini.gov.uk/together-towards-improvement/together-towards-improvement-post-primary.pdf.

Gross, S. J. (1998). *Staying Centred: Curriculum leadership in a turbulent era.* Alexandria, VA: Association for Supervision and Curriculum Development.

Gross, S. J. (2014). Using turbulence theory to guide actions. In Branson & Gross (Eds.), *Handbook of Ethical Educational Leadership* (pp. 246–262). New York and London: Routledge.

Gross, S. J. (2016). *Using turbulence theory as a metaphor in a volatile world.* Retrieved from http://marylandpublicschools.org/about/Documents/Promising-Principals/Resources/102016/2015TTonlytoMd.pdf

Harland, K., & McCready, S. (2012). *Taking boys seriously: A longitudinal study of adolescent male school-life experiences in Northern Ireland.* Bangor: Department of Education.

Harrison, J. A. (1998). School governance: is the clash between teachers and principals inevitable? *Journal of Educational Administration, 36*(1), 59–82.

Hughes, J., & Loader, R. (2015). Plugging the gap': shared education and the promotion of community relations through schools in Northern Ireland. *British Education Research Journal, 41*(6), 1142–1155.

Kezar, A. (2000). Pluralistic leadership: Incorporating diverse voices. *Journal of Higher Education, 71*(6), 722–743.

Lewis, S. G., & Naidoo, J. (2004). Whose theory of participation? School Governance policy and practice in South Africa. *Current Issues in Comparative Education, 6*(2), 100–112.

MacInnes, T., Aldridge, H., Parekh, A., & Kenway, P. (2012). *Monitoring poverty and social exclusion in Northern Ireland.* York: Joseph Rowntree Foundation.

Maulding Green, W., & Leonard, E. (2016). *Leadership Intelligence: Navigating to Your True North.* London: Rowman & Littlefield.

McGuinness, S. J. (2012). Education policy in Northern Ireland: A review. *Italian Journal of Sociology, 1*(1), 224.

National Governors' Association Manifesto. (2014). National Governors' association manifesto. Retrieved from https://www.nga.org.uk/getattachment/About-Us/NGA-manifesto_FINAL.pdf

Niens, U., O'Connor, U., & Smith, A. (2013). Citizenship education in divided societies: teachers' perspectives in Northern Ireland. *Citizenship Studies, 17*(1), 128–141.

Nolan, P. (2013). *The Northern Ireland peace monitoring report, Number Two.* Belfast: Community Relations Council.

Northern Ireland Executive. (2016).*Draft programme for government framework (2016–2021).* Belfast: NIE.

O'Connor, U., Beattie, K., & Niens, U. (2009). *An evaluation of the introduction of Local and Global Citizenship to the Northern Ireland Curriculum.* Belfast: CCEA.

OFMDFM, N. I.. (2009). *Strategy for victims and survivors.* Retrieved from https://www.executiveoffice-ni.gov.uk/sites/default/files/publications/ofmdfm_dev/strategy-for-victims-and-survivors-november-2009.pdf

Oliver, J. (1994). *Aspects of Ulster.* Antrim: Greystone Books Ltd.

Perry, C. (2011). *School Governors.* Research and Information Service Research Paper. Belfast: Northern Ireland Assembly.

Purvis, D. (2011). *Educational disadvantage and the protestant working class. A call to action.* Belfast: Dawn Purvis.

Roulston, S., Hansson, U., Cook, S., & McKenzie, P. (2016). If you are not one of them you feel out of place: Understanding divisions in a Northern Irish town. *Children's Geographies, 15*(4), 452–465.

Shapiro, J. P., & Gross, S. J. (2013). *Ethical educational leadership in turbulent times: (Re)Solving moral dilemmas* (2nd ed.). New York, NY: Routledge.

Taysum, A. (2012). A critical historiographical analysis of England's educational policies from 1944 to 2011. *Italian Journal of Sociology of Education, 4*(1), 54–87.

Tschannen-Moran, M., & Gareis, C. R. (2015). Principals, trust, and cultivating vibrant schools. *Societies, 5*(2), 256–276.

Tutu, D. (2004). *God has a dream. A vision of hope for our time.* New York, NY: Random House.

Wardlow, M. (2003). *In support of integrated education.* Belfast: Northern Ireland Council for Integrated Education.

Worden, E. A., & Smith, A. (2017). Teaching for democracy in the absence of transitional justice: The case of Northern Ireland. *Comparative Education, 53*(3), 379–395.

Chapter 7

Supervisors in the Arab Education System: Between Governability, Duality and Empowerment, through a State of Turbulence

Khalid Arar and Asmahan Masry-Herzallah

Abstract

The research aimed to clarify how supervisors in the Arab education system act to close the achievement gaps and to introduce learning programs that can empower students and improve their achievements. Qualitative research employed in-depth interviews with supervisors in the Arab education system, which constitutes a substantial element of the schools' governance. The research attempted to answer the following questions: (1) Which steps do education administrators in the Arab education system take to reduce students' underachievement, widen circles of cooperation and empower change agents during crises that deepen achievement gaps between Arab and Jewish students? (2) Do Arab school supervisors understand their interplay with government policies as empowering or disempowering them to improve students' achievements and ensure the curriculum's cultural relevance? (3) To what extent do the supervisors believe that cultural change is required to enable them to empower school communities to become societal innovators for equity, peace and renewal within existing administrative structures?

Research findings were interpreted through the lens of Turbulence Theory (Gross, 2014). Findings indicated that the supervisors strive to improve students' achievements. A major challenge is to ensure the relevance of learning programs to the school community, while mediating between local community demands and the technocratic accountability imposed by the Ministry of Education for the implementation of its policies. This leadership is isolated in its efforts to establish fairness and education for

Turbulence, Empowerment and Marginalisation in International
Education Governance Systems, 159–184
Copyright © 2019 by Emerald Publishing Limited
All rights of reproduction in any form reserved
doi:10.1108/978-1-78754-675-220181009

empowerment and coexistence in a divided society. Implications and directions for future research are discussed.

Keywords: Equity; peace; achievement gap; supervisors; Arab schools

Introduction

The growing sense of crisis that accompanies those working in education systems stems from tension between modern characteristics of the education system and the continuously rapidly changing reality of the post-modern world. In this context, the global spread of educational research and theory in more developed economies has had a tremendous impact on what is taught and tested in less developed countries and on the organisational forms of schooling (Arnova, Torres, & Franz, 2013; Waite, Rodríguez, & Wadende, 2015)

Yet in all countries, public education is a unique arena with a particular structure and characteristic processes. This arena is restricting and perhaps even prevents the attribution of professional responsibility in a simple manner to individuals, allowing those who wish to avoid responsibility to do just that (Moloi, Gravett, & Petersen, 2009).

Furthermore, school superintendents play a key role in mobilising school performance, especially when dealing with centralisation and accountability systems (Early et al., 2016). Schools and governing bodies are operating in constantly changing and challenging environments (Wait et al., 2015). Nevertheless, this macro-lens helps us to penetratingly examine the controversial role of the Arab education system, which serves a controlled native minority (Arar & Abu-Asbah, 2013; Jabareen & Agbaria, 2014). Further, a number of major challenges including the Arab education system's structural subordination to the Jewish state education system which determines the contents of its learning programs (Author & Other, 2013) can be addressed including continuous demands of 'loyalty' in exchange for government financial support (Abu-Saad, 2006; Author, 2012). The Arab education system also faces the challenge of inferior educational achievements reflecting a concentration of disadvantages due largely to the low socio-economic status of Arab society in comparison to Jewish society.

The difference between the two systems, Jewish and Arab, and the volatile environment in which the Arab education system exists leads us to adopt Turbulence Theory to better understand how those attempting to lead Arab education can overcome this constrictive reality. We use this theory to better understand how they can nevertheless initiate and sustain deep democratic reform in such a turbulent era, steering the Arab education system to greater success.

Gross (2014) attempted to measure the emotional climate of schools by likening it to different levels of turbulence experienced when flying an airplane ranging from light, through moderate and severe to extreme. For example, a light level of turbulence would occur when students had varied socio-economic statuses in the school; a moderate level would be produced when the school was required to assimilate reform and a severe or extreme level of turbulence would occur if parents vociferously opposed a particular learning programme. In these situations, the school would face a serious challenge, having to maintain control in order to avoid chaos (Harvey, Cambron-McCabe, Cunningham, & Koff, 2013). The level of turbulence is assessed in line with the stakeholders' positionality with regard to proposed changes, and the consequent cascading flow of change in the organisation. In other words, the reactions of stakeholders to the school's attempts to introduce change can increase the turbulence or the direction of its flow and eventually the extent to which the organisation manages to re-establish equilibrium or is halted in its tracks (Gross, 2004). Thus, a state of turbulence necessitates the leadership's intervention to ensure the continuation of smooth running of the organisation's daily life, functioning and outputs (Gross, 2014; Harvey et al., 2013).

This study aims to investigate a particular state of turbulence in the Arab education system in Israel. Despite the many studies that have discussed the deficiencies of the Arab education system in Israel, there has been little consideration of the challenges facing the leaders of this system when they attempt to cope with gaps in achievements between Arab and Jewish education and between the different schools of the Arab education system. This chapter aims to identify Arab supervisors' perceptions of the role they play to reduce gaps in achievements between Jewish and Arab students in national and international exams by adapting school-learning programs with the participation of various actors to advance the Arab education system, often with significant success. These attempts involve finding solutions to cope with the competing interests within the education system

To clarify the supervisors' perceptions of the role that they play in the Arab schools to reduce gaps between the Arab education system and the Jewish education system, we employed semi-structured in-depth interviews with the Arab supervisors, all of whom can potentially alter the appearance of the education system. More specifically, we posed the following research questions: (1) How do Arab supervisors understand their role as agents of change to improve pupils' achievements in the state of turbulence created by conflicting expectations of the Ministry of Education and the Arab community? (2) To what extent do the supervisors believe that they are capable of engendering a deep cultural change in order to improve students' achievements and empower school communities for social equity and renewal within existing administrative structures? (3) What steps do Arab supervisors take to reduce underachievement in the Arab education system and empower the students?

Theoretical Framework

Understanding the Challenges Facing Minority Education through the Lens of Turbulence Theory

In the attempt to build a conceptual framework to understand the forces acting on a complex social system during attempts to introduce change, Gross (2014) suggested that the Turbulence Theory (Gross, 2014) is a metaphor to describe upheaval and turbulence in educational organisations. It defines how and why organisational conditions become volatile and frames the world of educational innovation. Change always brings with it opposition, and dominant groups may only accept local-level proposed change (Ruşitoru, 2017) by marginalised groups if the change does not undermine the government dictated education programs and create oppositional education (Ball, 2007).

Gross tried to understand educational innovation and change through four key questions:

(1) How might the levels of disturbance facing innovating schools be described so that different degrees of challenge could be compared?
(2) How might the emotional strength of that disturbance be more thoroughly understood?
(3) How might the school look at its own disturbance in a measured way so that reasoned action could be more likely?
(4) Might there be a positive aspect to the disturbances facing schools that decide to innovate, or was turbulence always a detrimental force to be avoided or at least diminished?

Flight turbulence is generally described by four levels, which the theory applies to instability in educational organisations: *Light*: little or no movement of the craft, translated into current matters, little or no interruption to regular work, and minor signs of stress. *Moderate*: noticeable waves, translated into widespread awareness of the issue and specific sources. *Severe*: strong gusts that threaten control of the craft, translated into fear for the organisation, widespread community protests and a sense of crisis. *Extreme*: forces so great that control is lost and structural damage to the craft occurs, is translated into structural damage to the very functioning of the organisation.

Light or moderate levels of turbulence allow for observation, data gathering, and analysis, as a means of working through the problems, whereas severe or extreme turbulence extends no such opportunity, since the need for a speedy, well-considered response is crucial.

Another dimension that is able to strengthen or to remove the levels of turbulent flow, is 'stability'. A school with high levels of turbulence experiences reduced levels of academic achievements and an inability to retain the good reputation that previously characterised the school as a school striving for high achievements and realising this goal. A strong leader can regain stability if s/he ensures that the school succeeds in standing against this flow, so that after the performance of various programs it regains its old reputation. Thus, there are three main characteristics of stability: (1) relativity – meaning that the stability of the organisation is measured relative to a similar situation in another place, (2) stability which can be sustained through demanding external influences on education that bring changes, including shifts in ideologies and (3) ability to open a path for dynamic forces to act within the organisation. When these three forces are joined together they can influence the school organisation in either a positive or a negative manner, while they wait for the end of the turbulence. In this context, it should be noted that in distinction from Chaos Theory, Turbulence Theory constitutes a metaphor which is used in order to assist us to understand life in a far clearer manner, both at the micro-level and also at the organisational macro-level (Gross, 2014).

Turbulence Theory helps us to gain a more correct perspective concerning the movements that occur in school organisations, to see the potential benefits of the turbulence that hits the school and to maintain an appropriate level of necessary flexibility. The complex challenges of Arab minority education engen- der ethical dilemmas for the leaders of the Arab education system and the search for solutions for these dilemmas constitutes a difficult part of the school experi- ence. Challenges emerge as a result of an inbuilt tension between the entities that represent the same education system (Boyd, 2003). We therefore deemed it relevant to use the lens of Turbulence Theory to try to interpret and understand the strategies employed by Arab supervisors to cope with the challenges pre- sented when they attempt to transform moral purpose into moral action. Observation of the reality in the Arab education system reveals that this system is required to respond to conflicting expectations of different bodies and stake- holders, whose goals sometimes harmonise and sometimes clash.

Educational Leaders' Potential to Overcome the Shortfalls of the Arab Education System in Israel

The Context

The Arab minority in Israel constitutes approximately 20% of the state's popula- tion (Central Bureau of Statistics, 2016). Arab communities mainly live in differ- ent geographical areas separate from Jewish communities. In education, this is expressed by the existence of two separate education systems (Oplatka & Arar, 2016). Although the two communities live separately, this has not led to greater autonomy for Arab institutions, except for Arab local governments and religious bodies, although even this autonomy is limited.

With the establishment of the State of Israel in 1948, the Arab population lost the autonomy that it had enjoyed during the days of the British Mandate. The new state established a unified centralised controls over the state education system, neu- tralising the influence of the Arab minority over its children's education so that the Arab education system became a subsidiary state education system (Oplatka & Arar, 2016). The Ministry of Education set up a separate 'Department of Arab Education'. This department, subordinate to ministry regulations, has no auton- omy, apart from the technical adaptation of learning contents for the Arab system to the contents applied throughout the education system (Saban, 2002). Lack of an independent educational administration for the Arab population means a lack of real influence over the learning contents in Arab schools.

Structurally, the Israeli state education system to which the Arab education system is subordinated is divided into five geographical regions: Jerusalem, Southern Israel, Central Israel, Haifa and Northern Israel (Author, 2012). Each regional office is governed by a regional manager responsible for a staff of supervisors; Jewish supervisors serving the Jewish education system and Arab supervisors serving the Arab education system. Although the two education systems operate separately, as noted the Arab education system is subordinated to the Jewish education system. In the upper strata of the education system hierarchy, senior Jewish administrators man the Ministry of Education hierarchy descending from the ministry's Director General, through the deputy Director General and so on, to the person appointed as supervisor of Arab, Druze and Bedouin Education, a role that is in the main merely a symbolic and representative role (Author & Other, 2013). The ministry defines the school supervisor as the link between the Ministry of Education and the field.

Public school education in Israel is segregated, with three separate sectors for religious and secular Jewish children and for Arab children. Each sector includes both state and non-state schools, Jewish children study in Hebrew, and Arab children study in Arabic (Gibton, 2011). The Jewish state education system serves 73.9% of the whole Israeli education system, which is divided into the state secular system (45.1%) and the religious education system (28.8%). The Arab state education system serves 26.1% of the children in Israel (Central Bureau of Statistics, 2015). This latter system is almost entirely state-funded and supervised. It is subject to government control of educational contents, resources and organisational structure. Apart from government control and supervision of learning contents, the Arab education system endures discrimination in the allocation of budgets in comparison to the Jewish education system (Balas, 2015; Bleikopf, 2014).

The disparity in inputs for the Arab education system described previously is associated with inferior student achievements, especially in entry exams for the universities (dependent on eligibility for matriculation certificate and psychometric tests). In the academic year 2014, 41.7% of Arab high school students were eligible for a matriculation certificate in comparison to 52.1% of Jewish high school students (Central Bureau of Statistics, 2016). Yet another gap was found between the lower achievements of Arab speakers in comparison to the higher achievements of Hebrew speakers in psychometric test results. According to data from the Central Bureau of Statistics, in 2014, there was a mean gap of 96 points (476 points in comparison to 570 points) in psychometric test to the disadvantage of Arab students which limits Arab students' ability to acquire higher education (Oplatka & Arar, 2016).

In the Arab education school system, principals act under the constrictions of a reality full of contradictions. Observation of the reality in this education system reveals that this system is required to respond to conflicting expectations of different bodies and stakeholders, whose goals sometimes harmonise and sometimes clash. On the one hand, they are strictly regulated by the government's supervisors while, on the other hand, they are under pressure from local Arab governments with their own socio-cultural considerations and demands. In practice, 'hamulla' (extended families) politics in local governments strongly influence the patterns of the principal's functioning in Arab schools. Arar and Masry (2016, p. 23) state: 'The influence of strong 'hamullas' (extended families) often dictate appointments to school staffs and may prevent teacher dismissal irrespective of professional considerations'. This background also influences the patterns of parents' involvement in the schools, which is generally characterised by their

complaints about the school's lack of transparency and very little parent participation (Arar, Shapira, Azaize, & Herz-Lazarowitz, 2013).

This complex of challenges also engenders ethical dilemmas for the leaders of
the Arab education system and the search for solutions for these dilemmas constitutes a difficult part of the school experience. As these Supervisors seek to reconcile conflict Turbulence Theory as proposed by Gross (2014) is used here to
try to interpret this volatile situation and to understand the strategies employed
by the Arab supervisors to cope with this situation and transform moral purpose
into moral action.

The Supervisor's Role in Promoting a Discourse of Inclusion

The role of the supervisor is highly complex especially as already noted, the
supervisor is required to cope with contradicting demands of the different stakeholders in education, to do 'more' and 'better' (Maxfield, Shapiro, Gupta, &
Hass, 2010). The complex expectations from supervisors grow in parallel to their
own desire to react and function excellently in complex and often stormy environments (Lewis, Rice, & Rice, 2011). As part of the supervisors' duties they
need to understand and react appropriately to the demands from the field; they
are responsible for the identification and understanding of the challenges and
future opportunities that stem from the different government-imposed reforms
and they are also the leaders responsible for constant development of learning
streams, and foster learning and leadership in others.

Current research emphasises that regional leadership — especially that of the
supervisors — has the potential to influence the quality of teaching and learning
in the schools. This influence relies on two essential foundations: the supervisor
is a pedagogic leader focusing on improvement of teaching-learning processes
and, second, the supervisor is a systemic leader, who sees the schools under their
area of jurisdiction as a productive professional network working in cooperation
(Avney Rasha, 2010). As part of the supervisor's role, he/she acts to create work
and learning environments for principals and to develop the school according to
defined standards; pooling the resources of the schools in their area of jurisdiction and analysing the application of resources to develop essential learning
opportunities in the schools and bring all students up to the required achievements. They conduct supervisory and follow-up visits to check the schools' compliance with regulations, and guide schools to ensure the quality of students'
achievements. Furthermore, they put in place and operate shared work processes
between the schools' local governments and ensure that all students have opportunities to attain the required achievements (Ministry of Education, 2017).

The regional supervisor is a unique point of contact and there is no replace-
ment for this role that mediates between the headquarters office and the field.
The supervisor translates general policies of the Ministry of Education for the
particular needs of the different school, and this is especially important because
of the diversity and range of cultures in Israeli society. To do this, the supervisor
decodes and analyses unique local trends and uses this information to create a
comprehensive picture of the situation for their superiors that can help them to

understand the genuine status of the field in order to improve/sustain its policies and modify them as necessary. Thus the supervisor's work fulfils two roles, derived from two main types of interaction between supervisors and school principals as set out in the Government Education Regulations (Superintendence Orders) Clause 15: Functions of the General Supervisor (Nevo, 2014).

(1) Inspection – supervision and measurement. In other words, a largely regulatory role opposite the school principal, that in turn shapes the relations between the principals and their subordinates (Ofsted, 2012).
(2) Supervision – guidance and instruction, counselling and feedback concerning the school processes. This is a role constructed on and relying on trust and shapes the partnership with school principals (Fergusson, 1998).

A state of structured tension exists between these two different functions. As a result of the onerous burden imposed on the supervisors by their many functions, they naturally tend towards their regulatory role that involves supervision and control over the school, serving as a channel to pass down instructions from 'above' to the schools and delivering reports to their superiors on the extent of compliance with the stipulated goals. In parallel, the supervisors' ability to serve as a guide and partner for the school principals is weakened. They are seen more and more as external, threatening figures, who focus on outputs and results but are apathetic to the daily difficulties with which the schools have to cope. Figure 1 illustrates the role of the supervisor, a role that embodies ambivalence and the need to cope with contradictory expectations.

The concept of 'observational education' underpins the model shown in Figure 1. 'Observational education' is derived from the field of philosophy and connects with Plato's (1975) in the 'Allegory of the Cave'. One of the main ideas expressed in the allegory is that the philosopher or the person who undertakes the responsibility of teaching others must be able to observe and see things that seem to contradict what is seen as real and accepted in the socio-cultural context in which he/she acts. Figure 1 illustrates the perception in which the supervisor's role is defined and constructed as just such a professional. At the core of this perception lie the supervisor's skills for observational education. The supervisor forms the overall evaluation of the situation through observation and collection of data in different ways and through fruitful dialogue with the principal and the school staff with attentiveness, and empathy to resolve conflict and lead change and to assure good communication at all levels sustain threshold standards are met. All this helps the supervisor to shape and consolidate policies, to identify and expose conflicts and obstacles delaying change and to push it forward under the shared leadership of the principal and the supervisor towards the achievement of new goals.

Given the above-described constraints, this research aimed to examine perceptions of the supervisors who have succeeded in rising to superior positions within an education system that produces inferior achievements for Arab students. In this position, they are able to lead comprehensive scholastic changes to

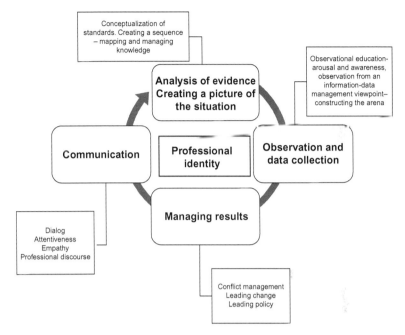

Figure 1. The Supervisor's Role.

enhance Arab students' achievements, yet as noted they face the challenges of serious turbulence within the Arab education system and complex expectations of different stakeholders in this system.

Methodology and Methods

The research aimed to clarify the perceptions of Arab supervisors who act to improve the achievements of the students in schools that they supervise, while collectively empowering the Arab education system in Israel.

Qualitative methodology was deemed appropriate for this research, since it can provide a detailed understanding of perceptions, meaning and intentions of administrative stakeholders (Cohen, Manion, & Morrison, 2011). The research tool was an in-depth semi-structured interview (Yin, 2009) conducted with seven Arab supervisors, people who can potentially alter the appearance of the Arab education system.

Each interviewee received an explanation of the objective of the study and was assured anonymity, and confidentiality, and consensual participation; they were able to terminate the interview if they chose to and withdraw from the research until point of publication. Interview questions included open questions, for example: 'How do you close the achievement gap between the Arab and Jewish education systems is'; probes aimed at clarifying the interviewee's descriptions such as 'Can you expand slightly on the steps you make in order to reduce the achievement gap'; and prompts that sought clarification such as 'If I have understood you correctly, in your view, the aim of Arab education policy is [...], is that correct?'.

All interviews were conducted in Arabic by two M.A students; each interview lasted between 90 minutes and two hours. All interviews were recorded with the interviewee's consent and transcribed. Table 1 describes the characteristics of the interviewees.

A detailed table was prepared that carefully documented the pseudonyms of the participants with their function, their age, their gender, their highest education qualification and their years of service. However, it was decided that confidentiality could not be assured with such a table. Thus, the pseudonyms we use for the purpose of the research are as follows: Karam, Besan, Muhammed Azal, Rafea, Aya and Ahmed with as close to a 50–50 gender split as is possible with a group of seven. The Arab supervisors' average age was 51 years with a range of 45–56, and their average length of time in their role was 11 years with a range of 6–18.

Data Analysis

Data were collected by January 2016 and since the collected data consisted of recorded interview transcripts, including varied responses to open questions, it was subjected to content analysis, organising the data according to themes and categories (Creswell, 2009). Inferences were drawn concerning the characteristics and meanings of the data. Interpretation followed the conceptualisation of Turbulence Theory using flight metaphors to describe the following levels of turbulence in schools: light, moderate, severe or extreme turbulence.

The interview transcripts underwent the four stages of content analysis suggested by Marshall and Rossman (2012): 'organisation of findings', 'construction of categories and themes, and associations between themes', 'examination of emergent hypotheses' and a search for 'different meanings of the themes'. The findings were organised and encoded through comparative analysis including comparison within categories, between their component themes and between the different categories as expressed in the interviewees' words. A comparison between all findings was conducted by the author in discussion with the interviewer, revealing insights and attributing meaning to the findings. This cross-checking of interpretations was employed to reinforce the reliability and internal validity of the findings, and eventually led to the formation of a set of inter-related categories (Marshall & Rossman, 2012). In order to articulate and highlight the major themes, representative voices and quotes that most accurately represent the themes are reported as follows in the description of the findings, providing fictive names to ensure the interviewees' anonymity. As the study is based on a small sample from a specific group of education system administrators, the reader should be aware of the limitations of the findings when deciding on the relevance of the findings and conclusions for other education systems.

Findings

Analysis of the findings revealed that the supervisor's role is considered by the supervisors and by many scholars (Nevo, 2014) as one of the most challenging roles in the education system, facing turbulence in their daily work life, which can become extreme when challenged by a reality of competing interests. The supervisors constitute a unique link in the chain of command between the headquarters office and the field staff. They work in coordination with many bodies such as the Ministry of Education, local government and other stakeholders in the education system in reality full of competing interests and extreme turbulence. Against this background, four categories emerged from the analysis of the findings:

Assimilation of a 'Foreign' Policy in the Arab Education System

The interviews revealed that the imposition of Ministry of Education policies on the Arab education system creates complex relations between the ministry and those who work in the field, and there is a feeling that there is a lack of transparency in these policies. Although the Arab education system is dependent on the Jewish system, there is a complete separation between the two systems, except for senior-level cooperation and discussion between Arab and Jewish supervisors (though some teachers and principals study together in the same teacher-training colleges, there are also separate Arab colleges). There is no shared pedagogic work between the schools in Arab communities and those in Jewish communities, while, on the other hand, they are both required to implement the same policies, the same programs that the Ministry of Education plans for the education system as a whole in Israel this creates a reality for the Arab supervisors which involves constant stress and turbulence. There is no separate Arab education system administrator in the Ministry of Education and no Arab administrator participates in the creation of the ministry's education programs (Author, 2012). This was explained by the supervisor Ahmed:

> As supervisors we are asked to implement programs and projects although we do not participate in the determination of their substance or have a say in the extent to which they are appropriate for the Arab education system. The system for which we are responsible suffers from deficient achievements. The learning programs are foreign, teachers' training takes place mainly in Jewish training colleges. Despite the complexity and particular differences of our education system, we are expected to implement uniform government policies in an optimal manner.

The supervisor Aya explained that she faced conflicting expectations as a supervisor:

> As a supervisor I am in the middle: I am the representative of the Ministry of Education opposite the Arab education system, I am

appointed to advance the ministry's policies in the field, in the
Arab education system with its unique features, cultural differences, and differences in human capital, structures, programs etc.

The respondents all agreed that there is a hiatus between the policies of the
Ministry of Education and their implementation in the Arab education system.
The supervisors saw their role as those responsible for supporting and advancing
the Arab education system, acting as agents for change and implementing the
ministry's policies in the field. Nevertheless, they found it difficult to perform
this role because of the gap between the ministry's demands and the reality in
the Arab education system, a situation which increases tension between different
stakeholders and engenders clashes which may often be − light turbulence and
overt confrontation − extreme turbulence. They stand at the crossroads between
the demands of the ministry that conflict with what they clearly see as the true
needs of their community, as explained by the supervisor Rafea:

> As part of its package of plans, the Ministry of Education
> declared its goals and aims for the year. To my regret, some of
> the matters that the ministry requires cannot possibly be imple-
> mented in the Arab education system, such as the incompatibility
> between the demands for professional development in compari-
> son to the profile of teachers in the Arab education system, the
> principals are unable to persuade the teachers to participate in
> courses outside their work hours.

Rafea explained the Arab teachers devote their time after school to extra clas-
ses to help their Arab students narrow the achievement gap in assessments in
additional language learning, and in disciplinary subjects, to enable them to
become college eligible. Similarly, Besan another supervisor pointed up another
gap between the ministry's policies and reality in Arab schools in schools under
his jurisdiction:

> The assimilation of computerization in education: in a large pro-
> portion of the Arab schools where there is no preparation of the
> necessary infrastructure, the teachers are not sufficiently familiar
> with this tool and in the end I am forced to confront my superiors
> to convince them that this policy is inappropriate. On the other
> hand, I also need to think how I am going to help those in the field
> to assimilate the program without the requisite infrastructure.

The tension evident in the abovementioned citation stems from the confrontation between internal stakeholders' concerns and a defensive attitude towards
the Ministry of Education policies when teachers are already exhausted from
working extra hours and their priority is their students rather than their professional development and when they do not have the computers or access to the

worldwide net to deliver the Information Technology curriculum. Thus, the Arab supervisors find themselves in a double bind because they need to meet policy to educate students concerning their roots, history and relevance, but only if they do not undermine the government dictated education programs and transform the school's programs into oppositional education (Ball, 2007). Evidence reveals an inbuilt tension between the entities that represent the same education system (Boyd, 2003; Gross, 2014). The words of the supervisors indicate that since government policies are constructed without input from the leaders of the Arab population, there is a gap between these policies as text, and the conditions and culture of the Arab education system that make their implementation as discourse very challenging without the appropriate infrastructure. This dissonance between government policies and the reality in the schools represents a state of severe turbulence, translated to confrontation between the different parties (Gross, 2014). The result is that it becomes difficult to implement government policies in the field without the correct infrastructure, which frustrates the staff of the Arab education system, and can lead to resistance born from a sense of a lack of equity within the system.

However, despite the lack of participation of the leaders of Arab education in the shaping of government education policies, there is cooperation between the supervisors of the two education sub-systems: Jewish and Arab, since both are subordinate to the Jewish managers of the ministry's regional offices. This coordination does permit some bridging of the gap and can help to ease confrontations and clashes between conflicting values, interests, and entitlement in the education system which are mirrored in a clash between different value systems in society.

Responsibility for the Reduction of Gaps

The Arab supervisors reported that they see themselves as responsible for the reduction of gaps between the Jewish and Arab education systems and between the different schools in the Arab education system (Muslim, Bedouin and Druze). Some of the supervisors try to pour special meaning into their roles, in an attempt to promote an agenda of first-degree educational change, including: empowerment of others and promotion of substantial equality and social justice (Harvey et al., 2013). They bring their own personal vision to their role, their power and experience as pedagogic experts, aiming to push forward social goals far beyond their official job description. They empower and educate others improving their professional prowess and act to enlarge teachers' success (Harvey et al., 2013).

The interviewees describe a difficult picture of gaps between Arab and Jewish education, gaps that are expressed on various levels as the supervisor Ahmed succinctly explained:

> The deficiencies of the Arab education system are as old as the existence of the State of Israel; this is expressed especially in unequal distribution of education resources, a lack of

suitable infrastructure for the schools and a deficient number of classrooms that we have to deal with each year, and a gap between the two systems [Jewish and Arab] in number of pupils per teacher, and in teaching hours for supplementary lessons. There is a gap in equipment and the local governments are weakened so that they cannot support the education system properly.

These findings indicate that the leaders of the Arab education system focus on the goal of reducing gaps and mark out operative objectives with the school principals. Yet the supervisors note that there is a serious problem concerning the traditional authoritarian and centralist managerial style of Arab school principals, and they need to help them to create mechanisms for teacher participation in the school's work, transforming the school into a learning organisation with a community of learners, as the supervisor Karem explained:

The first challenge that I face is to help principals to alter their perception and style of management, to share things, to support the teachers, to harness the teachers to participate in team work. They work alone, they feel overburdened, so I see it as part of my job to do this, to show the principals new methods of management and in this way to begin to reduce gaps.

He also added:

The role of the supervisor is considered one of the most challenging and essential in the education system. S/he is an asset for the Arab education system, S/he is the one that supports, listens to and calms the principals so that they can advance educational processes. I always hear that from the principals.

Similarly, the supervisor Besan added:

As supervisor of the counsellors, I begin with the empowerment of the principals, helping to change their perceptions about the substance of the counsellor's role in the school, and I also begin to reduce gaps, to enrich the principals' knowledge concerning the different role definitions and cooperation within the school.

These words reflect the lack of fit between head office policies and their implementation in the Arab education system which increases the sense of turbulence. Nevertheless, in some cases we can see how some of the external stakeholders, such as the supervisors from the Jewish-controlled education system help to increase capacity building in order to improve Arab students' achievement. Supervisors can ease the tension between competing values, by building circles of dialogue and demonstrating a caring attitude. They can guide principals who are required to implement government policies which are not always seen as appropriate for the Arab school. Rafea explained this role:

As the supervisor I guide the principals to successfully promote collaborative work in the school. Together with their staff they should map the school, and identify the difficulties. It should not be just the principal who thinks or sees. The moment that I ask the principal to meet with me together with staff members, this gives more power and meaning to the teachers. They are able to feel that they belong to the school, and are able to articulate their voice and in this way, I can reduce another gap, by empowering the principal and teachers to work in coordination with today's education system, in Israel and in the world, adapting themselves to changes in education.

The dissonance between the Managing-Director's circulars and the ministry's other instructions and policies and the reality of practice in Arab schools exemplifies a moderate level of turbulence, translated to awareness of the gap and specific resources that could help to close it, this gap between policies and practices is also expressed in socio-cultural differences as reflected in the words of the supervisor Aya:

I work with the school on their reports regarding difficult and complex cases. I guide them, showing them how to treat these cases appropriately in accordance with the Ministry of Education policies and the Managing-Director's circulars. Of course, there is some difficult sensitivity involved when discussing how to promote the policies in a school in Arab society, which is a traditional society and often resists compliance with laws and regulations that do not comply with its cultural values. For example: when there is a problem of violence in the family and we have a duty to involve the welfare services and the police. I have to work together with all the relevant authorities to make wise culture-appropriate decisions.

The superintendents' words suggest that in the sequence between policy-making and its assimilation through the supervisors and regulations, there is little consideration of the cultural context in which the principals work, and this engenders a sense of dissonance between the policies and the field.

At a more advanced level, the supervisors envisage their role as helping to reduce gaps through the widening of the principals' circles of activity with other bodies in their communities, in compliance with Ministry of Education guidelines; also, broadening the collaboration of the school with other schools in the community. The supervisors hold peer seminars for the principals to encourage them in this work, and organise joint learning seminars for principals together with teachers from various disciplines to the waves of moderate turbulence. They hold meetings for principals with other community role holders to present the school's work. These strategies help to reduce the distance and misunderstandings between the different stakeholders, and the principals learn from their successes and failures, as Rafea explained:

> In order to reduce the gaps between Jewish and Arab education you first have to present a statistically valid picture of things. The Ministry of Education policy is today very clear, they advocate work in cooperation with the local governments and with parents. In order to promote this work, I have to promote cooperation between all those involved. I encounter a special difficulty with the managers of the local government education departments especially regarding the use of privatized programs as part of the informal education system.

The interviewees indicated that there is insufficient pooling of resources and distribution of resources and a lack of multicultural networks for knowledge exchange and dialogue to develop deep understandings of the self in relation to the other. For the supervisors, the principal constitutes the school's backbone and s/he is expected to invest efforts to improve the students' achievements and to continuously enhance the school's achievements. This is because the supervisors see the learning resource as the sole tool that can improve the access of their minority, marginalised society to economic and social resources. Ahmed's description of the deficiencies of the Arab education system, supported also by Rafea's description of the difficulties, represent the severe turbulence that they navigate in their efforts to implement educational policy (Gross, 2004). Rafea explained how their acts to improve achievements in the schools for which they are responsible:

> At the supervisors' and principals' forum, I set out the goals and objectives of the region on two levels, the level of reduction of gaps in achievements and the level of development of an optimal learning climate. I divided the schools by communities and in each community, I tried to build a network of schools in the following manner: each school principal undertakes to take responsibility for one discipline, for example Arabic language. He maps the students' achievements and the teachers' profiles in each of the schools and begins, together with them, to construct a strategy and to follow-up on their activity. The principal is assisted by the regional mentor in the specific discipline. The work is then presented in the forum at the level of one compulsory discipline for all the schools in a particular local government area. In this way, the forum constitutes a professional discussion circle through which we can lead the pedagogy at the community level both for the basic disciplines, and also to produce an optimal learning climate together with the school counsellor and the supervisor for educational counselling

In line with Rafea's words, the supervisor Besan explained how they tried to further the policy of reducing gaps in schools' achievements:

> I have a female principal who holds discussion circles with parents from a socio-economically disadvantaged neighborhood. She enlisted the parents for a 'coffee and cake' project (she always prepared coffee and cakes) they discussed all the subjects relating to them and to the students and in this way, she managed to improve the students' behavior and achievements with the support of their parents.

The supervisors produced a light turbulence as defined by Gross, noting that reducing gaps in achievements and establishing an optimal climate are not easy tasks. The resistance that the supervisors encounter, stems among other things from the fact that they are seen as representatives of a mistrusted government, distanced from the interests of the Arab education system. Azal explained their difficulties in the same context:

Undoubtedly, there is a significant gap between the Arab and Jewish systems. To close this gap, I learn about everything that exists in the Jewish education system to understand how they act and then I learn in depth about the Arab education system and to understand what is missing. I usually succeed in this, but the problem that I face is not in attaining budgets to reduce gaps but how to plan the exploitation of the budgets in the most appropriate way to reduce existing gaps.

In conclusion, the gaps between government policies and conditions in the Arab education system are influenced by local factors including difficult relations with local government. These circumstances create a state of moderate turbulence which is exacerbated by deficient government resource allocations. The supervisors emphasised the challenges posed by the gaps between the Jewish and Arab education systems expressed in different dimensions: subordination of the Arab system to the Jewish system, lack of sufficient cooperation between different stakeholders, unequal budgets for the two systems and the fact that government policy is often foreign to the reality in which it is to be implemented (Oplatka & Arar, 2016). The next theme relates to the foreign nature of curricula imposed on the Arab education system.

Development of Culture-sensitive Curricula

The complex nature of the Arab education system means that it faces dilemmas regarding the development of learning programs suitable for the unique needs of Arab society. Such programs are not considered in the different Ministry of Education reforms. The supervisors talked about the difficulty they find in promoting government curricula due to the need to consider cultural sensitivities in their communities. The supervisor's role is often seen by their community as regulatory, supervising the implementation of the policies of the Ministry of Education, while completely ignoring the voices of the school's population. The supervisors pointed up this difficulty and the need to reduce this gap by adapting policies to ensure social justice for Arab children where social justice is a primary virtue (Adler, 1941), through investment in the improvement of a failing scholastic reality, and prudently learning from the ability of schools in the Jewish system to produce stronger academic achievements within the same compulsory education system. Again, prudence is a primary virtue identified by (Adler, 1941). Aya states:

> One of the most complex issues in the world of counselling is making treatment methods culturally-sensitive. In the Director-General's circulars, there are regulations that are culturally inappropriate for Arab culture, because of their cultural sensitivity. Therefore, in recent years I have formed a professional staff to work on the development of a set of programs for counselling that will be culturally sensitive for the Arab education system. Its impossible to simply copy existing programs from the Jewish education system for the Arab education system. I work very hard opposite my superiors to convince them how important this work is so that they will permit it. I explain how important it is to provide resources for the Arab education system to involve professionals who will help us to promote this process.

Similarly, the supervisor Aya clarified their position on the modification of government programs:

> I have worked hard in the last year to promote programs for according to the needs of Arab society. The problem begins with the training that is rather foreign, and professional development is subordinate to Jewish education. This all increases the gap [between the two systems] and makes it difficult for me to do my job and be relevant.

Some of the supervisors devoted attention to the design of culture-sensitive programs as Name inserted here explained:

> As part of their independent pedagogic and managerial flexibility, each school has the possibility to adapt 25% of their learning programs. Together with the principals I try to promote subjects which are important for each school. I encourage the principals to encourage the teachers to develop school programs, to highlight [their culture's] uniqueness, this is the only place where they can introduce unique cultural elements into the Arab education system.

The supervisors also note the essential nature of their role for Arab society. It is a significant role assisting the promotion of different reforms as appropriate for Arab society and culture, as noted by the supervisor Azal:

The supervisors have an important and meaningful role. They promote the computerisation reform while adapting it culturally for the needs of the Arab school and its culture. They relate to social and cultural aspects involved in the encounter between education and information technology in the Arab education system. They help to integrate this reform, it was not easy at all and the supervisors made a significant contribution to this, they worked together with the staff throughout the Arab Education System to form their vision on this issue with their limited budgets and infrastructure.

In this theme, it was clear that despite the perception of the supervisor's role as one that is tied to the implementation of regulations, a perception that makes them appear less trustworthy, the supervisors often acted as a mediator between government head office policies and the school, so that they dealt with the development of culturally-sensitive programs with pedagogic flexibility. This communication is also stretched in the direction of meditation between the two societies (Jewish and Arab) that live separately and often in conflict one with the other as shown in the next theme.

D. Moving towards Inclusion

Because of the multiplicity of groups that compose Israeli society and the way in which it has developed since the establishment of the state, it is perceived as a politically and socially split society with gaps between the different social groups. According to the Ombudsman's report (State of Israel Report, 2016, the management of the Ministry of Education has failed over the years to take the necessary steps to provide a pedagogic, financially operative foundation for the creation of long-term coexistence in the education system (State of Israel, 2016).

Despite this deficiency, the supervisors see themselves as agents of change for the promotion of coexistence. Each supervisor works to advance this subject according to their world perception but without any clear program from above. All the supervisors noted that their work in cooperation with Jewish colleagues was important. Arab supervisors hold meetings with their Jewish peers and learn about learning programs in Jewish schools and the extent of their success in order to try to modify these programs for Arab society. Rafea noted: 'Graduates of our education system will continue their studies in higher education institutions in Israel (through their additional language of Hebrew) and will integrate into the national employment market'. Besan spoke about their role in developing dialogue between the two peoples:

> I strongly believe in advancing co-existence, my role is to help the principals to understand our uniqueness and then to teach them about the 'other'. To learn from others how to maintain our identity, how to develop different programs from early childhood on

the subject of our values and identity. We are opening the gates of the system and allowing entry to teachers from each of the societies to the parallel education system.

The supervisor Ahmed also felt it important to open up both education systems, and sees their role as significant in promoting the Ministry of Education policies to integrate Jewish teachers in the Arab education system:

> In the last year, the Ministry of Education together with The Abraham Fund and Givat Haviva College have tried to strengthen coexistence through the integration of Jewish teachers in the Arab education system, I think that these programs cannot succeed without my help.

To sum up, some of the supervisors such as Besan clearly see themselves as having a mission to develop dialogues between the two societies as a tool to enable the gap in infrastructure, and the achievement gap between the Jewish Education System and the Arab Education System to be narrowed for equity, renewal and social mobility in Israeli society. Interestingly, this finding agrees with my previous research (Author & Other, 2017). In some of the supervisors' narratives, we witness their strong desire to dispel uncertainty while trying to ease the influence of unequal inputs and avoid the generation of a higher level of turbulence. We can also hear different pleas for support to ensure 'survival', reflecting the desires of school principals who aim to improve school functioning. The supervisors also helped the principals to cope with the feeling that they needed to 'fight' with the local authority which did not understand their needs or attempted to impose their agenda on the schools.

Concluding Remarks

The research described in this article aimed to understand the way in which supervisors in the Arab education system in Israel perceived their efforts to improve pupils' achievements in an era of dynamic change. The findings were interpreted through the lens of Turbulence Theory.

Analysis of the findings indicated that the role of Arab supervisors in the Arab education system is complex and subject to clashing discourses and expectations that positions them in a perpetual state of turbulence. The supervisors attempt to implement an educational policy that is determined by the government ministry at a distance from Arab society and find themselves facing continual resistance from different stakeholders, a situation that can be defined as a moderate state of turbulence. This resistance can easily accelerate and engender a state of severe turbulence especially when the Ministry of Education applies more stringent nationalist policies, which are resisted by the Arab public. An example of this is the demand of the Arab public to close Arab schools on Nakhba memorial day. Nakhba or 'the day of catastrophe' is normally the day after Israel celebrates their independence which began on 14th May 1948. On Nakhba the Arab people remember their exodus, and enforced refugee status of up to 700,000 people (Lubin, 2014).

Moreover, it is clear that the Ministry of Education ignores the need for the expression of the unique socio-cultural characteristics of Arab society as a native national marginalised minority that demands the realisation of collective rights awarded to other such minorities worldwide. The supervisor has to try to bridge this divide between the two entities: the Ministry of Education and their own community in order to ease turbulence between competing values and interests and widen circles of dialogue and capacity building.

The supervisors see themselves as those responsible for planning the educational future of the Arab education system yet in some cases they have to implement hostile policies built on the suspicion of the majority society towards its Arab citizens, and the government continually demands expressions of loyalty in exchange for the allocation of resources (Arar & Masry, 2016). They also point up the lack of their involvement as representatives of the Arab education system in the planning of policy as a text for their schools, or the allocation of funds for infrastructure to realise the policy in the real world. The supervisor is often therefore seen by Arab society as representing the interests of the establishment and not their own community, nevertheless some of the supervisors see their role as a public mission, working to reduce gaps between the Jewish and Arab societies and even providing tools for dialogue in order to strengthen peaceful coexistence (Author & Other, 2017). Additionally, some school principals adopted a creative approach to cope with the differences between values, needs and practices in the Arab and Jewish system. The supervisors point up the difficulties involved in applying government education policies without the required infrastructures and resources in the Arab education system. They also identify a lack of sensitivity to Arab culture and felt that they were 'in the middle' and had to find ways to bridge between these policies and the schools, for example in coping with cultural sensitivity with violence in the family. In at least one case, the supervisor felt the need to develop a professional discussion circle through which they sought feedback on strategies to improve community participation and produce an optimal learning climate together.

Although Arab society sees the Arab education system as almost the only tool that can help it to develop its human capital and absorb educated Arab academics (Abu-Saad, 2006), this system is often used in an unintelligent way for foreign interests such as the accumulation of power for particular local hamullas (Arar & Masry, 2016), a situation that can stir up moderate to severe turbulence with negative consequences for the cooperation between supervisors and local Arab government.

The supervisors also indicate the need for changes in the Arab school culture so that a more participatory model will be adopted and initiate projects and strategies to improve dialogue between the different school stakeholders and organise regional meetings and discussion between the principals. Furthermore, there are schools that stress the importance of building capacity for both professional capital and communities of practice to improve teacher quality and learning outcomes.

Almost all the interviewees noted that there are insufficient resources for the Arab education system, a fact that makes it difficult for them to perform their roles as necessary (Agnon, 2006). This seems to lead to differences in the level of work between Arab and Jewish local government education departments, to a large extent due to differences in available budgets (Author & Other, 2013). This inequality stimulates moral questions concerning the role of education policy-makers since it maintains the weakness of the Arab education system (Gibton, 2011; Golan-Agnon, 2006). This complex reality means that the school is almost continually positioned at the eye of the storm, and the ability to navigate such extreme turbulence varied according to the ability of those who lead educational change to overcome resistance to change. Without urgent correction, the gaps between the Jewish and Arab education systems will continue to grow and Arab youth will find it difficult to escape a future of disadvantage and weakness (Abu-Saad, 2006; Balas, 2015). There is also an obvious neglect of the specific difficulties and characteristics of the Arab education system by the Ministry and power struggles between head office and the field, a reality that does not help to improve collaboration or to build professional learning communities. Often the supervisors, as the main players in the field, are left with a sense of isolation (Waite *et al.* 2015). Some supervisors tried to bridge cultures and attempted to ensure equity, and entitlement by creating a mobilising reality within the school. They organised seminars and regional meetings of education staff, promoting collaboration and participation in the schools. They listened to the difficulties of the school principals and assisted them to cope with the complexity of their roles and to steer through situations of turbulence that threatened to cascade and undermine the principals' control. They expressed a deep awareness of their role in providing tools for their graduate educators to facilitate their social mobility. In terms of Turbulence Theory, they were the pilots who maintained stability in times of turbulence and in situations that threatened to undermine control they found the opportunities to engender change.

Figure 2 illustrates the different influences on the Arab school in Israel in an environment of ambivalence and conflicting expectations. Although the supervisors strive to create equal opportunities for Arab students, the lack of resources in the Arab education system, and the lack of their influence over ministry policy, often mean that they are only able to induce change inside their education system, creating a light or moderate turbulence (Gross, 2014). Thus, it is argued that as long as there is no significant change, that begins with setting the positionality of the system's leaders, the limited autonomy that is enjoyed by the local Arab education offices cannot produce any worthy results that could rescue the Arab education system from its present stagnation (Darling-Hammond & Lieberman, 2012; Kelly, 2009).

We see that the Arab education system functions as a national minority system, subordinate to an overriding majority education system, whose policies are mediated by regional supervisors. At the same time, the relationship between the local government and the school is characterised by the school's weak one-way

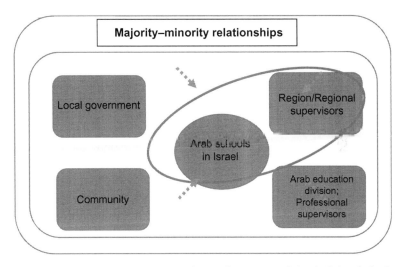

Figure 2.   Patterns of Influence on the Performance of Arab Schools in Israel
Under Conflicting Expectations.

dependence (on the local government) (Author & Other, 2013). The community
also maintains a weak relationship with the school, which often functions in isolation from its community (Gross, 2014). The relationship with the Arab
Education Department, represented by professional supervisors, also exhibits
weak dependence, which diminishes the place of an authentic curriculum vis-à-
vis the need for strong regulation. In view of the above, it seems that the Arab
school functions under strong centralist control, and lacks pedagogic autonomy
(Oplatka & Arar, 2016).

Furthermore, the supervisors indicated that, like other minority and marginalised groups throughout the world, the Arab marginalised minority in Israel is
under pressure to assimilate. The education system adopts the majority culture
as an informal norm, so that the supervisor is torn between the professional
sphere (as a representative of headquarters) and the personal sphere (as a member of the marginalised minority group) (Lewis et al., 2011). As Van Laer and
Janssens (2014) noted, the supervisors attempt to create a coherent identity that
marries the norms dictated by the Israeli-Jewish system's leaders, with the contradicting expectations of the Arab society from which they originated. Despite
this attempt to reconcile these two worlds, it is obvious that some of the supervisors feel they are between the hammer and the anvil and sense pressure from
both sides. Such a role that seeks to reconcile conflicting groups that may readily
turn their hostility on the person in the middle, requires the supervisor to have
the primary virtue of courage (Adler, 1941).

It seems that this marginal education system has still not translated its segregation into an advantage for its schools, failing to pool educational resources that
might enable it to strengthen its heritage, educational values and ideology and
organise and manage the educational resources more effectively (Harvey et al.,

2013). It is also true that the state education system suffers from the split between Jewish and Arab systems which severely disrupts coordination. Additionally, local politics produce an ineffective education system dominated by a culture of power conflicts (Arnova et al., 2013).

It is concluded that facilitating stakeholders' tight coordinated networking may turn out to be the most cost-efficient and effective method for optimising Arab students' learning in the Arab Education System. Moreover, and despite the need to reinforce Arab students' unique cultural identity, there should also be an attempt to move from competing ideals, and values that bring about competing political projects, towards projects that have common values and can enhance mutual understanding, shared world views, and multicultural education. This can be achieved through open and candid interaction and cooperation between the different stakeholders in the Arab education system in order to decrease distance and disagreement between them, and engender social cohesion through constructive dialogue and power-sharing instead of controlling governmental practices.

Although generalisation of the findings is limited due to its methodology, it is possible to point to several implications for Arab education policy and in similar developing and minority societies striving to achieve educational change through a bottom-up process. The findings also suggest the need for broader and more representative future research on these issues.

References

Abu-Saad, I. (2006). State-controlled education and identity formation among the Palestinian Arab minority in Israel. *American Behavioral Scientist, 49*(3), 1085–1100.

Adler, M. (1941). *A dialectic of morals: Towards the foundations of political philosophy*. Notre Dame: University of Notre Dame.

Arar, K., & Abu-Asbah, K. (2013). 'Not Just Location': Attitudes and perceptions of education system administrators in local Arab Governments in Israel. *International Journal of Educational Management, 27*(1), 54–73.

Arar, K., & Masry, A. (2016). Motivation to teach: The case of Arab teachers in Israel. *Education Studies, 42*(1), 19–35.

Arar, K., Shapira, T., Azaize, F., & Herz-Lazarowitz, R. (2013). *Arab Women into Leadership and Management*. New York, NY: Palgrave Mcmillan.

Arnova, R. F., Torres, C. A., & Franz, S. (2013). *Comparative education: The dialectic of global and local*. Lanham: Rowan & Littlefield.

Avney Rasha Institute. (2010). *The development and learning for the role of general superintendent* [Hebrew]. Retrieved from http://www.avneyrosha.org.il/Role/Pages/Inspector_development.aspx

Balas, N. (2015). Inequality in the education system, who opposes and who enjoys the gaps? In D. Ben David (Ed.), *Report on the Social, Economic and Political Status of the State* (pp. 435–467). Jerusalem: Taub Center. [Hebrew].

Ball, S. (2007). *Education plc: Understanding private sector participation in public sector education*. London: Routledge.

Bleikopf, M. (2014). *Gaps between Jews and Arabs in the education system – The physical infrastructure.* Jerusalem: Sikui Association for the Promotion of Civil Equality. [Hebrew].

Boyd, W. L. (2003). Public education's crisis of performance and legitimacy: Rationale and overview of the yearbook. In W. L. Boyd & D. Miretzky (Eds.), *American Educational Governance on Trial: Change and Challenges – The 102nd Yearbook of the National Society for Study of Education (NSSE)* (pp. 1–19). Chicago, IL: Chicago University Press.

Central Bureau of Statistics. (2015). *67th Independence Day - 8.3 million residents in the State of Israel.* Announcement to the press. Retrieved from http://www1.cbs.gov.il/reader/newhodaot/hodaa_template.html?hodaa=201511099

Central Bureau of Statistics. (2016). *Annual Statistical Abstract for Israel – No. 66.* Jerusalem: CBS. [Hebrew].

Cohen, L., Manion, L., & K. Morrison (2011). *Research methods in education* (7th ed.). New York, NY: Routledge.

Creswell, J. W. (2009). *Research design: Qualitative, quantitative, and mixed-methods approaches.* London: Sage.

Darling-Hammond, L., & Lieberman, A. (2012). *Teacher education around the world: Changing policies and practices. Teacher quality and school development.* Florence, KY: Routledge, Taylor & Francis Group.

Fergusson, V. (1998). *Supervision for the self-managing school: The New Zealand experience.* Paris: International Institution for Educational Planning.

Gibton, D. (2011). Post-2000 law-based educational governance in Israel: From equality to diversity. *Educational Management, Administration and Leadership, 39*(4), 434–454.

Golan-Agnon, D. (2006). Separate but not equal: Discrimination against Palestinian Arab students in Israel. *American Behavioral Scientist, 49*(3), 1075–1084.

Gross, S. J. (2014). Using turbulence theory to guide actions. In C. M. Branson & S. J. Gross (Eds.), *Handbook on Ethical Educational Leadership* (pp. 246–262). New York, NY: Routledge.

Harvey, J., Cambron-McCabe, N., Cunningham, L. L., & Koff, R. H. (2013). *The superintendent's fieldbook* (2nd Ed.). Thousand Oaks, CA: Corwin.

Jabareen, Y., & Agbaria, A. (2014). Autonomy for Arab education in Israel: Rights and possibilities. *Gilui Daat, 5*(1), 13–40.

Kelly, A. V. (2009). *The curriculum theory and practice.* London: Sage.

Lewis, T., Rice, M., & Rice Jr, R. (2011). Superintendents' beliefs and behaviors regarding instructional leadership standards reform. *International Journal of Educational Leadership Preparation, 6*(1), 1.

Lubin, A. (2014). *Geographies of liberation: The making of an Afro-Arab political imaginary.* Chapel Hill: University of North Carolina Press.

Marshall, C., & Rossman, G. (2012). *Designing Qualitative Research* (3rd ed.). Thousand Oaks, CA: Sage.

Maxfield, S., Shapiro, M., Gupta, G., & Hass, S. (2010). Gender and risk: Women, risk taking and risk aversion. *Gender in Management: An International Journal, 25*(4), 586–602.

Ministry of Education. (2017). *School administration: The superintendent and the school working according to standards.* Retrieved from http://cms.education.gov.il/EducationCMS/Units/Yesodi/Minhal/standards/Mefakeah.htm [Hebrew].

Moloi, K., Gravett, S., & Petersen, N. (2009). Globalization and its impact on education with specific reference to education in South Africa. *Educational Management Administration & Leadership, 37*(2), 278–297.

Nevo. (2014). *Government Education Regulations (superintendence orders) Clause 15: Functions of the General Superintendent.* Retrieved from https://www.nevo.co.il/law_html/law01/152_031.htm#Seif15 [Hebrew].

Ofsted. Children's Services and Skills. (2012). *The framework for school inspection in England under section 5 of the Education Act 2005 (as amended).* Manchester: The Office for Standards in Education, Children's Services and Skills (Ofsted). Retrieved from file:///C:/Users/user/Downloads/The%20framework%20for%20school%20inspection%20from%20September%202012%20(1).pdf

Oplatka, I., & Arar, K. (2016). Leadership for social justice and the characteristics of traditional societies: Ponderings on the application of western-grounded models. *International Journal of Leadership in Education, 19*(3), 352–369.

Plato. (1975). Politea. In *Writings of Plato*, Vol. B. trans, Yosef, G. Liebs. Tel Aviv: Shocken. [Hebrew].

Ruşitoru, M.-V. (2017). Le droit à l'éducation et les politiques éducatives. *Union européenne et Roumanie.* Paris: Harmattan.

Saban, A. (2002). The collective rights of the Palestinian Arab minority: What there is, what there is not and the taboo area. *Legal Studies, 26*(1), 241–319.

State of Israel. (2016). *Ombudsman and public complaints commissioner's special report* [Hebrew]. Retrieved from http://www.mevaker.gov.il/he/Reports/Report_545/92be6185-dbc9–44d9-8c97–98eead865fab/Life-together_Final_preview.pdf?AspxAutoDetectCookieSupport=1

Van Laer, K., & Janssens, M. (2014). Between the devil and the deep blue sea: Exploring the Hybrid identity narratives of ethnic minority professionals. *Scandinavian Journal of Management, 30*(2), 186–196.

Waite, D., Rodríguez, G., & Wadende, A. (2015). Globalization and the business of educational reform. In J. Zajda (Ed.), *Second International Handbook in Globalization, Education and Policy Research* (pp. 353–374). Dordrecht: Springer.

Chapter 8

Turbulence in Efforts at Curriculum Renewal for Educational Equity: A Critical Analysis of a Primary Curriculum Review Exercise in Trinidad and Tobago

Freddy James and June George

˙Abstract

This chapter reports on research work which was a component of an independent review of the primary school curriculum renewal exercise that was commissioned by the Ministry of Education in Trinidad and Tobago and executed during 2012–2013. It examines how agencies functioned to engender educational change through education governance systems in the process of revising the curriculum. Turbulence Theory (Gross, 2014) was the tool used to explore the interactions among agencies. The research shows that turbulence occurred at various stages and that the outcome of interactions among the agencies that were in pursuit of educational change and equity was largely dependent on the extent of the turbulence and how it was managed. For example, the local Curriculum Planning Team (CPT) was able to learn from external consultants while firmly maintaining that they were the ones who had a deep understanding of the local context and should therefore have a major say in what was included in the curriculum. However, the CPT could do little to offset the severe turbulence caused when the political directorate mandated that there should be full-scale implementation of the revised curriculum without the benefit of a pilot. The role of socio-political contextual factors in the curriculum development process is highlighted.

Keywords: Turbulence; curriculum renewal; educational change; equity

Turbulence, Empowerment and Marginalisation in International
Education Governance Systems, 185–203
doi:10.1108/978-1-78754-675-220181010

Introduction

The research reported in this chapter is based on a component of a larger research project that was an independent review of the primary school curriculum renewal exercise that was carried out in Trinidad and Tobago (T&T) under the Seamless Education System (SES), which is a programme sponsored by the Inter-American Development Bank (IDB). The actual curriculum renewal exercise occurred during the period December 2012 to July 2013, and the review was commissioned two years later. This component of the review examines the agencies charged with the responsibility to revise the curriculum. It further examines the interactions among these various agencies and uses this platform to explore how these agencies functioned to engender educational change through education governance systems in the process of revising the primary school curriculum. For purposes of this chapter, the term 'agencies' refers to sections/units/divisions and personnel within the national education governing body, the Ministry of Education (MoE) that were involved in the revision process.

At its core, change of any nature can be uncomfortable, disruptive or traumatic, even when it results in benefits to and for those persons and institutions that experience the change (Fullan, 2006). Educational change operates at different levels – classroom, department, school, district and state/system – and is articulated in different forms such as: renewal, transformation, reform, school improvement and school effectiveness. The educational change discussed in this study is that occasioned by the revision of the primary school curriculum in T&T. We have classified it as educational change taking place at the state/education governance system level and executed in the form of curriculum renewal

Educational change is both complex and complicated. It is complex in that it is usually an interconnected process, involving interaction among webs and networks of persons and agencies. It is complicated in that the interplay among agencies and the change process can be difficult and perplexing and this creates what Gross (2014) describes as 'turbulence'. The research sought to explore if/how turbulence occurred in the curriculum renewal process and to comment on the impact of any such turbulence on the main goal of engaging in equity-driven primary curriculum renewal. Data were gleaned from persons who reside at the lower and middle level of the education governance system in T&T groups that seldom get the chance to express how they experience the many educational change processes the country undergoes and their role in the outcome of such processes. Further, by evaluating the process of curriculum change, the research provided an opportunity for curriculum change agents and agencies to detail their experiences, iterations and interactions and in so doing, the research filled a gap by giving critical groups in the change process an opportunity to share their experiences of the process. Specifically, the research was guided by the following research questions:

- What were the agencies and where did the power lie in their interactions in the process of renewing the primary school curriculum in T&T?

- Which (if any) interactions among agencies produced turbulence during the primary school curriculum renewal process and what impact did any such turbulence have on the different agencies' navigation through curriculum renewal goals and related cultural changes?

We used qualitative research techniques to carry out this investigation and relied heavily on Gross' (2014) Turbulence Theory in making sense of the data generated. The expectation is that this chapter will add to the discourse on the use of Turbulence Theory in education, with a special focus on the attempt to empower professional educational leaders, and staff to empower young people, and their parents through the curriculum renewal process.

The Context of the Study

The Setting

T&T is a twin-island republic located at the southernmost end of the chain of Caribbean islands. T&T has a population of approximately 1.3 million, consisting mainly of persons of African descent (36.3%), East-Indian descent (37.6%), and mixed-race descent (24.2%). These islands were formerly a British colony and achieved independence in 1962. The country became a republic in 1976. Since gaining independence, the country has had a democratically elected central government operating under a bicameral system which is a legislative body that has an appointed Senate and democratically elected House of Representatives in two chambers (Online Dictionary, 2017). The central government is located in Trinidad, the larger of the two islands. Although this central government is responsible for the overall governance of the country, there are several aspects of the governance of Tobago for which another body, the Tobago House of Assembly (THA), has some responsibility. Education is one such area.

The education system in T&T spans the range from early childhood care and education, through the primary (elementary) school level, through the secondary (high) school level, to the tertiary education level, and lifelong learning. The MoE has overall responsibility for education at all of these levels, but, more specifically, at the first three levels. This chapter focuses on curriculum renewal at the primary school level. There are 455 primary schools in T&T and primary education is free and compulsory.

There are layers of governance structures that interact within the T&T context with respect to primary school curriculum change and innovation. The MoE is the national governing body and is headed by a cabinet Minister, the Minister of Education, who is responsible for the policy directives of the Ministry. There are several units/divisions within the MoE, one of which is the Curriculum Planning and Development Division (CPDD). Each unit/division is headed by a Director who reports directly to the Chief Education Officer (CEO). In turn, the CEO reports directly to the Minister. The Minister chairs the Strategic Executive Team meetings, which are held periodically, and the attendees include all Directors. At these meetings, policy is elucidated, ministerial directives are given, strategies are mapped out, and there is feedback on, and critical analysis of what is happening in the field with respect to curriculum and other matters.

The CPDD, headed by a Director, is responsible for all aspects of curriculum work, including curriculum design, development, implementation, monitoring and evaluation. The Director oversees the work of Curriculum Coordinators (CCs) and Curriculum Officers (COs) in the field. The CPDD has the prime responsibility for implementing curriculum-related policies and directives that emanate from the Strategic Executive Team meetings chaired by the Minister of Education. These policies and directives apply in both Trinidad and Tobago. The Division of Education Youth Affairs and Sport (DEYAS) is a unit within the Tobago House of Assembly with responsibility for education matters, including curriculum matters. DEYAS is bound by curriculum policy directives from the MoE that dictate what the nature of the primary school curriculum should be. It is expected that there would be collaboration between DEYAS and the CPDD in the design of the curriculum. DEYAS, however, has the responsibility for implementing, monitoring and evaluating the primary school curriculum in Tobago.

Planning for the Primary Curriculum Renewal

This most recent effort at revising the primary school curriculum in Trinidad and Tobago had its origins in a broader MoE project, the Seamless Education System (SES) programme. This was a three-phase programme, funded by the IDB, which was intended to ensure the country's competitiveness by investing in human capital (IDB, 2009). The first phase of the project was focused on improving the quality of education at the early childhood care and education and primary levels. The research questions of this chapter are bounded by the attempt to upgrade offerings at the primary level.

There was a long period of planning for the project, during which time several changes occurred. The main reason for the changes was the shifting of the seat of power from one political party to another due to the results of general elections in the country. These elections are held every five years. In the two-party system which exists in T&T, it is often the case that there are differences in education policy between the parties and it is not uncommon to find that when there is a change in government, existing education policy may be discarded and replaced. There may also be Cabinet reshuffles during a government's five-year term of office. Further, it is sometimes the case that public servants are shifted around, resulting in key posts in the MoE being filled by new persons from time to time. In the period of planning for the project, changes in personnel included two different governments, three ministers of education, five directors/acting directors of curriculum and several CEOs.

There was also a change in the level of the school system in which some CCs and COs were now expected to function. Many of these officers had come from a secondary school base and, hitherto, had functioned as officers for the secondary school curriculum. These officers were thus now placed in a situation where they had to make a shift in their thinking and operations. Further, there was a general feeling that the existing primary school curriculum was outdated and needed to be changed. Some of the concerns were that the curriculum was overloaded, not student-centred, content – rather than skills-focused and lacking in organised learning experiences in the visual and performing arts and physical education.

The climate within which curriculum renewal was embarked upon was thus a complex one. The MoE had engaged in some consultation and needs assessment activities in months prior to the commencement of the writing of the curriculum. It had used foreign consultants to do some of this background work and there was therefore a body of information available that could inform the direction of the renewal process. The MoE had contracted a foreign consulting firm to train local personnel in curriculum development and to lead the entire writing process. The MoE also organised itself into various teams prior to and during the writing exercise, with a Core Planning Team (CPT) providing general oversight, with guidance from the foreign consulting firm.

Some Issues Associated with Curriculum Change

Globally, governments have been initiating changes in their educational systems in ways that support student achievement and seek to close the inequity gaps in student outcomes (Levin, 2007). Often, these educational changes involve changes to the curriculum. Many of these efforts tend to be met with conflict that sometimes thwarts the improvement thrust (Levin & Fullan, 2008). Levin (2007) ascribes such conflict to educators' perceptions that they are blamed for discrepancies in the system and that they are forced to adopt what he terms 'undesirable practices'. However, by the same token, the catalyst for many educational change efforts is conflict, or what Gross (2014) calls 'turbulence'. The ensuing review of pertinent literature provides a critical analysis of the seemingly inter-twining concepts of curriculum change, equity and turbulence.

Curriculum Change Theory

The term curriculum is interpreted as an output of the curriculum development process that produces 'a plan for learning' (Thijs & van den Akker, 2009, p. 9). It is also viewed as a 'structured series of intended learning outcomes' that 'prescribes (or at least anticipates) the results of instruction' (Johnson, 1967, p. 130). We embrace the notion that the curriculum is planned and informs instruction through the statement of intended learning outcomes.

The writers acknowledge the nuanced difference between the concepts of *curriculum change and curriculum development*. In order to bring about change in the curriculum, the curriculum development process must take place. For purposes of this study, curriculum change refers to any conscious, deliberate attempt to engender change in the curriculum of a school or school system which should produce four key outcomes: a new structure, new teaching practices, new curriculum materials and change in beliefs or understandings (Patterson & Czajkowski, 1979). Curriculum change, like educational change, is a process with a number of elements that must be taken into consideration.

Fullan (2007), for example, identifies 'change agents' as one of the key elements and states that everyone is a change agent. The nature and context of the innovation are critical elements. The context of innovation includes issues such as: peoples' readiness for change, school culture and climate, parents and local community, school staff and administration and the state mandates and directives. Still, with regard to the issue of mandates, Fullan (2007) contends that these do not work. Other elements in the curriculum change process include equity and equality at both the individual and collective levels and planning and preparing for the implementation of change.

Thus, while curriculum change can be beneficial, its benefits are not a given since they depend on the purposes of the curriculum related to sharing knowledge and access to equitable opportunity for middle benefits and social mobility; the availability of resources; the competence and interactions of different agencies and their change agents/personnel; the commitment of persons to the curriculum development process and consultation where all have an opportunity to talk back to power; and the external forces including consultants who are attached to foreign finance packages. Parsons and Beauchamp (2012) caution that 'if a curriculum revision process is overly ambitious, is carried out within short timelines and is within an environment of low investment in teachers, problems will inevitably arise' (p. 29). Additionally, curriculum development does not happen in a vacuum; it is wedded and often driven by socio-political factors in a given context (Glatthorn, Boschee, Whitehead, & Boschee, 2012; Thijs & van den Akker, 2009), be it country, district or school context. The following section provides a discussion on issues of equity which, to some extent, illuminates how socio-political factors in a particular context might impact curriculum change.

Equity

According to (Levin, 2007) most education reform efforts have an underlying goal of realising equity in the system. We interpret equity as quite distinct from equality, whereby the former means giving everyone what they need to succeed, whereas the latter means giving everyone the same or treating everyone the same. While equality does have to do with fairness, it is not sufficient when it comes to educational reform, because not only does one size not fit all (Ohanian, 1999), but all schools, communities and societies are not equal (Gross & Shapiro, 2016). Economic and class differences differentiate schools based on resources and access. Then, there are ideological differences, such as essentialism versus market forces (Berliner & Biddle, 1995), which are often attached to financial packages. The main point about these differences is that they create and sustain achievement gaps in systems between dominant and marganalised groups like the Black-White achievement gap (Wagner, 2010). Thus, in the main, educational reform is an attempt to close these gaps. Still, Fullan (2010, p. 15) cautions that while 'an increase in the average level of achievement in a society is important [...] whether the gap between high and low achievers decreases as the overall average rises is equally as important.

Closing the gaps often means ensuring that education is inclusive (Ainscow, 2005) and that differentiated instruction is practised in the teaching and learning process (Tomlinson, 2014). In some countries and contexts such as parts of India, Africa and the Caribbean, inclusive education is considered as an approach to addressing the needs of disabled students. However, internationally it is articulated in broader terms to mean an approach to reform that supports and fosters diversity among all students (UNESCO, 2001). This chapter adopts this broader approach and in so doing acknowledges a position that education is a basic right and the basis of a just society. Differentiated instruction according to Tomlinson (2014) exists when teachers provide specific alternatives that allow each student to learn as deeply as possible, according to his/her learning ability. It assumes that each child has a different learning road map and therefore requires different teaching and learning tools to succeed. Thus a differentiated classroom is a nurturing environment in which learning is encouraged for all but not by setting one particular standard for all.

To achieve inclusive and differentiated instruction in classrooms, teachers must be adequately developed professionally in pedagogy and instruction. In *The Flat World and Education: How America's Commitment to Equity will Determine Our Future*, Darling-Hammond (2010) suggested that teacher quality is the most important influence on student learning (Desimone, 2009; Fullan, 2010; Mckinsey, 2007; Thrupp & Lupton, 2006). Thus, teacher training and development to ensure quality across the board is an essential aspect of educational reform. Nevertheless, many policymakers limit or eliminate the budget and time for professional development of implementers, thereby implying that schools and educators can deliver change without the requisite support (Darling-Hammond, 2010).

Turbulence Theory

Gross' (2014) Turbulence Theory provided a theoretical framework within this study to interpret the findings and make meaning of the interplay among and between agencies, governance structures and relationships in determining the outcome of the curriculum renewal process as empowering or disempowering educational leading professionals to Empower Young Societal Innovators for Equity and Renewal (EYSIER). According to Gross (2014), the purpose of Turbulence Theory is to provide a way of understanding and then navigating the disturbances during periods of change and innovation in educational institutions and organisations. Gross and Shapiro (2016, p. 151) further state that Turbulence Theory helps educational leaders to 'contextualise a given problem as they construct strategies to move to less troubled waters'. Still further, they suggest that turbulence may not necessarily be something to avoid when support for change is required, hence their suggestion to work with turbulence rather than trying to control it.

Gross (2014) identifies four levels of turbulence: light, moderate, severe and extreme. Light turbulence refers to little or no disruption in an ongoing situation. Although the disturbance is minimal, there is a cause for concern and attention needs to be paid. Moderate turbulence relates to more active disturbances, noticeable tremors with a specific cause that require specific and focused action. Moderate turbulence often necessitates action, creativity and sensitivity. Severe turbulence indicates strong movements that threaten a loss of control and unravelling of structures, which leads to a crisis situation. An examination of the levels of turbulence can lead one to believe that the impact of turbulence on innovation is all negative. However, this is not the case. In Gross's use of the comparison with the aeroplane, he contends that, turbulence that causes the aeroplane to move is positive, because without it the plane cannot fly. Similarly, turbulence in the education system may be what triggers innovation that can bring about much-needed change. This certainly was the case with the primary school curriculum renewal process in T&T.

Gross (2014) identifies three underlying dynamics of turbulence theory, which provide an organising framework to interpret how an organisation and its people experience turbulence and the implications of the impact of such experiences. These three dynamics can also determine whether the level of turbulence is high or low. He describes them as positionality, cascading and stability. It should be noted that these three dynamics can all exist at the same time; hence, their collective impact must be considered when examining a particular situation (Gross & Shapiro, 2016). Deeper expositions on the three underlying dynamics of turbulence are provided as follows.

Positionality
All turbulence is not experienced to the same degree by everyone in the organisation (Gross, 2014), which implies that the turbulence a person/agency experiences depends on one's/its position in the organisation. This, in turn, implies that turbulence has different meanings for different persons and agencies, depending on the position from which they are experiencing it and their own phenomenological interpretation of the source of the turbulence. Understanding positionality is important because it helps change agents calibrate the gravity and nature of the turbulence that different persons and agencies may experience, and therefore, actions can be taken to safeguard those most at risk. Within the educational change literature, this is addressed under the issues of planning, monitoring and constant critical and reflective evaluation that relate to the implementation process (Fullan, 2007).

Cascading
Cascading refers to instances whereby forces within the change environment advertently or inadvertently increase the level of the turbulence. For example, an organisation may be hit by one change and before it can grapple with this change it is hit by another and so on. The addition of each new turbulent event makes it seem as if the turbulence is mushrooming. Thus, according to Gross (2014, p. 254) 'understanding cascading is a matter of understanding context and the force of a series of turbulent conditions'.

Stability
Stability is described as a third force that determines how turbulence is experienced in an organisation. The more stable the organisation, the better it is to

adapt to change (Gross, 2014). Gross (2014, p. 255) defines stability as '[...] a relationship between the object we are examining (e.g. organisation, a bridge, a country, a person) and the dynamic forces confronting it'. Thus, stability under turbulence theory is a dynamic concept, acquired and sustained through action and flexibility. The degree of stability of the organisation, allows it to respond to change in measured, flexible ways that often take the form of dialogue or a commitment to continuous communication, democratic practices that foster equality and shared power and innovation to drive the mission (Gross & Shapiro, 2016). Still, Gross (2014) cautions that 'there are limits to stability', adding that 'nothing is stable in an unqualified sense', (p. 256) since it is relative to the dynamic forces that impact on it.

Summary

Curriculum change is one element in a wider field of the educational change processes (Parsons & Beauchamp, 2012) which is sometimes initiated by turbulence (Gross, 2014) and undergirded by a rationale to provide equity in the education system (Levin, 2007) by improving teaching and learning and, as a corollary, student outcomes. The review shows that turbulence is not necessarily a bad thing, since it can be a driver or catalyst for change and improvement, once it does not overwhelm the change agents and different agencies within the educational governance system. We agree with Levin and Fullan (2008) that the key to successful educational change, such as curriculum change, is to create an environment that fosters sustained commitment to change in school and classroom practices and not only through governance and accountability structures. As mentioned earlier, closing the gaps in education achievement requires inclusivity and changes in teaching and learning practices. Thus, curriculum change alone will not bring about equity in an education system. While sustained effort to change and improve teaching and learning practices is necessary, curriculum change does not occur in a vacuum. The socio/cultural/political contexts, within a legislative framework of human rights, accountability and responsibility, play a role in determining the impact and level of success of the change for equity, renewal, peace and social mobility. These ideas formed the backbone of the analysis which is described in the following section.

Methodology

We refer again to Parsons and Beauchamp's definition of curriculum development as being a process concerned with reviewing, planning, developing, implementing and maintaining curriculum (2012, p. 26). We also embrace the assertion by Patterson and Czajkowski (1979) that curriculum change refers to any conscious, deliberate attempt to engender change in the curriculum of a school or school system. We juxtaposed these ideas and concluded that the primary curriculum renewal process in which the MoE was engaged was a curriculum development process that was expected to result in curriculum change.

Although the conduct of this research study was only permissible after the curriculum renewal process had reached the implementation stage, we were still able to suspect very early in our research activity that both challenges and gains had been encountered in the curriculum renewal process. We therefore saw it fit to draw on Gross' Turbulence Theory in making sense of what had transpired. This, then, is a post hoc analysis of the curriculum renewal process that draws heavily on Turbulence Theory as a frame of analysis.

Design

This was a case study within the qualitative research paradigm (Merriam, 1988; Miles & Huberman, 1994). The phenomenon explored was the process of interaction between key stakeholders involved in the primary curriculum renewal process, which was occurring within the bounded context of the primary education system of Trinidad and Tobago. We further define the study as an instrumental case study in that the intention was to seek in-depth understandings of an issue (Merriam, 1988; Stake, 1995).

Data Collection

Semi-structured interviews were the main method of data collection used. Key stakeholders were identified and these were interviewed either individually, or in focus groups. The data-gathering exercise spanned a period of about three months. The interviews were all directed at gaining respondents' perceptions of being involved in the process of planning for, developing and implementing the revised primary school curriculum. The selection of interviewees was guided by a desire to gain the perceptions of stakeholders at the various levels where possible. Thus, the interviewees in Trinidad included the CEO; members of the CPT; the Director of the CPDD; three CCs, 14 COs and 17 practicing teachers who had functioned as members of writing teams. The interviewees in Tobago included the Student Support Services Coordinator, two primary school supervisors, seven principals and one teacher who was at the time deputising as principal. Convenience sampling was used in instances where access to stakeholders (particularly at the lower levels of the system) proved to be challenging. The foreign consultants were not interviewed as they had long completed their task and left the country.

Interview protocols were designed, peer-reviewed, and refined. Interviews were audio-taped, after first gaining permission from the interviewee(s) to do so. No interviewees objected to being audio-taped. Names of interviewees were concealed.

Data Analysis

Audiotapes were transcribed and the transcripts were subjected to thematic analysis. In the first round of analysis, attempts were made to identify incidents in the curriculum review process that were either reported as being significant, or else, their significance was alluded to. In the second round of analysis, these incidents were examined using Gross' Turbulence Theory, including the level of turbulence, the role of positionality, instances of cascading, and any effect of stability on the impact of turbulence.

Discussion of Findings

The analysis was done in response to the research questions:

(1) What were the agencies, and where did the power lie in their interactions in the process of renewing the primary school curriculum in Trinidad and Tobago?
(2) Which (if any) interactions among agencies produced turbulence during the primary school curriculum renewal process and what impact did any such turbulence have on the different agencies' navigation through curriculum renewal goals and related cultural changes?

The Main Actors

All the agencies referred to in the description of the context of the study mentioned previously were involved in the process of curriculum renewal. The directive for the commencement of the process came from the Minister of Education, and was further amplified in the meetings of the Strategic Executive Team. The Director of the CPDD, under the direction of the CEO, had the responsibility to ensure that the plan was executed. A CPT, made up of senior Curriculum staff, was appointed to guide the planning and the day-to-day operations of the project. The foreign consultants played a key role as they were involved, not only in the planning for the curriculum renewal, but also in training local personnel to be prepared for the work at hand. In this regard, the consultants worked closely with the CPT and also with the writing teams. Typically, a writing team was led by a CC or a CO and was made up of specially selected primary school teachers and, in some cases, other COs as well.

Exploring the Interactions

Turbulence Theory was the main tool used to explore the interactions among agencies. Gross (2014) recommends that the analysis should begin with an exploration of the contextual variables operating. In the introduction to this chapter, we outlined some of the contextual factors. We reiterate these factors here since they set the stage for exploring significant events and any turbulence experienced:

• There was an all-round desire for change at the time of the curriculum renewal process. Although the renewal process was initiated as a result of a policy directive from a new Minister of Education who had new policy ideas about the curriculum, there was also consensus among teachers, parents and MoE officials that the curriculum was outdated.

- The renewal process was facilitated by both financial and intellectual input from international agencies/organisations. Funding came in the form of a loan from the IDB and foreign consultants were employed to generate baseline documents and also to lead the curriculum writing process.
- The philosophical orientation for the revised curriculum, that is, *a thematic integrated approach*, was decided by Ministry officials and the foreign consultants. There existed an entrenched view from past secondary school curriculum development efforts that an integrated approach to the curriculum was best. The foreign consultants were also enthusiastic about an integrated approach. The thematic component was introduced by senior MoE personnel.
- Most of the CCs and COs responsible for the delivery of the curriculum had, hitherto, worked mainly within the secondary school sector. There were very few among them with a primary school curriculum background. In addition, very few had any primary curriculum development experience of note, given that the existing primary curriculum had been in use for over 20 years. The thematic integrated approach was new to almost all curriculum personnel.
- Curriculum development was not intimately linked to the supervisory structure for primary schools. The curriculum development process was managed by a CPT situated in the CPDD and writing teams comprised COs and CCs leading teachers in the writing of the curriculum. Neither the School Supervisors nor the Principals who report directly to the School Supervisors were directly involved in the curriculum development exercise.

With a full understanding of the context, Gross (2014) recommends that questions pertaining to positionality be asked to 'illuminate' turbulence by exploring how different groups and individuals in the organisation experience it. In addition, Gross and Shapiro (2016) highlight that positionality, cascading, and stability affect one another and therefore their combined impact should be explored. We therefore sought to use this framework to analyse interview data collected from the various stakeholders involved in the review of the primary school curriculum in the attempt to understand the degree of turbulence (if any) and its impact at the various stages of the exercise.

Interactions of the CPT in the Curriculum Writing Process

This team was central to the curriculum renewal exercise. It interacted with those above it in the chain of command, that is, the Director of the CPDD and the CEO, and also with those below it, that is, the CCs, the COs and the writing teams.

The Director of the CPDD explained that the focus on integration had been 'mandated' by consultants who had guided the revision of the lower secondary curriculum in the years preceding this exercise. The members of the CPT had done their own literature research and had themselves found a thematic integrated approach to be attractive. The coordinator of this team explained:

> And so, as we continued to meet and make inputs and so on, and do our own research, the merits of the integrated thematic

approach were clear to us. We had our own discussions about it
[...] and were very sold in no time (CPT Coordinator).

So, making decisions about the philosophical orientation of the curriculum
was a significant incident in the curriculum renewal process. There seems to
have been light turbulence among the top MoE officials at this initiation stage
about what the philosophical orientation for the curriculum would be.

The CPT had been given full responsibility for the execution of the writing
exercise by the Executive Management Team. To carry out the work, though,
they had to be trained and guided by the foreign consulting firm that had been
contracted and charged with this responsibility. Significant incidents occurred in
the interactions between the CPT and the consultants and these sometimes
resulted in severe turbulence. On the one hand, the consultants, who had very
little experience with the local context, were supposed to train and guide the
CPT. On the other hand, the members of the CPT were senior members of the
CPDD, with some advanced training in education. Perhaps more importantly,
they had a deep understanding of the local context, including the needs of the
teachers and children for whom the curriculum was being designed. There were
several instances where turbulence developed. The following excerpt illustrates
this phenomenon:

> They guided us. The two leads that we saw the most, were
> [Names given]. They came intermittently to Trinidad and we
> would have plenary sessions with them. They would offer ideas,
> but, a lot of times they wanted to know what we wanted. Things
> emerged through discussions – a lot of discussions – sometimes
> heated discussions. They had some set ideas of where they wanted
> to go. We had set ideas in terms of our educational context, our
> context, our culture, and so there were times when we were very
> heated and passionate in our discussions (CPT member).

It is interesting to note here that the CPT did not treat the consulting firm as
having more authority. Instead, they were determined to have their views considered and acted upon. Contextual factors such as lack of familiarity with the
local context on the part of consultants and what appears to have been some initial lack of flexibility on their part seem to have caused cascading to occur, to
the point where discussions were sometimes 'heated'.

Another significant occurrence experienced by the CPT involved the passing
on of the concept of a thematic integrated approach to writing teams and helping them to embrace this approach and work with it during the writing phase.
Interview data indicate that a fair amount of uncertainty about the focus of the
work prevailed for a while. Even at the end of the exercise, the uncertainty per-
sisted. For example, one writing team member declared after the writing exercise
had been completed: *We all need to question where the decision to make it a thematic integrated approach came from.* Indeed, we were never able to get clear,

theoretical explanations of the concept although the literal translation of focusing on themes and cutting across subject areas, rather than using a subject-based approach, was clearly enunciated. Nonetheless, the severe turbulence caused by using the thematic integrated approach also had some positive outcomes as there were other team members who remarked that though the task was difficult, it was rewarding, for example:

> Even though at times I found the process was a little disorienting, I appreciated it in the sense that they were asking us to make a paradigm shift from how we approach teaching and how you would approach even teaching at the primary school (Writing Team member).

From the perspective of positionality, the CPT had the level of authority to ensure that the use of a thematic integrated approach did, in fact, occur. However, there was some attempt at democratising some aspects of the remainder of the curriculum writing process. There was a wide discussion among CCs and COs about other factors that should impact the design. Although the curriculum writers (teachers) were simply told that they had to use the thematic integrated design, they were allowed to influence what actually went into the materials by being given the latitude to indicate what could and could not work in a primary school system. Thus, although turbulence existed, it was mitigated to some extent by the willingness of those in higher positions of authority (CPT) to allow for some degree of input from others with less authority.

Interactions between MOE Personnel and School Personnel
One of the goals of the curriculum review process was to create a curriculum that would better serve the needs of all students, albeit a curriculum that fostered equity by focusing on inclusivity and differentiated instruction. A member of the CPT explained: *Our system had evolved to a different place in terms of inclusivity where we were looking at a measure of students with challenges being mainstreamed* [...] Another member of the CPT also acknowledged that teacher training to implement the new curriculum was imperative and that *differentiated instruction was one of the pillars in an attempt to widen the training base.*

Interview data indicated that the CPT had a comprehensive plan for implementing the revised curriculum that included teacher training prior to implementation, monitoring, supervision and evaluation of the implementation process. This did not, however, go as planned. Rather, a plethora of events occurred that created moderate to extreme turbulence that thwarted the original implementation plan.

Moderate turbulence occurred when a new Government was voted into office and a new Minister of Education was installed, since the new Minister had different ideas of how the revision process should take place and issued directives accordingly. Changes included working with shorter timelines and a reduced budget. On a positive note, in response to the shortened timeline, the CPT coordinator and one of her co-leads from the curriculum writing teams used their creativity and edited some of the documents themselves. The coordinator's words mentioned below express both the tension that the changes in timelines caused and the creativity of their response to it, which indicate that there was some stability in this team.

> We wanted more time, more time in the writing process to do it more extensively, more deeply. We had seen a couple of typos. Even though we hired an editor he could not work with our time-lines. And myself and one of my co-leads [Name given] edited the entire document ourselves.

Three events occurred that, collectively, had a cascading effect, resulting in severe turbulence. First, the IDB loan that funded the project had been significantly expended, so that there were less funds available for the project than originally envisioned. Second, the new Minister changed the implementation plan that involved piloting the curriculum change with 60 selected schools for a period of three years, to going national with the implementation in all schools, all at once. This meant that the timelines for implementation moved from a three-year rollout plan to two weeks. This triggered a change in the planned teacher training, which changed from the planned two-week exercise, to one week and eventually to four days. Third, as a result of a lack of resources, the Curriculum Implementation Support Team (CIST) that was set up to supervise, monitor and evaluate the change was no longer operationalised. It can be said that the combination of these cascading events culminated in extreme turbulence, because the CIST, charged with the critical role of ensuring that the implementation process was monitored, supervised and evaluated was never operationalised. Below is how one member of the CIST team summarised the impact of the turbulence:

> Because those two factors (lack of resources and the political directive to go national with the implementation) simultaneously − that movement from small control group where we could have evaluated and could have seen what were the shortcomings and more specifically treat with teacher and teacher training support within that controlled environment, see where our needs were or where our plans were not meeting the needs of teachers [...] redirected certain elements that we would have planned for in a certain way − we were not able to do that.

Even more so, in terms of positionality, the turbulence affected schools and school staff, as they were not adequately prepared to implement the new curriculum and, in some cases, this resulted in partial or no implementation of the revised curriculum in some schools.

Interactions between MoE Personnel and THA DEYAS Education Personnel
Interview data on the interactions between THA DEYAS education personnel
and MoE personnel are conflicting. All persons interviewed from Tobago were of
the view that the level of consultation afforded them was unacceptable. As a
contextually and culturally homogenous group, Tobago Principals and School
Supervisors were in agreement that Tobago's input was not represented at the
initialising stage of the revision process. Neither Tobago School Principals nor
School Supervisors were represented on the MOE implementation team. This is
exemplified in the words of one Tobago principal who stated: *I only heard about it
when they start sending the rewrite to us. We did not have much of an input. We are
like little additives, the suffix.* Nevertheless, there is documentation that MoE personnel had apprised education officials in Tobago of their plans as early as 2009.
Additionally, interview data from MoE officials outlined measures that were
taken to ensure that Tobago was included every step along the way, for example:

> A full consultation of Tobago's stakeholders was held in August
> 2011 with the attendance of [Name given], Minister of Education
> and other heads of the Ministry of Education and The Tobago
> Division of Education, Youth Affairs and Sport. This event was
> chaired by [Name given] and Tobago's voice was well represented
> in the data taken into consideration for the review of the curricu-
> lum. (Member of CPT)

It would seem then that there was light turbulence in the interactions between
the MoE personnel and the Tobago education officials that might have affected
the curriculum development process. With regard to positionality, Tobago personnel expressed the view that they were disadvantaged because of their position
on the smaller of the two islands and because they were not allowed the opportunity to bring things that were specific to Tobago to the curriculum development table. This was in stark contrast to the perspective of the MoE officials
and it is not surprising that turbulence ensued.

Conclusion

The study sought to examine the agencies and interactions of these agencies
involved in the primary curriculum renewal process to determine which, if any,
brought about turbulence and the impact of such turbulence on the curriculum
renewal process. Turbulence initiated the move to renew the primary curriculum,
which was laudable, given the goals of the renewal to improve primary school
education by making it more inclusive by differentiating instruction and generally making it more equitable. The reports indicate that a great level of thought
and organisation had gone into the preparation and planning for the review
exercise, as exemplified by the creation of teams within the MoE to manage certain aspects of the review. There is evidence that stakeholders were consulted in
the early stages of the process, but the evidence was not forthcoming as to how
the views of stakeholders were incorporated into the curriculum development

process. Two key sets of change agents (school supervisors and principals) were not members of the curriculum planning team. This was a critical oversight because these two sets of stakeholders are responsible for supervising and monitoring policy implementation and leading and managing change at the site of change, that is, the schools.

The research shows that turbulence occurred at various stages of the review process. Gross and Shapiro (2016) submit that turbulence is a part of our lives and they advise that the best approach to deal with this force is to use it to our advantage and to work with it, rather than to try to control it. To some extent, this approach was taken by some of the agencies involved in the primary revision process. For example, the impetus for curriculum change was a result of taking advantage of the collective dissatisfaction by education stakeholders with a curriculum that was not realising equity by serving the needs of all students. Additionally, there is evidence that some members of the curriculum writing team felt that engagement in the curriculum development process was rewarding and that making a contribution to the development of a more meaningful primary curriculum was empowering, even though the process was taxing.

Still, the degree of turbulence at times was overwhelming and did thwart some of the change efforts. One example of this was the cascading that occurred within the writing teams, which did not have a full grasp of the concept of a thematic integrated curriculum. Further, there is the cascading and extreme turbulence that led to the abandonment of the CIST, which was an important agency for the implementation process of the curriculum renewal. The CPT was left powerless, having no resources to enable the work of the unit and having to follow the political directorate's mandate to roll out the curriculum at the national level instead of at the level of a pilot as had been planned. We highlight again the admonition by Parsons and Beauchamp (2012, p. 29) that 'if a curriculum revision process is overly ambitious, is carried out within short timelines and is within an environment of low investment in teachers, problems will inevitably arise'. We note that this was borne out in this primary curriculum renewal process.

Glatthorn et al. (2012) and Thijs and van den Akker (2009) argue that sociopolitical contextual factors can impact the curriculum development process. In this case, while the findings show that these socio-political contextual factors such as the voice of the political directorate and advice from international consultants provided much of the impetus for the curriculum renewal process, they also show that these very socio-political contextual factors complicated and to some extent inhibited the curriculum development process, causing much turbulence in the process.

References

Ainscow, M. (2005). Developing inclusive education systems: What are the levers for change? *Journal of Educational Change, 6*(2), 109–124.

Berliner, D., & Biddle, B. (1995). *The manufactured crisis: Myths, fraud, and the attck on America's public schools*. New York, NY: Perseus Books.

Darling-Hammond, L. (2010). *The flat world and education: How America's commitment to equity will determine our future.* New York, NY: Teachers College Press.

Desimone, L. M. (2009). Improving impact studies of teachers' professional development: Toward better conceptualizations and measures. *Educational Researcher, 38*(3), 181–199.

Fullan, M. (2006). Change theory: A force for school improvement (Centre for Strategic Education Seminar Series Paper No. 157). Retrieved from http://www.michaelfullan.ca/Articles_06/06_change_theory.pdf.

Fullan, M. (2007). *The new meaning of educational change* (4th ed.). New York, NY: Teachers College Press.

Fullan, M. (2010). *All systems go: The change imperative for whole school reform.* Thousand Oaks, CA: Corwin and Ontario Principals' Council.

Glatthorn, A., Boschee, F., Whitehead, B., & Boschee, B. (2012). *Curriculum leadership: Strategies for development and implementation* (3rd ed.). Los Angeles, CA: Sage.

Gross, J. (2014). Using turbulence theory to guide actions. In C. Branson & S. Gross (Eds.), *Handbook of Ethical Leadership* (pp. 246–262). Abingdon: Routledge.

Gross, S. J., & Shapiro, J. P. (2016). *Democratic ethical educational leadership: Reclaiming school reform.* New York, NY: Routledge.

Inter-American Development Bank. (2009, May). IDB backs Trinidad and Tobago's Seamless education system. Retrieved from http://www.iadb.org/en/news/news-releases/2009-05-20/idb-backs-trinidad-and-tobagos-seamless-education-system,5418.html

Johnson Jr., M. (1967). Definitions and models in curriculum theory. *Educational Theory, 17*(2), 127–140.

Levin, B. (2007). Sustainable, large scale education renewal. *Journal of Educational Change, 8*(4), 323–336. doi:10.1007/s10833-007-9041-y

Levin, B., & Fullan, M. (2008). Learning about system renewal. *Educational Management Administration & Leadership, 36*(2), 289–303.

McKinsey Report. (2007). *How the world's best performing systems come out on top.* London: McKinsey & Company.

Merriam, S. B. (1988). *Case study research in education: A qualitative approach.* San Francisco, CA: Jossey-Bass Publishers.

Miles, M. B., & Huberman, A. M. (1994). *Qualitative Data Analysis: An Expanded Source Book* (2nd ed.). Thousand Oaks: Sage.

Ohanian, S. (1999). *One size fits few: The folly of educational standards.* Portsmouth, NH: Heinemann.

Online Dictionary. (2017). Retrieved from https://www.google.tt/search?ei=zGWyW7OrA4XI5gLmxrHYDA&q=online+dictionary&oq=online+dictionary&gs_l=psy-ab.1.0.35i39k1j0i7i30k1l8j0i67k1.3272.4025.0.6595.5.5.0.0.0.0.188.320.0j2.2.0....0...1c.1.64.psy-ab..3.2.318....0.FN-O6mAK36c. Accessed on 2 January 2017.

Parsons, J., & Beauchamp, L. (2012). *From knowledge to action: Shaping the future of curriculum development in Alberta.* Alberta: Alberta Education and Standards Sector.

Patterson, J., & Czajkowski, T. (1979). Implementation: Neglected phase in curriculum change. *Educational Leadership, 37*(3), 204–206.

Stake, R. (1995). *The art of case study research.* Thousand Oaks, CA: Sage.

Thijs, A., & van den Akker, J. (Eds.). (2009). *Curriculum in Development*. Enschede: SLO—Netherlands Institute for Curriculum Development. Retrieved from http://www.slo.nl/downloads/2009/curriculum-in-development.pdf/

Thrupp, M., & Lupton, R. (2006). Taking school contexts more seriously: The social justice challenge. *British Journal of Educational Studies, 54*(3), 308—328.

Tomlinson, C. A. (2014). *The differentiated classroom: Responding to the needs of all learners*. North Garden VA: Association for Supervision Curriculum Development.

UNESCO (2001). *The open file on inclusive education*. Paris: UNESCO.

Chapter 9

Empowering Superintendents in the United States to Empower Societal Innovators for Equity and Renewal in the Community

Carole Collins-Ayanlaja, Warletta Brookins and Alison Taysum

Abstract

Superintendents' agency in the US is shaped by governance systems within education systems. These Education Governance Systems have been in a state of flux and experienced turbulence for twenty years. The professional challenge this research addresses is how do 14 credentialed educational professional African American women superintendents with doctorates and track records of school improvement, navigate the turbulence to empower families, and Empower Young Societal Innovators for Equity, Renewal (EYSIER), Social Mobility, and Peace.

This chapter identifies three aspects of a theory of knowledge to action to emerge from the empirical evidence presented. First, African American women superintendents need to know how to access policy and legislation, how to stay up to date with policy and need to be empowered to challenge policy. Policy has the back of African American women fighting institutionalised racism. Second, African American women superintendents need role models, and mentors with wisdom who can create proactive and mobilising networks across the state and the nation to advocate for and to support the teachers' and leaders' professional learning to be the best teachers, leaders and superintendents they can be. Finally, the African American women superintendents who have been self-selecting, or identified as potential future superintendents by current superintendents and schoolboards, need to be part of succession planning that transcends the short elected lives of district school boards. Newly incumbent African American women superintendents need to be empowered by Education Governance Systems to enable them to deliver on their manifestos and track records of

Turbulence, Empowerment and Marginalisation in International
Education Governance Systems, 205–233
doi:10.1108/978-1-78754-675-220181011

outstanding school improvement with the impact strategies they were employed to implement. The impact strategies include promoting high-quality home–school engagement and ensuring all students learn how to learn, are culturally sensitive, ask good questions and solve problems as Young Societal Innovators for Equity and Renewal. The chapter recommends a network of African American women superintendents implements this theory of knowledge to action and that their work is documented, and if successful in optimising students' learning, and outcomes, disseminated to build capacity for EYSIER.

Keywords: Democracy; equity; achievement gap; reparation; peace

Introduction

The Turbulence Superintendents Navigate

Superintendents' agency in the US is shaped by governance systems within education systems. These Education Governance Systems have been in a state of flux and experienced turbulence for twenty years. The professional challenge this research addresses is how do 14 credentialed educational professional African American women superintendents with doctorates and track records of school improvement, navigate the turbulence to empower families and Empower Young Societal Innovators for Equity, Renewal (EYSIER), Social Mobility and Peace.

The context is complex because superintendents are expected to play pivotal roles in navigating the turbulence and leading the change to optimise students' learning and student outcomes (Björk, Browne-Ferrigno, & Kowalski, 2014). Lassnigg (2016) identifies States' and Federal control of Education Governance Systems has increased by mechanisms of accountability made possible by data management introduced with The Programme for International Student Assessment (PISA). Pons (2017) calls such data management governance by numbers where the individual lives of each human being can be readily replaced by a string of exam results, a kind of DNA coding that, coupled with the post-code can predict, or even determine, the trajectory of a lived life. Alston (2012, p. 128) challenges the role of models to control and predict district outcomes because the lived lives of individuals who are discriminated against because of their race, or gender, need to be examined 'in order to discredit and discount misconceptions and beliefs held by dominant groups about people of colour'.

Decentralisation of power to school boards has appeared to reduce central control. However, the main change has been a loss of bureaucratic systems that were important for knowledge transfer, exchange and cascading. The main problem is the communication lines between the assessment of students' learning and their feedback which seek to reduce unpredictability through standardisation which undermines culturally relevant learning which is unpredictable and complex (Lassnigg, 2016). Ford and Ihrke (2016) suggest governance by the school board can be understood as mission to optimise academic outcomes, policy at academic, administrative and fiscal levels and administration which is the implementation of the policies to deliver on the mission. Another dimension is management of instruction, and assessment for learning which the school board can attempt to manipulate, but ultimately the superintendent and her or his principals and staff implement these policies as text on a day-to-day basis through policy as discourse in the classrooms (Ball, 2004). School boards in executing their duties may be dysfunctional, and/or change, resulting in high superintendent turnover despite the superintendents meeting their targets to raise exam scores (Grissom & Anderson, 2012). The aim of this chapter is to generate new understandings of the severity of the impact of different problems superintendents who are women of colour encounter, and to develop a theory of Empowerment through Governance Systems for Equity and Renewal. The authors recognise Nathan Glazer's (1987) essay 'Emergence of an American Ethnic Pattern', to identify the Black-White achievement gap as a global phenomenon (Wagner, 2010). Our research seeks to document patterns that emerge from the evidence and seeks to present an emerging Theory of Knowledge to Action which has implications for other minoritised communities. We focus on women of colour because there are an estimated 45,672, 250 Black residents in the United States (US Census Bureau, 2016). Although this number is smaller than the estimated 57,230,247 Hispanic population resident in the US, 50,218,265 of this Hispanic population identify as White (Ibid) and therefore need to be the focus of a separate study.

There is a dearth of qualitative research on women of colour in decision-making positions in education systems and particularly on their role as top Chief Executives of education system leadership. To address this gap, and to make a new contribution to knowledge, this chapter focuses on Black women superintendents as the sample aligns with the purpose of the book to generate new understandings of how these Black women navigate intersectionalities of discrimination. Horsford (2014) draws on Crenshaw (1989) to make the case that socially constructed identities include race, gender, cultural heritage, class, language, faiths and none, gay, lesbian, bisexual, queer and transgender (GLBQT), and those recognised as disabled by society. Superintendents are empowered, or otherwise, to lead curriculum transformation to support the educational success of Black young people, young people of Colour, religiously divided young people and all young people with protected characteristics in the UK Equality Act (UK Government, 2010) in a context of a Black-White achievement gap. Turbulence Theory allows the authors to categorise the impact of the interplay between the superintendent, policy and the school board. Gross (2014, p. 248) theory of turbulence states that 'turbulence can be described as 'light' with little or no movement of the craft. 'Moderate with Very noticeable waves. 'Severe' with strong gusts that threaten control of the aircraft. 'Extreme' with forces so great that control is lost and structure damage to the craft occurs'. The authors take a social constructivist approach to collecting fourteen narrative biographies of Black women superintendents using semi-structured interviews

(Denscombe, 2007). The strategy is case study (Yin, 2008). The research con-
formed to the British Educational Research Association (BERA) (2011)
Guidelines for Ethical Framework, and the American Educational Research
Association ethical framework (2010), the University of Leicester ethical Code
of Conduct, Governors State University Institutional Review Board and Eastern
Illinois University Institutional Review Board.

The authors' positions in the research is humanist, and all three authors are
Christians. Our values and behaviours are that we love God and that God has
invited us to follow his commandments. The first two of these commandments
are to love God, and the second is to love each one of his children which is every
human being regardless of their faith or none, their race, ethnicity or their cultural heritage and to advocate for social justice with courage and prudence on
this planet for each human being who was, is and is yet to come. We believe
that each child has rights (United Nations, 1948), and responsibilities in their
cultural and economic participation in a democratic education system and a
democratic society (Dewey, 2016) post desegregation and to realise the promised
freedom of the Brown V Board of Education (United States Supreme Court,
1954) that broke the strong hold of Jim Crow and racial segregation (Douglas
Horsford & Bell McKenzie, 2008). To address the aims of the chapter, the
authors ask three questions: first, how do the Black women superintendents
describe and understand their interplay with policy and how the school board
empowers or disempowers them to raise exam scores and optimise the cultural
relevancy of the curriculum for all? Second, how do they describe and understand the role mentors, and/or advocates play when they navigate the governance structures? Finally, to what extent do superintendents believe a cultural
change is required to empower them to empower school communities within
existing governance structures?

Policy Defends Human Rights?

Superintendents need to know policy and their preparation needs to include
courses in school law, and game changing judicial decisions that impact the integration or segregation of marginalisation groups (James & McCormick, 2009;
Tellerico & Blount, 2004). Further Tellerico and Blount (2004) identify that state
and federal benchmarking data that reveal subgroups identified by race,
GLBQT, language, special education, ethnicity, religion and special needs labels
need to be used by the superintendent and the school board when implementing
key works and what Pons (2017) call statistical equity which redefines social justice. Pons identifies, however, that powerful agents of change in education systems may interpret, and manipulate PISA data and disseminate it, but arguably
they will not be able to manipulate poverty indicators. Payne (2008) identifies
that poverty has a massive impact on education and that the post-code of a child
is a key determinant in their academic career trajectory regarding whether they
will or will not be college eligible and then attend college and complete. Yet
school funding itself is influenced by a policy which can change as the House of
Representatives and Senate swing from one ideology to another and thus change

policy because education funding is not A-political; the politicisation of funding is summed up by Björk et al. (2014, 458):

> With regard to adequacy, progressives believe the lack of financial resources needed to implement mandated reforms jeopardises accomplishing the task. With regard to efficiency, conservatives endorse the need to increase funding to produce higher levels of student academic outcomes but argue that broad-based competition will produce both efficiency and increased student learning. With regard to liberty, conservatives believe that local school taxes are preferable to increasing federal government support and accepting greater levels of control of education; however, they oppose tax increases. With regard to equity, the disparity among school districts to generate tax revenue has forced a majority of states legislatures to develop more equitable funding formulas. These disparate concerns reflect the collision between the individual and the public interest (Levin, 1999) and describe the rough-and-tumble world in which superintendents will invariably be forced to make unpopular decisions (Kowalski, 2013). Hence, continuous conflict among interest groups and contentious politics are redefining superintendents' work.

The politics can also play out between school board members and the superintendent where school board members' reasons for becoming school board members is altruistic, but may also be about having power over the superintendent, and playing out vendettas (Mountford, 2004). As such the relationships between school board members and the superintendent may be tedious, controversial and very turbulent which can distract from the school boards' key works in governance practices and prevent the superintendent from implementing change strategies to optimise students' learning supported by parents' full and free interactions and association with the school and school staff. Mountford (2004) goes on to argue there are few school board candidates and low voter turnout and a large number of board members are appointed by other board members outside elections. The school board have less power with increased state and federal control and find decision-making more difficult which can lead to apathy and the kinds of turbulence that is difficult to navigate to improve culturally relevant learning and improve student outcomes in the district. Yet Mountford identifies that one board member sought election so that they could sack the current superintendent because they thought they could do a better job. A board member may be less qualified with no experience in education, but may seek to usurp the superintendent for personal reasons, perhaps this is why there are such high superintendent turnovers (Grissom & Anderson, 2012).

Ehren, Honingh, Hooge and O'Hara (2016) suggest that school boards do not focus on the governance of instruction, the curriculum and learning and teaching, which they leave to the superintendents to work with principals and teachers. However, if the superintendents are engaged with power plays with turbulent boards, the superintendents do not have time for this important work. Ehren et al. (2016, 448) suggest: 'Additional improvements in the effectiveness of these school boards could be gained if school inspections motivate these school boards to focus on the governance of teaching and instruction in their schools'. Sheard and Avis (2011) and Bush and Coleman (2001) both make the point that pedagogic knowledge, or the art and science of learning and teaching (Garrison, 2009) and engaging with the knowledge, skills, experience and expertise of social systems in the locale of the district schools may become empowering at a strategic level. Phelan (2009) argues teachers who are free from fixed rules and technical, standardised teaching to the test may engage with the unpredictability in the classroom as diverse personalities from different cultural heritages to facilitate what Dewey called 'the grace and play of life' that engages with moral training of the immature child to the mature.

Arguably superintendents need to be empowered to mobilise collaborations and partnerships to connect their staff, with the students, the parents and the community. Connecting different groups may empower community members to build meaningful and worthwhile relationships and work for equity. Together, these different groups with different interests may explore what leading a good life is together and make informed choices about their values and behaviours so they can live a good life. Superintendents cannot empower young societal innovators to work for equity and renewal of this nature with intergenerational community members, if they are in a mode of 'protectionism' with a focus on keeping their post, rather than building capacity for sustainable instruction with the education systems they lead and manage and administrate (Alston, 2000). Indeed, protectionism does not only prevent superintendents from meeting this standard for superintendents; it prevents them from meeting the other standards that map back to their job description that is decided at state level. Carrasco and Fromm (2016) suggest that the positions of schools within the district can create turbulence for superintendents meeting standards whilst responding to market pressures and school boards who may build market competitive agendas which do not seek all children to optimise their learning. Rather, the markets can shape the values that underpin the school boards' policies and administration to meet their mission statement by undermining the larger community relationships by building greater entitlement for their students than other students in other schools get, due to different available funding. Ford and Ihrke (2016) identify that school boards with members who have served for five years or more are more effective. Ford and Ihrke identify stability is probably a key factor here, and working with one superintendent offers opportunities for both school boards and superintendents to develop their key work together and build trust and respect for each other's knowledge, skills, experience and expertise to deliver the mission, policies, administration and instructional dimensions day by day.

Mentoring African American Women for Mobilisation into Chief Executive Superintendency

Munoz et al. (2014) affirm that a key driver to women seeking and becoming superintendent role incumbent was their empowerment, and all superintendents had mentors. However, if their mentors were not powerful and did not possess the power relationships to help them create what Bhaskar (2010) calls real-world opportunities, the mentors could not be effective advocates for their mentees and secure their successful move into the top Chief Executive position of superintendent. Grant (2012) suggests that African American female aspiring superintendents experience intersectionalities of discrimination (Crenshaw, 1989). A qualifier for becoming superintendent is the doctorate and doing Predominantly White Institution's (PWIs) doctorates many African American women have negative experiences (Gay, 2004). Grant (2012) identifies these negative experiences follow them in their careers and manifest themselves in unfair treatment, being marginalised, isolated, misjudged, silenced, discouraged, dismissed, their intellect called into question and a limited access to building networks of same-race women, ethnic role models, and to mentors who can help them navigate the turbulence they experience from institutionalised racism in PWIs (Collins Ayanalaja, & Taysum, 2016). Tillman (2012) agrees with Grant and Gay and reveals Black females need mentoring that is constructive, purposeful and consistently develops the individual to reach their career goals. Networks of mentors across disciplines supports success as does participation in committees and making presentations in the district, state, nationally and internationally. Tillman (2012, p. 124) states:

> You must be purposeful and strategic in meeting, networking with, and being mentored by well-established senior scholars (and in some cases junior scholars). Talk with them about your goals. Get advice from them about the best strategies to accomplish your goals, and develop or revise your plan based on suggestions they make that can enhance your career [...] Networking also includes meeting, communicating with, and collaborating with scholars in your peer group. This can be beneficial to Black female early career scholars who want to establish a support group that will facilitate friendship and professional collaborations.

The integration and promise of a post-racial society post-Brown and Jim Crow has not empowered African American women, and Ladson-Billings (2005) suggests these women navigate the turbulence that exists between the social order that perpetuates White privilege and the degradation and oppression of their own racial group. The structures of institutions harbour the constructs of an old social order that legitimised stealing Black people from Africa and enslaving them and treating them brutally (De Gruy, 2005; Taysum & Murrel-Abery, 2017). The labour from the slaves built the wealth of the nation that was not shared with those that had laboured (Taysum & Murrel-Abery, 2017). Thus, the division of labour gave upper-class slave owners greater entitlement, and cultural, economic and political power than White middle-class people and White working-class people and these White people had greater entitlement and cultural and economic and political power than Black slaves. Reparation for the evil of slavery has not been made and is not being made in the social construction of society. The radicalised structures do not empower marginalised groups with the thinking tools they need to be independent, critical and reflective thinkers who have self-awareness (Taysum, 2012a, b). These people are potentially internalising the regulation of the markets that sustain the panopticon overview of those with power and prevents innovation that may seek to redistribute the division of labour through social mobility (Foucault, 1991). Thus, the opportunity to seek a golden balance between socialism and capitalism is not offered but may be if the future generations develop the knowledge skills and experience they need to become societal innovators for equity and renewal (Taysum, 2012a, b, 2013, 2014; Taysum et al., 2015, 2016, 2017) and are able to bridge to their true self Stansberry Beard (2012). In the beginning, such bridging may need to take place in conditions that do not recognise all people and how the pledge to the American Flag: 'one Nation under God, indivisible, with liberty and justice for all' is interpreted as important with regard to what Adler (1941) calls the virtue of social justice.

Meyer and Benavot (2013) suggest that the oppression and the financial differentials between funding of different schools have led to greater differences between schools which is affirmed by neoliberalism, market forces. The differentials are reaffirmed with superintendents and principals having more autonomy with the implementation of the curriculum. Thus, the inequalities are allowed to perpetuate, and the fear of managing a culture change, leading to a loss of greater entitlement by those that enjoy White privilege including working-class White folk and middle-class White folk can drive a projection of hatred towards those that appear to threaten a person's well-being (Taysum, 2017a). Potentially, a divide and conquer is at play between White working-class and White middle-class groups, White groups and Black groups, and Black working-class groups and Black middle-class groups. Tribes only come together to fight for their own well-being, and allegiances can shift if a person's greater entitlement within a social order, or institution, won through competition within neo-liberal market forces is threatened. Institutions may protect their privilege and perpetuate it (Kakos & Palaiologou, 2014). The fear of giving up their additional entitlement may be consciously or subconsciously protected by creating intersectionalities of discrimination between different groups of people and inviting those with less intersections of discrimination to rule over those with more intersections of discrimination (Taysum, 2017b). Munoz et al. (2014) reveal women superintendents cannot break through the ceiling preventing their promotion to superintendent and that communities, and the school board members are not yet ready to accept them in the top executive role of superintendent. Reed (2012) argues that formal and informal mentoring between older and younger Black women leaders may have a positive impact on intergenerational relationships and help develop bridging cultures with school boards, schools, staff and the communities.

McClellan (2012) suggests that understanding the self through auto-ethnography empowers everyone to interrogate intersectionalities of discrimination.

Greve and Reff Pedersen (2017) report on a Masters programme taken over a period of up to six years, developed by the Danish government and provided by Universities. The Master's programme is in Public Governance and seeks to cross organisational boundaries within the public sector and build collaborative partnerships and working networks between those responsible for executive public management. Evidence reveals public managers have learned more about each other's responsibilities and challenges in different divisions of public services, and this has been facilitated in a non-competitive arena. The programme has enabled managers to develop strategic joined up thinking in their missions, policies, administration and management of day to day activities and their consequences for building sustainable improvement, efficiency and innovations for equity and renewal. These are the kinds of programmes that may lead to culture changes but they need sustained government support and commitment that spans election and re-election terms if they are to deliver the culture change required to optimise all students' learning whilst navigating the negative impact of intersectionalities of discrimination including that of poverty (Payne, 2008). Such a programme connects with Ranson (2008) ideas that cosmopolitan civic society may emerge through a wider reconstitution of the public sphere that seeks equity and renewal through understanding how the education market place perpetuates the greater entitlement of some groups and promotes their interests leaving groups of losers in their wake.

Developing a Culture Change for Equity and Renewal

Culture changes that promote ideologies of inclusion of people of all faiths and none, and of diverse race, ethnicity and protected characteristics documented in the UK Equality Act (UK Government, 2010), and cultural heritages need to connect students' ability and motivations with feelings of belonging (Jenson, 2016). Belonging to a community is positively affirmed when community members from the school board and superintendent, to principals, to staff, to students, to parents and to community stakeholders can experience mutual respect, trust and have spaces of tolerance to agree to disagree and work together to co-create new solutions to old problems for equity and renewal (Taysum, 2017a, 2017b; Taysum, Collins-Ayanlaja, & Popat, 2017). Jenson (2016) suggests such approaches to and engagement with cultural change needs to have bridging strategies between worlds so that all students, parents and staff feel accepted. Brown (2014, p. 1) identifies that African American women superintendents when hired and able to sustain their role as top chief executive are: 'learning, teaching and modelling how to overcome racism, sexism and oppressive socio-politics' and the fact that they are in the role reveals they have successfully navigated the turbulence of intersectionalities of discrimination to become superintendent. Horsford (2014) identifies Black women navigate the severe turbulence of clashing opposite forces of: 'separatism vs. assimilation, nationalism vs. integration, gender equality vs. racial justice. In order to ensure their own rights, they had to fight for both gender equality (from which they would not entirely benefit because of racism) and racial justice (which would be limited by sexism), and bridge divisions within the white women's movement and Black national and power movements, respectively'. The Black women navigated through these seemingly impossible choices to bridge build between the opposing forces (Blackmore, 1999; Fitzgerald, 2010).

Stansberry Beard (2012) develops the idea of bridge building for re-culturing and suggests that perhaps the most important bridging an African American woman superintendent can do is develop self-awareness to be a bridge to one's true self. A superintendent who is true to themselves may be clear about the kinds of social change that is required and can role model learning to learn (James & McCormick, 2009), ask good questions and solve problems (Wagner, 2010). Such clarity of purpose is important because Apple (2013) asks can education change society? Apple identifies that neoliberal agendas and education becoming more closely connected with the needs of corporate society. Such connections drive more and more disconnections between people, their communities, the institutions and the governance systems. The division of labour and the divide and conquer strategies to protect greater entitlements and privilege begs the question who is changing society using education? Brunila and Ryynänen (2017) suggest that disadvantaged young people are being directed to become entrepreneurial and self-regulated within structures that do not allow them to be entrepreneurial due to the many restrictions and regulations that favour corporations. The kinds of entrepreneurial activity that may be realised is through self-employment in zero hours contracts that prevent young people from making rent, getting married, having a family and planning for their retirement. The impact of this is a 'lost generation' who will face their own societal and personal challenges whilst not being able to effectively support a growing elderly population in the future (Castellani, 2012).

Douglas Horsford (2012) argues that for real cultural change educational leaders, school boards and those responsible for developing and recruiting superintendents require greater cultural literacy for re-culturing (Carter, 2008; Stanton-Salazar, 2010; Taysum, 2017b). These superintendents can then act as a bridge when connecting different communities to share different cultures (Taysum, 2017b). These different cultures include the academy and scientific knowledge, the community and members of all faiths and none in the real world that connects with the metaphysical world and those with intersectionalities of discrimination (Dewey, 1929; Helve, 1991). Garrison (2009) identifies such re-culturing may help de-couple the technical accountability models from the critical and reflective approaches. The latter allows teachers to develop unpredictable, culturally relevant full and free interactions in a classroom to optimise learning. Such learning transcends a technical reductionist model of teaching to the test, with highly structured lesson planning, that is not developed by the teacher themselves with the students' participation (Harrison, Taysum, McNamara, & O'Hara, 2016). Phelan (2009) agrees that superintendents need teacher education programmes that help teachers challenge policies and help ethical impartialities to be explored where fear can be addressed by understanding the nature of the fear, such as giving up greater entitlement and privilege, and re-imagining new futures (Taysum, 2017a). Firestone (2009) argues no magic bullet can enable state or federal policy makers to bring about such changes in learning cultures working with education governance systems. For this to occur, the will of the community needs to be aligned with a Board empowering the superintendent to act, and the superintendent needs to mobilise this authority with top district leadership.

Methodology

The research draws its data set from the purposive sampling of 14 African American superintendents currently seated or retired within the last academic year prior to the commencement of the study. Their pseudonyms include Denise, Rachel, Rhonda, Sarah, Nancy, Anita, Theresa, Vickie, Michelle, Grace, Anna, Bessie, Joan, and Helena. The research connects with the call to engage with research of Black leaders' lived experiences in the US who advance social justice agendas in education (Douglas, Horsford, 2016). The respondents were seasoned educational leaders with, on average, twenty plus years in high- level administration and five or more years in the position of superintendent. The study assumes a social constructivist approach and is interpretive. The protocol, comprised of semi-structured open-ended questions (Denscombe, 2007) allowed for guided, open-ended inquiry that welcomed rich, in-depth responses that reflected the participants' attitude and perceptions. The interviews lasted on average one hour, and took place in a location of the interviewee's choice that facilitated comfortable communication. Venues included the respondents' homes, offices, restaurants and coffee shops. During the visits, the researchers recorded the interviews which were transcribed and sent to the participants for respondent validation. When the recording was not agreeable, the researchers took field notes of the interviews. The field notes also detailed background information on the respondent including the number of years in educational leadership and in the role of superintendent, the demographics of the district(s) served and currently serving and a description of significant accomplishments in those districts, and the composition of the school-boards for which the leader worked previously and currently works, most specifically the racial composition of the boards. The background information provided a point of reference for the superintendents and engaged the researchers in understanding the respondent's exposures and range of experiences. Sample size decisions in qualitative research offer leverage depending on the researcher need.

For the purposes of this research, 14 respondents were identified. In ethnography, the recommended sample size is approximately 30−50 interviews, whereas in phenomenology, the recommended sample size is 'six interviews' (Mertens, 1998, p. 271). The interview schedule was robust and the number of respondents for this study was sufficiently placed between both ethnographic norms and phenomenological norms. According to Kilbourn (2006), the phenomena that we aim to understand are filtered through a point of view in a qualitative study. Thus, the theoretical frameworks aforementioned are important as guideposts for the analysis. Interpretations are always filtered through one or more lenses or theoretical perspectives that we use for "seeing"; reality is not something that we find under a rock (p. 545). As researchers we acknowledge our constructs influence the research. Through a collaborative approach to analysis with independent decision-making and group dialogue, three researchers launched the data analysis by depositing the full transcripts to a secure password protected drop box of which each researcher had access. The goal was to conduct multiple reads on each transcript, and then begin to identify themes relative to the overarching questions.

The readers coordinated analyses in categories of thought that reflected the direction set by the questions that had been posed. First, the macro level of categorisation and theme identification prompted the researchers to attempt To identify a common thread that flowed through the interviews. The process of data analysis began to take a more micro approach as the researchers divided data into smaller, meaningful categories that aligned with the research questions. Four key themes emerged:

(1) the superintendent's approach to policy;
(2) the superintendent's perception of board roles;
(3) the superintendent's access to mentorship; and
(4) the superintendent's perspective on the nature of their work and what factors impact their ability to propel the mission and vision of their organisations.

The primary goal throughout the data review and analysis was to cross-check themes that emerged and avoid assumptions. As a reflective process, qualitative analysis grows out of the researcher interaction with the data. For this study, the researchers activated the constant comparative method (Mertens, 1998). Conclusions arose through reflection whereby the researchers were aware of the need to construct and revisit categories, look for similarities, uncover negative evidence and notice patterns (Mertens, 1998; Stainback & Stainback, 1988). Following Huberman's (1994) approach to qualitative analysis, the researchers created a descriptive picture of the superintendent responses. As Patton (2015) suggests, the analysis grew out of a creative process that determined what was significant and what was insignificant. The researchers were two African American women and a White, and non-American woman. The balance created by the diversity of the three researchers participating in data analysis enhanced the quality dimensions and the trustworthiness of the warrants for the claims made (Oancea & Furlong, 2007).

Through collaborative discourse and shared analyses, the researchers provided checks and balances to one another and maintained awareness of subjectivity which offers a more accurate perspective (Peshkin, 1988). The researchers actively approached this project with the desire to gain insight into the data that recognises multiple mindsets and honours the diverse experiences of Black women educational leaders in the superintendent role.

Findings

Policies Defend Human Rights

All fourteen superintendents identified that policy enabled them to work for social justice, and seek funding that was owed through legislation and the law. Three representative quotes on this position are presented:
Denise stated:

> With regard to ed policy. It is extremely important that the superintendent provide the key leadership looking at national, international, and state policy. The district is [...] has an understanding of what the trends are and where they should be going to best serve the children and students of that particular district. So as a superintendent, I always made it my business to read, subscribe, use digitally, the policy making agencies, the Brookings institute, Harvard education Journal, Ed Leadership, AASA Journal, Phi Delta Kappan so that I keep abreast of the state and national stage, also international. I also make sure that my board is abreast of what they need to know particularly at the state level [...] on a weekly basis I would inform them of legislation, proposed legislation that would affect district policy. I had a great deal to do with STEM education where I would hold district and administrative retreats regarding STEM education, innovation. We would literally take 2–3 days before school started and we would read together, discuss together [...] the bigger picture of how we would want that to look in our own district. I did that with the board, administrative staff, then my principals would do that with their staff.

Rachel stated:

> I don't have to spend a huge amount of time creating policies, there are lawyers that develop the policy. What it has allowed me to do is have a board member that the board has selected as policy chair to work with me and the community and to look at those policies to see how strongly they will assist us in impacting the district. Really, there are three jobs of a board: to hire a qualified superintendent, to approve the school budget, and to develop policy and I look at governance as it relates to policy. That is the board's main job, to govern. The board is in the balcony and I am on the dance floor with the staff. And the board should stay in the balcony while I am on the floor implementing, creating, directing, and working with a team of effective professionals and that is a given.

Rhonda stated:

> I work very closely with the legislatures. I can pick up the phone
> at any time to discuss an unfunded mandate. I can say this is how
> it will harm our district. And what the cost will be. When it
> comes to our community, I call together the 5 mayors [...] this is
> a district that prior to my coming had been taken over by the
> state for 10 years due to finances being poor. So with me being
> the first superintendent African American superintendent, people
> are watching to see what direction is the district going to go in
> having a Black female superintendent. The district has gone very
> well. I have been able to pull the mayors together have conversa-
> tion about the need of the school district, how can we partner
> together to get things done, even so far as salt to put down in the
> winter, how can we share in the cost and go in jointly [...] how
> can we take a look at utilities also when it comes to the police
> departments.

> I have called in the police chiefs to talk to them about how we
> can improve our students' relationship with the police department
> especially in light of what is happening in (city unnamed) con-
> cerns about the police and fears of the police and now with the
> talk of immigration with our new president and talk of charter
> schools with the Governor, State Education Secretary and
> Secretary of Education at the federal level. These decisions are
> really not favouring those who have been disenfranchised and do
> not have an opportunity to really handle things on their own. We
> have kids who are coming to school every day because of what
> the president is saying about deporting Mexicans back to
> Mexico. They are in fear, our parents are in fear. We have had to
> bring people to come in to talk to our parents, our students, to
> try to alleviate some of the fears they have regarding some of the
> social issues in our society today.

Sarah stated:

> Following on from a split Board when 3 did not pay the bills and
> a 7th left for past crimes. I did seek legal council. There was school
> code that stated that it was my fiduciary responsibility to make
> sure that the bills were paid. I could be in trouble for not paying
> the bills. It is a truth faith walk for anyone in this position. If they
> do not have faith in this position, they will not make it.

The findings agreed with Tellerico and Blount (2004) that the superintendents
knew the power of policy and law and were able to operationalise policy for
social justice. However, superintendents navigated turbulence with school

boards that were not following policy, for example if the school board was split, which agrees with Pons (2017). The findings reveal more experienced superintendents were able to secure the financial resources needed to implement mandated reforms which agrees with Björk et al. (2014). Superintendents were able to align the shift in learning cultures with working with top district leadership, such as mayors which agrees with Firestone (2009). However, other superintendents had to navigate turbulence with split school boards who did not want to follow policy and the example cited from the evidence is the refusal of a split Board to pay bills.

All fourteen superintendents identified that navigating the turbulence within a school board ranged from severe to light, and those that identified light turbulence also identified they were aware of superintendents who had experienced severe turbulence. Those that experienced severe turbulence are represented by Theresa who stated:

> If I could change that structure of that board, I would. Because I think that in so many instances, the children lose because the board is out of control. They don't understand their role as a governance. They want to, like I said, jump into the running of the school system. Which is not their job and so when you find stuff like that happening there needs to be something that the superintendent can do to, you know what I am saying [...] But the way that it is set up now, there is nothing you can do, but accept it and move on. And that is the unfortunate part because it really isn't about us [...] as individuals as the superintendent, it involves what is happening to our children and so often I believe the board loses sight of that [...] why we are here, it is all about the kids, so very often, I believe, they lose sight of that and it becomes about them, power and stuff like that. So, if I could change anything, I would change that structure.

Denise stated:

> I think key to that is your School Board in the system that we operate under [...] you must have the support of the school board to let you do your job [...] I have found that the politics of education in Name of State can prevent you from doing that. There are times they get in the way of what is best for education [...] I think what helps to be an effective superintendent is to know how to get around those issues [...] something that actually when you are training [...] they do not do a lot of training of how to make that happen [...] Interestingly enough, my school board was 100% African American [...] I got some of my greatest opposition from African American women on the school board. Not necessarily about my professional expertise. Many of the parents and

families that I would meet and form relationships with, it was not so much of an issue. But the people that hired me, who were over me, supervised me, I being their one employee, which had a lot to do with how I think they were educated, number one, number 2, their level of employment, and their level of exposure and ability to read, discern, facts and data and not how they felt. That to me is a huge dilemma and it is impacting what can be done for African American children within the community. I strongly believe we were held up in terms of moving forward as a district by the lack of vision of the school board and their lack of under-standing about quality education-in many cases because I firmly believe they didn't have a quality education. They want it, but they don't know what it looks like or how to get it. I had School board members who complained about too much homework, school board members who said they didn't like to help their kids in the evening with a project, that's the responsibility of schools … lack of understanding. They want to be like certain white sub-urban districts but don't necessarily want to do the things that their parents do. I have struggled with the concepts of elected vs appointed school boards. I am not sure one is any better than the other. All have political ramifications. I do think certain things have been put in place to require school boards to have certain training. Yet, I have seen people skirt it, go and not listen like kids in the classroom and still get credit for it with no actual transformation of how they do public education. I am at a quan-dary right now in terms of how to can make that happen. The bottom line is that you have to have an informed public [...] par-ents and community members actively engaged in the dialogue about what education should look like. What I saw in my old dis-trict was a superintendent's ability to have dialogues in the larger community and bring about individuals to enculturate them as potential school boards [...] actively involved, energy, hopefully not as much politicization in terms of seeing their true roles and responsibilities.

The findings connect with Mountford (2004) who suggests school boards may enjoy having power over superintendents, and this may be connected with school board members having little power in other parts of their lives, coupled with having few formal educational qualifications themselves. Such school board members recognise they will not be able to get the position of superintendent. The empowered superintendent tool kit found on The school superintendents' Association Website (2018) appears to present quick fixes, along with references that are technical, standards based, with a view to providing some districts supremacy over others in a competitive high stakes market. The evidence reveals the superintendents are 'at a quandary right now in terms of how we can make 'good education' happen and what it would look like. Perhaps a new kind of bridge is needed between the board and the superintendents that empowers superintendents to operationalise their track records of leadership skills as critical reflective practitioners who: listen carefully and believe that working together with trust and respect can challenge policy; have the confidence to advocate for their communities full, free and successful participation in the education system when the communities have traditionally been segregated, marginalised and oppressed. One of the superintendents in the research identifies they are in this position and Nancy stated:

> I have enjoyed working with my school board basically because they first became good listeners. They listened to what I had to say and I in turn listened to them and then we could talk on the same level, not the same level, but with an understanding. I really did appreciate my board. My board set up a system of protection for me. They kind of built a wall so that I would not have the sting by myself. If someone disagreed with my decision, rather than to think that I had to shoulder it by myself, my board would defend the decision I had to make publicly. I had the public support from my board and I appreciated that. That is how I was able to lead my principals. They knew I had the support of the board. If I made a decision with them, and was trying to get them on board, I was able to demonstrate I cared about them [...] empowering them to do the job that I can't do alone. I believe in teaching and learning, and I thought they should join me facing the journey [...] I can't do it alone. I had the board's protection in terms in helping me speak with my voice, make decisions/policy, implement policies/programs; I had the support of the majority of my principals. Now I have had a few nay-sayers, those that would not come on board, but when they saw that did not stop us, I was not going to dwell on the negatives, then they too had to come aboard and put in their best effort or not, but they were cooperative.

Key to Nancy's position is that the school board has her back and protects her, and she has worked with the same Board for 11 years. In many ways, this school board is visionary and provides the conditions a superintendent needs to optimise students' learning and empower them to be college eligible and college completes to become future societal innovators for equity and renewal. This connects with Ford and Ihrke (2016) who identify that school boards with members who have served for five years or more are more effective because they are more stable and have built trusting relationships hallmarked by respect for each other's knowledge, skills, experience and expertise. These kinds of relationships are important to deliver the mission, policies, administration and instructional dimensions day by day as the school board and superintendent learn together.

Mentoring African American Women for Mobilisation into Chief Executive Superintendency

All fourteen Black Women Superintendents identified mentoring was important along with networks that were supportive, but their experiences of mentoring was varied. Vickie stated:

> I would say […] really I think promoted by a district superintendent that had a group of seven young women that he really worked to support us from an academic perspective, an operational perspective so that we could keep the balance. There were times when folks were struggling for supplies in schools he would say, give them the supplies they need. You do not want that to be a deterrent to your focus in moving the children forward. Those were key things that really stuck with me during the years. When I first became the chief officer, a foundation provided a mentor from Harvard. He was here visiting – we would talk via telephone. What are the issues facing urban school settings? How were they solving problems elsewhere that could be applied to the district? Although I didn't have access to all the resources to do everything we thought was important, I was able to secure some grant funding in literacy that made a huge difference in helping to meet the needs of students that needed that extra boost.

Rhonda stated:

> One of my biggest mentors was a university professor that I had in my doctorate program. I was the only African American in my program, he was very determined, […] he was a Caucasian male […] now the head of the department at a university, but very vested in my success. So much so that even when I graduated and brought down two vans of family for the graduation, he had a reception for me on his lawn at his home and so he was invested in my success, did everything that he could and said that you will be successful with this degree, you will get your dissertation, and we will work together to see that this happens. […] My husband worked two jobs so that I did not have to work and I could go to school full time. So that was someone who was a mentor who believed in what I was doing and supported and encouraged me, even though I was getting tired with two small children to take care of and I was changing jobs, to special education supervisor, special education director, to a building principal-over the course of the time that I was enrolled at Penn State in my doctorate program, also enrolled at Grand Valley State working on my supervisory certificate. At the same time, I was enrolled at two universities raising small children and changing jobs.

[...] I also have superintendent colleagues who are mentors. As they say it is lonely at the top so you need someone to talk to who you can trust, confide in, and who has your back. I have one friend, in particular [...] she is a colleague and someone who works very closely with me [...] an African American female. We are supportive of each other and know that when we are dealing with something then we are looking at how to help each other. Also, she and I work with an aspiring superintendent institute. We are in the 7th year this summer. Through that work, there are other superintendents across the nation that we work with very closely and we mentor each other and we also make it our job to mentor aspiring superintendents, especially aspiring superintendents of color who have no one to advocate for them, who don't know how to navigate the waters, in order to get to the superintendency. We have made it our work to say that we need more superintendents of color throughout this nation because right now there are less than 4%, so what do we need to do? Not just talk about the shortage but make sure we are instrumental to eradicate the shortage. So we have taken it upon ourselves to really train people from the principal level and central office on the road to the superintendent. We have had 25 of the aspiring superintendents become superintendents over the course of the six years we have been doing this work.

Anita stated:

What I have encountered is undereducated administrators coming out of our universities. They don't have the training or understanding to recognize excellent instruction in classroom, they don't have the training to know what they must do to offer alternative strategies. It is a greater problem because if you do have teachers at the mastery level, master teachers, and an administrator comes in who has no concept of curriculum, no concept of structure; it is demoralizing to teachers who at the top of their game and what they are doing at the classroom. My fear and the greatest problem I have is really not on the parent side, it is the fact that I am not finding/seeing educators at the administrative level that I feel are trainable. If you are not trainable, then I am not sure what we are seeing. Because I am building for the future and you have to build on a base [...] I am inviting colleagues to come in and present to cohorts on campus. The issue is if you have a masters, type 75, and you've gone to someone's doctoral program, that doesn't have standards [...] they think, 'I am doctor someone', and the fact that I use poor grammar, sentence structure, and split verbs, is not an issue. It is an issue.

Sarah stated:

> First time I had a mentor for about a week or so then they dismissed me for no cause.
>
> Second time I didn't have a mentor I asked attorneys when I had questions. We had high legal bills, but I had to do things that I knew was right within the law.

The superintendents' experiences agree with Tillman (2012) Grant (2012) and Gay (2004) and reveal Black females need mentoring that is constructive, purposeful and consistently develops the individual to reach their career goals and optimise students' learning. Superintendents who do not have critical mentors who can role model making bridges to their true selves and to different world views within the same community and between communities, potentially internalise the regulation of the markets that sustains the panopticon overview of those with power, and White supremacy. Critical mentors are therefore essential for empowering innovative superintendents to work for equity and renewal to redistribute the division of labour through social mobility (Foucault, 1991). Preventing innovation sustains the status quo and prevents social mobilisation and social justice and is a barrier to EYSIER (Taysum, 2012a, b, 2013, 2014; Taysum et al, 2015, 2016, 2017). Further, networks of mentors are essential to support these Black women superintendents to succeed and build further networks across disciplines with agents with power such as Mayors and politicians to support successful participation in committees and build capacity for equity and renewal in the district, state, nationally and internationally. A culture change is needed in schools to empower innovative superintendents to work for equity and renewal and thereby provide returns on investment in education systems.

Transformation through Bridging between the Work, the True Self and the Students' Cultures

All fourteen Black women superintendents agreed that they needed to be culturally sensitive and start where the students and the communities are and build shared world meanings together in safe spaces of respect, trust and tolerance. The position is revealed with the following representative quotes. Rhonda stated:

> You have to understand the culture and be culturally sensitive and meet kids where they are and form a relationship with kids. It's important for adults to have relationships. We talk about this, provide training, we are taking surveys on emotional intelligence to understand who we are and how we relate and what we need to do to be more successful with the work we do with staff, students and parents. When African American parents and

parents of color come in we find that staff assume that they can talk to the parents the way they would talk to someone from their own neighborhood, and not realize that the parents in their culture are different. And not realize that the parents in their culture are different. You have to be able to relate [...] willing to be a listener [...] understand how to form a relationship [...] not just hit them with problems, but form a relationship first.

Nancy stated:

Charters have more flexibility and freedom to do what is necessary rather than testing all day [...] or teaching to the test or have the stress of reaching all the mandates. If you could take away all the mandates [...] if they were not funded, or underfunded [...] that would help the situation. I think I would be able to do more with less if I had the opportunity to take away the mandates.

Theresa identified she has built a network of Black women superintendents who train the principals who train the teachers to develop cultural literacy and to transform through bridging between world views; between dominant cultures and marginalised cultures. The staff act as role models for the students and she states:

We pool our resources together to provide professional development for teachers and staff [...] its building our students up so that they are successful when they go out building that compassion and empathy for others and supporting and respecting other cultures and so forth. It also gives us an opportunity for our kids to come and perform, and to showcase what they have learned [...] and gives an opportunity for our teachers to do the same. We build capacity by providing professional development, through what we call workshops. We show best practices of what is working [...] for children of color; children of poverty.

The findings connect with Douglas Horsford (2012) who argues that for real cultural change educational leaders, school boards and those responsible for developing and recruiting superintendents require greater cultural literacy for re-culturing. The superintendents need to work as a bridge between different communities, and they need to ensure that their staff have cultural literacy and that they use their cultural literacy to engage the participation of parents and the will of the parents. They can do this by celebrating cultural histories using evidence-informed positions logically and with a moral compass to guide an ethical framework (Carter, 2008; Firestone, 2009; Stanton-Salazar, 2010; Taysum, 2017a). Garrison (2009) identifies such re-culturing may help de-couple the technical accountability models from the critical and reflective approaches that bridge between scientific knowledge, the true self that may include the metaphysical including all faiths and none, and the real world (Bhaskar, 2013). The latter allows teachers to develop unpredictable, culturally relevant full and free interactions in a classroom to optimise learning that provides space for flow.

Anita has the same position as the other twelve respondents but she explicitly states she has seen returns on investment in change strategies that focus on bridging between different world views, the true self and the real world to offer social mobility and middle-class benefits to African American communities and states:

> I was asked a question when I interviewed coming into the Superintendency [...] 15 years ago by the board president. He asked me did I think that a school district could become strong enough that it could influence a community and the direction that the community was going and stabilize a community. He asked me if I thought a school district even in the face of some of the things going on nationally, if a school district could establish its own standards and those of the community. Coming out of Chicago I said no, absolutely no. I see now and I see that based on the fact that we have stopped movement out of the community because people want their children to be in the school district, I understand the complexity of community, the whole community and their relationship as a school district and their relationship with me. I have the same responsibility to nurture, teach, and be involved with the community as I have with my staff. Having said that, that is the reason my schedule is structured so that if there is an activity that occurs after school that is parent/community based, I am present. I am present, not only because I am laying eyes on [...] but I am present because of the fact that I realize in the African American community specifically, we have a need to identify with a person; persons that we feel has a connection to our children. One of the reasons over time that they have had less violence and disruptive behavior (here), is because I believe our values have permeated and people begin to understand that we understand. There is a threat to the African American middle-class that is real. It is real. And I know that others look at it in another way. The only reason our men are violent and they misbehave is because they have lost hope. The reason families are so splintered is because they have lost hope. They have lost hope in many different reasons. Who do they turn to if they feel their child is not getting a good education? They don't have the resources to put their child in a private school. You can't test into alternative schools, selective enrolment schools. Parents don't have the money to send their kids to college, yet they know that this is the pattern for success.

Theresa affirms the position of all the superintendents in this study and identifies that African American educators and communities must fight for social justice, and democracy and states:

> We have some very talented African American educators and leaders and I have space for them here because my kids deserve them. When we speak of developing young people for social renewal we are developing young people to make this a more civil society. They are fighters for equity, and renewal in their communities, they want to be connected with their community, they want to make a difference [...] sustain a more civil society where they have more opportunities.

The evidence connects with Apple (2013) who asks can education change society? Apple identifies that neoliberal agendas and education are becoming more closely connected with the needs of corporate society. Such connections drive more and more disconnections between people, their communities, the societal institutions, and the governance systems. The division of labour and the divide-and-conquer strategies to protect greater entitlements and privilege directs people to become self-regulating within structures that favour corporations (Ball, 2017; Foucault, 1991). Creating opportunities to build local communities based on growing food, which supplies cafe cultures and restaurants which require building, and maintenance, and decorating, which attracts people who like to build their homes near to the emerging vibrant small and medium enterprises need could be part of the school curriculum. Here the school could be the hub of the community with the superintendent bridging between different groups and their interests for full and free interactions and cooperations for democracy in education (Dewey, 2016).

Discussion, Concluding Comments and Recommendations

Navigating Turbulence Drawing on Gross (2014) Theory of Turbulence

Gross's (2014, p. 248) Turbulence Theory states that 'turbulence can be described as "light" with little or no movement of the craft. "Moderate" with Very noticeable waves. "Severe" with strong gusts that threaten control of the aircraft. "Extreme" with forces so great that control is lost and structure damage to the craft occurs'. The findings reveal that the turbulence is extreme where superintendents have been sacked because the school board has personal vendettas, and because the school board have no knowledge, skills, experience or qualifications in education. Such members of the Board want a good education for their district, but they do not know how to get it, and prevent the superintendent from achieving a cultural transformation that delivers opportunities for social mobility and middle-class benefits to African American communities trapped in poverty. Extreme turbulence has also been felt because of the institutionalised racism that the African American women superintendents have had to fight and have acted as bridges between.

A Theory of Knowledge to Action

A theory of knowledge to action is to assure that all African American women in teacher training, and throughout their careers as teachers, and leaders in education need to be aware of school policy, how to access policy and legislation, how to stay up to date with policy and how to challenge policy (James & McCormick, 2009). Policy provides them with the human rights that some who may benefit from White privilege might forget about in their day to day work in education systems. Policy has the back of African American women fighting institutionalised racism (Collins Ayanlaja & Taysum, 2016). African American women need role models, and mentors who are superintendents, and who create proactive and mobilising networks across the state and the nation to advocate for and to support the teachers' and leaders' professional learning to be the best leaders and superintendents they can be which is what students and families in the US deserve. Finally, the African American women who have been self-selecting, or identified as potential future superintendents by current superintendents and school boards, need to be part of succession planning that transcends the short elected lives of district school boards. Newly incumbent African American women superintendents need to promote learning how to learn so that their students will learn how to learn (James & McCormick, 2009), be culturally sensitive, ask good questions and problem solve as Young Societal Innovators for Equity and Renewal (Taysum, 2012a, b, 2013, 2014; Taysum et al., 2015, 2016, 2017). We recommend that a network of African American women superintendents puts this knowledge to action and that their work is documented, and if successful, disseminated to build capacity for EYSIER.

References

Adler, M. (1941). *A dialectic of morals: Towards the foundations of political philosophy*. Notre Dame: University of Notre Dame.

Alston, J. (2000). Climbing hills and mountains: Black females making it to the superintendency. In C. C. Bruner (Ed.), *Sacred Dreams: Women and the Superintendency* (pp. 79–90). Albany, NY: State University of New York Press.

Alston, J. (2012). Standing on the promises: A new generation of Black women scholars in educational leadership and beyond. *International Journal of Qualitative Studies in Education*, 25(1), 127–129.

American Educational Research Association. (2010). Code of ethics. *Educational Researcher*, 40(3), 145–156.

Apple. (2013). *Can education change society*. London: Routledge.

Ball, S. (2004). *Education policy and social class: The selected works of Stephen J. Ball*. London: Routledge.

Ball, S. (2017). *Edu.net: Globalisation and education policy mobility*. London: Routledge.

Bhaskar, R. (2010). *Reclaiming Reality: A critical introduction to contemporary philosophy*. London: Routledge.

Bhaskar, R. (2013). *Reclaiming reality*. London: Routledge.

Björk, L., Browne-Ferrigno, T., & Kowalski, T. (2014). The superintendent and educational reform in the United States of America. *Leadership and Policy in Schools*, *13*(4), 444–465.

Blackmore, J. (1999). *Troubling women: Feminism, leadership and educational change.* Buckingham: University Press.

British Educational Research Association. (2011). British Educational Research Association (2011). *Ethical Guidelines for Educational Research.* London: BERA.

Brown, A. (2014). The recruitment and retention of African American women a public school superintendents. *Journal of Black Studies*, *45*(6), 573–593.

Brunila, K., and Ryynänen, S. (2017). New rules of the game: Youth training in Brazil and Finland as examples of the new global network governance. *Journal of Education and Work*, *30*(4), 353–366.

Bush, T., & Coleman, M. (2001). *Leadership and strategic management.* London: Sage.

Carrasco, A., & Fromm, G. (2016). How local market pressures shape leadership practices: Evidence from Chile. *Journal of Educational Administration and History*, *48*(4), 290–308.

Carter, P. L. (2008). Teaching students fluency in multiple cultural codes. In M. Pollock (Ed.), *Everyday Antiracism* (pp. 107–112). New York, NY: The New Press.

Castellani, M. (2012). *Young people in Europe from 'lost generation' to 'sacrificed generation'.* Retrieved from theeuros.eu. Accessed on 16 August 2014.

Collins Ayanlaja & Taysum. (2016). Institutionalised racism in world education research association annual conference, Washington, DC, April.

Crenshaw, K. (1989). Demarginalizing the intersection of race and sex: A Black Feminist critique of antidiscrimination doctrine, feminist theory, and antiracist politics, University of Chicago Legal Forum, 1989, 139–167.

De Gruy, J. (2005). *Post traumatic slave syndrome.* Portland: Joy De Gruy Publications Inc.

Denscombe, M. (2007). *The good research guide (3rd ed.).* Milton Keynes: Open University Press.

Dewey, J. (2016). *Democracy and education.* New York, NY: Macmillan.

Dewey, J. (1929). *Experience and Nature.* Kindle Edition.

Douglas Horsford, S. (2012). This bridge called my leadership: An essay on Black women as bridge leaders in education. *International Journal of Qualitative Studies in Education*, *25*(1), 11–22.

Douglas Horsford, S. (2016). This bridge called my leadership: An essay on Black women as bridge leaders in education. In S. Douglas Horsford & L. Tillman (Eds.), *Intersectional Identities and Educational Leadership of Black Women in the USA.* London: Routledge.

Douglas Horsford, S., & Bell McKenzie, K. (2008). Sometimes I feel like the problems started with desegregation': Exploring Black superintendent perspectives on desegregation policy. *International Journal of Qualitative Studies in Education*, *21*(5), 443–455.

230   *Carole Collins Ayanlaja et al.*

Ehren, M., Honingh, M., Hooge, E., & O'Hara, J. (2016). Changing school board governance in primary education through school inspections. *Educational, Management, Administration and Leadership, 44*(2), 205–223.

Firestone, W. (2009). Accountability nudges districts into changes in culture. *Phi Delta Kappan, 90*(9), 670–676.

Fitzgerald, T. (2010). Spaces in-between: Indigenous women leaders speak back to dominant discourse and practices in educational leadership. *International Journal of Leadership in Education, 13*(1), 93–105.

Ford, M., & Ihrke, M. (2016). Do school board governance best practices improve district performance? Testing the key work of school boards in Wisconsin. *International Journal of Public Administration, 39*(2), 87–94.

Foucault, M. (1991). *Discipline and punish. The birth of the prison.* London: Penguin Social Sciences.

Garrison, J. (2009). The art and science of education. *Journal of Curriculum Studies, 41*(1), 17–20.

Gay, G. (2004). Navigating marginality en route to the professoriate: Graduate students of color learning and living in academia. *International Journal of Qualitative Studies in Education, 17*(2), 265–288.

Glazer, N. (1987). *Affirmative discrimination ethnic inequality and public policy.* Harvard: Harvard University Press.

Grant, C. (2012). Advancing our legacy: A Black feminist perspective on the significance of mentoring for African-American women in educational leadership. *International Journal of Qualitative Studies in Education, 25*(1), 101–117.

Greve, C., & Reff Pedersen, A. (2017). Denmark's master of public governance program: Assessment and lessons learned. *Teaching Public Administration, 35*(1), 22–37.

Grissom, J., & Anderson, S. (2012). Why superintendents turn over. *American Educational Research Journal, 49*(6), 1147–1180.

Gross, S. (2014). Using turbulence theory to guide action. In C. Branson & S. Gross (Eds.), *Handbook on ethical educational leadership* (pp. 246–262). New York, NY: Routledge.

Harrison, K., Taysum, A., McNamara, G., & O'Hara, J. (2016). The degree to which students and teachers are involved in second-level school processes and participation in decision making: an *Irish Case Study. Irish Educational Studies, 35*(2), 155–173.

Helve, H. (1991). The formation of religious attitudes and worldviews: A longitudinal study of young Finns. *Social Compass, 38*(4), 373–392.

Horsford, S. D. (2014). This bridge called my leadership: An essay on Black women as bridge leaders in education. In S. D. Horsford & L. C. Tillman (Eds.), *Intersectional identities and educational leadership of Black women in the USA* (pp. 11–22). Abingdon: Routledge. [Reprint of article in *International Journal of Qualitative Studies in Education*].

Huberman, B. (1994). *Qualitative data analysis: An expanded sourcebook.* London: Sage.

James, M., & McCormick, R. (2009). Teachers learning how to learn. *Teaching and Teacher Education, 25*(7), 973–982.

Jenson, S. (2016). Institutional governance of minority religious practices: Insights from a study of Muslim practices in Danish schools. *Journal of Ethnic and Migration Studies, 42*(3), 418–436.

Kakos, M., & Palaiologou, D. (2014). Intercultural citizenship education in Greece: Us and them. *Italian Journal of Sociology of Education, 6*(2), 69–87.

Kilbourn, B. (2006). The qualitative doctoral dissertation proposal. In *Teachers College Record.* Retrieved from https://www.tcrecord.org/AuthorDisplay.asp?aid= 16939. Accessed on 05 January 2018.

Kowalski, T. (2013). *The school superintendent. Theory, practice, and cases in educational leadership faculty publications.* Paper 44. Retrieved from https://pdfs.semanticscholar.org/8a7d/5f4bc1675493ef90568255870a0330064b92.pdf. Accessed on October 20, 2018.

Ladson-Billings, G. (2005). *Beyond the big house: African American educators on teacher education.* New York, NY: Teachers College Press.

Lassnigg. (2016). When complexity meets evidence in governance. *European Journal of Education, 51*(4), 441–446.

Levin, H. M. (1999). The public-private nexus in education. *American Behavioral Scientist, 43*(1), 124–137.

McClellan, P. (2012). Race, gender, and leadership identity: An auto ethnography of reconciliation. *International Journal of Qualitative Studies in Education, 25*(1), 89–100.

Mertens, D. (1998). *Research methods in education and psychology.* London: Sage.

Meyer, H., & Benavot, A. (2013). *PISA, power, and policy: The emergence of global educational governance.* Oxford: Symposium Books.

Mountford, M. (2004). Motives and power of school board members: Implications for school board-superintendent relationships. *Educational Administration Quarterly, 40*(5), 704–741.

Munoz, A., Pankake, A., Murakami, E., Ramalho, S., Mills, S., & Simonsson, M. (2014). A study of female central office administrators and their aspirations to the superintendency. *Educational Management Administration and Leadership, 42*(5), 764–784.

Oancea, A., & Furlong, J. (2007). Expressions of excellence and the assessment of applied and practice-based research. *Research Papers in Education, 22*(2), 119–137.

Patton, M. (2015). *Qualitative research and evaluation methods integrating theory and practice.* London: Sage.

Payne, C. (2008). *So much reform, so little change: The persistence of failure in urban schools.* Harvard: Harvard Education Press.

Peshkin. (1988). In search of subjectivity-one's own. *Educational Researchers, 17*(7), 17–21.

Phelan, A. (2009). The ethical claim of partiality: Practical reasoning, the discipline, and teacher education. *Journal of Curriculum Studies, 41*(1), 93–114.

Pons, X. (2017). Fifteen years of research on PISA effects on education governance: A critical review. *European Journal of Education, Research Development and Policy, 52*(2), 131–144.

Ranson, S. (2008). The changing governance of education. *Educational Management, Administration, and Leadership, 36*(2), 201–219.

Reed, L. C. (2012). The intersection of race and gender in school leadership for three Black female principals. *International Journal of Qualitative Studies in Education, 25*(1), 358–389.

Sheard, M., & Avis, J. (2011). Schools, governance and community: A next practice intervention. *Educational Management, Administration, and Leadership, 39*(1), 84–104.

Stainback, S., & Stainback, W. (1988). Understanding and conducting qualitative research. US Council for Exceptional Children.

Stansberry Beard, K. (2012). Making the case for the outlier: Researcher reflections of an African-American female deputy superintendent who decided to close the achievement gap. *International Journal of Qualitative Studies in Education, 25*(1), 59–71.

Stanton-Salazar, D. (2010). A social capital framework for the study of institutional agents and their role in the empowerment of low status students and youth. *Youth and Society* (first published online then in 2011) *43*(3), 1066–1109.

Taysum, A. (2012a). *Evidence informed leadership in education.* London: Continuum.

Taysum, A. (2012b). *Convener of a large symposium in two parts: 'Globalization, Policy and Agency: Eight Nation states working together to Further Understand their Political Sociologies of Education'.* European Conference for Educational Research, Cadiz, September.

Taysum, A. (2013). *Convener of a large symposium in two parts; 'International Boundary Crossing Study of Teachers' and Students' Participation in Institutional Processes and Practices".* European Conference for Educational Research. Istanbul, September.

Taysum, A. (2014). *Convener of a large symposium in two parts: 'International Boundary Crossing Study Of Higher Education Institutions working in Partnership with Schools To Improve Participation In Processes And Practices Chair: Jan Heystek (Stellenbosch University) Discussant: Carole Collins Ayanlaja (Chicago, Superintendent).* ECER, Porto.

Taysum, A. (2015). *Convener of a large symposium in two parts: 'A Theory of Young People's Participation in Systems and Learning from International Boundary Crossing Action-Resarch Project Arar, K., Collins-Ayanlaja, C., Harrison, K., Imam, H., Murrel-Abery, V., Mynbayeva, A., Yelbayeva, Z.* European Conference for Educational Research. Budapest, Hungary. September.

Taysum, A. (2016). *Convener of a large symposium in two parts: McNamara (Chair), Risku, M., Collins Ayanlaja, C., Iddrisu, M.T., Murrel-Abery, J.V., Arar, K., Masry-Herzallah, A., Imam, H., Chopra, P., McGuinness, S. Theoretical underpinnings of an education and skills model for participation and cooperation in the Youth Field; empowering Europe's young innovators.* European Conference for Educational Research, Dublin, Ireland, August.

Taysum, A. (2017). *Convener of a large symposium in two parts: Arar, K., Masry-Herzallah, A., Collins Ayanlaja, C., Brookins, W., McGuinness, S., Bates, J., Roulsten, S., O'Connor, U., James, F., and George, J., Taysum, A. Turbulence in Six International Education Governance-Systems: Comparing Knowledge to Action for Equity, Peace and Renewal.* European Conference for Educational Research, Copenhagen, Denmark, August.

Taysum, A. (2017a). A Deweyan blueprint for moral training for Democracy in Education presentation Oxford University Symposium, April.

Taysum, A. (2017b). Systems theory and education: A philosophical enquiry into education systems theory. In P. Higgs & Y. Waghid (Eds.), *A Reader for Philosophy of Education* (Vol. 1, p. 1). South Africa: Juta.

Taysum, A., Collins-Ayanlaja, C., & Popat, S. (2017). Developing school leaders' characters as critical educators for social justice through a lens of Agape in T. Fawssett The Feast (Chair) *Community Cohesion Symposium*. Brahma Kumaris World Spiritual University, Leicester.

Taysum, A., & Murrel-Abery, J. V. (2017). 'Shifts in education policy, administration and governance in Guyana 1831−2017, Seeking 'a political' agenda for equity and renewal' in A. Taysum (Ed.). *Italian Journal of Sociology of Education* 9(2), 55−87.

Tellerico, M., & Blount, J. (2004). Women and the superintendency: Insights from theory and history. *Educational Administration Quarterly*, *40*(5), 633−662.

The School Superintendents Association Website. (2018). Toolkits. Retrieved from http://www.aasa.org/home/. Accessed on 1 April 2018.

Tillman. (2012). Inventing ourselves: An informed essay for Black female scholars in educational leadership. *International Journal of Qualitative Studies in Education*, *25*(1), 119−126.

United Nations. (1948). *Universal Declaration of Human Rights* (General Assembly Resolution 217 A). Retrieved from http://www.un.org/en/universal-declaration-human-rights/. Accessed on 29 April 2018.

UK Government. (2010). *Equality act*. London: HMSO.

United States Supreme Court. (1954). Brown v. Board of Education, 347 U.S. 483 (1954). Retrieved from http://caselaw.lp.findlaw.com/scripts/getcase.pl?court=US&vol=347&invol=483. Accessed on October 22, 2018.

US Census Bureau. (2016). Residential vacancies and homeownership in the fourth quarter 2015. Retrieved from http://www.census.gov/housing/hvs/files/currenthvspress.pdf. Accessed on 26 April 2016.

Wagner, T. (2010). *The global achievement gap*. New York, NY: Basic Books.

Yin, R. (2008). *Case study research: Design and methods (Applied Social Research Methods)*. London: Sage.

PART III
TURBULENCE, EMPOWERMENT AND MARGINALISATION: KNOWLEDGE TO ACTION

Chapter 10

Turbulence, Empowerment, and Marginalised Groups: A comparative analysis of five International Education Governance Systems

Alison Taysum and Khalid Arar

Abstract

This chapter presents a comparative analysis of the English, Northern Irish, Arab Israeli, Trinidad and Tobago and the US cases. The focus is what we have learned from the research about: the relationships within Education Governance Systems to navigate turbulence; building capacity for empowering senior-level leaders to deliver on their manifestos and outstanding track records for school improvement; reducing the achievement gap between dominant groups and marginalised groups in International Governance Systems. The chapter identifies that all cases require participatory multi-stakeholder action to develop and support collaborative networked learning communities in practice. Such communities of and for practice need to Empower Young Societal Innovators for Equity and Renewal (EYSIER). Policy and Education Governance Systems have the potential to synthesise the best of what has been said and done in the past, with innovative ways of working by empowering networks of knowledge building and advocacy. These networks co-create opportunities for action learners to work together to describe intersectionalities of discrimination and begin to remove fear of discrimination and marginalisation from Education Governance Systems. From this position, senior-level leaders can work with their leaders, teachers, parents and students to optimise how learning about the self, and learning how to learn improves community education for all students and EYSIER.

Keywords: Democracy; equity; achievement gap; reparation; peace

Turbulence, Empowerment and Marginalisation in International
Education Governance Systems, 237–274
Copyright © 2019 by Emerald Publishing Limited
All rights of reproduction in any form reserved
doi:10.1108/978-1-78754-675-220181012

The aim of this research and our book was to examine the extent to which an Education Model; Empowering Young Societal Innovators for Equity and Renewal (EYSIER) our international team had developed would have the potential to build capacity through Education Governance Systems. We wanted to find out if senior level leaders in Education Governance Systems including superintendents, MATs CEOs, and equivalent leaders were empowered as professional autonomous experts with track records of outstanding school improvement, to act as the bridge between legislation, education governance systems, top district administrators, School Boards, schools and colleges, communities and the University to build capacity for the community model.

The innovative EYSIER offers a Charter Mark and has been developed over five years with a team from twenty three different nation states (Taysum, 2012a, 2012b, 2013, 2014; Taysum et al., 2015, 2016, 2017) from Europe and internationally. The team has since grown to thirty different nation states who are now included in a research proposal and represent many different cultural heritages of people moving to Europe and throughout the world. The five first principles of the EYSIER Model are as follows:

(1) Inclusion to realise social justice and recognition for all (Adler, 1941; Fraser, 2000; Marshall & Gerstl-Pepin, 2005);
(2) respect to realise social justice (Barnett, 2000; Taysum & Gunter, 2008; Carter, 2005, 2008);
(3) trust in the search for truth (Barnett, 2000; Möllering, 2001; Pring, 2000; Wagner, 2010);
(4) courage to engage in prudent dialogue to co-create constructive cross-cultural critique of alternative world views to arrive at a shared multicultural world view (Adler, 1941; Darling-Hammond & Rothman, 2013; Gerstl-Pepin & Aiken, 2012; Ishii, Klopf, & Cooke, 2007); and
(5) the generation of new knowledge that prudently synthesises traditional and new knowledge to enable the re-imagining of new futures where young people are mobilisers of stable and sustainable social change for equity and renewal (Harrison, Taysum, McNamara, & O'Hara, 2016; Taysum, 2012a, 2012b).

This comparative analysis chapter seeks to affirm if these first principles of EYSIER currently exist in Education Governance Systems. The evidence from the senior leaders from marginalised groups in this book, including superintendents in Trinidad and Tobago, and the US, superintendents and supervisors in Arab Israel, chief executive officers (CEOs) of Multi Academy Trusts (MATs) in England and Principals in Northern Ireland find clashes between these primary virtues, and the prioritisation of secondary intellectual virtues revealed through a focus on exam outcomes students achieve (Van Deuren, Evert, & Lang, 2015).

The comparative analysis addresses four research questions: first, how do these senior-level leaders who are from marginalised groups and lead both marginalised groups, and/or dominant groups, describe and understand how education governance systems and education commissioners/school boards, and centralised political powers empower them to develop school communities as societal innovators for equity, and renewal? Second, how do these senior-level leaders of marginalised groups describe and understand the role mentors and/or advocates play to support their navigation through any turbulence? Third, to what extent do these senior-level leaders believe a cultural change is required to empower them in school communities to EYSIER? Finally, what impact strategies emerge of knowledge to action to assure senior-level leaders in edu- cation governance systems are empowered to stabilise their schools, colleges, and communities to successfully navigate turbulence to deliver the EYSIER Model? The chapter first presents a review of the literature. Next the findings from each of the five international case studies from the book are presented and compared and contrasted and synthesised with the literature. Finally, we present the conclusions of the comparative analysis of these five case studies and impact strategies of knowledge to action.

Understanding Theories of Knowledge to Action for Senior Leaders as Bridges; A Review of the Literature Informed by the International Case Studies

First rules, first principles and verifiable theories shape the scientific world view (Helve, 1991), and curricula are developed to meet particular bodies of knowledge from the scientific world view. There are many tensions between what counts as evidence from which first rules and first principles, and verifiable theories with proof of concept can emerge (Pring, 2000; Taysum & Iqbal, 2012). The first rules and verifiable theories can only be provisional taking Popper's (1963) approach of connections and refutations in that they help us make sense of the world until new knowledge proves them false. Kuhn's notion that a new paradigm needs to be developed when first principles are found to be false arguably keeps the scientific world view forever young and starting again. Popper, on the other hand, suggests that we will always be in a position of starting again if we do not build on previous knowledge handed down from generations before. Starting again may help empiricists' egos because they may not wish to state that they were wrong, finding it easier to find fault in the paradigm and starting a new one. Arguably, Popper did not find fault with social scientists, rather the problem was with the lack of respect for learning from history, and learning from all community members including the marginalised. The pragmatic consequences of each generation not learning from history, and not including all voices in the construction of provisional first principles is that humanity is condemned to be ever immature. The immature will make the same mistakes of previous generations by not organising infrastructures and human agency to approach and engage with the causes of a clash of different interests that can lead to war (Dewey, 1918; MW11). The route to peace is arguably describing the causes of the clashes and then working together to develop strategies for equity, renewal and peace.

As Taysum argues drawing from Plato (2018) in the English case study, learning from, and respecting history is vital as a moral imperative in *Timaeus in p. 16376:*

> Thereupon one of the priests, who was of a very great age, said: O Solon, Solon, you Hellenes are never anything but children, and there is not an old man among you. Solon in return asked him what he meant. I mean to say, he replied, that in mind you are all young; there is no old opinion handed down among you by ancient tradition, nor any science which is hoary with age...

and by Plato (2018) in *Critias*, p. 17765:

> By such reflections and by the continuance in them of a divine nature, Like the qualities which we have described grew and increased among them; but when the divine portion began to fade away, and became diluted too often and too much with the mortal admixture, and the human nature got the upper hand, they then, being unable to bear their fortune, behaved unseemly, and to him who had an eye to see grew visibly debased, *for they were losing the fairest of their precious gifts (their virtue)*; but to those who had no eye to see the true happiness (*found through right*), they appeared glorious and blessed at the very time when they were full of avarice and unrighteous power.

Dewey (2016) echoes this claim and suggests when diverse communities seek first principles together, they might look to good people of past epochs from diverse cultures, races, ethnicities, the marginalised, and people of all faiths and none for examples of good first principles, *of people with the precious gift of virtue.* Our International comparative analyses therefore include perspectives of leaders from marginalised groups from different faiths and none, diverse cultures, races, ethnicities, and different genders (Equalities and Human Rights Commission, 2010). We have deliberately listened to the voices of senior leaders from marginalised groups who lead marginalised groups with different intersectionalities of discrimination and may or may not include dominant groups. Our methodologies also call on us to consider the extent to which our methods include an appreciation for competition that prevents feudalism and master–slave relationships that stimulate innovation, entrepreneurialism that protects citizens' rights, with a welfarist approach to societal associations that prevent elites developing master–slave relationships, which, in turn, stimulates innovation and protects citizens' rights.

The Metaphysical Shapes the World View

Reflective thinking and reasoning without an empirical, or scientific base shape a metaphysical world view (Helve, 1991). The metaphysical world view is based on faith and if it were verifiable, then faith would be undermined, but those taking a leap of faith might find their own verifiable truth, found through right. Adler (1941) suggests primary virtues, or cardinal virtues are prudence, fortitude and social justice. These primary virtues perfect a human being's nature, not to a limited good, but to all good things that will contribute to making them a good person who lives a happy life because they can order their goods and the production of the goods. Secondary virtues are intellectual virtues and grant an aptitude for good work that can be verified through student exam outcomes. These exam outcomes might be a result of learning for the test and may not be evidence of being able to apply the knowledge that has been tested. Certainly, these exam outcomes are not evidence of good acts that may become good habits. Together, the primary virtues and secondary virtues enable humanity to develop the right order of goods and their production as a key to leading a good life in becoming and can stabilise a human being. Stable human beings who are virtuous have the dispositions to encounter unexpected situations and can rely on themselves, as autonomous mature adults, to behave with virtue within those situations. Such responses are logical, empirically informed, moral and ethical, and ensure that people together do not harm each other, or themselves, and they can live lives with the potential for a happy ending (Adler, 1941; Taysum, Forthcoming). Here, a happy ending is that someone can look back on their life and be happy with their values and acts. A former US superintendent and current University Professor articulated acts that may be regretted are those that have a 'shoot from the hip' response to unexpected situations (Taysum, 2012a, 2012b).

Building a life of character with primary virtues and secondary virtues requires reflective thinking which connects with Stenhouse (1975) reflective thinking and is subjected to knowledge that is not part of a recognised set of scientific rules and verifiable theories. There are no manuals for everyday life experiences a human being will encounter over a lifetime, but there are primary principles, primary virtues and secondary virtues, habits and logical, empirical, moral and ethical responses that can be put to good use. Adler (1941) identifies acquiring virtue is challenging because logical engagement with virtues lacks practical empirical application, and practical empirical application of virtue lacks engagement with primary and secondary virtues which leads to a loop and a mystery of how anyone can become virtuous. So we return to Plato who suggests 'no old opinion is handed down among you by ancient tradition', and Adler's solution lies therein. Adler suggests humans need a mentor, or mentors of virtue. Virtuous mentors, who are not perfect because no human being is perfect, have gained practical empirical knowledge of virtue over a lifetime, drawing from the best that has been thought and said throughout the ages. These mentors of virtue have theorised the best that has been thought and said about human codes of behaviour and their underpinning values. Using logic, they have then compared and contrasted their own values and acts with those of what Plato calls 'old opinions' from their mentors from previous generations found between the lines of texts. The 'old opinions' may be found in the codes of human behaviour held in the holy books of all faiths and none and the philosophical books of different traditional classical texts such as the Greek myths,

Asian philosophies, in the United National Declaration of Human Rights (United Nations,1947) and in anthropologies that celebrate cultural heritages from different groups of people, including marginalised groups of people which exist in the world today, or have existed in the world in the past.

Reflective thinking on old opinions that can be talked through with mentors and within networks of mentors and peers may require thinking past the many misrecognised intentions, and actions throughout time that empirical evidence reveals. Moving beyond misrecognised intentions that can lead to a breakdown of trust and relationships may aim to get to the possibilities of uncontaminated 'primary virtues, or primary principles' (Taysum, 2012a, 2012b). Moving towards a state of becoming that fully recognises the purity of primary virtues is arguably only possible through reason, and logic (Logos) and critiquing the empirical evidence of good people throughout history from all faiths and none (pathos). Describing, understanding and celebrating these good people's first principles, and virtues, and how their behaviours revealed these primary virtues or revealed others may help people to learn more about themselves which may underpin their process of becoming autonomous mature citizens. These people may compare and contrast their moral compass that informs their ethical framework with Adler's primary principles of prudence, fortitude and social justice (ethos) (Taysum, 2017a).

Such political philosophical inquiry may help individuals develop their own primary principles as they develop their own identity in becoming. Analysing the empirical evidence of all events and of all people, by definition, will include that which is not good such as the exploitation of human beings, slavery, denying human beings their human rights and marginalising human beings, which may give dominant Masters greater entitlement than others. Further, masters may justify their greater entitlement by arguments that they had earned their greater entitlement because they had won it competitively. However, a fair game has not been played if it involves exploitation, slavery, denying human beings their rights and marginalising voices (United Nations, 1948). Critiquing such empirical evidence from history may enable the continuous misrecognitions of secondary intellectual virtues of doing things right to be revealed and mapped and integrated with primary virtues which is to do the right thing, or as Plato says 'to do right' (De Gruy, 2005).

Primary virtues may potentially produce the purest acts of 'what is' and enable human beings to glimpse into the possibility for each person to become the best they can be and develop gifts they have. The gifts here might connect with Robinson's notion of education enabling the finding of a human being's 'element' (Robinson, 2014). Thus, organising education is about not just teaching skills but also meeting externally determined standardised test scores through secondary intellectual virtues, though clearly student outcomes are important. Rather, the priority for peace in our time and to challenge a divide and conquer agenda (Taysum & Murrel-Abery, 2017) is also about helping young people developing attitudes and behaviours applying the primary virtues of social justice, courage and prudence. Through the combination of first the primary virtues, and the secondary virtues, they are empowered to discover their gifts and qualities.

Nurturing gifts empowers young people to become the people they have been gifted to be. In other words, education is about EYSIER (Taysum, 2012a, 2012b, 2013, 2014; Taysum et al., 2015, 2016, 2017). These gifts can only be developed with the power of the community in mobilising students and school capacity. Although there are different types, structure and power dynamics of different communities: East, West, indigenous groups, minority groups, majority groups, marginalised groups, migrants, refugees, traditional groups, progressive groups, developed groups, and underdeveloped groups, groups with advanced technologies and groups without, bridging the gaps between these different groups has never been more important for peace in our time (Banks, 2017; Dewey, 2016). As Dewey (1918) identifies 'Warlikeness is not of itself the cause of war; a clash of interests due to absence of organisation is its cause' ('Morals and the Conduct of States', MW11, p. 125). Prioritising secondary intellectual virtues and data management that focuses on raising exam outcomes prevents the description of the acts that reveal primary virtues in community that seek to describe and overcome clashes of interests of different groups. Without a description of primary and secondary virtues, and their associated acts such as supporting a charity, community work or raping someone or murdering some-one, it is not possible to compare and contrast them with other frameworks of primary and secondary virtues from history, or Adler's (1941) prudence, forti-tude and social justice and those and the EYSIER Model. Bridging communities needs to mobilise the primary principles of the EYSIER: inclusion, respect, trust and courage to engage in prudent dialogue to build shared world views and synthesise the traditional and the innovative to re-imagine new futures where young people are mobilisers of stable and sustainable social change for equity and renewal.

Arguably, this means a bridge needs to be built to overcome a clash between; on the one hand, developing students' secondary intellectual virtues through raising exam outcomes to underpin social mobility and access to middle-class benefits; on the other hand, developing students' primary virtues of prudence, fortitude and social justice (EYSIER), and any other primary virtues that emerge, or groups bring to the table to be recognised and to talk about. The bridge work seeks to empower members of communities as mature citizens for full institutional civic engagement (Dewey, 2016).

Bridge work has the potential to synthesise the primary virtues and secondary intellectual virtues. A mentoring mechanism and networks may position the senior-level leaders of marginalised groups as bridges between different groups, policy-makers, top district and state administrators and states people, school boards, diverse communities of tax payers including parents and their children, all students including those in care, the academy as an Institution of knowledge generation, knowledge mobilisation and knowledge preservation, and all involved in Education Governance Systems. The networks that the senior-level leaders build explore primary and secondary virtues in policy as text and policy as practice at different levels of the community including the governance layers, the community layers, the economic layers and the independent states-people who quality assure all decisions in the pursuit of democracy in education and peace in our time (Dewey, 1916).

Supervisors of Postgraduate Research Programmes may play an important role in supporting leaders' critiques of literature throughout history of different 'good' acts of 'good' people and their primary and secondary virtues from different world views. The Higher Education Institutions' Postgraduate Research Programmes are locations for the democratisation of knowledge (Delanty, 2001) where senior leaders with different world views, diverse cultures, races, ethnicities, the marginalised and people of all faiths and none may work together to describe and understand interpretations of the divine and a world view that does not recognise the divine. Through their work together, they may learn to understand themselves better in relation with the other (Socrates; Kakos & Palaiologou, 2014) and are well positioned to connect their synthesised understandings of primary virtues, secondary intellectual virtues and their understandings of shared world views as political philosophers and legislators (Adler, 1941).

Senior-level leaders may then develop as educational legislators who can work with policy-makers and Education Governance Systems to organise education to describe clashes of interests and clashes that may be described as clashes of provisional first principles, or primary virtues. The descriptions may reveal discrimination in communities and/or intersectionalities of different levels of discrimination that have their own hierarchies (Crenshaw, 1989; Glazer, 1987). Together, these senior leaders can then develop impact strategies that stabilise communities and build community cohesion. For this, citizens need the thinking tools to make decisions based on logos, pathos and ethos and optimise the development of their tool box of resources of impact strategies and their critical evaluations that may empower them to learn how to learn as lifelong learners for social mobility, access to middle-class benefits and quality assure the values and behaviours of the elites.

A metaphysical world view may not be overtly spoken about in the classroom, schools or Education Governance Systems. At the same time, pretending individuals and groups do not hold such views of the divine, or of harmony, as central to their lives, is denying full and free interactions and cooperations with the state and institutions that recognise them fully as human beings (Dewey, 2016). Equally, those who do not believe in the divine are not able to realise virtues within a curriculum that celebrates universal human rights. Thus, curricula need to do more than focus on the secondary intellectual virtues realised through students' exam outcomes that lack a moral compass that assures an ethical framework. Recognising the significance of primary virtues connected to people of all faiths and none may offer young people opportunities to engage with their learning, particularly if they are frustrated because they are finding a particular aspect of the curriculum challenging to understand and apply in their real world. Therefore, Education Governance Systems arguably need to take metaphysical world views from throughout history, of all faiths and none, because they need to recognise that members of school communities may build their lives on their metaphysical relationship to primary virtues, their traditions and the divine which informs their associated ideologies, beliefs, acts and may provide internal motivation for intellectual virtues.

Engaging with first principles, primary virtues, and secondary intellectual virtues, and seeking provisional consensus on these within diverse communities, invites senior-level leaders to help different groups describe discrimination which Glazer (1987) identifies is required before the work can be done to address these intersectionalities of discrimination. Evidence that these barriers to social justice have been removed is when all citizens can enjoy full and free interactions and cooperations with institutions, the economy, and the states people who they are able to vote for to represent and serve them (Dewey, 2016).

The thinking back, or what Stenhouse (1975) calls reflective thinking to first virtues that sees beyond misrecognitions, or in other words, regressive abstraction through reason and logic, is very important because, although often unspoken, such ideals shape a metaphysical world view that is very powerful. Regressive abstraction is an important part of Socratic Dialogue (Saran & Niesser, 2004) because it affords the chance to go back to primary virtues without getting confused by the much intentional and unintentional misrecognitions and their pragmatic consequences that are part of daily human life. This has connections with the virtuous world view that Artistotle suggests young people are inculcated into without explanation of how, and Kant's notion that a lived world view can be rationalised (Taysum, 2016). However, it is important to note that many of Aristotle's rich manuscripts have been completely lost or re-authored by those with their own interpretation of the writings.

There is always the potential for philosophical inquiry to offer communities of diverse groups the opportunity to develop a shared world view, through dialogue with first principles and habits that all can provisionally agree on. Through such dialogue with a purpose and particular parameters, outlined previously, Aristotle suggests the immature can be inculcated into communities of praxis and habits that are inclusive, recognise diversity of the individual as a person and are constantly open to critical rationalisation as Kant suggests. Researchers who are philosophers of education, psychologists, sociologists, historians, economists, engineers and scientists can work through the clashes of values, and world collisions together, because as professional researchers this is their role. Here, the senior-level leaders as bridge people are very important to help researchers discuss their findings as the interface between policy and Education Governance Systems.

Senior-level leaders from marginalised groups are well positioned to bridge new knowledge about empowerment through Education Governance Systems and mobilise it into action in their own contexts to EYSIER and peace with parents, staff, stakeholders and all members of Education Governance Systems. School improvement is only possible through understanding and mobilising the power of the community (Morales, 2011).

To begin to do this, the aim of this chapter, and this book, is to provide senior-level leaders from marginalised groups, and majority groups with an opportunity to connect their own narrative biographies with that of other senior-level leaders in their nation state and beyond. We invite them, and all readers to consider the extent to which the first principles and theories that emerge from the comparative analysis of the five cases presented here from England, Northern Ireland, Palestine, Trinidad and Tobago and the United States is knowledge that can be put into action as impact strategies in their contexts.

However, it is not only that senior-level leaders may be disempowered by constantly protecting their jobs and navigating the turbulence caused by a clash of values between different groups within different layers of education systems and how they are organised, they can also be disempowered through a lack of funding for infrastructure. Taking the US case, it is interesting to note that Scott Walker signed the Wisconsin Act 10 (Wisconsin State Legislature, 2011) which limited collective bargaining for public workers which included educational administrators which connects with Daarel Barnette (2018) who stated some states ban superintendents from campaigning for funding for infrastructure. The evidence reveals how some public Education Governance Systems are making policy that may disempower educational administrators, including superintendents. Such disempowerment prevents what Dewey (2016) calls full and free participation with state institutions which is a barrier to social justice.

Fair funding formulas make transparent how different communities share their budgets, for example Cohen (2018) identified that US schools cannot rely on GoFundMe campaigns to keep water fountains lead free, school air conditioning in the summer, heating in the winter, rooves sturdy and windows intact. Daarel Burnette in an interview with the Washington Journal (2018) identifies that Americans need to consider how they share their tax dollars with their poorer next door neighbour to meet the Every Student Succeeds Act (2015) such that specified infrastructure threshold standards for all schools are met. Perhaps the only way future generations will get fair funding for equity and renewal is when young people in school systematically engage with developing primary and secondary virtues in a process of describing any fears that exist in institutional systems that may be caused by intersectionalities of discrimination (Taysum, Forthcoming). Such description may empower young people to put their primary virtues such as prudence, courage and social justice to work with their secondary intellectual virtues (Adler, 1941). The focus of their work to compare and contrast (critique) innovative theories (thesis), with old traditional opinions of the best that has been thought and said throughout time (antithesis), to co-create new solutions (synthesis) to old problems for equity, renewal and peace.

Findings

Empowering Young Societal Innovators for Equity and Renewal

First, the leaders who are navigating the governance systems find that different groups experience different levels of empowerment and disempowerment linked directly to intersectionalities of discrimination including being Black, Asian, Minority Ethnicity, female and part of a marginalised group based on their faith or not having a faith. These leaders identify there is a gap in achievement linked to marginalised groups who experience intersectionalities of discrimination.

Each category of discrimination listed previously has a hierarchy in terms of the impact of the discrimination on the individual, which puts different people who experience the same discrimination, or intersectionalities of discrimination against each other in a struggle for greater entitlement (Taysum & Murrel-Abery, 2017). Creating conflict within a system through different levels of marginalisation prevents groups and individuals working together to define and address the intersectionalities of discrimination and remove them. These senior-level leaders all confirmed that a common factor of those experiencing discrimination of any kind was linked to greater poverty.

The Arab Israeli Case finds a gap between the Arab students in Israel and the Jewish students in Israel and identifies that the way in which education aims to address these inequities needs to be first described and then revised:

> The transformation from modernity to post-modernity necessitates re-examination of the substance of education, its goals, teaching methods, learning programs, evaluation methods and organizational structures, and consequentially ethical and political considerations also need revision.
>
> Arnova, Torres, & Franz, 2013; Waite, Rodriguez, & Wadende (2015)

The Northern Ireland case identifies that there is an enduring gap in achievement based on religion and calls for the implementation of the legislation for shared education by describing the lasting impact of segregation and working together to implement shared education:

> The commitment to develop common shared spaces in education, housing and society in general is highlighted in the Programme for Government as essential for the development of a tolerant, respectful and equitable Northern Ireland (NIE, 2016). In particular, the enduring gap in educational and social outcomes for some pupils is a key challenge for government and policy makers (Harland & McCready, 2012; Nolan, 2013). This inequity has strong historical roots in the conflict of Northern Ireland; the geography of its worst extremes is closely aligned to those areas where social disadvantage and marginalisation were most prevalent, so that poverty, poor housing, limited social and educational opportunities and unemployment co-existed with entrenched views of the 'other' community (Deloitte, 2007). Whilst some communities have flourished more than others, an intergenerational pattern of poor educational outcomes and reduced social opportunity has tended to prevail in spite of successive community and education-based initiatives.
>
> MacInnes, Aldridge, Parekh, & Kenway (2012); Purvis (2011)

Segregation can have a lasting impact across society, and in particular, on young people (Roulston , Hansson, Cook, & McKenzie,

2016). The Northern Ireland *Strategy for Victims and Survivors* (Office of the First Minister and Deputy First Minister (OFMDFM), 2009) 'recognises the impact of the Troubles/Conflict on Children and Young People' (Commission for Victims and Survivors, 2016), and states: 'An important area to be addressed is likely to be the intergenerational impact of the troubles on children and young people and the need to promote cross-community work with children and young people.'

OFMDFM (2009, p. 12)

The US case agrees with the Arabs in Israel and the Northern Ireland position regarding the importance of identifying and describing segregation before it can be systematically addressed through legislation and praxis:

Resh and Benavot (2009) suggest that the oppression, and the financial differentials between funding of different schools has led to greater differences between schools which is affirmed by Neo liberalism, and market forces. The differentials are reaffirmed with Superintendents and principals having more autonomy with the implementation of the curriculum. Thus the inequalities are allowed to perpetuate, and the fear of managing a culture change, leading to a loss of greater entitlement by those that enjoy White privilege including working class White folk and Middle class White folk can drive a projection of hatred towards those that appear to threaten a person's well being (Taysum, 2017a). Potentially a divide and conquer strategy is at play between White working class and White middle class groups, White groups and Black groups, and Black working class groups and Black middle class groups. Tribes only come together to fight for their own well being, and allegiances can shift if a person's greater entitlement within a social order, or institution, that has been won through competition within Neo-liberal market forces is threatened. Institutions may protect their privilege and perpetuate it (Kakos & Palaiologou, 2014). The fear of giving up additional entitlement may be consciously or subconsciously protected by a very small number of elite citizens who may create intersectionalities of discrimination in different groups of people, and invite those with less intersections of discrimination to rule over those with more intersections of discrimination (Taysum, 2017a). Muñoz, Pankake, Shirley, and Simonsson (2017) reveal women superintendents find it very challenging to break through a ceiling of discrimination, and that communities, and School Board members are not yet ready to accept them in the top executive role of Superintendent.

The comparative analysis also revealed that the Trinidad and Tobago case needs the intersectionalities of discrimination to be carefully described:

> While equality does have to do with fairness, it is not sufficient when it comes to educational reform, because not only does one size not fit all (Ohanian, 1999), but all schools, communities and societies are not equal (Shapiro & Stefkovich, 2016). (These differences need to be described) Economic and class differences differentiate schools based on resources and access; ideological differences, such as essentialism versus market forces (Berliner and Biddle, 1995), which are often attached to financial packages. The main point about these differences is that they create and sustain achievement gaps in systems between dominant and marganalised groups linked to the Black-White achievement gap (Wagner, 2010). Thus, in the main, educational reform is an attempt to close these gaps. Fullan (2010, p. 15) cautions that while 'an increase in the average level of achievement in a society is important, [...] whether the gap between high and low achievers decreases as the overall average rises' is equally as important.

The English case also calls for different forms of discrimination to be described so that they can be addressed:

> The co-creation and renewal of participatory institutions such as the legal system, the governance systems, and the economy would benefit from citizens seeing people who 'look like me' to believe they will be respected in truth (Sleeter & Carmona, 2017). The people who 'look like me' need to participate in leading these institutions as role models who have succeeded in making their dreams, ideals, and spiritual longings a reality (Gordon, 1993). Further, the cultural change may benefit from describing, and deepening understandings of how some have greater entitlement than others in a divide and conquer context resulting in White privilege, and a hierarchy of power from middle class White people and working class White people, Working class White people and Black people (McIntosh, 1997). A dominant group may understand the institutions that reproduce their 'unnatural supremacy' that appears 'natural'. Describing, and then critically analysing, and reflecting upon closed reproductive systems of culture that replicate inequity, may underpin a cultural change to open systems of informed consent, underpinned by the Empowerment of Young Societal Innovators for Equity and Renewal. The CEOs interacting and cooperating with Corporate Public Governance Systems and the principals, staff, parents and students, may benefit from connecting communities together

through engagement with the physical scientific knowledge, and its application for innovation to grow Small and Medium enterprises with high-end Unit Labour Costs (ULCs). The physical scientific knowledge may be connected with the spiritual understandings of meanings, social interactions and social cooperation, with the self, the other, the community, and the states people who pen the rules (Dewey, 1929; Shook & Good, 2010). Taysum's (2017b) synthesis of Dewey's (1909) moral training with Dewey's democracy for education provides a framework that may help CEOs understand how to participate as political philosophers in full and free interactions and cooperation with societal institutions (Taysum, Forthcoming).

A comparative analysis reveals that all senior-level leaders from marginalised groups in the five nation states experience discrimination that segregates. Their contexts of segregation as marginalised groups is one of the intersectionalities of discrimination including sectarianism, race, socio-economic status and gender underpinning marginalisation, an education achievement gap for students and a perpetual cycle of poverty for students and their families with no concrete opportunities for social mobilisation. All cases identify that the intersectionalities of discrimination need to be described which agrees with Glazer (1987) and Crenshaw (1989) and then critiqued using the first principles of EYSIER Model; inclusion to realise social justice (Marshall & Gerstl-Pepin, 2005), respect to realise social justice (Barnett, 2000) and trust in the search for truth to realise social justice (Barnett, 2000; Möllering, 2001; Wagner, 2010). These first principles of the EYSIER Model connect with a primary virtue of social justice (Adler, 1941) which is currently not being realised in the five education governance systems.

Second, Senior Leaders of Virtue, Supported by Wise Mentors and International Networks, Can Bridge Different Groups, Describe Intersectionalities of Discrimination and Address Causes of Fear and Marginalisation within a System

Our comparative analysis secondly reveals there is a growing sense of crisis and fear that accompanies those working in Education Governance Systems. The crisis stems from a tension between modern characteristics of leaders of public Education Governance Systems with no educational professional credentials who are controlling and preventing the professional educational senior-level leaders with track records of school improvement from implementing their manifestos for school improvement. The clash of cultures is played out with regard to which values and virtues are primary, and which are secondary in the organisation of education.

In public Education Governance Systems those with no professional experience of leading education institutions from failing to excellence, have the financial and structural power to make decisions, and organise education. There is no transparent, participatory process by which these leaders of public Education Governance Systems are required to demonstrate the primary and secondary virtues of their manifestos, or strategies to organise education that aligns with diverse communities to EYSIER, Social Mobility and Peace.

Evidence reveals professional credentialed educational senior-level leaders with track records of moving educational institutions from failing to excellence are, in the main, excluded from power through forced takeovers, or changes of leadership of Educational Governance Systems that bring shifts in political ideologies underpinned by different values. Senior-level leaders from marginalised groups and advocating for marginalised groups articulated they feared they may be ousted from their role and recruited as consultants, or short-term advisers who are paid to do the hard, back breaking work in the field to improve education, with no permanent contractual employment rights, or associated pension. Those in public Education Governance Systems who can hire and fire these professional credentialed educational senior-level leaders, with track records in school improvement, and recruit them as consultants may take the credit for the school improvement and demand high renumeration or point the finger of blame at them for any 'poor' performance.

The senior-level leaders with professional educational credentials and track record of school improvement articulated the current Education Governance System is generating fear in the system, which distracts them from their mission and vocational calling to mobilise their track records of outstanding school improvement. Their time is taken up 'watching their backs' (Evert, Van Deuren, & Lang, 2015) to protect their careers so that they can protect their families and plan for the future with a pension.

The senior-level leaders articulated the fear is symptomatic of a *break down of trust and respect for the educational professional expert, and a break down of trust of the professional expert within the public Educational Governance System.* Increasing temporary part-time consultants and external advisers in an Education Governance System has an impact on loyalty and commitment to the system. This is evidence of *not including Senior-level Leaders with outstanding track records of school improvement who advocate for social justice with prudence and courage.* Indeed, building fear into an Education Governance System may reveal a strategy to purposely 'divide and conquer' (Taysum & Murrel-Abery, 2017). *People competing with each other to keep their jobs are less likely to have the courage to spend time working together with prudence to generate new knowledge to describe the fear caused by intersectionalities of discrimination they experience and put knowledge to action together to find new solutions to old problems for social justice (Taysum, forthcoming).* The findings agree with Gunter, Hall and Mills (2015) who identify consultancy and short-term contracts reduce loyalty and commitment of those individuals to the communities and to improving the system (Gunter et al., 2015).

Rapidly dismantling Education Governance Systems and rebuilding them, and/or implementing rapid change without senior-level leaders with professional educational credentials, and track records of school improvement organisation the change is dangerous. The danger lies in limiting the opportunity for senior-level leaders of the educational profession who have earned the mantel of expert and gained wisdom as enlightened mature organisers of education, to engage with succession planning. Without succession planning by the educational profession for the education profession, the education profession is weakened, which will impact on the quality of learning, student outcomes and their economic, political and cultural participation as mature citizens.

There is a fear that a focus on students' exam outcomes prioritises secondary intellectual virtues and doing things right, but does not prioritise primary virtues of social justice, prudence and courage which underpin what Plato calls doing the right thing. Organisations in competition with one another for funding and to get the best exam outcomes have little opportunity for identifying and sharing talent through succession planning for the common good, and the strength, and wealth of the nation. The senior-level leaders from marginalised groups and advocating for marginalised groups identify that the competition within areas and between areas contributes to public Education Governance Systems being populated by those who want their school to succeed and do not want all children to succeed, leaving some failing schools 'untouchable'. Such an unenlightened approach connects with Plato who states: 'there is no old opinion handed down among you by ancient tradition, nor any science which is hoary with age' that is hallmarked by what Plato calls the divine and what may be called in a framework of all faiths and none: 'virtue'. The findings accord with Dewey (2016, p. 1920) who states:

> We must depend upon the efforts of enlightened humans in their private capacity [...] the full development of private personality is identified with the aims of humanity as a whole and with the idea of progress [...] and the very idea of education as a freeing of individual capacity in a progressive growth directed to social aims.

The Arab education case identifies there is a systemic clash in values and states:

> The role of the professional in organising education is clashing with the role of the non-professional public manager organising education. In particular, the globalization of education has had a tremendous impact on what is taught and tested in less developed countries and on the organizational forms of schooling (Nir, 2014; Waite et al., 2015). Many scholars have studied the functioning and outputs of these less developed national education systems, noting the extent of their adaptation to the international community; while others have warned against intellectual and cultural colonization and the potential commodification of 'Western' education in contexts where it is less appropriate (Arnova et al., 2013; Darling-Hammond & Lieberman, 2012).

Public education is a unique arena with a particular structure and characteristic processes. This arena is restricting and perhaps even prevents the attribution of professional responsibility in a simple manner to individuals, allowing those who wish to avoid responsibility to do just that.

The Northern Ireland case identifies that there was a clash of values in Education Governance Systems, when those leaders without professional credentials and track records confused their responsibilities with those of the professional senior-level leaders with professional education credentials and a track record for school improvement employed to organise education:

The Education Reform Order (1989) introduced autonomous self-managed schools with significant changes in curriculum, budget formula allocations and the emergence of various government educational policies and initiatives. This transition reflected challenges elsewhere - for school leaders who were resistant to engaging with a more scrutinising form of governance (Blase, 1997; Harrison, 1998) and for governors who could potentially confuse their strategic responsibilities with the management responsibilities of the head teacher and senior leaders (Allen & Mintrom, 2010). More recently, a new single statutory support agency across Northern Ireland (the Education Authority) was established to provide a more cost-effective model for the delivery of education services, although the current economic situation presents funding challenges creating further turbulence for governing bodies. (Shapiro & Gross, 2013)

The findings from the US case agree with the other cases:

The findings agreed with Tellerico and Blount (2004) that the superintendents knew the power of policy and law and were able to operationalise policy for social justice. However, superintendents navigated turbulence with School Boards that were not following policy, for example if the School Board was split, which agrees with Pons (2017). The findings reveal more experienced Superintendents were able to secure the financial resources needed to implement mandated reforms which agrees with Björk, Browne-Ferrigno and Kowalski (2014). However, other Superintendents had to navigate turbulence with split School Boards who did not want to follow policy, or respect the professional values of the Senior Level Leader, and the example cited from the evidence is the refusal of a split Board to pay bills.

All fourteen superintendents identified that navigating the turbulence within a School Board ranged from severe to light and those that identified light turbulence also identified they were aware of superintendents who had experienced severe turbulence.

The Trinidad and Tobago case identifies there is a clash in values, and professional senior-level leaders did not participate in the curriculum planning:

> There was a long period of planning for the project, during which time several changes occurred. The main reason for change was the shifting of the seat of power from one political party to another due to the results of general elections in the country. In the two-party system which exists in Trinidad and Tobago, it is often the case that there are differences in education policy between the parties and it is not uncommon to find that when there is a change in government, existing education policy may be discarded and replaced. There may also be Cabinet reshuffles during a government's five-year term of office. Further, it is sometimes the case that public servants are shifted around, resulting in key posts in the Ministry of Education (MoE) being filled by new persons from time to time. In the period of planning for the project, changes in personnel included two different governments, three Ministers of Education, five directors/acting directors of curriculum, and several CEOs. The MoE also organized itself into various teams prior to and during the writing exercise, with a Core Planning Team (CPT) providing general oversight, with guidance from the foreign consulting firm.

The English case identifies a clash of values in Education Governance Systems, not just between senior-level leaders without professional educational credentials, and a track record of school improvement, and those with these qualities, but also a clash of values in the public financing of education:

> The findings connect with the values of a Private Equity Fund manager (Diamond, 2012) that seeks to make as much money before making a swift withdrawal or exit with no responsibility for duty of care and the rights of the human beings left behind (BBC News, 2017). Without financial decisions being made drawing on policy memory (Hodgson, and Spours, 2006) that are empirical, logical, moral and ethical, and regulated by Ofsted, there is no opportunity to 'hand down old opinion by ancient tra- dition' which Plato identifies as vital in *Timaeus and Critias*, balanced by innovation for equity and renewal, in a public Education Governance System. Taysum (2017a) suggests engaging with decision making with a moral compass that assures an ethical framework (ethos), empirical evidence that informs decisions (pathos) and logical decision making (logos) is possible when applying the thinking tools found in Taysum (2012a,

2012b) Learning to Critically Analyse and Reflect for Emancipation, or Enlightenment (CARE). These tools are also applied in Taysum's (Forthcoming) synthesis of John Dewey's framework Moral Training for Democracy in Education (Dewey, 2008, 2016) that seeks to identify injustice in a system and eradicate it (May, 2017). Thus, the public can engage with unexpected situations such as Carillion, that builds Private Finance Investment Schools in partnership with the public sector that has seen share prices drop by 90% in just over the last year (The Guardian, 2018). The Guardian (p. 1) states: In 2016 it had sales of £5.2bn and until July boasted a market capitalisation of almost £1bn. But since then its share price has plummeted from 40p per share, to 14p per share, and it is now worth just £61m. 27,500 employee's pensions were part of Carillion at a value of circa £900 million. Questions are being asked regarding how the Carillion Annual Accounts (2016) showed dividends of circa 18p per share, that is a return on investment per share, for one year of almost 50%, could have been made when there was a short fall in the pension, and in 12 months time Carillion is bankrupt owing £1.3 billion with contracts that are not being honoured (BBC, 2018a, 2018b), and when interest rates for tax payers' savings, including pension pots were 2.5% or less.

Collinson (2018) identifies small enterprises will feel the worst impact of Carillion going bankrupt because they will be last to get payment, leading to collapse, and to many having to sack their employees. Collinson (2018, p. 1) states:

Rather than just look to government *we should be taking a hard look at the corporate governance structures* in place at the firm; *these should have changed the strategy and structure well before we got to this disappointing and damaging end point.*

The BBC (2018c, p. 1) identified Carillion: 'employed 43,000 people worldwide, 20,000 in the UK, and had 450 contracts with the UK government. The government has said that staff and contractors working on public sector service contracts will continue to be paid. But there is concern that big projects, including the construction of hospitals and roads, will be delayed while the details are worked out. There are also big worries for an estimated 30,000 smaller firms which have been working on Carillion projects in the private sector.

The findings reveal that all senior-level leaders of marginalised groups in the research experienced a clash of values in the system where virtues of prudence courage and social justice were not valued, which has allowed those who Plato describes as 'full of avarice' to exercise 'unrighteous power'.

The senior-level leaders in this research wanted to be empowered to enable them to deliver their manifesto for school improvement and to be fully included in the organisation of education, build respect and trust in the system and work with primary virtues of courage, prudence and social justice (Adler, 1941). They wanted to connect the primary virtues with secondary intellectual virtues to create new knowledge and mobilise it for social justice, equity, renewal and peace. The findings agree with the first principles of the Education Model: EYSIER.

A first principle is that the senior-level leaders from marginalised groups with professional credentials wanted to be empowered to describe the fear caused by intersectionalities of discrimination in the system and work as bridges between public Education Governance Systems and the public to put this knowledge to action by building inclusionary processes and practices together for social justice (Marshall & Gerstl-Pepin, 2005; Taysum, Forthcoming).

A second principle is that these senior-level leaders wanted to be empowered to act as bridges between public Education Governance Systems and the public to put knowledge to action to build respect in the system for social justice (Barnett, 2000).

A third principle is that these senior-level leaders from marginalised groups wanted to be empowered to act as bridges between public Education Governance Systems, and the public to put knowledge to action together to build trust in the system for social justice (Barnett, 2000; Möllering, 2001; Wagner, 2010).

A fourth principle is that these senior-level leaders from marginalised groups wanted to be empowered to act as bridges between public Education Governance Systems, and the public, to put knowledge to action with courage to provide opportunities to bring diverse members of the community with different intersectionalities of discrimination together through conferences, workshops, concerts, dancing, sharing all faiths and none, open days, sports days, watching sport together, sharing fun events, sharing different interests and building open home-school relationships. They wanted to build bridges to shared world views and participation in the Education Governance Systems including in elected roles (Darling-Hammond & Rothman, 2013; Gerstl-Pepin & Aiken, 2012; Ishii et al., 2007).

A fifth principle is that these senior-level leaders from marginalised groups wanted to be empowered to act as bridges between public Education Governance Systems, and the public to put knowledge to action to engage with prudent philosophical inquiry to generate new knowledge that critiques and reflects upon these five principles to work towards democracy in education. They articulated such work would benefit from being supported by a networked professional body of national and international experts as mentors. All participating in this critical reflection need to have the thinking tools for such philosophical political inquiry to assure what Plato calls the 'retention of the greatest of all gifts: virtue' (Taysum, Forthcoming, 2017a, 2017b, 2012a, 2012b). In other words, to reject being enlightened, individuals need to have opportunities in the curriculum to make logical, evidence-informed, moral and ethical choices about what enlightenment is, and why they do, or do not want to become enlightened.

Reading these findings through a turbulence theory identifies that a definition of turbulence is to contextualise; '[...] the only sure way to avoid turbulence is to stay on the ground. Those who journey into the sky must be prepared' (Gross, 1998, p. 140). All cases reveal that senior-level leaders of marginalised groups have experienced a clash in values working in partnership with others who do not have professional educational credentials, or track records of school improvement. These senior leaders with track records of outstanding school improvement want to be empowered by public Educational Governance Systems that aim to raise standards so that they can do what they are experts of, and have outstanding track records of; improve education for equity, renewal, peace and improve student exam outcomes for social mobility and access to middle-class benefits.

Third, Senior-level Leaders of Marginalised Groups Need Mentoring and Networks to Help Them Navigate Turbulence

Third instability is caused by high stakes testing and the curriculum requiring the development of intellectual skills that do not nurture each individual's gifts, or value spending time on building relationships of trust hallmarked by virtue. These senior-level leaders articulated they wanted high-quality mentoring, and participation in the building of networks of expert mentors and peers who, as senior-level leaders, have track records of improving education so that they can pass on 'old opinion' that successfully improves effective education and its organisation with proof of concept.

In the Arab education in Israel, senior-level leaders are disempowered because they have to deliver a centralised curriculum where focus on intellectual outcomes distracts from time to build networks of expert mentors that support the senior-level leaders in developing strategies to nurture individual students' gifts:

> The Arab education system [...] is subject to government control of educational contents, resources and organizational structure. Golan-Agnon (2006) showed how Israel's centralized education system effectively controls and unifies and critiques activity in schools, maintaining a lack of equal educational opportunities for the Arab minority, due to a 'concentration of disadvantages' in its resources. Arab and Jewish education are thus not only separated but also unequal both in means and outputs.

The Northern Ireland case identified senior leaders need to be empowered to navigate high stakes testing regimes that focus on intellectual virtues demonstrated by student outcomes, but limit the time spent on building a shared education that builds harmony between diverse and segregated communities:

Concepts of community and individual rights come from widely divergent sources. Tutu (2004) explains the community concept of Ubuntu, the Nguni Bantu term meaning 'humanity towards others', in this way: 'In the end, our purpose is social and communal harmony and well-being. Ubuntu does not say, 'I think therefore I am.' It says rather: 'I am human because I belong. I participate. I share" (p. 27). Kept in balance, the forces of community standards and individual rights can complement one another and make a relatively free society feasible. The same pursuit of harmony between community and the individual can be found in the history of education (discussed in the introduction of this book) and, it is hoped, in Northern Irish schools [...] One principal also mentioned the need for middle leadership training, as this would help develop better support structures within the school as well as helping develop relationships with others in school leadership roles across Northern Ireland, which would also extend the support network. Another school principal referred to being able to discuss ideas with and have the support of local religious leaders, (as mentors), and that this was invaluable in terms of support for empowering young people.

The US case identifies that superintendents want to be empowered, mentored and supported by networks to overcome the segregation of marginalised community members:

> The superintendents' experiences agree with Tillman (2012) Grant (2012) and Gay (2004) and reveal Black females need mentoring that is constructive, purposeful, and consistently develops the individual to reach their career goals and develop school staff to optimise students' learning. Superintendents who do not have critical mentors who can role model making bridges to their true selves, and between different world views within the same community and between communities, potentially internalise the regulation of the markets. This kind of internalisation sustains the panopticon overview of those with power, and White supremacy, and prevents innovation that may seek to redistribute the division of labour through social mobility (Foucault, 1991). Preventing innovation to sustain the status quo prevents social mobilisation and social justice and is a barrier to Empowering Young Societal Innovators for Equity and Renewal (EYSIER) (Taysum, 2012a, 2012b, 2013, 2014; Taysum et al., 2015, 2016, 2017). Further, networks of mentors are essential to support these Black Women Superintendents to succeed and in turn, build further networks across disciplines with agents with power such as Mayors and politicians. The Superintendents may then support successful participation in committees and build capacity for equity and

renewal in the district, state, nationally and internationally. A culture change is needed in schools to provide returns on investment in education systems.

The Trinidad and Tobago case identifies that the curriculum limits how the Senior Level Leaders can empower the teachers to develop individual students' gifts, and develop differentiated culturally relevant learning opportunities:

> To achieve inclusive and differentiated instruction in classrooms, teachers must be adequately developed professionally in pedagogy and instruction. In *The Flat World and Education: How America's Commitment to Equity will Determine Our Future*, Darling-Hammond (2010) suggested that teacher quality is the most important influence on student learning (Desimone, 2009; Fullan, 2010; Mckinsey, 2007; Thrupp & Lupton, 2006). Thus, teacher training and development to ensure quality across the board is an essential aspect of educational reform. Nevertheless, many policy makers limit or eliminate the budget and time for professional development of implementers, thereby implying that schools and educators can deliver change without the requisite support networks of educational experts (Darling-Hammond, 2010).

The English case identifies Black, Asian and Minority Ethnicity senior-level leaders are able to engage the community, but they had to fight the infrastructure to be able to improve education standards for all:

> The chances for legal differences between general rules and the potential changes at the local application could mean strengthening or undermining human rights, which depends on the power and the ethos, logos and pathos of those who have the right to organise education (Harris, O'Boyle, & Warbrick, 2009; Ruşitoru, 2017). Those who have the right to organise education are currently not the BAME CEOs of Small, Medium, and Empty Multi Academy Trusts (MATs) who have educational professionals' credentials, have met the DfE (2015) educational leaders' values, and have track records for improving schools. Rather these BAME CEOs have to fight for the right to mobilise their track records of school improvement and they have to fight for the right to bring an 'untouchable' school into their MAT that they have improved, because once it is improved, it is very attractive to large MATs.

The evidence reveals that the senior leaders in this research are best placed to organise education in their contexts as *enlightened humans* who focus on education as a freeing of individual capacity growth directed to social aims (Dewey, 2016). However, they articulate they want to have the support of expert mentors and networks of experts and peers that will help them navigate turbulence (Gross, 2014). They identify turbulence presents itself through the prioritisation of secondary intellectual virtues in Education Governance Systems that focus on: economies of scale; controlling what senior-level leaders can and cannot do; quantitative data on dashboards of students' outcomes on high stakes testing. Rather these senior-level leaders want to be empowered to mobilise their track records for school improvement and focus on the primary moral virtues combined with the secondary intellectual virtues to Empower Communities and Young People to become Young Societal Innovators for Equity, Renewal, Social Mobility and for Peace in our time (Adler, 1941; Taysum, Forthcoming). Evidence reveals that disempowering senior-level leaders, which is what is happening now, has not closed the Black-White Achievement Gap, is not closing the Black-White Achievement Gap, and unless senior-level leaders are empowered to deliver their manifestos, and mobilise their track records of school improvement the Black-White Achievement Gap is unlikely to close in the future.

Fourth, Infrastructures for Cultural Change; Empowering Educational Professionals for Empowering Young Societal Innovators for Equity, Renewal and Peace

Infrastructures are required for cultural change with transparent and open pathways that enable professional credentialed educational senior leaders to organise education for equity, renewal, peace and optimise students' learning, and learning outcomes for social mobility, and middle-class benefits. Public education is a unique arena with a particular structure and characteristic processes. This arena is restricting and perhaps even prevents the attribution of professional responsibility in a simple manner to individuals who have done the hard work of improving schools, allowing those who wish to be credited for school improvement and receive large renumeration to get the credit and the large renumeration, whilst simultaneously avoiding responsibility for any failure.

The Arab education case identifies the superintendents are unable to affect any cultural change because:

> A lack of an independent educational administration for the Arab population means a lack of any influence over the learning contents in Arab schools.

The Northern Ireland case identifies that dialogue and working together is required for culture change and that different groups need to come together to co-create positive intergroup relations hallmarked by primary virtues that recognise progress towards peace, rather than focus on the secondary intellectual virtues of exam results:

Hughes and Loader (2015), among others, contend there is broad agreement that interaction between schools can facilitate positive intergroup relations. Over the past thirty years in Northern Ireland, there has been a drive to encourage schools of all sectors and types to form learning communities. This is particularly evident through the formation of formal partnerships at a local level in Area Learning Communities (ALCs). In Northern Ireland, every post-primary school is part of an ALC which can also involve colleges of Further Education, in order to 'maximise(s) the opportunity to meet the needs of pupils across the [given] area'. *McGuinness (2012) states: 'Where schools once competed with each other, they increasingly collaborate through the growth of Area Learning Communities (ALCs) [...], it is with these ALCs that our greatest hope may lie'* (2012, p. 232).

We would sit down as a leadership team and look at how we are going to drive this or that initiative forward, [...] it's your middle leaders who are on the real frontline and they are leading departments of maybe eight people in a school as big as this [...] so, they're the people that you really need on board (Interviewee H). This might suggest where the drivers may lie in achieving the empowerment of the school community.

In relation to Shared Education, one of the school principals emphasised the need to avoid having too rigid a structure and a 'one size fits all' approach as there would be variation in terms of best approaches to Shared Education across Northern Ireland depending on the locality and particular local contexts. The need for structural change was also identified, for example: '*I just think we need a different language, to be more inclusive, to be more respectful and it is about equity and it is about equity in terms of recognising the progress that our children have made, recognising stages of progression and recognising progression rather than recognising these landmark ages, when we expect them all to have got this standard*'. Establishing trust in a post-conflict society can be challenging. As Tschannen-Moran and Gareis (2015) recognise '*trust becomes salient when people enter into relationships of interdependence, where the outcomes one desires cannot be met without the involvement and contribution of others*'.

The US case identifies that where superintendents have been able to affect a cultural change the result has been:

returns on investment when change strategies focus on bridging between different world views, the true self, and the real world to offer social mobility and middle class benefits to African American communities (and marginalised groups who have experienced oppression/segregation by White supremacists).

The Trinidad and Tobago case identifies that the planned culture change experienced a critical oversight; those responsible for implementing the cultural change were *excluded* from participating in the planning of the culture change:

> Data were gleaned from persons who reside at the lower and middle level of the education governance system in Trinidad and Tobago, groups that seldom get the chance to express how they experience the many educational change processes the country undergoes and their role in the outcome of such processes. Two key sets of change agents (school supervisors and principals) were not members of the curriculum planning team. This was a critical oversight, because these two sets of stakeholders are responsible for supervising and monitoring policy implementation and leading and managing change at the site of change, that is, the schools.

The English case findings reveal:

> Black Asian, Minority Ethnicity (BAME) Chief Executive Officers (CEOs) of Multi Academy Trusts (MATs) who have a track record of improving schools from Requires Improvement to Good, and Outstanding are prevented from growing their MATs (and improving more schools) because they do not have the infrastructure. Without an infrastructure, their professional expertise as key agents of change, to develop John Dewey's desirable rules or right acts that shape good character and virtue are prevented from flourishing (Adler, 1941). The BAME CEOs are also concerned that if they take on an additional school, they may leave their colleague's good or outstanding school down the road, vulnerable to a rapid forced takeover from a large MAT. The pragmatic consequences would be the connections between the community, parents, students, school staff and CEOs will be lost, along with the chances to debate, and develop a shared world view of what it is to lead a good life with the community. The BAME CEOs wish to move slowly when growing their MATs, and ensure that all their academies in their MATs are 100% good or outstanding before building capacity and taking on more failing schools to improve them. The findings connect with the Government Report on MATs (2017) that cautions that the growth of MATs does not compromise raising standards and improving performance. MATs with demonstrated infrastructure,

but not 100% good and outstanding schools, and have not had an Ofsted inspection, are allowed to take on more schools (Schools Week, 2017). The current processes and practices for growing MATs are preventing the realisation of the aims of Morgan (2016), the then Education Secretary who stated MATs that cannot demonstrate a 'strong track record' in improving schools will not be allowed to take on more schools (p. 1). The Guardian (2016, p. 1) has identified that: 'England's largest academy chains have 'serious weaknesses' as bad as the local authorities they were intended to replace, Sir Michael Wilshaw has told the education secretary, Nicky Morgan, in strong criticism of the government's flagship school improvement programme'.

The senior-level leaders from marginalised groups reveal Education Governance Systems focus on developing students' intellectual virtues. Curricula are underpinned by a high stakes testing regime, which prevents senior-level leaders developing a culture change to connect communities with their institutions, through full and free participation in a shared education for equity, renewal, improved student outcomes, social mobility, and raising communities out of poverty in a step by step way to build peace. The senior-level leaders identify they need expert mentors and networks of expert mentors and peers to help them navigate this severe and extreme turbulence.

Conclusions; A Comparative Analysis of Five International Education Governance Systems; Turbulence, Empowerment and Marginalised Groups

The senior-level leaders who participated in this research, from marginalised groups identify there is a clash of values in Education Governance Systems. The clash of values prevents them from mobilising their outstanding track records of improving education, disconnects the community from their schools and colleges, and prevents raising students' exam outcomes for social mobility. The pragmatic consequence is fear is built in Education Governance Systems. The senior-level leaders are not empowered to operationalise their track records of, and manifestos for school improvement which creates fear that they will be blamed for a lack of school improvement, or be forced into leaving their roles as outstanding senior-level leaders of school improvement. Fear is distracting and destabilising and prevents these senior-level leaders, school staff and parents from working together to address the root causes of their disempowerment within the Education Governance System. Indeed evidence reveals that the struggle for survival can lead to competition between senior-level leaders and MATs which may echo a divide and conquer strategy where different groups with different levels of entitlement are set up to compete with each other to improve their entitlement (Taysum & Murrel-Abery, 2017). Such conflict distracts them from addressing real moral and ethical problems of colonisation within their Education Governance Systems of those without professional educational credentials and without outstanding track records of school improvement.

Distracting senior-level leaders and MAT communities by creating fear in the system also prevents individuals from having the time to think about and fully understand how current regulation and accountability structures allowed Carillion Annual Accounts (2016) to show dividends of circa 18p per share; that is a return on investment per share for one year of almost 50%, when there was a short fall in the pension, and in 12 months of time Carillion is bankrupt owing £1.3 billion with contracts including those for schools, hospitals and prisons not being honoured (BBC, 2018b), and when interest rates for tax payers' savings, including pension pots were 2.5% or less. BBC (2018d, p. 1) report: 'The chairman of trustees of Carillion's pension scheme, Robin Ellison, has suggested in a letter to a committee of MPs that there was a *funding shortfall of around £990m* with Carillion's defined benefit pension schemes by the end'. Thus, the real losers are the Small and Medium Enterprises (SMEs) in local communities that Carillion subcontracted the work to, the tax payer who worked for Carillion and has now lost their job and their pension, and may need to seek work as a temporary part-time contractor, and all stakeholders of the PFI contracts Carillion are not honouring in schools, hospitals and prisons (Collinson, 2018).

Fear of the other causing conflict prevents groups working together for Societal Innovation, Equity, Renewal, and social mobility that lifts people out of poverty and builds peace. Gross (2014) Turbulence theory has provided a useful lens through which to examine the experiences of the professional and credentialed educational senior-level leaders working in divided, and/or marginalised societies or communities. The senior-level leaders have experienced severe and extreme levels of turbulence and they require expert mentors and networks of expert mentors and peers to navigate such turbulence. Indeed some senior-level leaders in each case report that in their struggles, they have become experts in school improvement and are well positioned to be mentors to others to navigate such turbulence in their school improvement journeys.

Networks empower senior-level leaders to work together and not against each other and to draw on 'old opinion' that has proof of concept, coupled with logical and evidence-informed, moral and ethical innovations for improving education and navigating turbulence. The evidence reveals that curriculums may claim inclusion, but the senior-level leaders articulate children from marginalised groups in their schools and colleges are educated in separate, or segregated schools. The political will to provide curricula to celebrate diverse cultural heritages and share world views of people of all faiths and none, has been largely absent (although this may change in the Northern Ireland case with the publication of the Department of Education report *Integration Works. Transforming Your School*, in December 2017). The senior-level leaders in this research organise education as political, philosophical, legislators and enlightened human beings, but they do so as isolated individuals.

The evidence from all cases connects with Apple (1995) who asks can education change society? Our evidence reveals that these senior-level leaders 'response to this question is; 'yes, we can', but the evidence reveals this is happening only one school at a time by isolated individuals. The findings connect with Dewey (2016, p. 1920):

> We must depend upon the efforts of *enlightened humans* in their private capacity [...] The full development of private personality is identified with the aims of humanity as a whole and with the idea of progress [...] and the very idea of education as a freeing of individual capacity in a progressive growth directed to social aims.

To build capacity these isolated individuals need to be supported by expert mentors, and networks of expert mentors and peers. These networks can be brokered by the academy taking a 'not for profit' approach as Higher Education Institutions, which are institutions of knowledge creation, mobilisation, and preservation that serve the interests of the public (Duncan, 2011; Morales, 2011; Taysum, 2011). The networks can empower the senior-level leaders to be bridges between Education Governance Systems, the public, and the academy.

The evidence has revealed that neo-liberal agendas and education are becoming more closely connected with the needs of corporate society, and are driven by intellectual virtues, and evidence reveals 'avarice' rather than the primary virtues that might critique corporate intellectual virtues and find them wanting. Without curricula that balances primary virtues of prudence, courage and social justice, with secondary intellectual virtues, different groups of people may continue to feel more disconnected from their communities, societal institutions, and Education Governance Systems that do not recognise or respect their world views. The division of labour and the divide and conquer strategies to protect greater entitlements and privilege, directs people to become self-regulating with the values of corporations as they seek to protect themselves from systemic fear (Ball, 2017; Foucault, 1991; Taysum, 2017a; Taysum & Murrel-Abery, 2017). Opportunities to become self-regulating as mature citizens are not afforded to them in curricula that only focuses on developing intellectual virtues[1]. Chances to build the problem solving skills required for innovation, and to build sustainable local communities by, for, and of members of local communities who, taking a liberal approach to growing SMEs, offer authentic competition to large corporations are diminished. Schools that could teach the value of the environment through sustainable farming skills, and growing small orchards, and fruit trees in communities' streets could in turn lead to young entrepreneurs building SMEs that, properly regulated, could supply local cafe cultures, old people's care residences, hospitals and restaurants and develop local economies and inter-generational relationships within communities that foster commitment and

---

[1]Research is recommended into how school business managers and administrators in academies are affected by such clashes in cultures, and this professional challenge has not been the focus of this research.

loyalty to local communities (Taysum, 2017a, 2017b). These kinds of infrastructures require building, and maintenance, and decorating, which attracts further SMEs who are paid directly by the public Education Governance System, and not by a large public Corporation such as Carillion who subcontract the work out to SMEs. SMEs are well positioned to work directly and closely with senior-level leaders and their staff to build trust, and not, as a senior-level leader identified in the English case in chapter five:

> deliberately put the soap dispenser and the hand dryer in the wrong places because they knew it would increase the likelihood for the need for repairs and it would increase the likelihood of failure of those components which in turn would mean the service contractors would always have something to do.

In this scenario, the public Education Governance System does not pay the public corporations through PFIs to potentially pay local community small and medium enterprises, and 'top slice' large amounts of money for 'managing the outsourcing of hard back breaking work in the field, to local small and medium *contractors*' (Collinson, 2018; Taysum, 2017b).

The new infrastructure, in turn, may attract people who like to build their homes near to emerging vibrant small and medium communities. Here, the untouchable academy, transformed to outstanding by a senior-level leader and their staff, and community, could be the stable hub of a sustainable community. The senior-level leaders bridge between different groups and their interests for full and free interactions and cooperations for democracy in education (Dewey, 2016; Taysum, 2017a).

The conclusions reveal enlightened senior-level leaders with educational professional credentials, mapped to professional standards located within an education profession, recognised by the nation states' authoritative bodies, and who have outstanding track records of school improvement, have the desire to, and are capable of organising education to EYSIER for Social Mobility that lifts people out of poverty, and builds peace with the following primary principles, that include primary, and secondary virtues:

(1) Inclusion to realise social justice and recognition for all (Adler, 1941; Fraser, 2000; Marshall & Gerstl-Pepin, 2005; Morgan, 2018)
(2) respect to realise social justice (Barnett, 2000; Taysum & Gunter, 2008)
(3) trust in the search for truth (Barnett, 2000; Carter, 2005; Möllering, 2001; Wagner., 2010; Pring, 2000);
(4) courage to engage in prudent dialogue to co-create constructive cross-cultural critique of alternative world views to arrive at a shared multicultural world view of how to live together for peace in our time (Adler, 1941; Darling-Hammond & Rothman, 2013; Gerstl-Pepin & Aiken, 2012; Ishii et al., 2007);

(5) the generation of new knowledge that prudently synthesises traditional and new knowledge to enable the re-imagining of new futures where young people are mobilisers of stable and sustainable socio-economic change for equity and renewal (Harrison et al., 2016; Taysum, 2012a, 2012b).

The book contributes to the discussion of how senior-level leaders with educational professional credentials, and track records of outstanding school improvement, from marginalised groups articulate they want to be empowered, supported by networks of expert mentors, and peers, and supported by legislation so that they can organise education to, as Plato says, 'do right'.

The evidence reveals that these enlightened senior-level leaders have been appointed based on their professional credentials as educational leaders, their track records of improving educational outcomes and social mobility, their success in connecting communities with their schools, and they are people who enjoy the respect and trust of their communities using their primary and secondary virtues. The evidence reveals these senior-level leaders are enlightened individuals who can free individual capacity in a progressive growth directed to social aims (Dewey, 2016).

A central part of sustaining work in school and system improvement is developing the capacity of our school and system leaders to recognise, foster and implement innovative change within the learning communities. Education Governance Systems can be uniquely placed to do the work of empowering and developing leaders and contribute to the diffusion of innovation in research and practice. By creating and empowering collaborative networked learning communities and supporting the ongoing professional learning and development of individual practitioners, and professional associations, opportunities emerge to strengthen existing and emergent pathways for bridging the knowledge-practice gap in senior-level leadership of Education Governance Systems (Duncan, 2011; Morales, 2011; Taysum, 2011).

Evidence reveals how Education Governance Systems can encourage educational senior-level leaders to close the Black-White achievement gap (Wagner, 2010) while engaging effectively in evidence-informed, logical, moral and ethical praxis that help school communities gain deeper understanding of how to connect with school empowerment through participative processes and practices and distribution of power/ power sharing (Taysum, Forthcoming).

This chapter has presented what we have learned about the relationships within Education Governance Systems to build capacity. The themes are: multistakeholder action for scaled knowledge to action impact strategies that foster and support collaborative networked learning communities in practice. Such communities of and for practice, and innovation-facilitating dialogue among practitioners that mobilises research to practice, and practice to research, underpins continued engagement between different stakeholders. The focus is on improving students' achievements for equity, renewal, improved students outcomes, social mobility and middle-class benefits. Policy and Education Governance Systems have the potential to synthesise the best of what has been said and done in the past with new innovations through networks of knowledge building and advocacy (Taysum, 2017a, 2017b, Forthcoming). These networks co-create action learners working together to describe intersectionalities of discrimination and begin to remove discrimination and marginalisation from Education Governance Systems, to optimise learning and improve success for all students and EYSIER.

Recommendations are that Education Governance Systems, that may confuse their governance responsibility with the responsibility for organising education systems, stop distracting senior-level leaders with educational professional credentials and outstanding track records of school improvement from organising educational effectiveness, improvement, and transformation. Rather, leaders of Educational Governance Systems need to diminish the impact of any turbulence on the Educational, Credentialed, Professional senior-level leaders that diminishes their ability to deliver their manifesto of school improvement.

These are the predicates for Education Governance Systems, and communities legitimately holding these senior-level leaders accountable for cultural change that EYSIER for Social Mobility and for working together for Peace. The strategies and infrastructures need to be fully and fairly resourced, and all funding needs to be published in the public domain with realistic Key Performance Indicators that reveal returns on investment over a five-year period with annual reviews, and regular meetings at all levels of the Education Governance System. The senior-level leaders organising education, if they are to be fairly held to account need to be empowered by: policy; infrastructure and relevant agents to act as bridges between different groups and networks; top district administrators; leaders of Education Governance Systems; the layers of committees that make decisions on policy, infrastructure, agency and/or provide quality assurance of the decision-making; parents; students; stakeholders within the community; the academy, which provides fully integrated postgraduate research programmes, and non-accredited courses for Initial Teacher Education, mid career educational professionals, educational professional leading experts, and educational professional gatekeepers.

We also recommend if senior-level leaders are authentically empowered to implement cultural change, that the EYSIER Education Model be implemented (Taysum, 2012a, 2012b, 2013, 2014; Taysum et al., 2015, 2016, 2017), supported by resources for each standard that meet each of the five primary principles.

Finally we recommend an Anthropology of Intersectionalities of Discrimination for professional educationals and adults interested in developing cultural literacy is developed with Intended Learning Outcomes that map back to primary moral virtues and secondary intellectual virtues (Adler, 1941), supported by a website with a tool box of differentiated resources for different aged children with different abilities for teachers to adapt. The website is supported by a platform for classrooms from different nation states to connect and optimise intercultural literacy and the development of shared world views.

References

Adler, M. (1941). *A dialectic of morals: Towards the foundations of political philosophy*. Notre Dame: University of Notre Dame.

Allen, A., & Mintrom, M. (2010). Responsibility and school governance. *Educational Policy, 24*(3), 439–464.

Apple, M. (1995). *Education and power*. New York, NY: Routledge.

Arnova, R. F., Torres, C. A., & Franz, S. (2013). *Comparative education: The dialectic of global and local*. Lanham: Rowan & Littlefield.

Ball, S. (2017). *Edu.net: Globalisation and education policy mobility*. London: Routledge.

Banks, J. A. (2017). *Citizenship education and global migration: Implications for theory, research and teaching*. American Educational Research Association.

Barnette, D. (2018). Education week state policy reporter: Failing Infrastructure in US Schools. *Washington Journal C-Span*. Retrieved from https://www.c-span.org/video/?439566-5/washington-journal-daarel-burnette-discusses-failing-infrastructure-us-schools. Accessed on October 31, 2018.

Barnett, R. (2000). *Higher education: A critical business*. Buckingham: The Society for Research into Higher Education & Open University Press.

Berliner, D. C., & Biddle, B. J. (1995). The Manufactured crisis: Myths, fraud, and the attack on America's Public Schools. *NASSP Bulletin, 80*(576), 119–121.

Björk, L., Browne-Ferrigno, T., & Kowalski, T. (2014). The superintendent and educational reform in the United States of America. *Leadership and Policy in Schools, 13*(4), 444–465.

Blase, J. (1997). *The fire is back!: Principals sharing school governance*. Thousand Oaks, CA: Corwin Press.

BBC News. (2017). Wakefield city academies trust pulls out of 21 schools. Retrieved from http://www.bbc.co.uk/news/uk-england-leeds-41198403"http://www.bbc.co.uk/news/uk-england-leeds-41198403. Accessed on December 22, 2017.

BBC. (2018a). Carillion: Banks call for government help. Retrieved from https://www.bbc.co.uk/news/business-42680585. Accessed on October 30, 2018.

BBC. (2018b). Carillion was left with just £29 million before going bankrupt. Retrieved from http://www.bbc.co.uk/news/business-42710795. Accessed on 1 May 2018.

BBC. (2018c). Andrea Albutt: Carillion has left our prisons in a terrible state. Retrieved from https://www.theguardian.com/society/2018/jan/23/carillion-prisons-terrible-state-andrea-albutt-prison-governors-chief. Accessed on October 30, 2018.

BBC. (2018d). Carillion: Are pensions on the brink? Retrieved from http://www.bbc.co.uk/news/business-42705641. Accessed on 18 February 2018.

Carillion. (2016). Carillion annual report and accounts; making tomorrow a better place. Retrieved from http://www.annualreports.co.uk/HostedData/AnnualReports/PDF/LSE_CLLN_2016.pdf. Accessed on 18 February 2018.

Carter, P. L. (2005). *Keepin' it real: School success beyond Black and White*. New York, NY: Oxford University Press.

Carter, P. L. (2008). Teaching students fluency in multiple cultural codes. In M. Pollock (Ed.), *Everyday antiracism*. (pp. 107–112) New York, NY: The New Press.

Cohen, R. (2018). Kids are freezing: Amid bitter cold, Baltimore schools, students struggle. *The Washington Post*. Retrieved from https://www.washingtonpost.com/

news/posteverything/wp/2018/01/08/public-school-buildings-are-falling-apart-and-students-are-suffering-for-it/?noredirect=on&utm_term=.0a4c2fc82610. Accessed on October 31, 2018.

Commission for Victims and Survivors. (2016). To improve the lives of all victims and survivors of the conflict. Retrieved from https://www.cvsni.org. Accessed on 20 April 2018.

Crenshaw, K. (1989). Demarginalizing the Intersection of Race and Sex: A Black Feminist Critique of Antidiscrimination Doctrine, Feminist Theory, and Antiracist Politics, University of Chicago Legal Forum, 1989, 139–167.

Darling-Hammond, L. (2010). *The flat world and education: How America's commitment to equity will determine our future.* New York, NY: Teachers College Press.

Darling-Hammond, L., & Lieberman, A. (Eds.) (2012). *Teacher education around the world: Changing policies and practices (Teacher quality and school development).* London: Routledge.

Darling-Hammond, L., & Rothman, R. (2013). *Teacher and leader effectiveness in high performing education systems.* Stanford, CA: SCOPE.

De Gruy, J. (2005). *Post traumatic slave syndrome.* Portland: Joy De Gruy Publications Inc.

Delanty, G. (2001). *Challenging knowledge the university in the knowledge society.* Buckingham: SRHE and Open University Press.

Desimone, L. M. (2009). Improving impact studies of teachers' professional development: Toward better conceptualizations and measures. *Educational Researcher,* *38*(3), 181–199.

Dewey, J. (1909). *Moral principles in education.* New York, NY: The Riverside Press Cambridge.

Dewey, J. (2016). *Democracy and education.* New York, NY: Macmillan..

Dewey, J. (1922). Morality is social. In *Human nature and conduct: An introduction to social psychology* (pp. 314–332). New York: Modern Library.

Dewey, J. (1929). *Experience and nature.* Peru, IL: Open Court Publishing Company.

Deloitte. (2007). *Research into the financial cost of the Northern Ireland divide.* Belfast: Deloitte.

Diamond, S. (2012). Beyond the Berle and means paradigm: Private equity and the new capitalist order. In C. Williams & P. Zumbansen (Eds.), *The embedded firm: Corporate governance, labor and finance capitalism* (pp. 151–176). Cambridge: Cambridge University Press.

Duncan, S. (2011). Improving the nutritional value of the food served and the dining experience in a primary school. *Management in Education, 25*(4), 142–145.

Equalities and Human Rights Commission. (2010). UK Equality Act. Retrieved from https://www.equalityhumanrights.com/en/equality-act/equality-act-2010. Accessed on 10 May 2016.

Evert, T., Van Deuren, A., & Lang, B. (2015). *Working towards success. Board, and superintendent interactions, relationships and hiring issues.* London: Rowman and Littlefield.

Foucault, M. (1991). *Discipline and punish; the birth of the prison.* London: Penguin.

Fraser, N. (2000). *Justice interruptus: Rethinking key concepts of a post-socialist age.* London: Routledge.

Fullan, M. (2010). *All systems go: The change imperative for whole school reform.* Thousand Oaks, CA: Corwin and Ontario Principals' Council.

Gay, G. (2004). Navigating marginality en route to the professoriate: Graduate students of color learning and living in academia. *International Journal of Qualitative Studies in Education, 17*(2), 265–288.

Gerstl-Pepin, C., & Aiken, J. (2012). *Social justice leadership for a global world.* Charlotte, NC: Information Age Publishing.

Glazer, N. (1987). *Affirmative discrimination ethnic inequality and public policy.* Harvard: Harvard University Press.

Golan-Agnon, D. (2006). Separate but not equal: Discrimination against Palestinian Arab students in Israel. *American Behavioral Scientist, 49*(8), 1075–1084.

Gordon, J. (1993). Why did you select teaching as career? Teachers of color tell their stories. Retrieved from https://files.eric.ed.gov/fulltext/ED383653.pdf. Accessed on October 31, 2018.

Grant, C. (2012). Advancing our legacy: A Black feminist perspective on the significance of mentoring for African-American women in educational leadership. *International Journal of Qualitative Studies in Education, 25*(1), 101–117.

Gunter, H., Hall, D., & Mills, C. (2015). Consultants, consultancy, and consultoracy in education policymaking. *England Journal of Education Policy, 30*(4), 518–539.

Harland, K., & McCready, S. (2012). *Taking boys seriously: A longitudinal study of adolescent male school-life experiences in Northern Ireland.* Bangor: Department of Education.

Harris, D., O'Boyle, M., & Warbrick, C. (2009). *Law of the European convention on human rights.* Oxford: Oxford University Press.

Harrison, K., Taysum, A., McNamara, G., & O'Hara, J. (2016). The degree to which students and teachers are involved in second-level school processes and participation in decision making: An Irish case study in Irish studies in education. *Irish Educational Studies, 35*(2), 155–173.

Helve, H. (1991). The formation of religious attitudes and worldviews: A longitudinal study of young Finns. *Social Compass, 38*, 373–392.

Hodgson, A., & Spours, K. (2006). An analytical framework for policy engagement: The contested case of 14–19 reforms in England. *Journal of Education Policy, 21*(6), 679–696.

Hughes, J., & Loader, R. (2015). Plugging the gap': Shared education and the promotion of community relations through schools in Northern Ireland. *British Education Research Journal, 41*(6), 1142–1155.

Ishii, S., Klopf, D., & Cooke, P. (2007). Worldview in intercultural communication: A religio-cosmological approach. In L. Samovar, R. Porter, & E. McDaniel (Eds.), *Intercultural communication a reader.* Boston, MA: Wadsworth Cengage Learning.

Kakos, M., & Palaiologou, N. (2014). Learning from international education policies to move towards education systems that facilitate sustainable full economic, cultural and political participation. *Italian Journal of Sociology of Education, 6*(2), 68–87.

MacInnes, T., Aldridge, H., Parekh, A., & Kenway, P. (2012). *Monitoring poverty and social exclusion in Northern Ireland.* York: Joseph Rowntree Foundation.

McIntosh, P. (1997). White privilege and male privilege: A personal account coming to see correspondences through work in Women's Studies. In R. Delgado & J.

Stefancic (Eds.), *Critical white studies: Looking behind the mirror* (pp. 291–299). Philadelphia, PA: Temple University Press.

McKinsey Report. (2007). *How the world's best performing systems come out on top.* London: McKinsey & Company.

Marshall, C., & Gerstl-Pepin, C. I. (2005). *Re-framing educational politics for social justice.* Boston, MA: Pearson/Allyn and Bacon.

Möllering, G. (2001). The nature of trust. From Georg Simmel to a theory of expectations, interpretation, and suspense. *Sociology, 35*(2), 403–420.

Morales, S. (2011). A study of parent participation at an international school in Spain offering the British curriculum. *Management in Education, 25*(4), 146–148.

Morgan, D. (2018). *An unbroken educational apartheid legacy: Chicago's south suburban predominantly black communities of color.* Kindle Edition.

Morgan, N. (2016). *Academy trusts without 'strong track record' can't have more schools. Schools Week.* Retrieved from https://schoolsweek.co.uk/morgan-academy-trusts-without-strong-track-record-cant-have-more-schools/. Accessed on February 22, 2018.

Muñoz, J., Pankake, A., Shirley, A., & Simonsson, M. (2017). Nurturing leadership: Equitable mentoring for the superintendency. *International Journal of Leadership in Education, 21*(3), 1–9.

Nolan, P. (2013). *The Northern Ireland peace monitoring report, Number Two.* Belfast: Community Relations Council.

Northern Ireland Executive. (2016). *Draft programme for government framework* (pp. 2016–2021). Belfast: NIE.

OFMDFM, NI. (2009). *Strategy for victims and survivors.* Retrieved from https://www.executiveoffice-ni.gov.uk/sites/default/files/publications/ofmdfm_dev/strategy-for-victims-and-survivors-november-2009.pdf.

Ohanian, S. (1999). *One size fits few: The folly of educational standards.* Portsmouth, NH: Heinemann.

Plato, J. B. (Ed.) (2018). *Timaeus and Critias in The Complete Works of Plato.* Olymp Classics: Kindle Edition.

Pons, X. (2017). Fifteen years of research on PISA effects on education governance: Acritical review. *European Journal of Education, Research Development and Policy, 52*(2), 131–144.

Popper, K. (1963). *Conjectures and refutations: The growth of scientific knowledge.* London: Routledge.

Pring, R. (2000). *Philosophy of Educational Research.* London: Continuum.

Purvis, D. (2011). *Educational disadvantage and the protestant working class. A call to action.* Belfast: Dawn Purvis.

Resh, N., & Benavot, A. (2009). Educational Governance, school autonomy, and curriculum implementation: Diversity and uniformity in knowledge offerings to Israeli pupils. *Journal of Curriculum Studies, 41*(1), 67–92.

Robinson, K. (2014). *Finding your element: How to discover your talents and passions and transform your life.* London: Penguin.

Roulston, S., Hansson, U., Cook, S., & McKenzie, P. (2016). If you are not one of them you feel out of place: Understanding divisions in a Northern Irish town. *Children's Geographies, 15*(4), 452–465.

Ruşitoru, M.-V. (2017). *Le droit á l'éducation et les politiques éducatives. Union européenne et Roumanie.* Paris: Harmattan.

Saran, R., & Niesser, B. (2004). *Inquiring minds; socratic dialogue in education.* Stoke-on-Trent: Trentham Books Ltd.

Shapiro, J. P., & Gross, S. J. (2013). *Ethical educational leadership in turbulent times: (Re)solving moral dilemmas* (2nd ed.). New York, NY: Routledge.

Shapiro, J., & Stefkovich, J. (2016). *Ethical leadership and decision making in education.* New York, NY: Routledge.

Shook, J., & Good, J. (2010). *John Dewey's philosophy of spirit with the 1897 lecture on Hegel.* New York, NY: Fordham University Press.

Sleeter, C., & Carmona, J. (2017), *Un-Standardizing curriculum: Multicultural teaching in the standards-based classroom (Multicultural Education Series).* New York, NY: Teachers College Press.

Stenhouse, L. (1975). *An introduction to curriculum research and development.* London: Heinemann.

Taysum, A. (2011). Strengths of postgraduate research in continuing professional development for professional educationalists. *Management in Education*, 25(4), 138–141.

Taysum, A. (2012a). *Convener of a large symposium in two parts: 'Globalization, Policy and Agency: Eight Nation states working together to Further Understand their Political Sociologies of Education'.* European Conference for Educational Research, Cadiz, September.

Taysum, A. (2012b). *Evidence informed leadership in education.* London: Continuum.

Taysum, A. (2013). Convener of a large symposium in two parts; 'International Boundary Crossing Study of Teachers' and Students' Participation in Institutional Processes and Practices". *European Conference for Educational Research.* Istanbul, September.

Taysum, A. (2014). Convener of a large symposium in two parts: 'International Boundary Crossing Study Of Higher Education Institutions working in Partnership with Schools To Improve Participation In Processes And Practices Chair: Jan Heystek (Stellenbosch University) Discussant: Carole Collins Ayanlaja (Chicago, Superintendent) *ECER, Porto.*

Taysum, A. (2015). Convener of a large symposium in two parts: 'A Theory of Young People's Participation in Systems and Learning from International Boundary Crossing Action-Research Project Arar, K., Collins-Ayanlaja, C., Harrison, K., Imam, H., Murrel-Abery, V., Mynbayeva, A., Yelbayeva, Z. *European Conference for Educational Research.* Budapest, Hungary. September.

Taysum, A. (2016). *Rationalising Kant with Aristotle's habits – The complexity of becoming virtuous.* Workshop, Almaty, Kazakhstan, November.

Taysum, A. (2016). *Convener of a large symposium in two parts: McNamara (Chair), Risku, M., Collins Ayanlaja, C., Iddrisu, M.T., Murrel-Abery, J.V., Arar, K., Masry-Herzallah, A., Imam, H., Chopra, P., McGuinness, S. Theoretical underpinnings of an education and skills model for participation and cooperation in the Youth Field; empowering Europe's young innovators.* European Conference for Educational Research, Dublin, Ireland, August.

Taysum, A. (2017). *Convener of a large symposium in two parts: Arar, K., Masry-Herzallah, A., Collins Ayanlaja, C., Brookins, W., McGuinness, S., Bates, J., Roulsten, S., O'Connor, U., James, F., and George, J., Taysum, A. Turbulence in Six International Education Governance-Systems: Comparing Knowledge to Action for Equity, Peace and Renewal.* European Conference for Educational Research, Copenhagen, Denmark, August.

Taysum, A. (2017a). Systems Theory and education: A philosophical enquiry into education systems theory. In P. Higgs & Y. Waghid (Eds.), *A reader for Philosophy of Education* (Vol. 1, p. 1). South Africa: Juta.

Taysum, A. (September, 2017b). Educational leadership for a global society. In *Inspiring School Leaders.* Cambridge: University of Cambridge.

Taysum, A. (Forthcoming). A Deweyan framework for moral training for democracy in education. In C. Lowery & P. Jenlink (Eds.), *Handbook of Dewey's educational theory and practice.* The Netherlands: Sense Publishers (in press).

Taysum, A., & Gunter, H. (2008). A critical approach to researching social justice and school leadership in England. *Education, Citizenship and Social Justice, 3*(2), 183–199.

Taysum, A., & Iqbal, M. (2012). What counts as meaningful and worthwhile policy analysis. *Italian Journal of Sociology of Education, 4*(1), 11–28.

Taysum, A., & Murrel-Abery, G. V. (2017). Shifts in education policy, administration and governance in Guyana 1831–2017. Seeking 'a political' agenda for equity and renewal. *Italian Journal of Sociology of Education, 9*(2), 55–87.

Tellerico, M., & Blount, J. (2004). Women and the superintendency: Insights from theory and history. *Educational Administration Quarterly, 40*(5), 633–662.

Thrupp, M., & Lupton, R. (2006). Taking school contexts more seriously: The social justice challenge. *British Journal of Educational Studies, 54*(3), 308–328.

Tillman, L. C. (2012). Inventing ourselves: An informed essay for Black female scholars in educational leadership. *International Journal of Qualitative Studies in Education, 25*(1), 119–126.

Tschannen-Moran, M., & Gareis, C. R. (2015). Principals, trust, and cultivating vibrant schools. *Societies, 5*(2), 256–276.

Tutu, D. (2004). *God has a dream. A vision of hope for our time.* London: Random House.

United Nations. (1948). *Universal declaration of human rights* (General Assembly Resolution 217 A). Retrieved from http://www.un.org/en/universal-declaration-human-rights/. Accessed on 14 October 2018.

Van Deuren, A., Evert, T., & Lang, B. (2015). *The board and superintendent handbook: Current issues and resources.* Lanham, MD: Rowman and Littlefield.

Wagner, T. (2010). *The global achievement gap.* New York, NY: Basic Books.

Waite, D., Rodriguez, G., & Wadende, A. (2015). Globalization and the business of education reform. In J. Zaida (Ed.) *Second International Handbook in Globalization, Education and Policy Research.* (pp. 353–374) Dordrecth: Springer.

Wisconsin State Legislature. (2011). Wisconsin Act 10 2011. Retrieved from http://docs.legis.wisconsin.gov/2011/related/acts/10.

Chapter 11

Conclusions: Turbulence, Empowerment and Marginalised Groups

Alison Taysum and Khalid Arar

Abstract

The aim of this book is to set an agenda and address a gap in the literature regarding Turbulence, Empowerment and Marginalisation in International Education Governance Systems and its relationship with narrowing the global phenomena of a Black-White achievement gap.

The aims are met by addressing the following questions. First, how do senior leaders of Educational Governance Systems who are from and represent marginalised groups in society, describe and understand how School Governance Systems empower or disempower them to develop school communities as societal innovators for equity, and renewal? Second, how do these senior-level leaders within Education Governance Systems describe and understand the role mentors and/or advocates play to support their navigation through the turbulence? Third, to what extent, do these senior-level leaders of Education Governance Systems believe a cultural change is required to empower them in school and college communities including staff, families, students and community partnerships to Empower Young Societal Innovators for Equity and Renewal (EYSIER)? Finally, what theories of knowledge to action emerge regarding how these senior-level leaders might successfully navigate turbulence to empower marginalised groups for equity and renewal for all in Public Corporate Education Governance Systems?

We identified in Chapter 1 that the context is one of colonisation between different groups. In Chapter 2, The review of literature focused on turbulence in Education Governance Systems and identified the global distribution of knowledge concerning education from cash-rich countries has had a tremendous impact on what is taught and tested in schools. Nation states that are not cash rich are marginalised in a global politics. International Testing Industries examine the output of national education systems

Turbulence, Empowerment and Marginalisation in International
Education Governance Systems, 275–294
doi:10.1108/978-1-78754-675-220181013

through a global lens. These studies do not shed light on: the socio-economic, or political context that shape the values, primary moral virtues and secondary intellectual virtues and acts of particular legislation; the fair funding formulas that underpin the allocation of funds to the construction of infrastructure; the Education Governance Systems structures and agencies; and the organisation of processes and practices of the education system within the international community. Intellectual and cultural colonisation that may lack what Adler calls moral and ethical frameworks may accelerate the commodification of education. Chapter 3 critically discussed how we implemented the same research design in each case taking a humanistic approach and identified that the research adopts a shared world view and seeks to recognise scientific, intellectual knowledge, and metaphysical moral and empirical knowledge. Chapters 4 through 9 presented the English, Northern Irish, Arab-Israeli, Trinidad and Tobago and the United States cases, and each case identified a clash of values between the professional educational credentialed senior-level leaders with track records for outstanding school improvement, and those in Educational Governance Systems with: no professional credentials; no track record of school improvement; a tendency to promote competition rather than cooperation; a desire for internal succession planning, rather than succession planning to achieve national education goals. The clash of cultures put senior-level leaders into a mode of protectionism with a focus on keeping their post and 'watching their backs', rather than building capacity for sustainable instruction within the Education Governance Systems they lead manage and administrate to optimise students' learning, students' outcomes and social mobility.

These senior-level leaders with Professional Credentials, and outstanding track records of school improvement need Education Governance Systems to empower them to do their job and create realistic opportunities to develop networks of professional experts in partnership with the academy to support them navigate any clash of world views. Funding is required for professional learning to ensure 'old opinion is handed down among them by ancient tradition' that is rationalised with logic, compared and contrasted with empirical evidence, and synthesised with innovations guided by a moral compass within an ethical infrastructure. These senior-level leaders need to be empowered to empower their staff as autonomous professionals to empower the parents and the students to gain the thinking tools they need to be lifelong learners with the capability to be self-legislating. This requires a culture change that prioritises the moral virtues of learning how to learn as moral citizens in becoming, above the secondary intellectual virtues demonstrated through success in high stakes tests.

Knowledge to action reveals young people need Education Governance Systems that EYSIER and underpin success in student outcomes for social mobility. Success in both these spheres will enable them to break their chains that have kept them dependent on the guidance of others who may seek to exploit them (De Gruy, 2008).

Further research is recommended to implement the knowledge to action impact strategies that emerge from all five cases.

Keywords: Democracy; equity; achievement gap; reparation; peace

The aim of this book was to set an agenda and address a gap in the literature regarding how Education Governance Systems empower or disempower key agents of change within a global phenomenon of a Black-White achievement gap (Apple, 2013; Payne, 2008; Wagner, 2010). The agenda focuses on delivering increased grade scores, and providing culturally relevant curriculums to bridge marginalised communities (and dominant communities within an education system (Epstein, 2015). Such empowerment is hallmarked by social justice, prudence and courage (Adler, 1941; Dewey, 2016) that may be found in all faiths and none and philosophical traditions as discussed in Chapter 3 of this book. We presented an International Comparative Analysis of turbulence in five nation states' Education Governance Systems and how senior educational leaders who represent marginalised groups Empower Young Societal Innovators for Equity, and Renewal (EYSIER) to improve student outcomes for social mobility that lifts people out of poverty and gives them the opportunity to escape struggling for survival and to work together for peace in our time (Taysum, 2012, 2013, 2014; Taysum et al., 2015, 2016, 2017).

The focus of the book was on the narrative biographies of senior-level leaders from marginalised groups. In England, the focus was Black, Asian, Marginalised Ethnicity (BAME) chief executive officers (CEO) of Multi-academy Trusts (MATs). In Northern Ireland, the principals were marginalised by sectarianism, and in Arab Israel, the superintendents/Administrators were marginalised by sectarianism. In Trinidad and Tobago, the focus was on those who had to implement curriculum reforms who had been marginalised from the curriculum planning and creation process. The marginalisation was further complicated by marginalisation of different groups within Trinidad and Tobago based on claims of power and extra entitlement for indigenous people, former colonisers or those from a cultural history of being slaves and/or indentured labourers (Taysum & Murrel-Abery, 2017). In the US, the focus was on Black African American Women Superintendents who were marginalised based on at least three intersectionalities of discrimination (Crenshaw, 1989) that included their race, their gender and a recent history of being part of an apartheid system until the 14th Amendment in 1968.

We decided to read the enablers and challenges these senior-level leaders experience through Gross' (2014) Turbulence Theory. Turbulence Theory provides a typology that allows us to categorise the level and the impact of the challenges these senior-level leaders, and key agents of change need to navigate as they mediate between the Education Governance Systems. Gross (2014, p. 248) theory of turbulence states that 'turbulence can be described as "light" with little or no movement of the craft; "Moderate" – with Very noticeable waves; "Severe" with strong gusts that threaten control of the aircraft; "Extreme" with forces so great that control is lost and structure damage to the craft occurs'. Reading the findings through the theory of turbulence reveals the state of the Education Governance Systems and their impact on empowering cosmopolitan citizens (Waghid & Smeyers, 2014) to participate fully and freely in societal interactions and cooperations between diverse groups. Thus, this research, and its dissemination was imperative because we cannot move forward with the EYSIER Education Model until:

- we have described and understood the turbulence in Education Governance Systems in different nation states as experienced by Professional Credentialed Educational senior-level leaders;
- we have described and understood how the turbulence empowers or disem-powers the Professional Credentialed Educational senior-level leaders to work for school improvement, equity and renewal, and social mobility that lifts young people out of poverty and offers the chance for them to work together for peace;
- we have considered what support these Professional Credentialed Educational senior-level leaders need to implement educational leadership, learning and change to EYSIER, underpin social mobility and access to middle-class bene-fits, and provide the chance to work together for peace in our time.

Our findings reveal in Chapter 1, that over time, with epochs sometimes span-ning thousands of years, the five different nation states that feature in this book have played different roles within the Karpman's Triangle (1968). Karpman's Triangle has three roles; oppressor, victim and rescuer. Through a process of coloni-sation or being colonised, or intervening in the colonisation of others, these nation states have experienced one or more of the roles. These social, economic and political histories still act as external influences on education today, but citizens are not given the thinking tools to engage with how these invisible characters, and invisible infrastructures from past epochs shape human values, habits and codes of behaviour nowadays that are manifested in marginalisation of particular groups.

The evidence in Chapter 1 reveals that those seeking to oppress others through colonisation do so from a position of being a victim of previous coloni-sation. DeGruy (2005) identifies that human beings who are dominated through slavery, or colonisation are not able to protect their families from harm and pos-sible annihilation because they are dominated by the colonisers who do not rec-ognise them (Payne, 2008). Those that have been colonised may go on to seek to protect their group's interests from the threat of annihilation. If they are unable to do this, De Gruy suggests they may oppress other groups to get a sense of power after being disempowered by the coloniser. A strategy to effect colonisa-tion is to implement a 'divide and conquer strategy' where different groups prevent each other from addressing the root cause of their marginalisation; challenging the coloniser. Rather the strategy of 'divide and conquer' builds inequity within a system between different groups so that they compete with each other for extra entitlement, and prevent their own growth into mature citizens whilst the coloniser need do very little except assure the inequity within the system continues, to continue their extra entitlement is never questioned (Taysum & Murrel-Abery, 2017). At this stage of the Earth's evolution, our research reveals that an outcome of colonisation is marginalisation of different groups where marginalisation is characterised by:

- a lack of cultural, economic and political inclusion and recognition (Marshall & Gerstl-Pepin, 2005; Fraser, 2000; Adler, 1941; Carter, 2008) leading to low socio-economic status (Boseley, 2017);
- unequal interactions and cooperation between members of a marginalised group and state institutions (Dewey, 2016) as a barrier to respect and social justice (Barnett, 2000);
- no confidence in building trust between different groups in the search for truth (Barnett, 2000; Möllering, 2001; Wagner, 2010);
- no dialogue to co-create cross-cultural critique of alternative world views with the courage to arrive at a shared multicultural world view (Adler, 1941; Darling-Hammond & Rothman, 2011; Gerstl-Pepin & Aiken, 2012; Ishii, Klopf, & Cooke, 2007);
- the perpetuation of fear that distracts citizens from applying logical, evidence-informed, moral and ethical knowledge prudently to their own lives on a rainy afternoon in November (Bridges, 2016), and applying philosophical inquiry with confidence to synthesise traditional knowledge, and new knowledge to enable the re-imagining of new futures where young people gain good student outcomes, social mobility, and are mobilisers of stable and sustainable social change for equity, renewal and can work together for peace in our time (Dewey, 2016).

The review of literature that focused on turbulence in Education Governance Systems identified the global distribution of knowledge concerning education from cash-rich countries, has had a tremendous impact on what is taught and tested in schools. Nation states that are not cash rich are marginalised in a global politics (Moloi, Gravett, & Petersen, 2009). Comparative studies focusing on statistics, for example, the Programme of International Students Assessment (Organisation for Economic & Cooperation & Development, 2017) and Trends in International Mathematical and Science Study (TIMSS) (Institute of Educational Assessors, 2017), and Progress in International Reading Literacy Study (PIRLS) (Institute of Educational Assessors, 2017) examine the output of national education systems through a global lens. However, these studies do not shed light on the socio-economic, or political context that shape: the values, primary moral virtues, and secondary intellectual virtues and acts of particular legislation; the fair funding formulas that underpin the allocation of funds to the construction of infrastructure; the Education Governance Systems structures and agencies; the organisation of processes and practices of the education system within the international community (Taysum & Iqbal, 2012). Intellectual and cultural colonisation that may lack what Adler (1941) calls moral and ethical frameworks may accelerate the commodification of education (Darling-Hammond & Lieberman, 2012; Waite, Rodríguez, & Wadende, 2015). Given the research basis described previously, it would seem reasonable for principals coping with the rapidly changing socio-economic and technological dynamics of the present era to heed the call to enhance their school's capacities to support student growth and empower their staff to EYSIER, to underpin high student outcomes, social mobility and working for peace. However, it cannot be assumed that all staff are willing or able to assume greater leadership roles (Woods & Roberts, 2018). Nor, we suggest, should it be assumed that all principals are willing to work with the senior-level leaders to develop primary moral virtues and secondary intellectual virtues in their curriculums without assurances that policy will support such a culture change. Rather, we concur with Leithwood, Day, Sammons, Harris, and Hopkins (2008) who advocate for a thoughtful and purposeful approach to developing leadership for school improvement. Perhaps it is time to trust the professional credentialed educational senior-level leaders with outstanding track records of school improvement to organise education and, as Leithwood et al. (2008) suggest trust them to make: 'intentional intervention on the part of those in formal leadership roles' (p. 279).

We implemented the same research design in each case taking a humanistic approach as set out in Chapter 3. We have chosen to conduct this International Comparative Education study to reveal a cross-disciplinary approach drawing on history, philosophy, psychology and sociology to help us understand the marginalisation of human beings over time. The International Comparative Education presents knowledge to action that mobilises knowledge and its critique (Paulston, 2000) from which impact strategies emerge to address turbulence, empowerment and marginalisation in international Education Governance Systems.

Our position in this research is that we believe we need to hold a mirror up to ourselves and our thoughts and actions, as we interpret and present to you, the reader, the findings from holding up a mirror to the thoughts and actions of elements of society. We then wish to engage in dialogues about power to explore the institutional legacy of why different dispositions, including the dispositions of the marginalised, exist.

Our comparative education of international perspectives focused on seeking a theory of governance for empowerment that uses a dialogic approach to the research that is conducted in partnership between those within the school communities and the academy. Evans and Robinson-Pant (2010) call for such innovative approaches to comparative education and international perspectives. We also generate new knowledge focusing on issues of power within comparative education and are mindful of how adults and young people's agency is shaped by structures that position them (Apple, 2013). We seek to understand culture and identity and reveal through comparative education analysis, the extent to which particular group's interests are marginalised and why (Arnova, Torres, & Franz, 2013). We therefore draw on Crossley (1999) and focus on the position of culture and policy context; both policy as text and policy as discourse and impact (Ball, 2004) in our approach to this comparative educational study. Although generalisation of the findings is limited due to our qualitative methodology, it is possible to point to three areas for Knowledge to Action in each case, and to find similarities between cases regarding how to empower Professional Credentialed, Educational senior-level leaders to empower marginalised groups to achieve educational change through a bottom-up process (Taysum, 2017a; Taysum, Forthcoming). The findings also suggest the need for broader and more representative future research on these issues.

The English case identified a clash of values between the professional educational credentialed senior-level leaders with track records for outstanding school improvement, and those in Educational Governance Systems with: no professional credentials; no track record of school improvement; a tendency to promote competition rather than cooperation; a desire for internal succession planning, rather than succession planning to achieve national education goals.

Three key areas for knowledge to action emerged: First, BAME CEOs with professional education credentials, and with Department for Education (2017) values, with a track record for improving schools to good and outstanding, need to be supported by legislation. The legislation needs to allow BAME CEOs to grow their groups of schools within their MATs slowly, moving one failing school to 'Good' or 'Outstanding' at a time. Arguably, no CEOs of any sized MAT should take on a new failing school to improve it, until all their current schools are 'Good' or 'Outstanding'. 'Good' and 'Outstanding' schools need to build high-quality relationships within communities (DfE, 2017) to bridge cultural differences within communities to EYSIER, improved student outcomes leading to social mobility that lifts individuals out of poverty and provides opportunities for working together for peace (Taysum, 2012, 2013, 2014; Taysum et al., 2015, 2016, 2017).

Second, An 'A' political educational professional body needs to be developed and connected to professional learning networks connected between the Academy and schools. This professional body overseas the development of networks, provides mentoring, and identifies and develops talent in long-term succession planning. The succession planning needs to transcend the local competitive needs of a school, and needs to focus on the good of all schools in England and the UK.

Third, all BAME CEOs of MATs need to be mentored by enlightened professionals with professional educational credentials and outstanding track records of school improvement, within an educational professional body. These enlightened professionals need to organise education as gatekeepers of wisdom, traditional knowledge, and innovation through educational professional constructive networks underpinned by a moral compass that assures an ethical framework (ethos), empirical evidence (pathos), and logical arguments (logos) (Taysum, 2017a, 2017b, Forthcoming). The mentoring needs to support decision making that connects individuals to each other and their communities to build peace, and optimise learning, social mobility, access to middle-class benefits and support transitions from immaturity to maturity (Dewey, 2016; Taysum, Forthcoming). Mentors need to be fully employed in the system with educational professional credentials and DfE (2017) values of educational leaders, rather than marginalised through temporary, part-time contracts. Mentors and wise enlightened professional, credentialed educational senior-level leaders with outstanding track records of school improvement should not be squeezed out of full-time permanent employment with a pension by a large MAT through a forced take over, and then re-employed by the large MAT as a temporary consultant with no long-term formal contractual connection to the school and MAT.

The Northern Ireland Case identified a clash of values between senior educational leaders with professional credentials and a proven track record for school improvement, and governors who could potentially confuse their strategic responsibilities with the management responsibilities of the head teacher and senior leaders (Allen & Mintrom, 2010). The Northern Ireland case also identified three areas for Knowledge for Action. First, strong relationships, resilience and collaboration were viewed as ways out of turbulence. However, the issue of collaboration, which is at the heart of shared education, is a complex one. As one of the senior-level leader interviewees explicitly acknowledged, a school may well be in competition with other neighbouring small schools for pupil enrolment and to attract pupils like a magnet, yet through shared education are expected to work together. In addition to collaboration through shared education, other networks which proved fruitful for participants included a school leader/principal network within their school sector and relationships developed through the area learning community.

Second, the role and support of mentors and advocates equips professional educational credentialed senior-level leaders with outstanding track records of school improvement, with the tools they need to deal with turbulence. The findings agreed with Gross (2014) who also emphasised the value of strong relationships with or between mentors. Relationships varied in terms of the formality of the relationship and the senior-level leaders (principals in the Northern Irish Education Governance System) would appear to value both formal and informal mentor relationships as part of their wider support network.

Third, evidence revealed identifying and recruiting senior-level leaders with passion in their work who can clearly articulate clarity in terms of their vision for building relationships with the community were best able to implement culture change and empower their young people to be drivers for social change. The culture change was further supported by developing networks of senior-level leaders across Northern Ireland facilitated by Higher Education Institutions, which extended the support network.

The Arab education in Israel Case also identified clashes of cultures (Arar, 2015; Arar & Massry-Herzallah, 2016). The role of the supervisor is highly complex especially as already noted, the supervisor is required to cope with contradicting demands of the different stakeholders in education, to do 'more' and 'better' (Maxfield, Shapiro, Gupta, & Hass, 2010). The complex expectations from supervisors grow in parallel to their own desire to react and function excellently in complex and often stormy, turbulent environments (Gross, 2014;

Lewis, Rice, & Rice, 2011). As part of the supervisors' duties, they need to understand and react appropriately to the demands from the field; they are responsible for the identification and understanding of the challenges and future opportunities that stem from the different government-imposed reforms and they are also the leaders responsible for constant development of learning streams and to foster learning and leadership in others. Three areas for Knowledge to Action emerged from the case. First, the need to reinforce Arab students' unique cultural identity through legislation whist moving from competing ideals, and values in the Education Governance System to common values that can enhance mutual understanding and multicultural education.

Second, bridging cross-cultural shared views can be achieved by building open and candid interaction and cooperation between the different stakeholders in the Arab education system to engender social cohesion through constructive dialogue and power-sharing instead of controlling hierarchical governmental practices.

Third, senior-level leaders need to have the tool box to support parental full and free participation in their child's learning and in Educational Governance Systems to realise educational change through a bottom-up process (Epstein, 2015).

The Trinidad and Tobago case identifies a clash in values and interests in the Education Governance Systems' structures. Curriculum change can be beneficial, but its benefits are not a given since they depend on: the purposes of the curriculum related to sharing knowledge and access to equitable opportunity for middle-class benefits, and social mobility; the availability of resources; the competence and interactions of different agencies and their change agents/personnel; the commitment of persons to the curriculum development process and consultation where all have an opportunity to talk back to power; the external forces including consultants who are attached to foreign finance packages. The clashes can be overcome, but it does mean recognising the educational professional in the learning and teaching process, and empowering them to use their professional knowledge, skills and experience, rather than de-professionalising them by excluding them from the curriculum planning process that is more likely to result in delivering the curriculum rather than being part of the planning of the curriculum process that will be carefully interpreting and shared with students through meaningful and worthwhile, culturally relevant learning experiences for the students in the classroom. Three areas for Knowledge to Action emerged.

First, when implementing curriculum change, it is important to have legislation that decrees the participation of those implementing the change at the conceptual stage, and the writing stage and that implementation should be piloted for proof of concept before national implementation.

Second, adequate resources need to be allocated to the education project to assure networks across agencies are operationalised to promote collaboration and knowledge exchange. Opportunities for succession planning during the reforms are part of the agenda.

Third, the planned success of reforms for a culture change recognises the importance of participation of parents of children and a bottom-up approach that includes students, teachers, principals and all senior-level leaders and policy makers.

The US case identified there can be clashes of values between Black African American Women Superintendents and their School Boards. Ehren, Honingh, Hooge and O'Hara (2016) suggest that School Boards do not focus on the governance of instruction, the curriculum and learning and teaching, which they leave to the Superintendents to work through with principals and teachers. However, if the Black African American Women superintendents are distracted by having to engage with power plays with turbulent boards, they do not have time to mobilise their manifesto of, and outstanding track records for school improvement, which they were appointed to do. Ehren et al. (2016, p. 448) suggest: 'Additional improvements in the effectiveness of these school boards could be gained if school inspections motivate these school boards to focus on the governance of teaching and instruction in their schools'. Sheard and Avis (2011) and Bush and Coleman (2001) make the point that pedagogic knowledge, or the art and science of learning and teaching (Garrison, 2009) and engaging with the knowledge, skills, experience and expertise of social systems in the locale of the district schools, may become empowering at a strategic level. Phelan (2009) argues teachers who are free from fixed rules and technical, standardised teaching to the test may engage with the unpredictability, and potential chaos in the classroom as diverse personalities from different cultural heritages to facilitate Dewey's synthesised framework; 'Moral training for Democracy in Education' (Taysum, 2017a, 2017b, Forthcoming). The Framework supports the transition of the immature child to the mature adult with primary moral virtues and secondary intellectual virtues for democracy in education (Adler, 1941; Dewey, 2016). A mature adult has the thinking tools that empowers them to learn how to learn, on a journey of choices regarding what living a good life means to them as enlightened citizens who critique what it means to be enlightened (Lie, 2011). Enlightened, mature citizens in becoming have the thinking tools to innovate their communities for equity, and renewal, gaining improved student outcomes, and social mobility that lifts young people out of poverty. Young people who are not struggling for survival in conditions of poverty, and who enjoy full-time permanent contacts in the labour market that allows them to plan for the future, have a family and have a pension are well positioned to have more time to think. As they think about the future, and the opportunities for their own children, they may be concerned about sustainable ways of living a good life for them and for their children with other groups in their community, nationally and globally. Such critical and reflective thinking may motivate them to work together and lobby their states people to represent their interests by working for diplomatic solutions, in trustworthy ways, for peace in our time (Dewey, 2016; Murray, 2018).

Evidence reveals professional credentialed educational senior-level leaders with outstanding track records of school improvement want to be empowered to mobilise collaborations and partnerships to connect their staff, with the students, the parents and the community (Epstein, 2015). Connecting different groups may empower community members to build meaningful and worthwhile relationships and shared world views whilst recognising each other's diverse identities (Banks, 2017). Together, these different groups with different interests may explore what leading a good life is together and make informed choices about their values and behaviours so they can live a good life (Adler, 1941). Black African American Women Superintendents cannot empower young societal innovators to work for equity and renewal, and improved student outcomes of this nature with intergenerational community members, if they are in a mode of 'protectionism' with a focus on keeping their post and 'watching their backs', rather than building capacity for sustainable instruction within the Education Governance Systems they lead and manage, and administrate.

Three areas for Knowledge to Action emerged. First, all African American Women in teacher training, and throughout their careers as professional credentialed teachers, and leaders in education need to be aware of school policy, how to access policy and legislation, how to stay up to date with policy and how to challenge policy (James & McCormick, 2009). The policy provides them with the human rights that some who may benefit from White privilege might forget about in their day to day work in Education Governance Systems. The policy has the back of African American Women fighting institutionalised racism (Collins Ayanlaja & Taysum, 2016).

Second, African American Women educational professionals need role models, and mentors who are Superintendents, and who create proactive and mobilising networks across the state and the nation to advocate for and give support to the teachers' and leaders' professional learning to be the best leaders and Superintendents they can be and that their communities, state and nation deserve.

Third, the African American Women educational professionals who have been self-selecting, or identified as potential future Superintendents by current Superintendents and School Boards, need to be part of succession planning that transcends the short elected lives of District School Boards. Newly incumbent African American Women Superintendents need to promote learning how to learn (Swaffield & MacBeath, 2009) so that their students will learn how to learn, be culturally sensitive, ask good questions and solve problem as Young Societal Innovators for Equity and Renewal (Taysum, 2012, 2013, 2014; Taysum et al., 2015, 2016, 2017). Succession planning may be facilitated by a network of African American Women Superintendents who put this knowledge into action as impact strategies. The implementation of the strategies needs to be documented, and, if successful, disseminated to build capacity for EYSIER (Taysum, 2012, 2013, 2014; Taysum et al., 2015, 2016, 2017).

A comparative analysis revealed that all cases found the Education Governance Systems had a clash of values. Critical, reflective thinking and reasoning without an empirical, or scientific base shape a metaphysical world view (Helve, 1991). The metaphysical world view is based on faith and if it were verifiable, then faith would be undermined, but those taking a leap of faith might find their own verifiable truth, found through right. Adler (1941) suggests primary virtues, or cardinal virtues are prudence, fortitude/courage and social justice. These primary virtues perfect a human being's nature, not to a limited good, but to all good things that will contribute to making them a good person who lives a happy life because they can order their goods, and the production of the goods. Secondary virtues are intellectual virtues and grant an aptitude for good work that, in the case of education, may be verified through student exam outcomes. These exam outcomes might be a result of learning for the test, and may not be evidence of being able to apply the knowledge that has been tested in the real world. Certainly, these exam outcomes are not evidence of good acts that may become good habits leading to a good life.

Together, the primary virtues and secondary virtues enable human beings and humanity to develop the right order of goods and their production as a key to leading a good life in becoming and can stabilise a human being. Stable human beings who are virtuous have the dispositions to encounter un-expected situations and can rely on themselves, as autonomous mature adults, to behave with virtue within those situations. Pring (2000) suggests that the virtues of a teacher are essential if the noble teaching profession is to optimise students learning for a good life. Such responses are logical, empirically informed, moral and ethical (Taysum, 2017a, 2017b, Forthcoming), and ensure that people together do not harm each other, or themselves, and they can live lives with the potential for a happy ending (Adler, 1941). Here, a happy ending is that some-one can look back on their life and be happy with their values, and acts. A former US Superintendent and current University Professor articulated acts that may be regretted are those that have a 'shoot from the hip' response to un-expected situations (Taysum, 2012).

Building a life of character with primary virtues and secondary virtues requires critical, reflective thinking which connects with Taysum's (2012) Learning to Critical Analyse and Reflect for Emancipation (Learning to CARE) Framework and Stenhouse (1975) reflective thinking and includes knowledge that may not be a part of a recognised set of scientific rules and verifiable theo-ries. There are no manuals for everyday life experiences a human being will encounter over a lifetime, but there are primary principles, primary virtues and secondary virtues, habits, and logical, empirical, moral and ethical responses that can be put to good use through asking good questions and problem-solving collaboratively. Such collaborative problem-solving may take place in the class-room guided by an expert teacher, guided by expert school leadership, guided by expert educational professional credentialed senior-level leaders with outstand-ing records of school improvement, empowered by Education Governance Systems, authorised by inclusive policy hallmarked by ethos, pathos and logos (Taysum, 2017a, 2017b, Forthcoming).

Adler (1941) identifies acquiring virtue is challenging because logical engagement with virtues lacks practical empirical application, and practical empirical application of virtue lacks engagement with primary and secondary virtues which leads to a loop, and a mystery of how anyone can become virtuous. In other words, how does a human being know an act is good or evil if they have no experience of the act to theorise, and they have no theory of the act to put into practice?

So we return to Plato who suggests there is: 'no old opinion handed down among you by ancient tradition', and Adler's (1941) solution lies therein. Adler suggests humans need a mentor, or mentors of virtue which connects with our findings in all five cases. Virtuous mentors, who are not perfect because no human being is perfect, have gained practical empirical knowledge of virtue over a lifetime, drawing from the best that has been thought and said throughout the ages, ideally in a professional body. A professional body provides a network of people with logical, evidence-informed, moral and ethical threshold levels for novice professional, senior professional, expert professional and mentor/gatekeeper professional (Eraut, 2002). These mentors/gatekeeper professionals of primary and secondary virtues (Adler, 1941) have theorised practice and practiced theories using logos, pathos and ethos (Taysum, 2017a, 2017b, Forthcoming). They have then compared and contrasted their own values and acts with those of what Plato calls 'old opinions' from their mentors from previous generations. Moreover, these 'old opinions' may be found in the codes of human behaviour held in the holy books of all faiths, books of no faith, and the philosophical books of different traditional classical texts such as the Greek myths and Asian philosophies, the United National Declaration of Human Rights (1948), anthropologies that celebrate cultural heritages from different groups of people including marginalised groups of people who exist in the world today, or have existed in the world in the past.

The comparative analyses identify the transformation from modernity to post-modernity necessitates re-examination of the substance of education. The re-examination needs to focus on the moral and ethical logic, and empirical evidence that informs the goals, teaching methods, learning programs, evaluation methods and organisational structures of education, and of those who organise education. Consequentially ethical and political considerations also need revision (Arnova et al., 2013; Waite et al., 2015).

Perhaps professional, credentialised educational senior-level leaders, and those in professional public Education Governance Systems and Public Governance Systems, legislators, civil servants, and states people need to be role models to young people, and their parents, by navigating clashes in cultures. Listening to each other and understanding different life narratives connected to the divine, or moves from backstabbing, to overcoming conflict with courage (Conroy et al., 2013). Without role models from leaders regarding how to share power and build relationships of trust, and gain confidence in these relationships, then as McGuinness et al. say in their chapter in this book, how can we hope the next generation of young people will do better than our generation in working for equity, renewal and peace? This is reaffirmed by Ishii et al. (2007, p. 34):

> All world views require some degree of adjustment if the species (of human beings) is to survive. Tracing the beliefs and assumptions underlying them is the first step in making social change possible.

Thus if young people are to become Young Societal Innovators for Equity and Renewal (Horizon, 2020, 2015; (Taysum, 2012, 2013, 2014; Taysum et al., 2015, 2016, 2017)) first they will need to trace the underpinning ideologies, principles, virtues, values, normative assumptions and behaviours of their world views together (Ishii et al., 2007). Our findings in this research agree with Rubin and Paplau (1975) that Education Governance Systems play significant roles in the development of human beings' world views and their opportunity to live with the Other peacefully. The senior-level leaders with Professional Credentials who were generous enough to give their time to talk to us, and to have worked with such grit and determination to educate our future generations, require legislation to let them lead their educational institutions including the infrastructure, the budgets, the interface with the educational institutions, the bridging between the Universities/Academy and the schools, and the mentoring and networks to build capacity for cultural change.

These senior-level leaders with Professional Credentials need Education Governance Systems to empower them to do their job, and to overcome any clash of world views so that 'old opinion is handed down among them by ancient tradition' that is rationalised with logic, compared and contrasted with empirical evidence that is synthesised with innovations guided by a moral compass within an ethical infrastructure. These senior-level leaders need to be empowered to empower their staff as autonomous professionals to empower the parents and the students to gain the thinking tools they need to be self-legislating (Taysum, Forthcoming). In an education system that provides young people's learning experiences that teaches to the text, or teaches to the test, the young people do not get to guide their own articulation of personal problems in the real world, such as marginalisation (Dewey, 2016). Young people need education governance systems that EYSIER, or they will not gain the thinking tools they need to be self-legislating, and they will continue to be dependent on the guidance of others who may seek to exploit them (De Gruy, 2008).

Gross (2014, p. 248) theory of turbulence states that: 'turbulence can be described as 'light' with little or no movement of the craft. 'Moderate with Very noticeable waves. 'Severe' with strong gusts that threaten control of the aircraft. 'Extreme' with forces so great that control is lost and structure damage to the craft occurs'. The findings reveal that the turbulence is severe to extreme where clashes exist between professional educational senior-level leaders, and Education Governance Systems, and/or a clash in values between a dominant group and a marginalised group based on intersectionalities of discrimination that can be based on professional values, race, gender, religion, culture, language and socio-economic status, and/or a clash in values between those who seek to empower individuals with the thinking tools they need to become mature, self-legislating individuals and those whose actions cause individuals to be dependent on them for guidance without understanding this is the pragmatic consequence, or because they want to exploit them.

Knowledge to Action

First in all five cases, senior-level educational leaders need legislation that empowers them to EYSIER. The innovative EYSIER offers a Charter Mark and has been developed over five years and represents many different cultural heritages of people moving to Europe and throughout the world with histories of being colonised and colonising over the past 5000–10,000 years.

The five first principles of the EYSIER Model are as follows:

(1) inclusion to realise social justice and recognition for all (Adler, 1941; Fraser, 2000; Marshall & Gerstl-Pepin, 2005);
(2) respect to realise social justice (Barnett, 2000; Carter, 2005; Taysum & Gunter, 2008),
(3) trust in the search for truth (Barnett, 2000; Möllering, 2001; Pring, 2000; Wagner, 2010);
(4) courage to engage in prudent dialogue to co-create constructive cross-cultural critique of alternative world views to arrive at a shared multicultural world view (Adler, 1941; Darling-Hammond & Rothman, 2011; Gerstl-Pepin & Aiken, 2012; Ishii et al., 2007);
(5) the generation of new knowledge that prudently synthesises traditional and new knowledge to enable the re-imagining of new futures where young people are mobilisers of stable and sustainable social change for equity and renewal (Harrison, Taysum, McNamara, & O'Hara, 2016; Taysum, 2012).

Second, senior-level leaders need mentors and networks to support their work to EYSIER in partnership with parents, principals, staff and students.

Third, senior-level leaders need support to develop the tools required for the philosophical inquiry to ask good questions about any fear any members of the community have of the system and work together to problem solve to EYSIER for Peace in our time.

We now seek proof of concept and are presenting our strategies of knowledge to Action through the EYSIER Model and seeking feedback on their impact to networks of senior-level leaders in the following forums:

- British Educational Leadership, Management and Administration Society Doctoral Research Interest Group (BELMAS DRIG) for BELMAS members at South Side Chicago Public Schools (See Appendices 5 and 6) drawing on Dr Carole Collins-Ayanlaja's networks;
- The American Educational Research Association, 2018, New York drawing on the networks of the John Dewey Society, BELMAS, UCEA, CESJ, and Leadership networks;
- European Conference for Educational Research, 2018, Italy;
- BELMAS Annual Conference 2018, Windsor;
- British Educational Research Association, 2018, Newcastle.

Further research is recommended to build capacity for EYSIER (Taysum, 2012, 2013, 2014; Taysum et al., 2015, 2016, 2017) within networks of Senior-level leaders, Education Governance Systems, Academics and all those interested in building capacity for school improvement for equity, renewal and social mobilisation for all.

References

Adler, M. (1941). *A dialectic of morals: Towards the foundations of political philosophy.* Notre Dame: University of Notre Dame.

Allen, A., & Mintrom, M. (2010). Responsibility and school governance. *Educational Policy, 24*(3), 439–464.

Apple. (2013). *Can education change society.* London: Routledge.

Arar, K. (2015). 'A Theory of Young People's Participation in Systems and Learning from International Boundary Crossing Action-Resarch Project A case of Arab Education in Isreal. *Part of a two part large symposium European Conference for Educational Research.* Budapest, Hungary, September.

Arar, K., & Masry, A. (2016). Motivation to Teach: the case of Arab teachers in Israel. *Education Studies, 42*(1), 19–35.

Arnova, R. F., Torres, C. A., & Franz, S. (2013). *Comparative education: The dialectic of global and local.* Lanham: Rowan & Littlefield.

Ball, S. (2004). *Education policy and social class: The selected works of Stephen J. Ball.* London: Routledge.

Banks, J. A. (2017). *Citizenship education and global migration: Implications for theory, research and teaching.* American Educational Research Association.

Barnett, R. (2000). *Higher education: A critical business.* Buckingham: The Society for Research into Higher Education & Open University Press.

Boseley, S. (2017). Poverty in the UK jeopardising children's health, warns landmark report. *The Guardian.* Retrieved from https://www.theguardian.com/society/2017/jan/25/poverty-in-the-uk-jeopardising-childrens-health-warns-landmark-report. Accessed 23 April 2017.

Bridges, D. (2016). *Philosophy in educational research: Epistemology, ethics, politics and quality.* E-book: Springer.

Bush, T., & Coleman, M. (2001). *Leadership and strategic management.* London: Sage.

Carter, P. L. (2005). *Keepin' it real: School success beyond Black and White.* New York, NY: Oxford University Press.

Carter, P. L. (2008). Teaching students fluency in multiple cultural codes. In M. Pollock (Ed.), *Everyday Antiracism.* New York, NY: The New Press.

Collins Ayanlaja and Taysum. (2016). Institutionalised Racism in World Education Research Association Annual Conference, Washington, DC, April.

Conroy, J., Lundie, D., Davis, R., Baumfield, V., Barnes, P., Gallagher, T., Lowden, K., Bourque, N., & Wenell, K. (2013). *Does religion work?* London: Bloomsbury.

Crenshaw, K. (1989). Demarginalizing the intersection of race and sex: A Black Feminist critique of antidiscrimination doctrine, feminist theory, and antiracist politics. *University of Chicago Legal Forum, 1989,* 139–167.

Crossley, M. (1999). Reconceptualising comparative and international education. *Compare a Journal of Comparative and International Education, 29*(3), 249–267.

Darling-Hammond, L., & Lieberman, A. (Eds.) (2012). *Teacher education around the world:Changing policies and practices (teacher quality and school development)*. London & New York, NY: Routledge.

Darling-Hammond, L., & Rothman, R. (2011). (Eds.), *Teacher and leader effectiveness in high-per forming education systems.* Washington, DC: Alliance for Excellent Education and Stanford, CA: Stanford Center for Opportunity Policy in Education.

DeGruy, J. (2005). *Post traumatic slave syndrome: America's legacy of enduring injury and healing.* Portland: Joy DeGruy Publications.

De Gruy, J. (2008). *Post traumatic slave syndrome.* Portland: Joy De Gruy Publications Inc.

Department for Education. (2017). National professional qualifications (NPQ) content and assessment framework. Retrieved from https://www.gov.uk/government/uploads/system/uploads/attachment_data/file/653046/NPQ_Content_and_Assessment_Framework.pdf. Accessed 25 February 2018.

Dewey, J. (2016). *Democracy and education.* New York, NY: Macmillan.

Ehren, M., Honingh, M., Hooge, E., & O'Hara, J. (2016). Changing school board governance in primary education through school inspections. *Educational Management, Administration and Leadership, 44*(2), 205–223.

Epstein, J. (2015). *School, family, and community partnerships, student economy edition: Preparing educators and improving schools.* London: Westview Press.

Eraut, M. (2002). *Developing professional knowledge and competence.* London: Routledge.

Evans, K., & Robinson-Pant, A. (2010). Compare: Exploring a 40-year journey through comparative education and international development. *Compare: A Journal of Comparative and International Education, 40*(6), 693–710.

Fraser, N. (2000). *Justice interruptus: Rethinking key concepts of a post-socialist age.* London: Routledge.

Garrison, J. (2009). The art and science of education. *Journal of Curriculum Studies, 41*(1), 17–20.

Gerstl-Pepin, C., & Aiken, J. (2012). *Social justice leadership for a global world.* Charlotte, NC: Information Age Publishing.

Gross, S. J. (2014). Using turbulence theory to guide actions. In C. M. Branson & S. J. Gross (Eds.), *Handbook on Ethical Educational Leadership* (pp. 246–262). New York, NY: Routledge.

Harrison, K., Taysum, A., McNamara, G., & O'Hara, J. (2016). The degree to which students and teachers are involved in second-level school processes and participation in decision making: An Irish case study in Irish Studies in education. *Irish Educational Studies, 35*(2), 155–173.

Helve, H. (1991). The formation of religious attitudes and worldviews: A longitudinal study of young Finns. *Social Compass, 38*, 373–392.

Horizon 2020. (2015). CO-CREATION-01–2017: Education and skills: Empowering Europe's young innovators. Retrieved from https://ec.europa.eu/research/participants/portal/desktop/en/opportunities/h2020/topics/co-creation-01–2017.html. Accessed on 30 May 2017.

Institute of Educational Assessors. (2017). *Progress in international reading literacy study.* Retrieved from http://www.iea.nl/pirls. Accessed on 18 March 2018.

Ishii, S., Klopf, D., & Cooke, P. (2007). Worldview in intercultural communication: A religio-cosmological approach. In L. Samovar, R. Porter, & E. McDaniel (Eds.), *Intercultural Communication a Reader*. Boston, MA: Wadsworth Cengage Learning.

James, M., & McCormick, R. (2009). Teachers learning how to learn. *Teaching and Teacher Education*, *25*(7), 973–982.

Karpman, S. (1968). Fairy tales and script drama analysis. *Transactional Analysis Bulletin*, *7*(26), 39–43.

Leithwood, K., Day, C., Sammons, P., Harris, A., & Hopkins, D. (2008). *Seven strong claims about successful school leadership*. Nottingham: Department for Education and Skills.

Lewis, T., Rice, M., & Rice Jr., R. (2011). Superintendents' beliefs and behaviors regarding instructional leadership standards reform. *International Journal of Educational Leadership Preparation*, *6*(1), 1.

Lie, J. (2011). Modern peoplehood: On race, racism, nationalism, ethnicity, and identity. UC Berkeley. Retrieved from https://escholarship.org/content/qt73c5 c0cg/qt73c5c0cg.pdf. Accessed on 30 March 2018.

Marshall, C., & Gerstl-Pepin, C. I. (2005). *Re-framing educational politics for social justice*. Boston, MA: Pearson/Allyn and Bacon.

Maxfield, S., Shapiro, M., Gupta, G., & Hass, S. (2010). Gender and risk: Women, risk taking and risk aversion. *Gender in Management: An International Journal*, *25*(7), 586–602.

Möllering, G. (2001). The nature of trust. From Georg Simmel to a theory of expectations, interpretation, and suspence. *Sociology*, *35*(2), 403–420.

Moloi, K., Gravett, S., & Petersen, N. (2009). Globalization and its impact on education with specific reference to education in South Africa. *Educational Management Administration and Leadership*, *37*(2), 278–297.

Murray, D. (2018). War without violence? Dewey's insights on modern warfare. John Dewey Society Annual Meeting, Dewey and Philosophy PanelI, Nationalism: War and Peace in American Educational Research Association, New York, April.

Organisation for Economic and Cooperation and Development. (2017). *Programme of International Students Assessment*. Retrieved from http://www.oecd.org/pisa/. Accessed on 18 March 2018.

Paulston, R. (2000). Imagining comparative education: Past, present and future. *Compare: A Journal of Comparative and International Education*, *30*(3), 353–367.

Payne, C. (2008). *So much reform, so little change: The persistence of failure in urban schools*. Harvard: Harvard Education Press.

Phelan, A. (2009). The ethical claim of partiality: Practical reasoning, the discipline, and teacher education. *Journal of Curriculum Studies*, *41*(1), 93–114.

Plato, J. B. (Ed.) (2018). *Timaeus and Critias in The Complete Works of Plato*. Olymp Classics: Kindle Edition.

Pring, R. (2000). *Philosophy of educational research*. London: Continuum.

Rubin, Z., & Paplau, L. (1975). Who believes in a just world. *Journal of Social Issues*, *31*(3), 65–89.

Sheard, M., & Avis, J. (2011). Schools, governance and community: A next practice intervention in educational management. *Administration, and Leadership*, *39*(1), 84–104.

Stenhouse, L. (1975). *An introduction to curriculum research and development.* London: Heinemann.

Swaffield, S., & MacBeath, J. (2009). Leadership for learning. In J. MacBeath & N. Dempster (Eds.), *Connecting leadership and learning: Principles for practice* (pp. 32–52). Abingdon: Routledge.

Taysum, A. (2012). *Convener of a large symposium in two parts: 'Globalization, Policy and Agency: Eight Nation states working together to Further Understand their Political Sociologies of Education'.* European Conference for Educational Research, Cadiz, September.

Taysum, A. (2012). *Evidence informed leadership in education.* London: Continuum.

Taysum, A. (2013). *Convener of a large symposium in two parts; 'International Boundary Crossing Study of Teachers' and Students' Participation in Institutional Processes and Practices".* European Conference for Educational Research. Istanbul, September.

Taysum, A. (2014). *Convener of a large symposium in two parts: 'International Boundary Crossing Study Of Higher Education Institutions working in Partnership with Schools To Improve Participation In Processes And Practices Chair: Jan Heystek (Stellenbosch University) Discussant: Carole Collins Ayanlaja (Chicago, Superintendent).* European Conference for Educational Research, Porto.

Taysum, A. (2015). *Convener of a large symposium in two parts: 'A Theory of Young People's Participation in Systems and Learning from International Boundary Crossing Action-Resarch Project Arar, K., Collins-Ayanlaja, C., Harrison, K., Imam, H., Murrel-Abery, V., Mynbayeva, A., Yelbayeva, Z.* European Conference for Educational Research. Budapest, Hungary. September.

Taysum, A. (2016). *Convener of a large symposium in two parts: McNamara (Chair), Risku, M., Collins Ayanlaja, C., Iddrisu, M.T., Murrel-Abery, J.V., Arar, K., Masry-Herzallah, A., Imam, H., Chopra, P., McGuinness, S. Theoretical underpinnings of an education and skills model for participation and cooperation in the Youth Field; empowering Europe's young innovators.* European Conference for Educational Research, Dublin, Ireland, August.

Taysum, A. (2017). *Convener of a large symposium in two parts: Arar, K., Masry-Herzallah, A., Collins Ayanlaja, C., Brookins, W., McGuinness, S., Bates, J., Roulsten, S., O'Connor, U., James, F., and George, J., Taysum, A. Turbulence in Six International Education Governance-Systems: Comparing Knowledge to Action for Equity, Peace and Renewal.* European Conference for Educational Research, Copenhagen, Denmark, August.

Taysum, A. (2017a). A Deweyan blueprint for moral training for Democracy in Education presentation Oxford University Symposium, April.

Taysum, A. (2017b). Systems theory and education: A philosophical enquiry into education systems theory. In P. Higgs & Y. Waghid (Eds.), *A reader for philosophy of education* (Vol. 1, p. 1). South Africa: Juta.

Taysum, A. (Forthcoming). A Deweyen framework moral training for democracy in education. In C. Lowery & P. Jenkin (Eds.), *A Dewey handbook of Dewey's education theory and practice.* Rotterdam: Sense Publishing.

Taysum, A., & Gunter, H. (2008). A critical approach to researching social justice and school leadership in England. *Education, Citizenship and Social Justice, 3*(2), 183–199.

Taysum, A., & Iqbal, M. (2012). What counts as meaningful and worthwhile policy analysis. *Italian Journal of Sociology of Education*, 4(1), 11–28.

Taysum, A., & Murrel-Abery, G. V. (2017). 'Shifts in education policy, administration and governance in Guyana 1831–2017. Seeking 'a political' agenda for equity and renewal'. In A. Taysum (Ed.), *Italian Journal of Sociology of Education*, 9(2), 55–87.

United Nations. (1948). *Universal declaration of human rights* (General Assembly Resolution 217 A). Retrieved from http://www.un.org/en/universal-declaration-human-rights/. Accessed on 29 April 2018.

Waghid, Y., & Smeyers, P. (2014). Re0envisioning the future: Democratic citizenship education and islamic education. *Journal of Philosophy of Education*, 48(4), 539–558.

Wagner, T. (2010). *The global achievement gap*. New York, NY: Basic Books.

Waite, D., Rodríguez, G., & Wadende, A. (2015). Globalization and the business of educational reform. In J. Zajda (Ed.), *Second International Handbook in Globalization, Education and Policy Research* (pp. 353–374). Dordrecht: Springer.

Woods, P., & Roberts, A. (2018). *Collaborative school leadership; A critical guide*. London: Sage.

About the Contributors

Editors

Dr Alison Taysum is a Lecturer in Educational Leadership and Management, Director for the MSc Educational Leadership and supervises PhD students at the University of Leicester, UK. Her international collaborative boundary-crossing research includes building capacity in Higher Education, collaborative research with leaders to Empower Young Societal Innovators for Equity and Renewal (EYSIER), implementing A Blueprint for Character Development (ABCD). She has worked as a consultant in Russia, Kazakhstan, Japan and Japanese Ministry of Education, South Africa, Pakistan, the UK, Indonesian Embassy, London and authored Taysum, A. (2012) *Evidence informed leadership in education*. London: Bloomsbury, and edited Taysum, A. and Rayner, S. (2014) *Investing in Our Education? Leading, Learning, Researching and the Doctorate*. Scarborough: Emerald. She is Treasurer for BELMAS, convenes funded educational leadership networks, serves on editorial boards and reviews for International peer-reviewed journals, book publishers, funding councils, International Conferences and the BELMAS Doctoral Thesis Award Panel.

Dr Khalid Arar is an Associate Professor of Educational Leadership and Higher Education at Al-Qasemi Academic College of Education, Israel. His studies focus on issues of diversity, equity and ethnicity in educational leadership and higher education. He has published extensively in the last years in issues of educational leadership and higher education in scholarly journals, and his most recent books include *Life Stories of Arab Women in Leadership and Management: Challenges and Changes* (with Tamar Shapira, 2015, in Hebrew), *Arab Women in Management and Leadership* (2013, Palgrave, with Tamar Shapira; Faisal Azaiza and Rachel Hertz Lazarowitz) and *Higher Education among the Palestinian Minority in Israel* (2016, Palgrave, with Kussai HajYehia). Additionally, he is an Associate Editor of *International Journal of Leadership in Education*.

Contributors

Dr Carole Collins Ayanlaja is an Assistant Professor of Educational Leadership, Eastern Illinois University, USA. She holds a PhD in Educational Policy and Administration from University of Illinois at Chicago. Her research interests include teaching, leadership and school intersections with race and culture. She is co-author of *African American Parents and Effective Parent Involvement*

Programs (2017) and serves on the editorial board of the *International Journal of Leadership in Education.*

Dr Jessica Bates is a Lecturer, School of Education, Ulster University, Northern Ireland and Senior Fellow of the Higher Education Academy. Dr Bates' research interests relate to education and inclusion, education systems and education policy in Northern Ireland, digital literacy, and improving library and information services. She is the Course Director for Library and Information Management at Ulster University.

Dr Warletta Brookins is Superintendent, Madison Community Unit School District #12, USA. She is an adjunct Professor in Educational Leadership at Governors State University and holds numerous awards, including (among others) the Madison IL NAACP Education Leadership Award, 2017, and the East St Louis, IL NAACP Innovative Educator Award.

Dr June George, PhD, is a retired Professor of Science Education. She served for 30 years at the School of Education, The University of the West Indies (UWI), Trinidad, taking various roles including lecturer, research fellow, senior research fellow, deputy dean for graduate studies and research, head of the department and professor. Over the years, her research work has been located largely in the areas of the intersection of science education and culture, programme evaluation, teacher education and assessment of student performance. She has published widely in these areas.

Professor Hauwa Imam is a Professor of Educational Administration in the Department of Education Managmement, University of Abuja, Nigeria. She is an avid researcher and writer.

Dr Freddy James is a Lecturer in Educational Leadership, The University of the West Indies, Trinidad. Her background is in secondary education and her research focuses on leadership, innovation, change and improvement in educational settings. She has published widely in international, regional and local peer-reviewed journals.

Dr Asmahan Masry-Herzallah is a Senior Lecturer, College for Academic Studies, Israel. She is a Head of Programme for the MA in Educational Administration and Head of the teaching committee. Her research interests relate to migration and education, social mobility and issues of planning in Arab education in Israel.

Dr Samuel McGuinness is a Lecturer in Educational Leadership and Management, Ulster University, Northern Ireland. His research interests are in education leadership and education policy; he has published on policy issues in Northern Ireland associated with the effects of the accountability agenda on schools and their leaders, and the growth and development of area learning communities.

Dr Una O'Connor is a Senior Lecturer, UNESCO Centre, School of Education, Ulster University, Northern Ireland, and a Senior Fellow of the Higher

Education Academy. Her research reflects an interest in social inclusion and focuses particularly on special educational needs, children's rights and well-being, citizenship education and education policy in Northern Ireland.

Dr Catherine Quinn is a Senior Lecturer in Science and Course Team Leader, St Mary's University College, Queen's University Belfast, Northern Ireland. Her research interests include loss of science from the NI Primary Curriculum; the current state of STEM ITE in NI, the importance of quality educational leadership and governance and gender balance in STEM.

Dr Stephen Roulston is a Course Director for PGCE Geography, Ulster University, Northern Ireland. His research interests include assessment, the use of ICT in education and the impact of a divided society and education system on school leadership and, ultimately, on young people. He is a Senior Fellow of the Higher Education Academy and a Fellow of the Royal Geographical Society.

Mr Brian Waring is a Senior Teacher (with responsibility for School Improvement), Royal Belfast Academical Institution, Northern Ireland. His research interests focus on the creation of settings and strategies that are conducive to learning and the development of a deeper understanding of effective school self-evaluation. He is particularly interested in comparing and contrasting approaches adopted towards school strategic development planning in a variety of different states and in furthering his understanding of the central role played in these processes by the development of human capital.

Appendix 1 Sample Invitation Letter to Interview to the Researched

Name of Researcher
Address of Researcher

Date

Name of Researched
Address of Researched

Dear (Name)

I am writing to ask if it would be possible for me to interview you about how you describe and understand your role as a key agent of change within educational governance systems. I would like to ask you about three key aspects. First, how you define opportunities and challenges of working for equity and renewal within educational governance systems. Second, how you navigate these and how you are supported to navigate these. Third, how you would like to be empowered within governance systems to empower students to be societal innovators for equity and renewal.

This research is part of an international comparative education study to understand changes in governance systems in different nation states. The aim is to present a symposium at the European Conference for Educational Research in Copenhagen, 2017 and to publish the findings in a book to categorise similarities and differences in how key agents of change, like yourself, are empowered through governance systems to empower students to be societal innovators for equity and renewal.

The research also focuses on the Black-White achievement gap as a global phenomenon, and the population and sample in each nation state will be key agents of change from marginalised communities.

If it is possible to talk with you then I am able to come to your Institution at your convenience. However I thought it would be helpful if I suggested some dates: insert dates and times: [...]

If these dates are not suitable, then please do suggest alternatives and perhaps we could talk on the telephone about any questions you may have about my work and/or any arrangements which we would need to make. My telephone number is: (work) or you may wish to email me on: [...]

I do hope that you are able to spare the time to talk with me. I look forward to hearing from you.

Yours sincerely

Researcher's name.

Appendix 2

University Address

Informed Consent Form

**This form must be used if you wish to participate in this
education research**

Dear

As part of a research investigation, and international comparative study, I would like to interview you about your role as a senior-level educational leader focusing on how you describe and understand your role as a key agent of change within educational governance systems. I would like to ask you about three key aspects. First, how you define opportunities and challenges to working for equity and renewal within education governance systems. Second, how you navigate these and how you are supported to navigate these. Third, how you would like to be empowered within governance systems to empower students to be societal innovators for equity and renewal.

I would like to audio record the interview, transcribe it, and return the transcript to you for respondent validation.

Any views expressed would be given in confidence, and any quotes used would be anonymised. Data will be stored securely on a password protected computer and backed up in accordance with the Data Protection Acts 1998 and 2003.

Please note that you can withdraw from the research by contacting me up to the date of publication of the research.

If you are willing to take part in this research, and for the interviews to be audio recorded, would you please sign below. If you would like to ask any questions concerning this process, please feel free to email me on:

Signature: Date:

Print name:

Appendix 3

Guide for Semi-Structured Interview Schedule for participants international comparative educational research project: Turbulence, Empowerment, and Marginalisation. Part of education project Empowering Young Societal Innovators for Equity and Renewal.

1a. Please can you tell me what you enjoy about working within the governance systems?

Prompt: Working with School commissioners, the school board, education policy, principals, and governing bodies.

Probe: Can you give me a concrete example of that?

1b. Can you tell me what opportunities you face to empower school communities to empower students to be societal innovators for equity and renewal?

Prompt: Mentoring educational leaders and staff, professional development opportunities, developing networks

Probe: Can you give me a concrete example of that please.

1c. Can you tell me what challenges you face to empower school communities to empower students to be societal innovators for equity and renewal?

Prompt: Time and space for developing culturally relevant curriculums, time and space for ITE and CPD to develop cultural alignment within education systems.

Probe: Can you give me a concrete example of that please.

2a. Reflecting on your answers (above), can you tell me how you navigate these?

Prompt: Can you tell me about the dynamics of power you navigate when working to empower staff and students in the education system?

Probe: Can you give me a concrete example of that?

2b. Who mentors you, or acts as an advocate to support you with curriculum transformation?

Prompt: Is there formal support or informal support?

Probe: Can you give me a concrete example of this please?

3a. How would you like to be empowered through governance systems to empower staff to empower students to be societal innovators for equity and renewal.

Prompt: What changes would you like to see happen in governance systems to empower you to empower staff and students to develop bridging cultures to develop multicultural identities for community cohesion?

Probe: Can you give me an example of that please?

3b. How might these changes be implemented?

Prompt: Who needs to be involved to enable these changes, and what do they need to do?

Probe: Can you tell me more about how such a cultural change can be operationalised?

Thank you very much for your time.

Digital recorder turned off.

Appendix 4

University

Name of Researcher

Date

Name of Researcher

Dear

I write to thank you for agreeing to be interviewed on Insert Date.

I have transcribed the recording which is attached for you to review and return to me so you can edit out areas you do not want included through respondent validation, or you can add sections as you wish.

I consider myself privileged to have had the chance to learn more about how you define opportunities and challenges to working for equity and renewal within education governance systems. Second, how you navigate these and how you are supported to navigate these. Third, how you would like to be empowered within governance systems to empower students to be societal innovators for equity and renewal.

Thank you for supporting this research.

Once again, many thanks,

In Partnership,

Name
Email:

Appendix 5

Doctoral Research Interest Group (DRIG)

Empowering Young Societal Innovators for Equity and Renewal (EYSIER)

Call to an Interactive Leadership Seminar to:

Review Strategies to Improve Education in Diverse Communities

Review a Deweyan Framework to Improve Democracy in Education

Global Kitchen, Mexico Room, 11722 S. Western Ave. Chicago, IL 60643

Wednesday, April 11 8:30 am–3:30 pm

Keynote Speakers:

Dr Alison Taysum, University of Leicester, UK

Dr Carole Collins Ayanlaja, Eastern Illinois University, USA

We seek the feedback and input of established superintendents and principals on the potential effectiveness of strategies that co-construct and/or join our international networks of nations/states to support higher levels of capacity building and autonomy for educational leaders improving schools.

To accept your invitation and register, please contact:
ast11@le.ac.uk

Keynotes of the event will be recorded for International BELMAS Members

Program

8.30 Registration and full breakfast

9:30 Welcome – Dr Carole Collins Ayanlaja and Dr Alison Taysum

9:35 First Keynote

Empowering Superintendents in the United States to Empower Young Societal Innovators for Equity and Renewal in the Community – Research Findings, Strategies and Future Directions for Research and Practice – Dr. Carole Collins Ayanlaja.

10:30 Coffee break and dialogue

11.00 Dr Carole Collins Ayanlaja and Dr Alison Taysum

12:00 Lunch and dialogue

1:00 Second Keynote

Dewey Framework; Moral Training for Democracy in Education – A Strategy for Empowering Young Societal Innovators for Equity and Renewal (EYSIER) – presenting strategies to put knowledge to action with the academy, BELMAS, Postgraduate Research, and Professional Learning Networks for Educational Organisational Effectiveness, Improvement and Transformation – Dr. Alison Taysum

2:00 Coffee break and dialogue

2:15 Workshop – Strategic plan review and feedback session – Strategies for Educational Organisational Effectiveness, Improvement and Transformation.

3.10 Plenary – Putting Knowledge to Action to Support the Work; Next Steps

3:30 Closing

Appendix 6

BELMAS
Northchurch Business Centre
84 Queen Street
Sheffield
S1 2DW

Date

Name of Delegate
Chicago Senior-level Leader
South Side Chicago Public Schools

Dear

I write to you in my capacity as the convener of the British Educational Leadership, Management and Administration Society Doctoral Research Interest Group (BELMAS DRIG) and Director/Treasurer of BELMAS for the last 15 years. **BELMAS** was established to maintain, promote and extend public education by advancing the practice, teaching, study of and research into educational leadership, management and administration. The organisation aims to provide a **distinctive, independent and critical voice** in the pursuit of quality education through effective leadership and management. We are concerned with **ideas** and **practice** and the inter-relationship between the two. Currently as Director of the International MSc Educational Leadership programme at the University of Leicester and Dissertation Supervisor, my engagement with BELMAS propels my leadership scope and engages me in progressive leadership philosophy and practice.

My research partner Dr. Carole Collins Ayanlaja, Assistant Professor of Educational Leadership at Eastern Illinois University and former principal, chief academic officer and superintendent has joined me to invite you to attend a BELMAS DRIG one-day seminar on 11 April 2018 from 8:30 am–3:30 pm. Held at Global Kitchen, 11722 S. Western, Chicago, the event includes breakfast and lunch. Your name was referred by Dr. Collins Ayanlaja based on your professional background and longstanding interest and engagement in educational equity and access.

The event is free to members of BELMAS and I invite you to join BELMAS free for one year, if you join by 1 April 2018. For membership benefits and to join please follow this link: https://www.belmas.org.uk/member-benefits. You may discontinue your membership with no penalty after the year if you so choose. The aims of BELMAS and of the BELMAS DRIG are realized by bringing together accomplished educational leaders like yourself, with different Research Interest Groups to be innovators for equity and renewal. Your expertise informs educational organizations and drives effectiveness, improvement and transformation.

Our research into educational governance systems has identified that aspiring and seasoned professional superintendents, principals and middle leaders in education need wise mentors like yourself to counsel them on how to improve education for all. We seek your input as an expert senior-level leader to advise us on the potential effectiveness of the two strategies to empower educational leaders. The strategies emerge from our forthcoming book *Turbulence, Empowerment, and Marginalised Groups in International Education Governance Systems* in the US, England, Arab-Israel, the West Indies and Northern Ireland.

Strategy 1
Superintendents and principals improve education in diverse communities with staff, parents and students by using postgraduate research, Massive Online Open Access Courses and BELMAS networks to describe and understand how policy supports professional educational leaders fighting institutionalized racism and social marginalization to raise children out of poverty.

Strategy 2
Taysum's synthesized Deweyan Blueprint of Moral Training for Democracy in Education seeks to offer Superintendents and Principals best practices to empower diverse communities to become societal innovators for equity and renewal by giving them access to the tools they need to develop character and virtues to access middle class benefits.

Our strategies need your feedback and input. As top leaders in our field, your voices and insight are crucial to advance quality educational leadership.

We look forward to seeing you on April 11th. Please confirm your attendance by responding directly to this letter of invitation by emailing ast11@le.ac.uk by March 12.

In Partnership,

Dr. Alison Taysum, and Dr. Carole Collins Ayanlaja.

Index